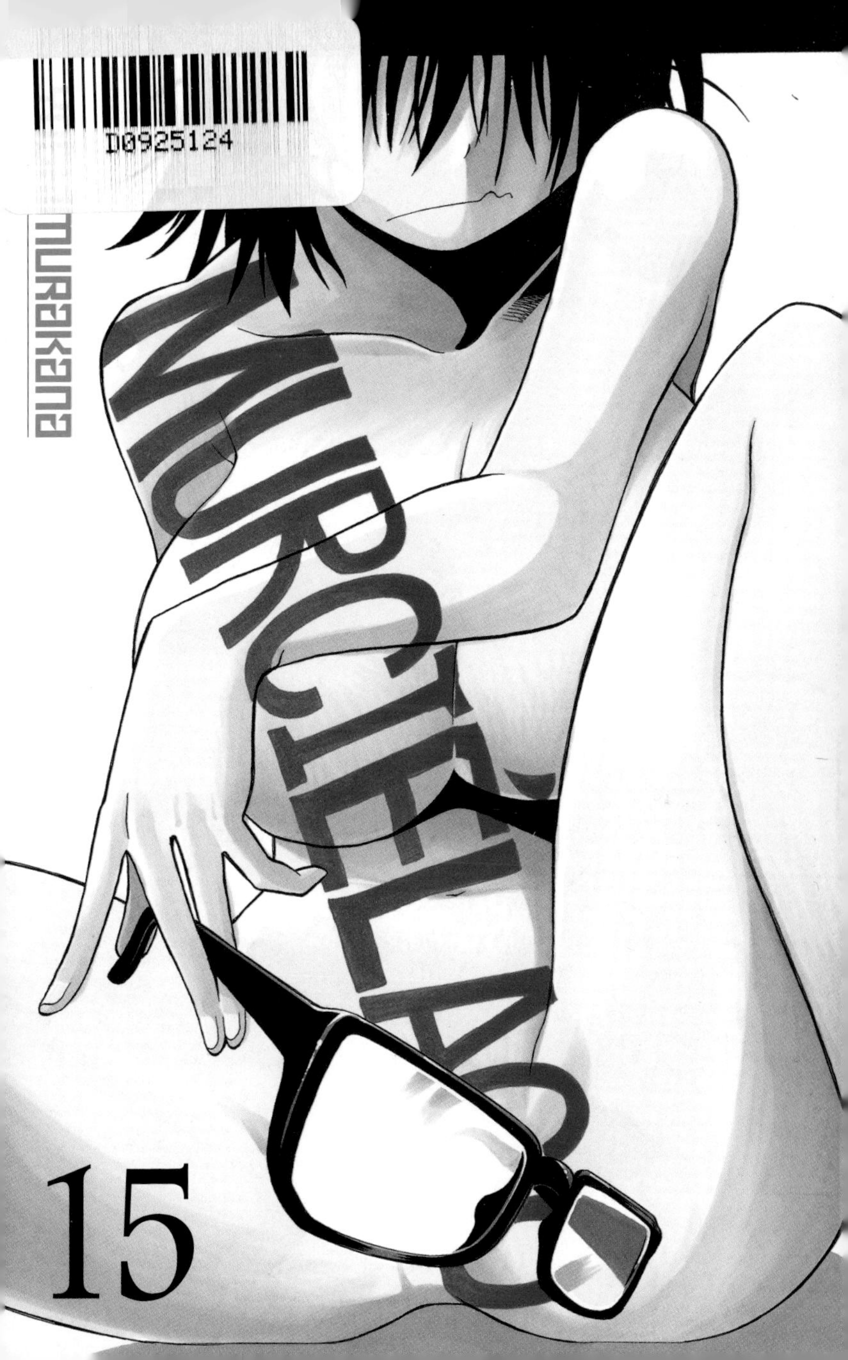
murakana
MURCIELAGO
15

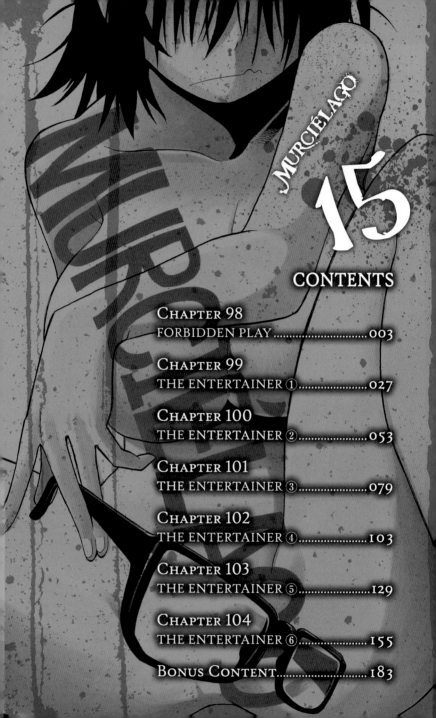

MURCIÉLAGO

# 15

## CONTENTS

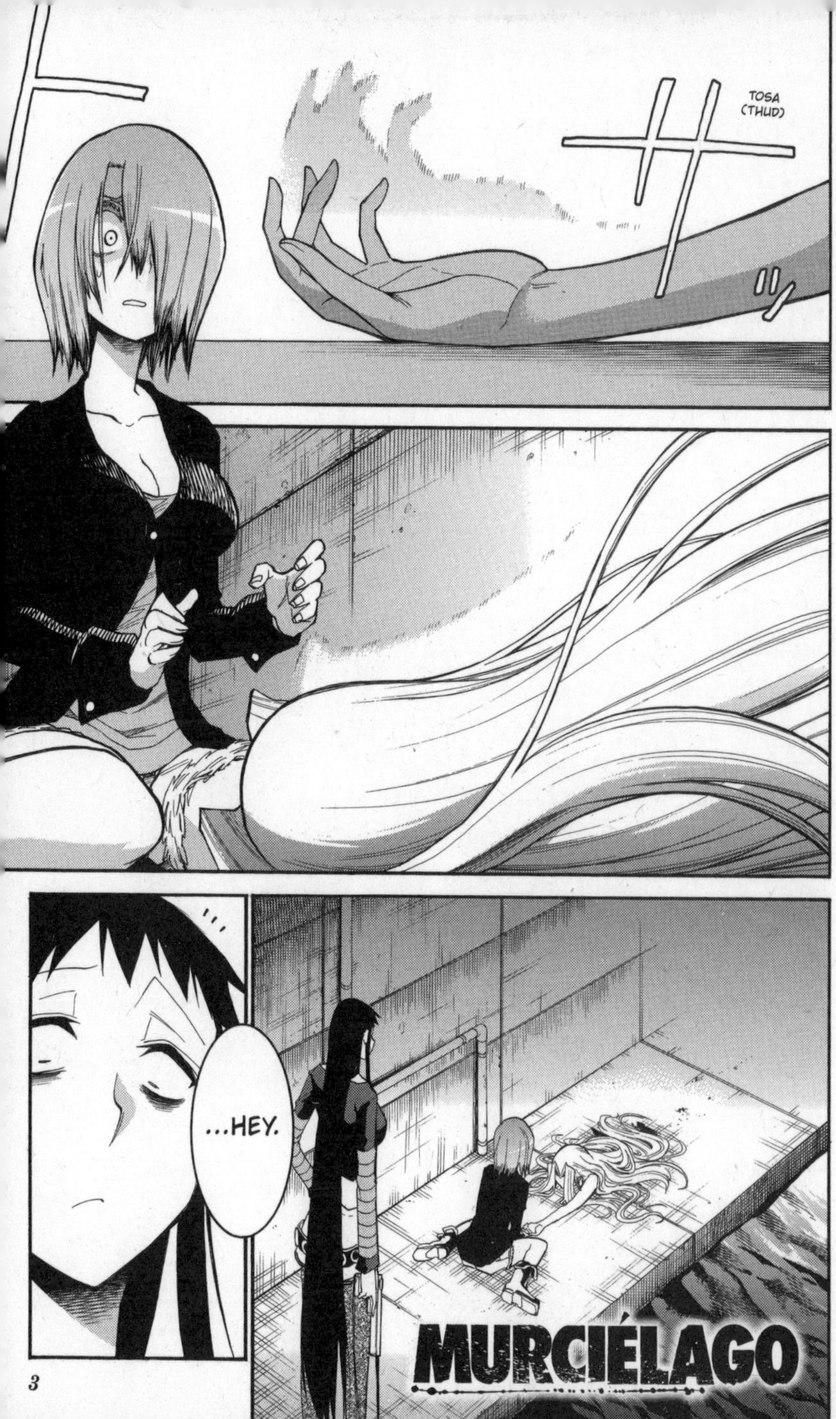
TOSA
(THUD)
...HEY.
MURCIÉLAGO

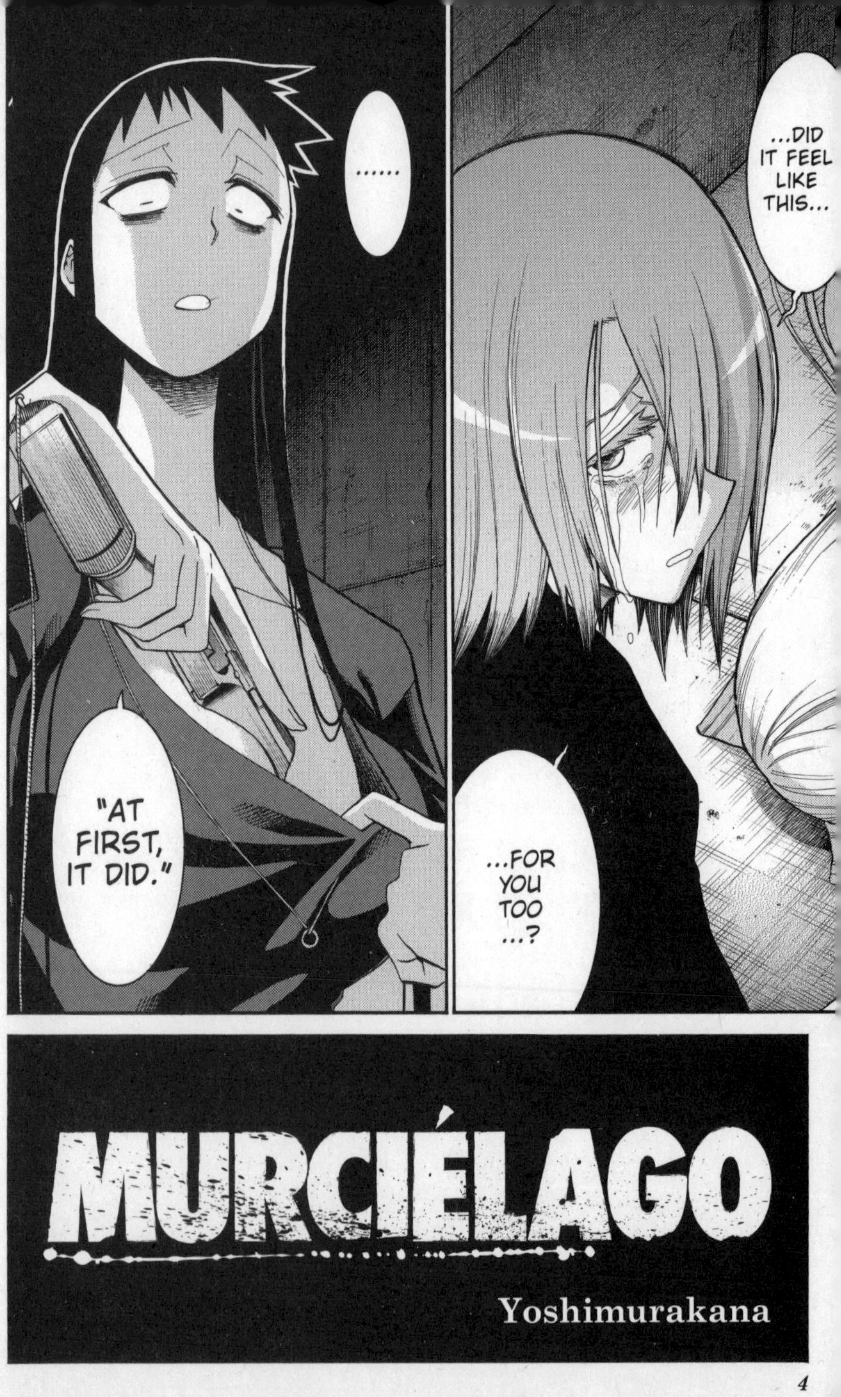
...DID IT FEEL LIKE THIS...
...FOR YOU TOO ...?
......
"AT FIRST, IT DID."

# MURCIÉLAGO

Yoshimurakana

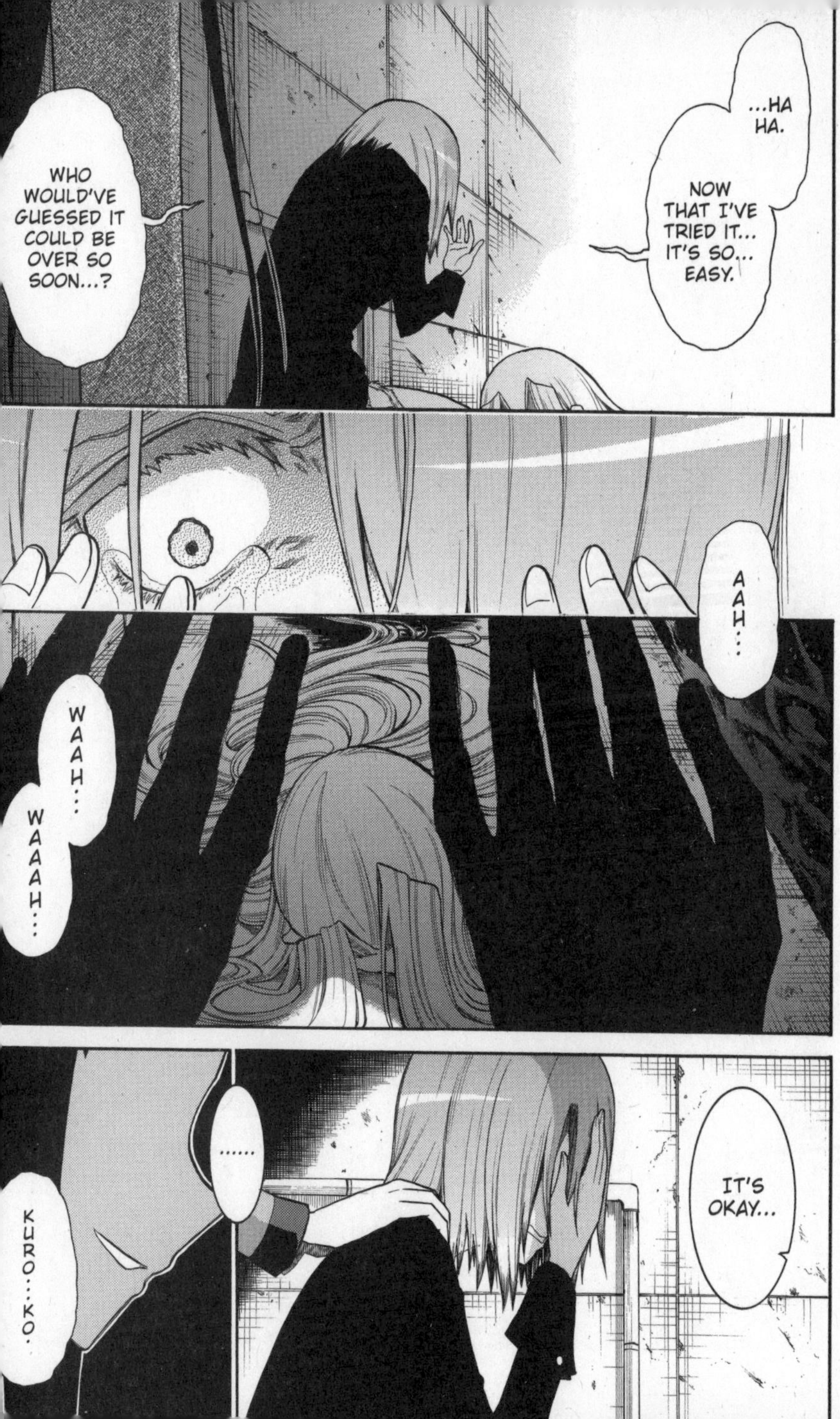
...HA HA.
NOW THAT I'VE TRIED IT... IT'S SO... EASY.
WHO WOULD'VE GUESSED IT COULD BE OVER SO SOON...?
AAH...
WAAAH...
WAAAAH...
IT'S OKAY...
......
KURO...KO.

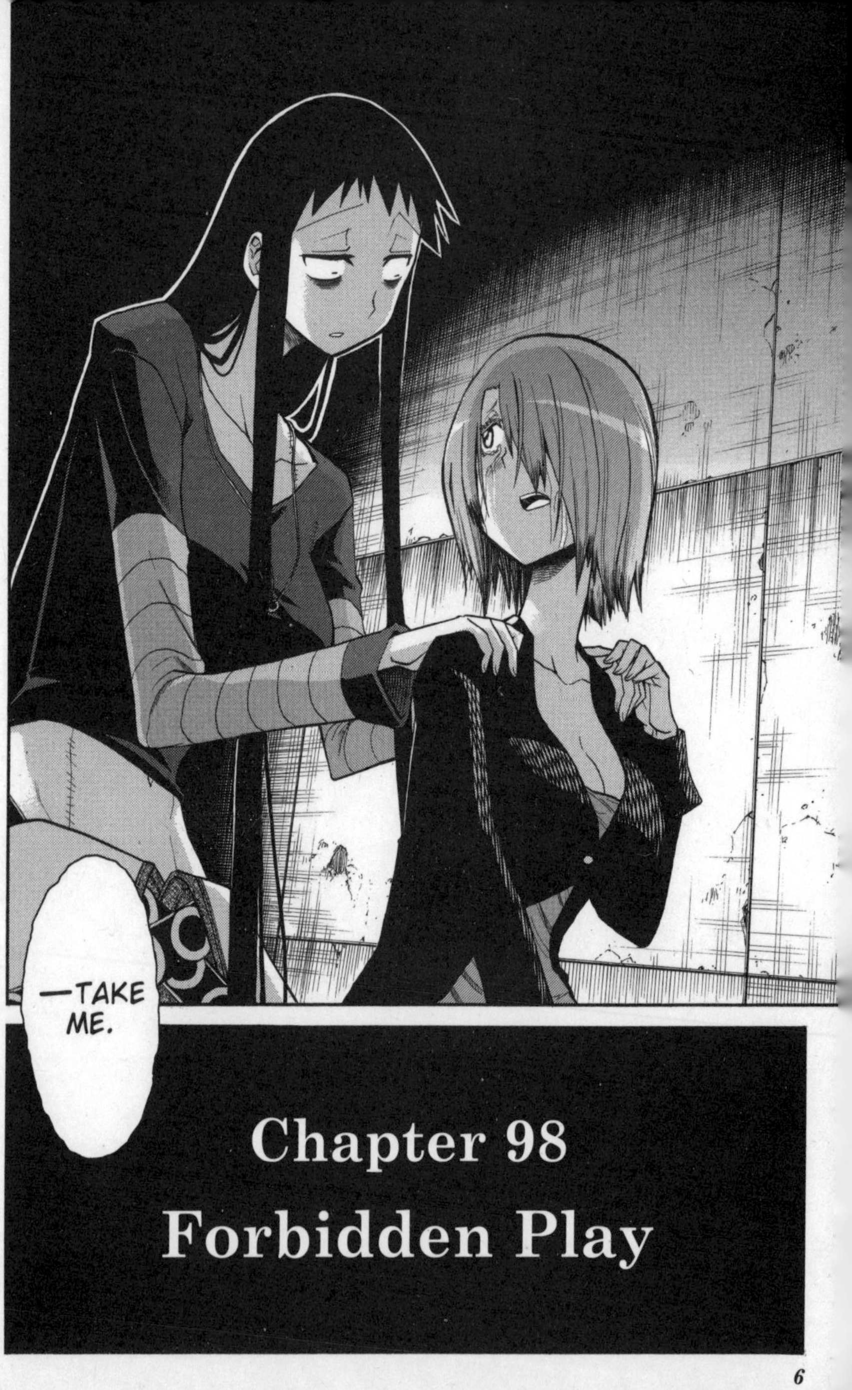
—TAKE ME.

# Chapter 98
# Forbidden Play

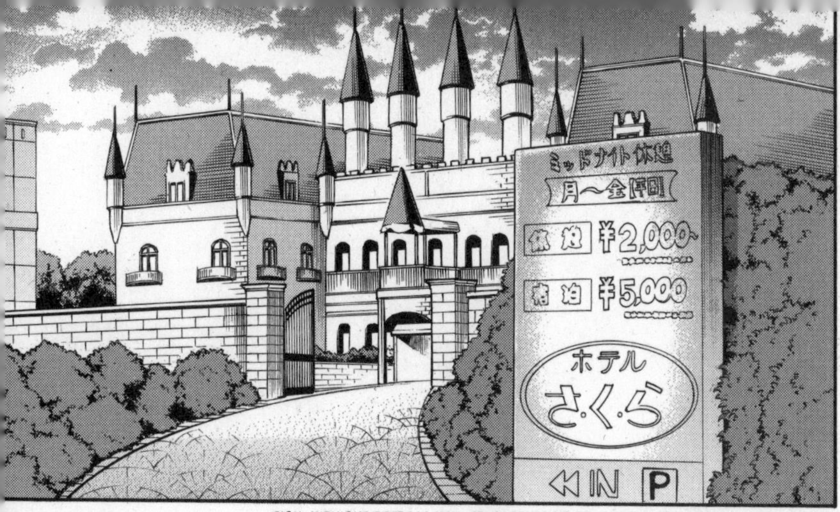
ミッドナイト休憩
月～金【平日】
休憩 ¥2,000~
宿泊 ¥5,000
ホテル
さくら
IN
P

SIGN: MIDNIGHT RETREAT, MON-FRI (WEEKDAYS) REST ¥2000, STAY ¥5000, HOTEL SAKURA

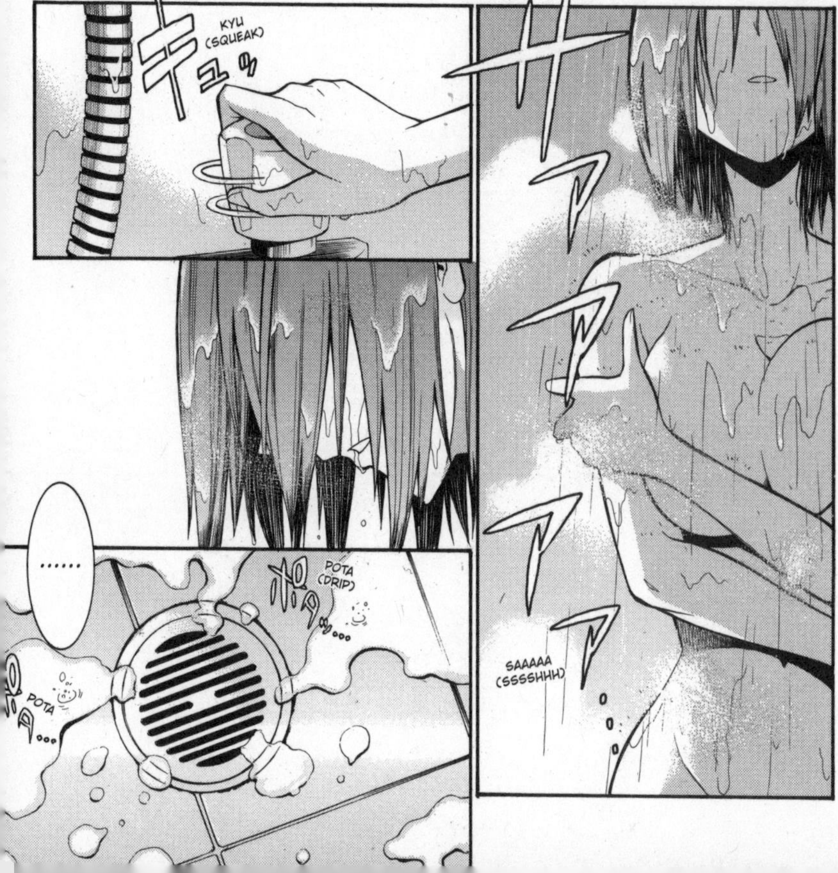
サァァァァ
SAAAAA (SSSSHHH)
キュッ
KYU (SQUEAK)
......
ポタッ...
POTA (DRIP)
ポタ...
POTA

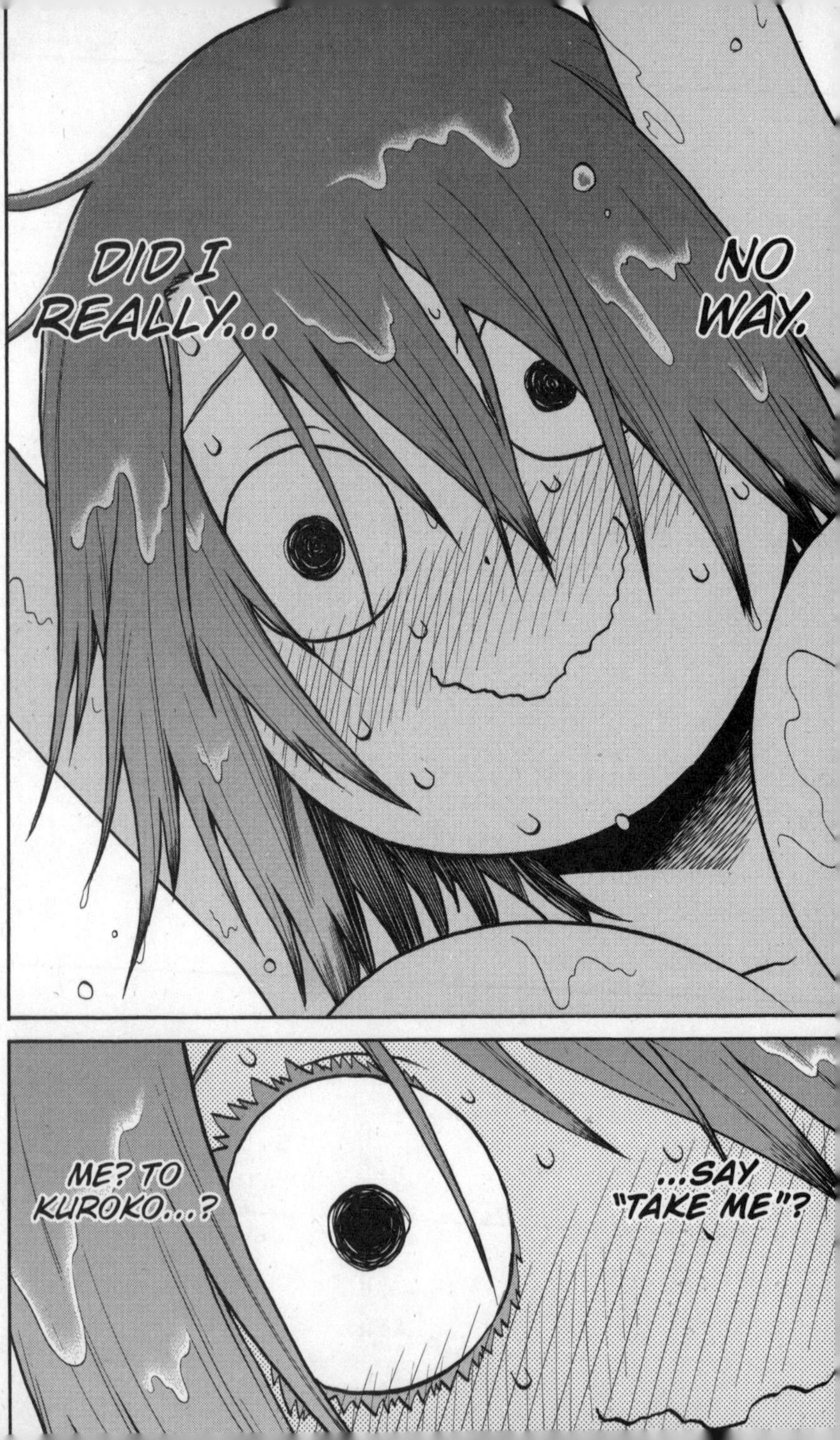
NO WAY.
DID I REALLY...
...SAY "TAKE ME"?
ME? TO KUROKO...?

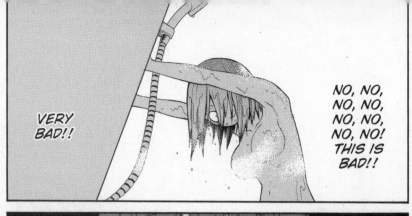

VERY BAD!!

NO, NO, NO, NO, NO, NO, NO, NO! THIS IS BAD!!

...OFF-LIMITS!!

AFTER ALL, YOU'RE......

I KNOW IT'S NOT FAIR TO KUROKO, BUT I REALLY...

PETA (STEP)

HYOKO (PEEK)

...UM, KUROKO?

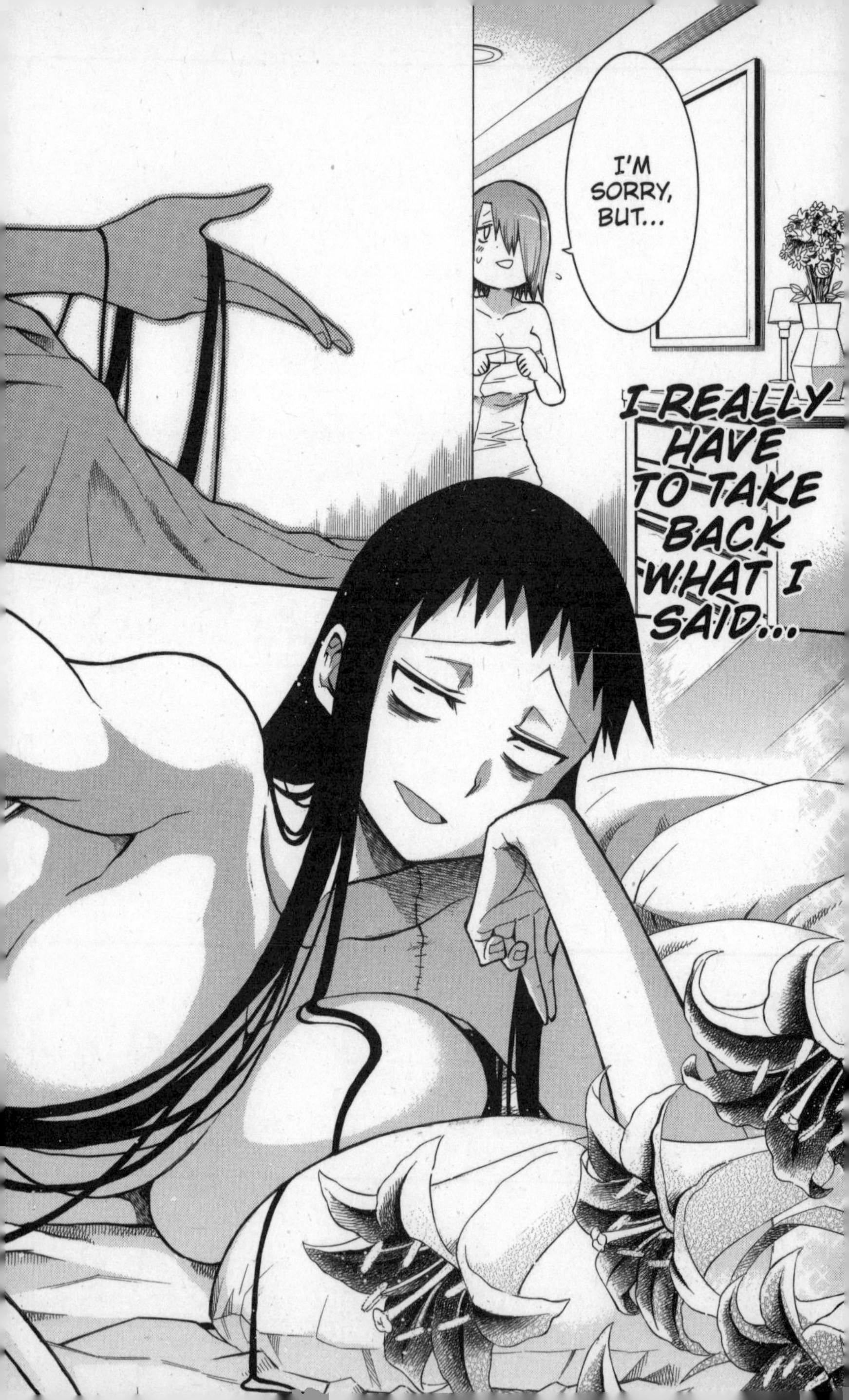
I'M SORRY, BUT...
I REALLY HAVE TO TAKE BACK WHAT I SAID...

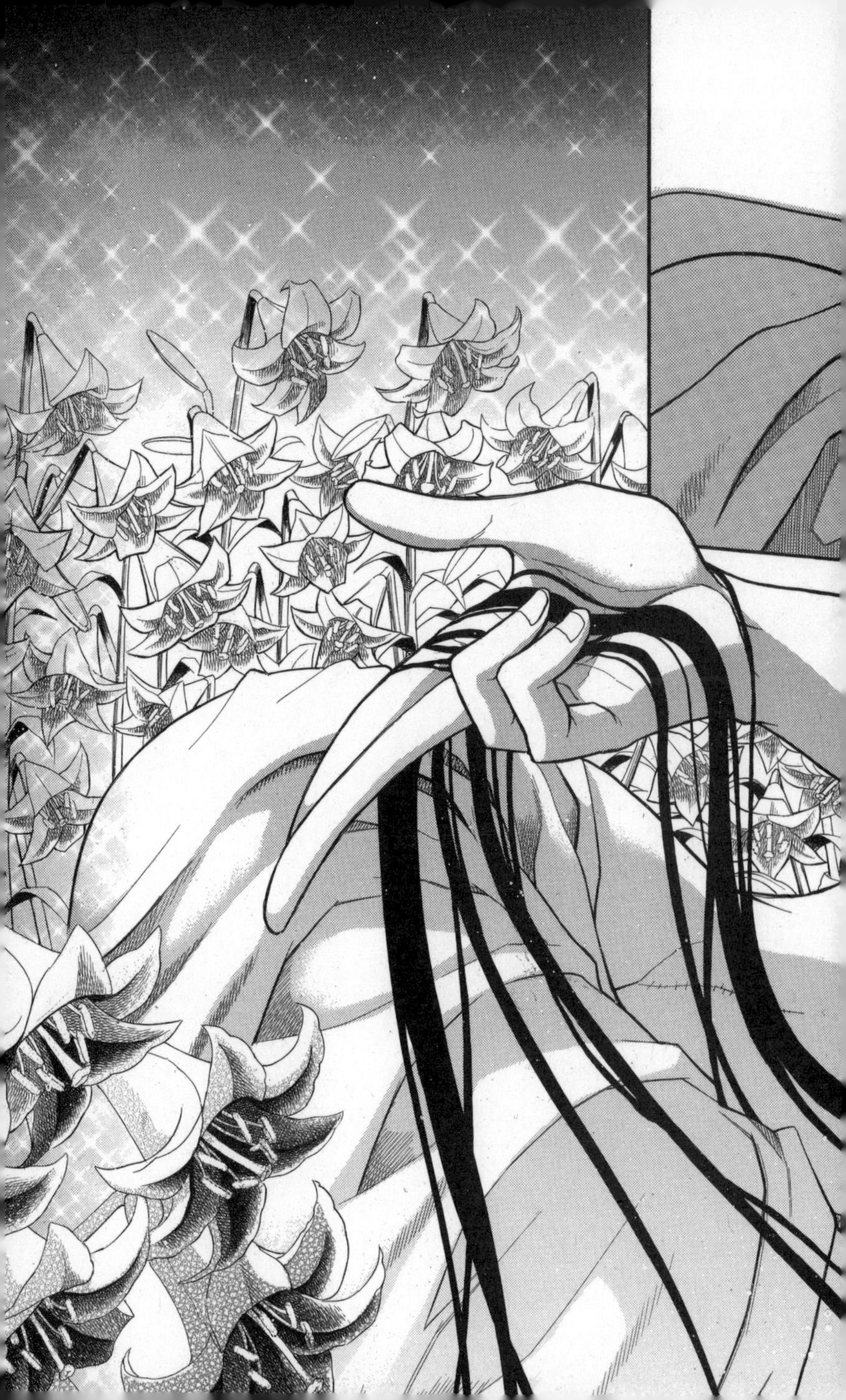

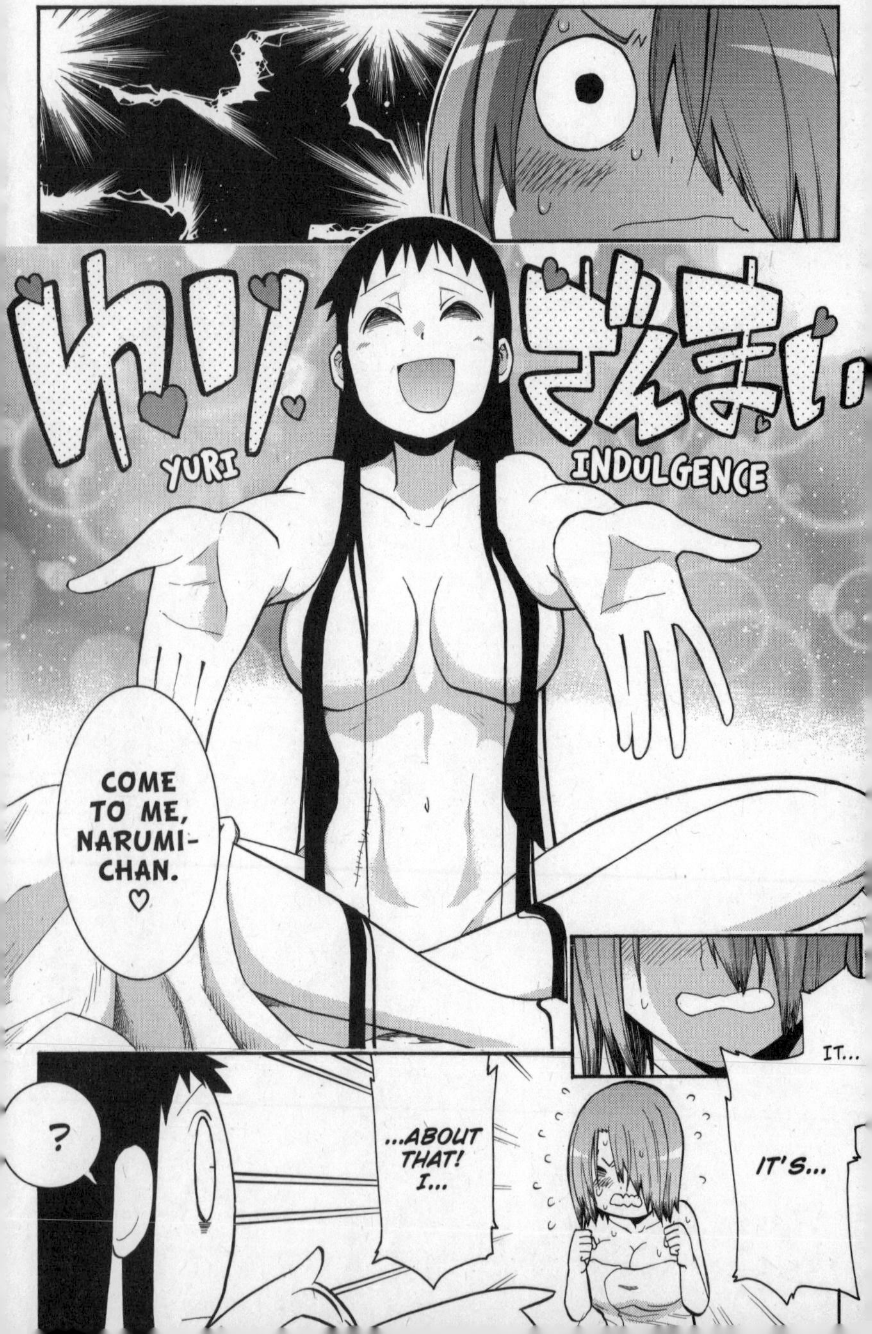
ゆり ぎんまい
YURI INDULGENCE
COME TO ME, NARUMI-CHAN. ♡
IT...
IT'S...
...ABOUT THAT! I...
?

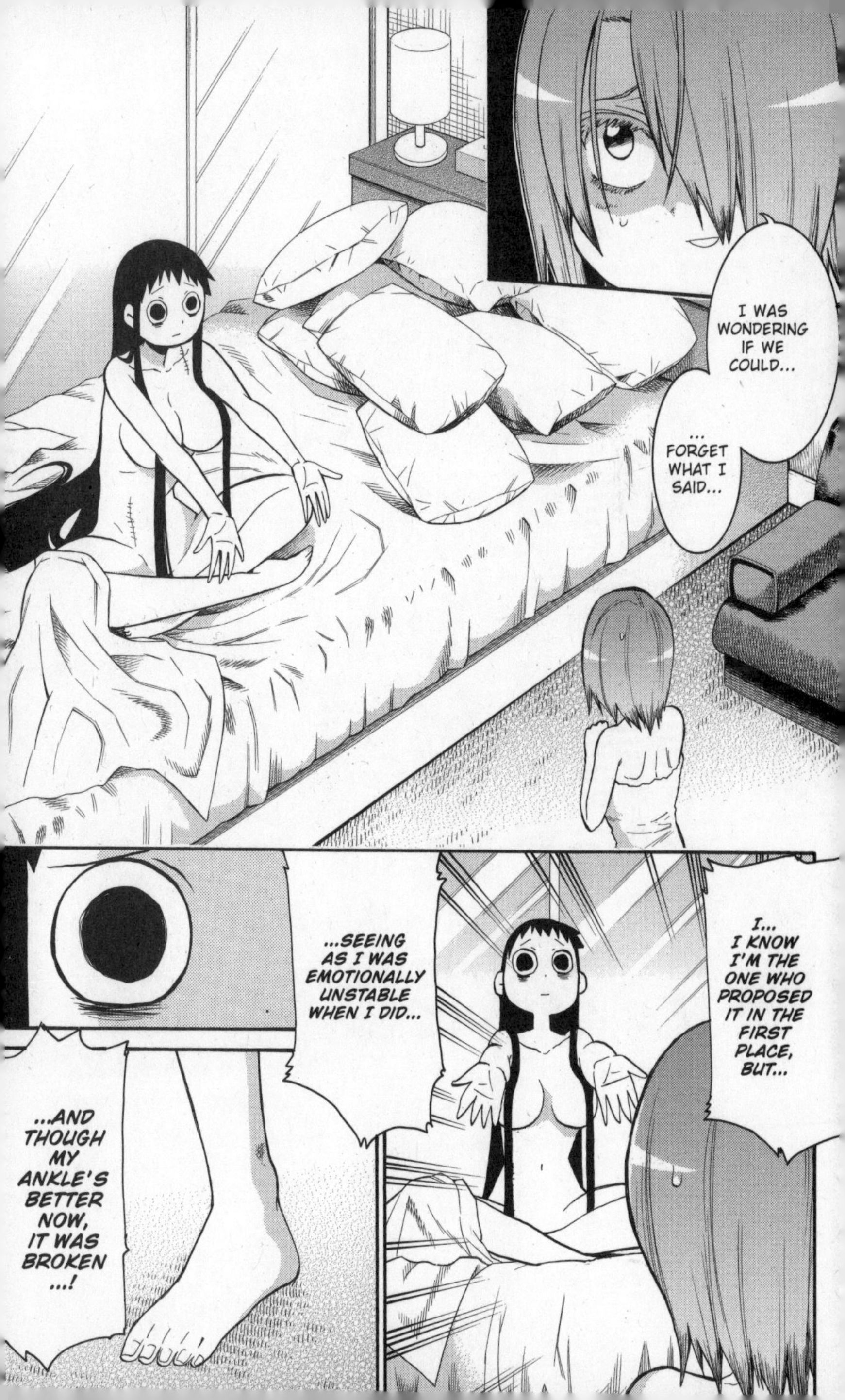
I WAS WONDERING IF WE COULD...
...FORGET WHAT I SAID...
I... I KNOW I'M THE ONE WHO PROPOSED IT IN THE FIRST PLACE, BUT...
...SEEING AS I WAS EMOTIONALLY UNSTABLE WHEN I DID...
...AND THOUGH MY ANKLE'S BETTER NOW, IT WAS BROKEN ...!

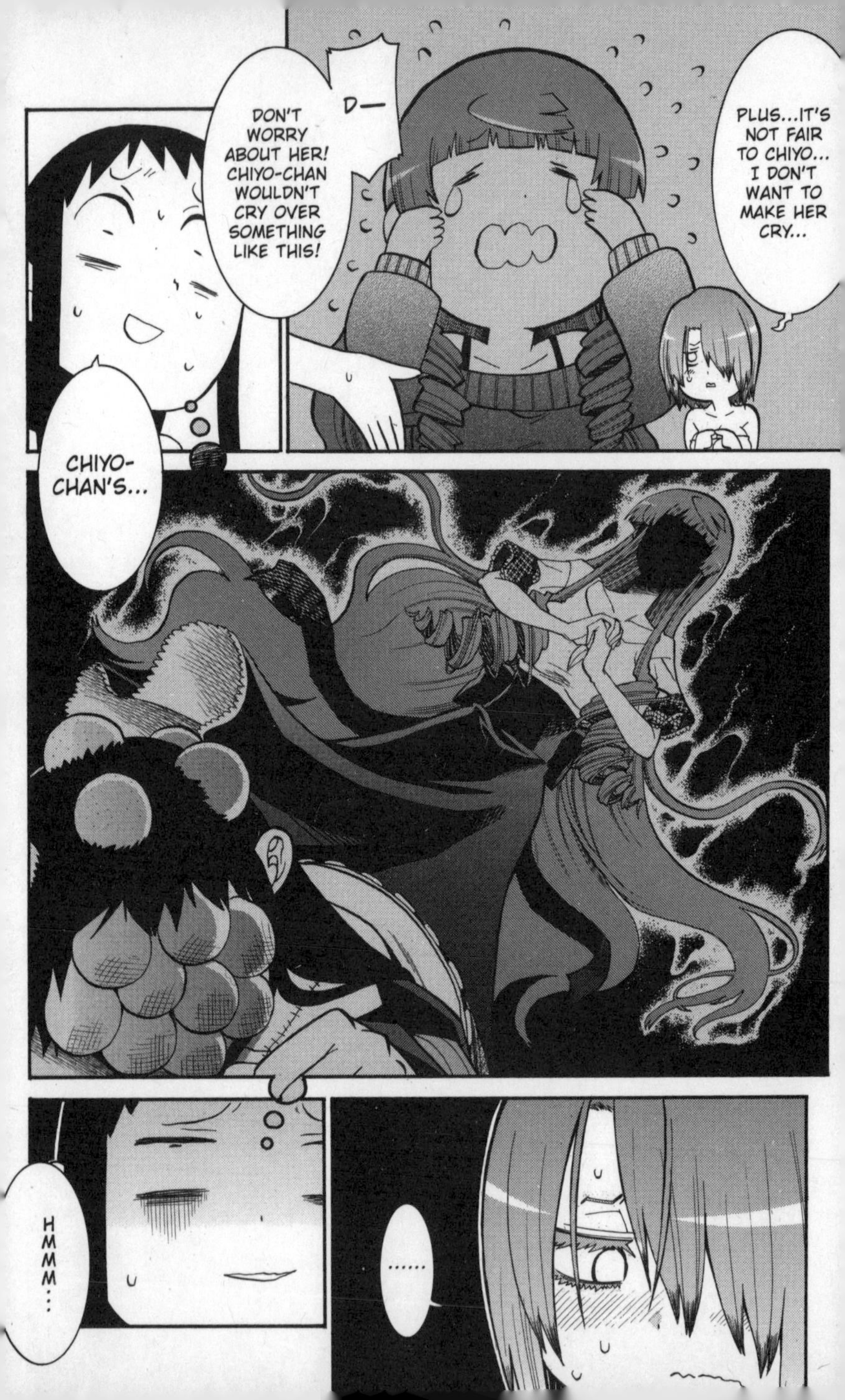
PLUS...IT'S NOT FAIR TO CHIYO... I DON'T WANT TO MAKE HER CRY...
D—
DON'T WORRY ABOUT HER! CHIYO-CHAN WOULDN'T CRY OVER SOMETHING LIKE THIS!
CHIYO-CHAN'S...
......
HMMM...

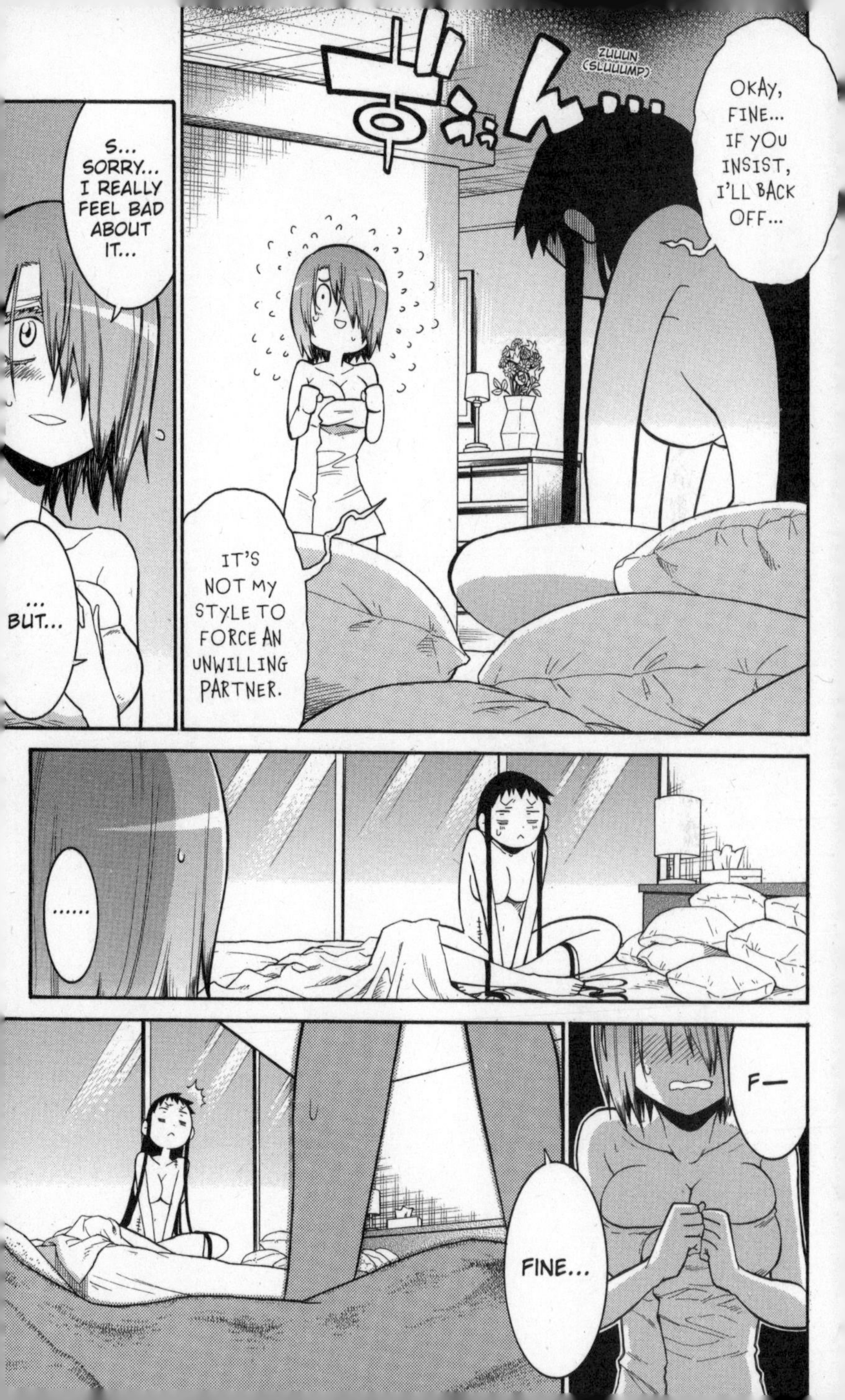
ZUUUN (SLUUUMP)
OKAY, FINE... IF YOU INSIST, I'LL BACK OFF...
IT'S NOT MY STYLE TO FORCE AN UNWILLING PARTNER.
S... SORRY... I REALLY FEEL BAD ABOUT IT...
... BUT...
......
F—
FINE...

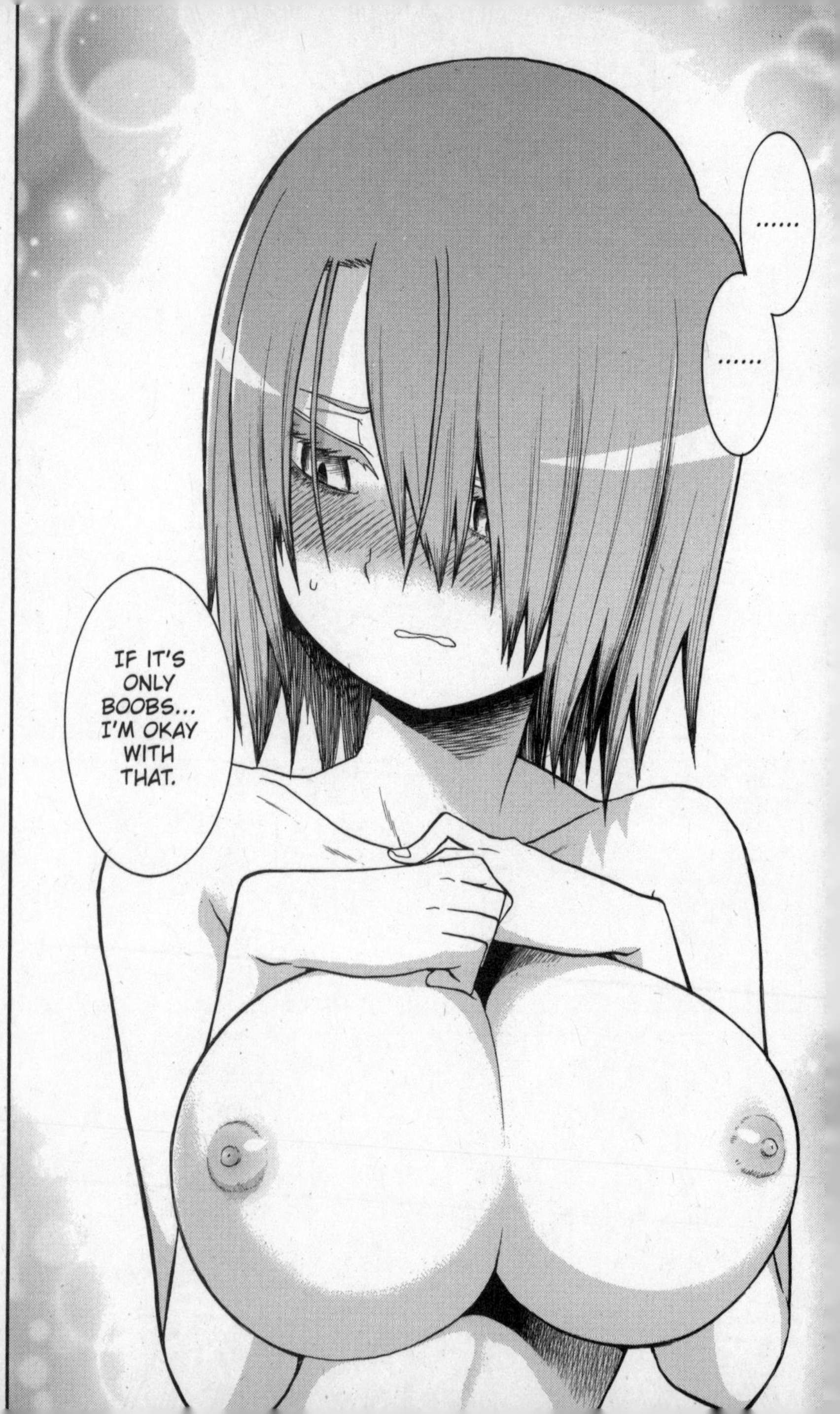
......
......
IF IT'S ONLY BOOBS... I'M OKAY WITH THAT.

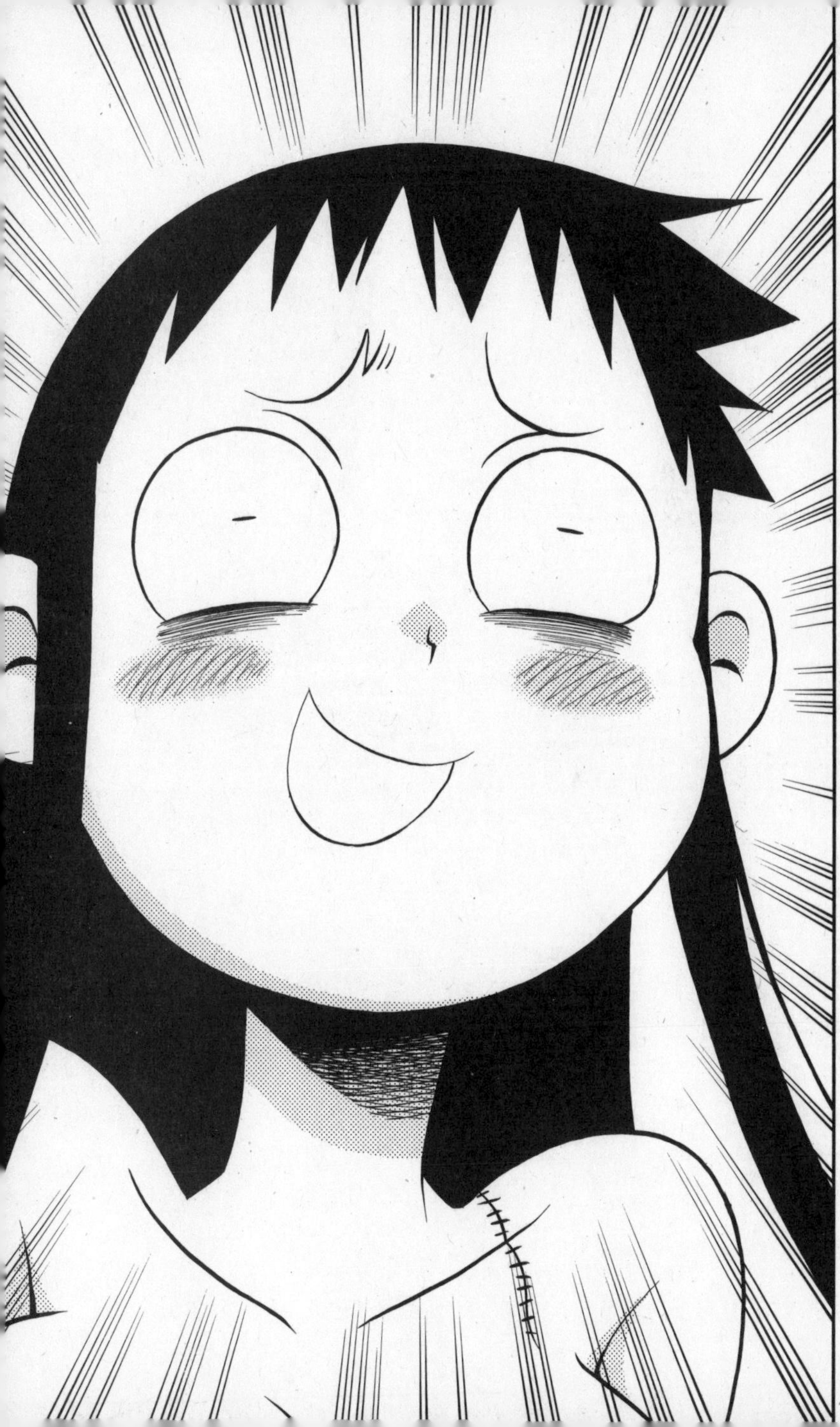

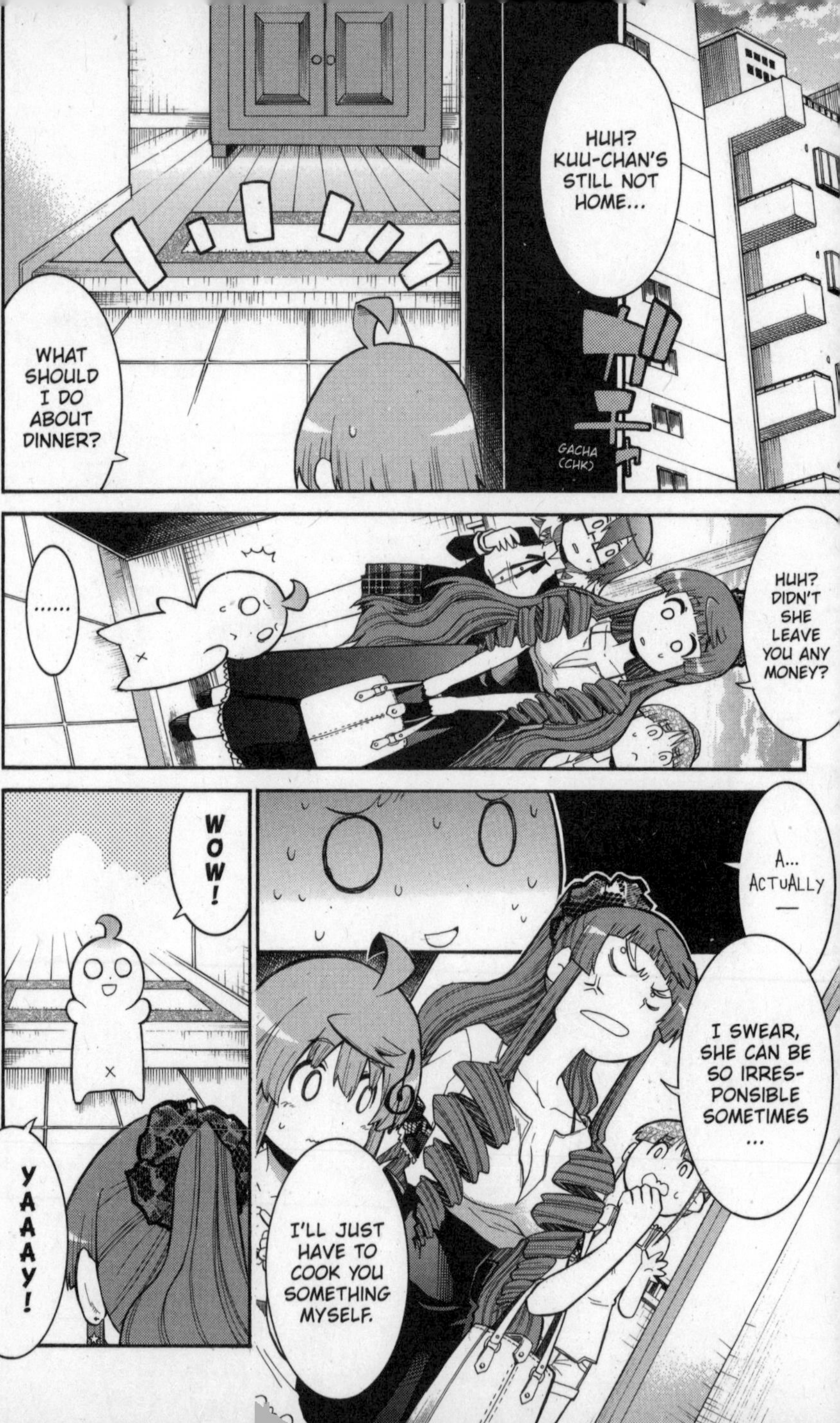
HUH? KUU-CHAN'S STILL NOT HOME...
GACHA (CHK)
WHAT SHOULD I DO ABOUT DINNER?
HUH? DIDN'T SHE LEAVE YOU ANY MONEY?
......
A... ACTUALLY—
I SWEAR, SHE CAN BE SO IRRES-PONSIBLE SOMETIMES...
I'LL JUST HAVE TO COOK YOU SOMETHING MYSELF.
WOW!
YAAAAY!

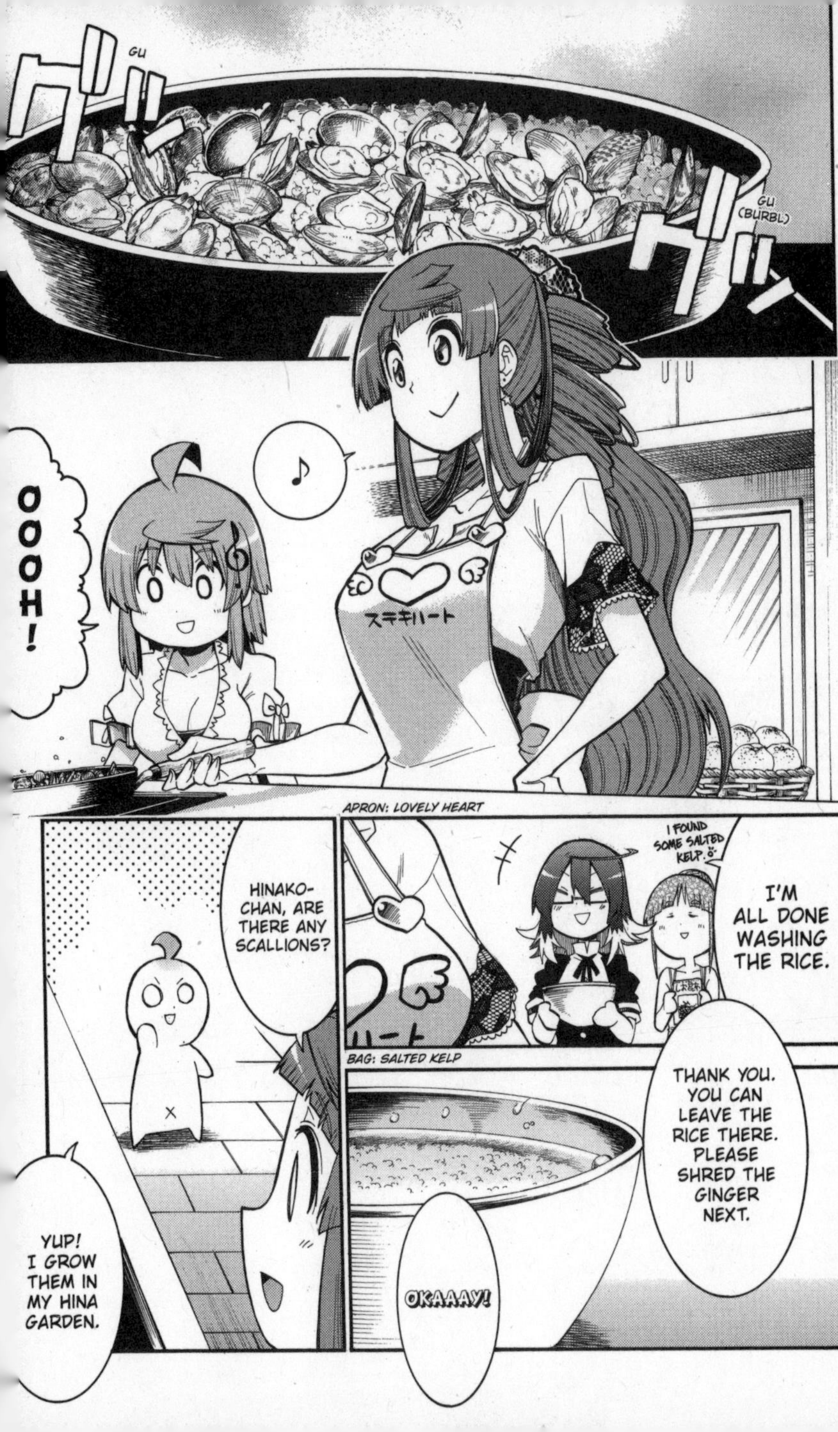
GU
(BURBL)
GU
♪
OOOOH!
ステキハート
APRON: LOVELY HEART
I'M ALL DONE WASHING THE RICE.
I FOUND SOME SALTED KELP.
BAG: SALTED KELP
THANK YOU. YOU CAN LEAVE THE RICE THERE. PLEASE SHRED THE GINGER NEXT.
OKAAAY!
HINAKO-CHAN, ARE THERE ANY SCALLIONS?
YUP! I GROW THEM IN MY HINA GARDEN.

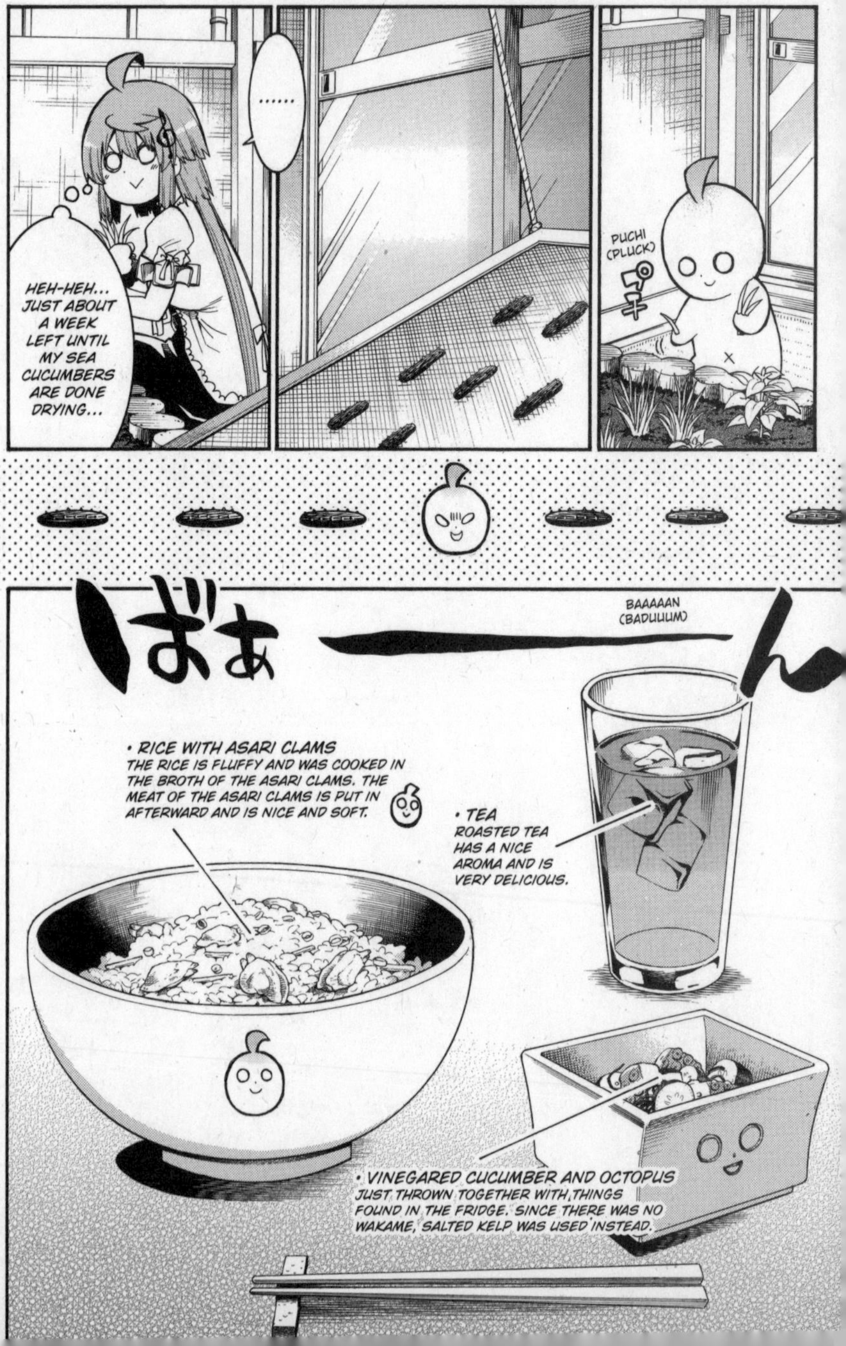
PUCHI (PLUCK)
......
HEH-HEH... JUST ABOUT A WEEK LEFT UNTIL MY SEA CUCUMBERS ARE DONE DRYING...
ばぁーーん
BAAAAAN (BADUUUM)
• RICE WITH ASARI CLAMS
THE RICE IS FLUFFY AND WAS COOKED IN THE BROTH OF THE ASARI CLAMS. THE MEAT OF THE ASARI CLAMS IS PUT IN AFTERWARD AND IS NICE AND SOFT.
• TEA
ROASTED TEA HAS A NICE AROMA AND IS VERY DELICIOUS.
• VINEGARED CUCUMBER AND OCTOPUS
JUST THROWN TOGETHER WITH THINGS FOUND IN THE FRIDGE. SINCE THERE WAS NO WAKAME, SALTED KELP WAS USED INSTEAD.

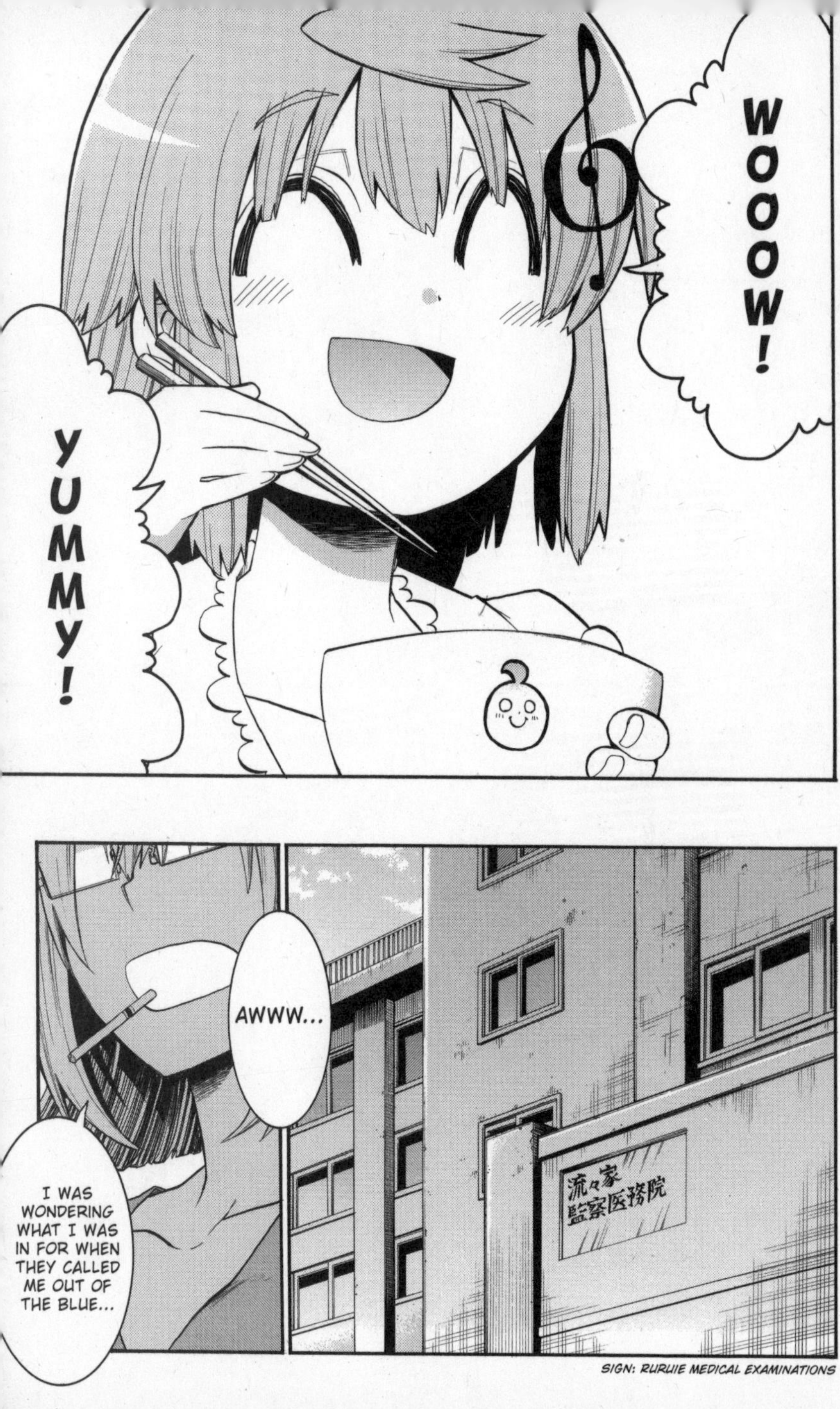
WOOOW!
YUMMY!
流々家
監察医務院
AWWW...
I WAS WONDERING WHAT I WAS IN FOR WHEN THEY CALLED ME OUT OF THE BLUE...
SIGN: RURUIE MEDICAL EXAMINATIONS

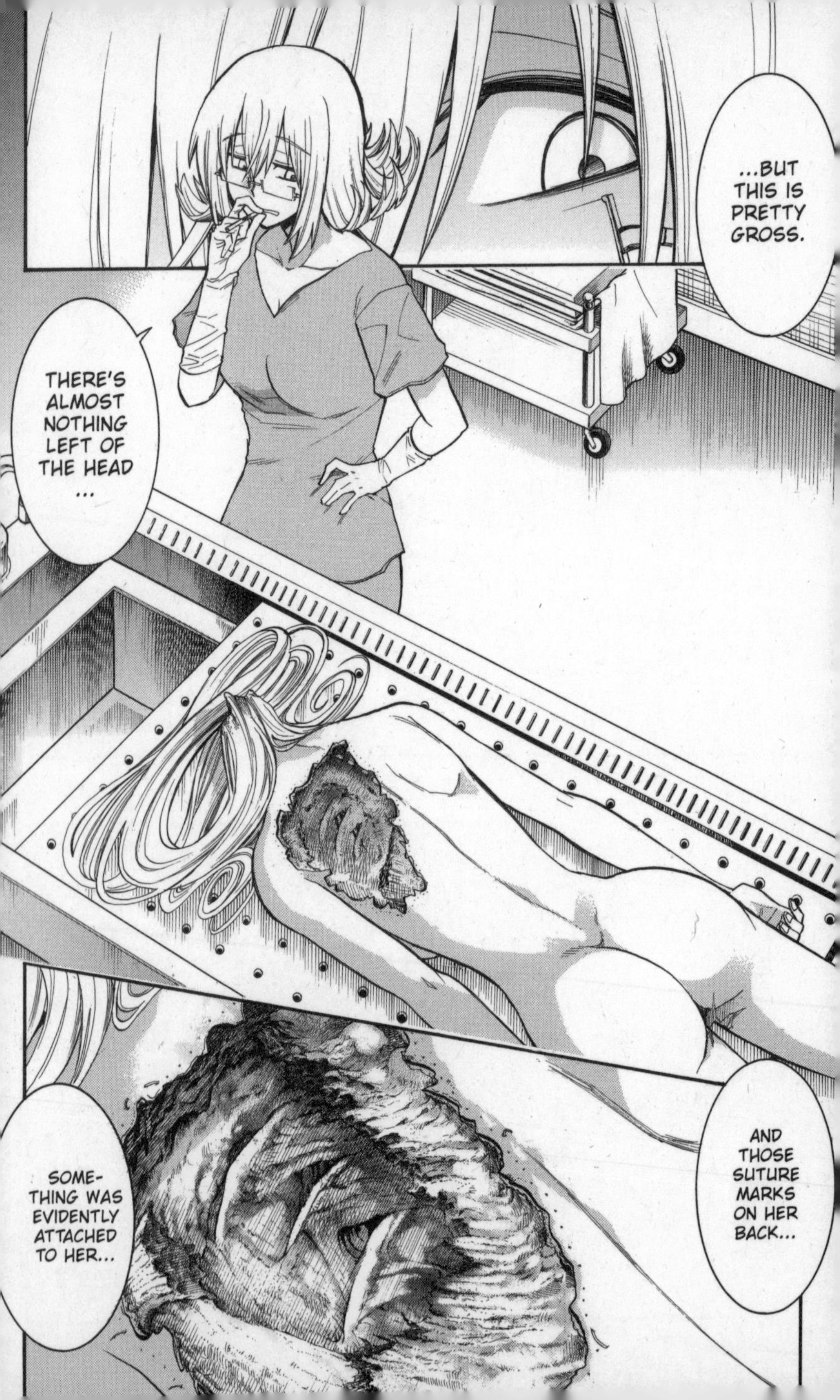
...BUT THIS IS PRETTY GROSS.
THERE'S ALMOST NOTHING LEFT OF THE HEAD...
AND THOSE SUTURE MARKS ON HER BACK...
SOME-THING WAS EVIDENTLY ATTACHED TO HER...

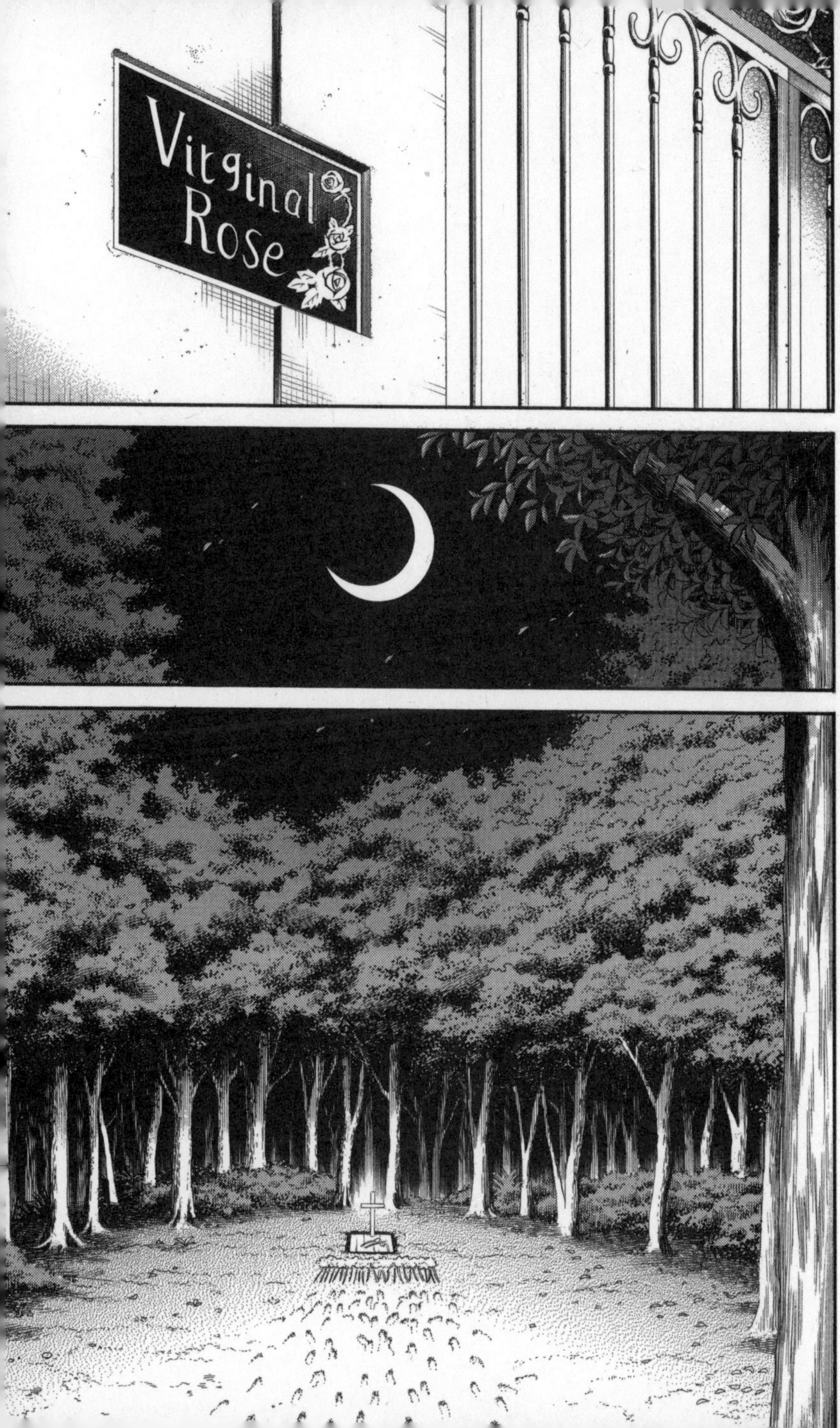
Virginal Rose

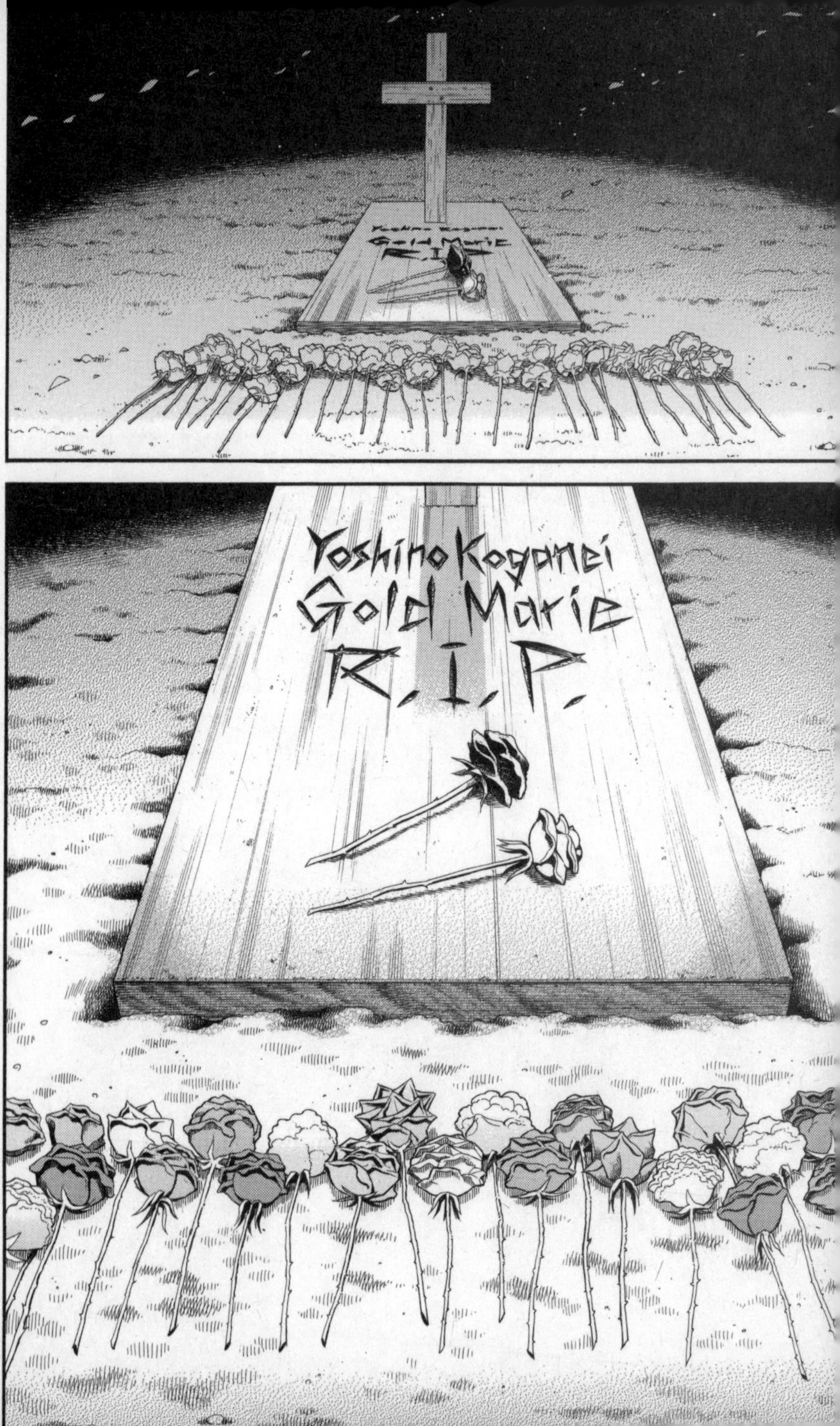
Yoshino Koganei
Gold Marie
R.I.P.

**MURCIÉLAGO**

MURCIÉLAGO

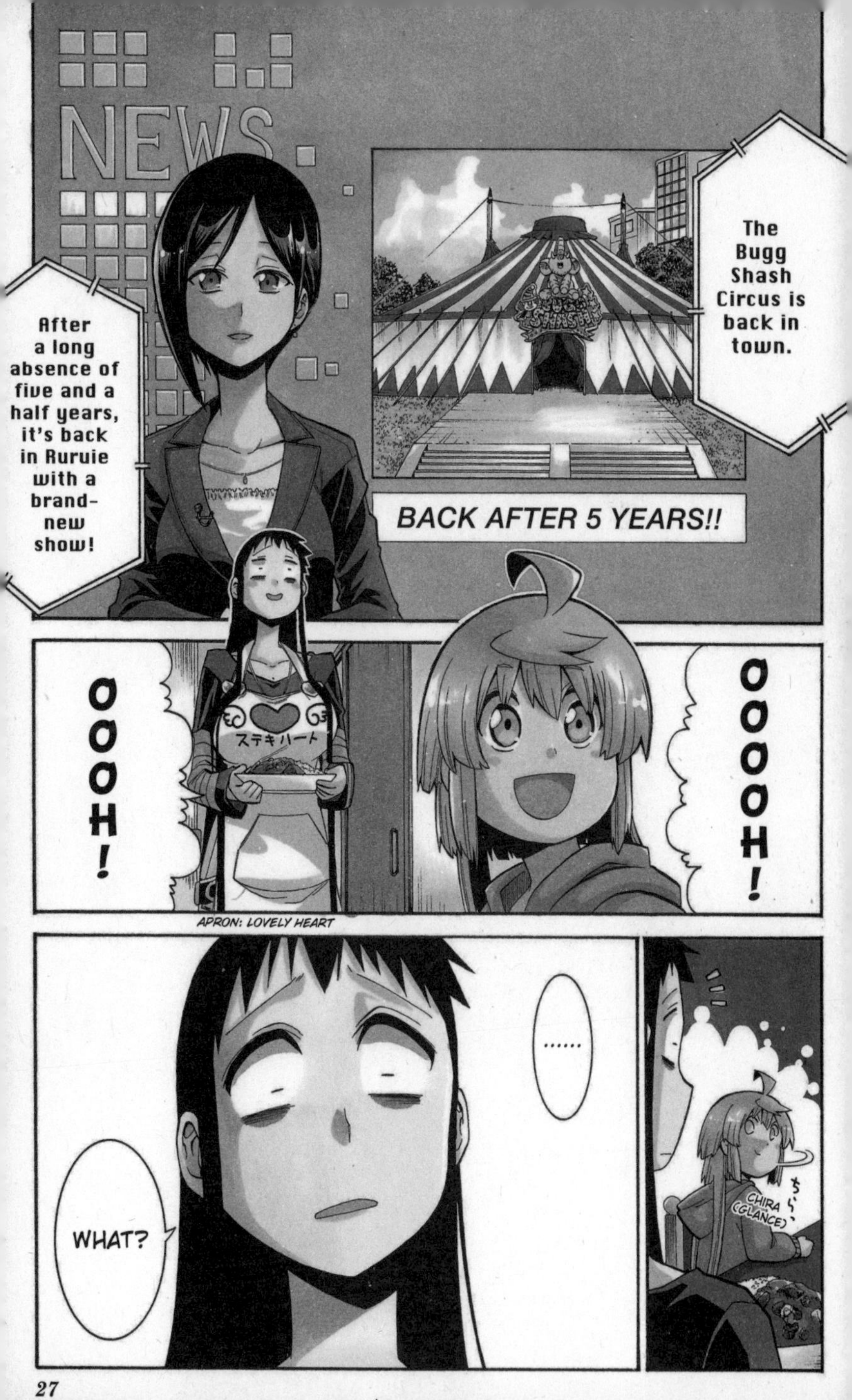
NEWS
The Bugg Shash Circus is back in town.
BACK AFTER 5 YEARS!!
After a long absence of five and a half years, it's back in Ruruie with a brand-new show!
OOOOH!
OOOH!
ステキハート
APRON: LOVELY HEART
ちら
CHIRA (GLANCE)
......
WHAT?

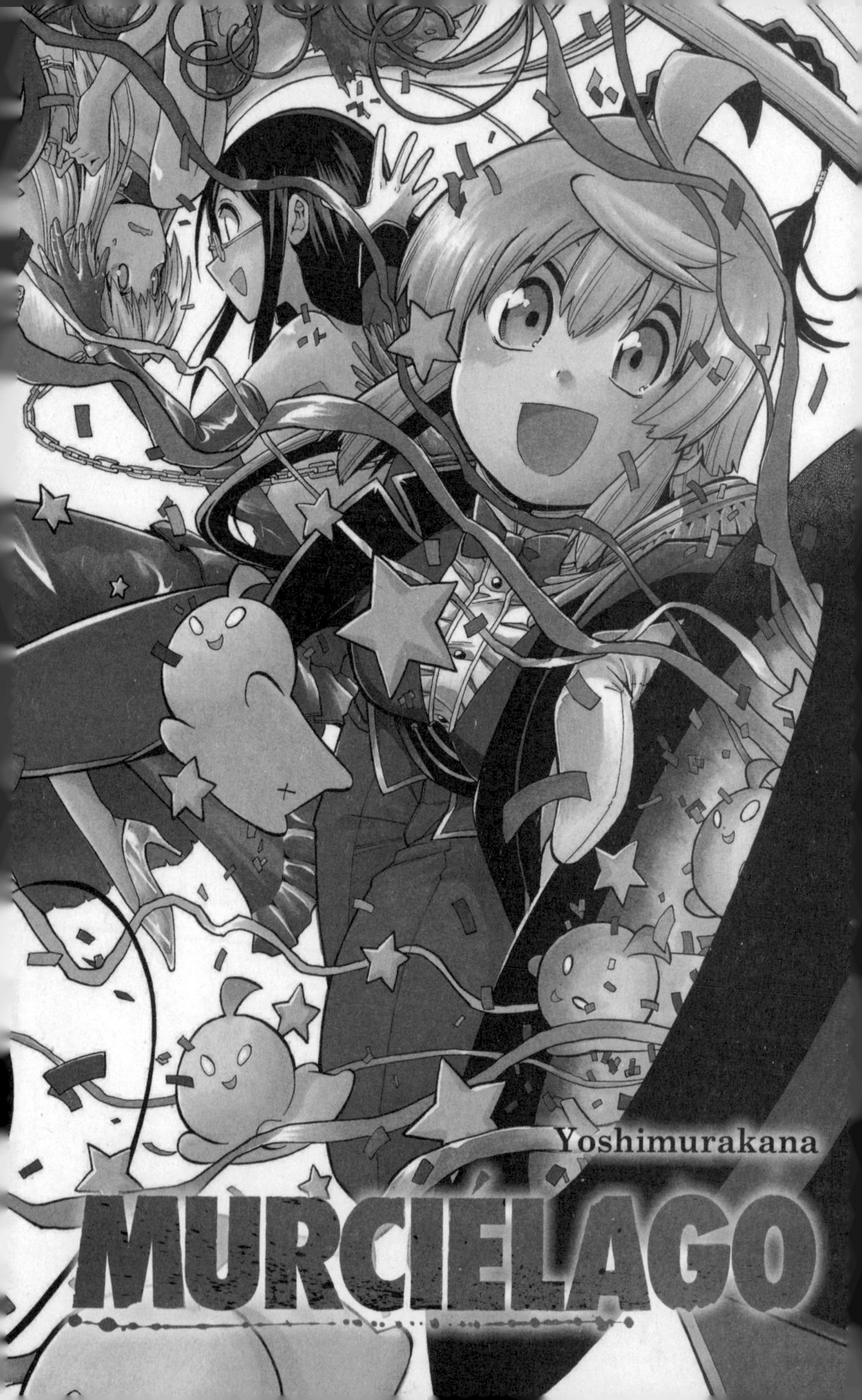
Yoshimurakana
MURCIELAGO

# Chapter 99 The Entertainer

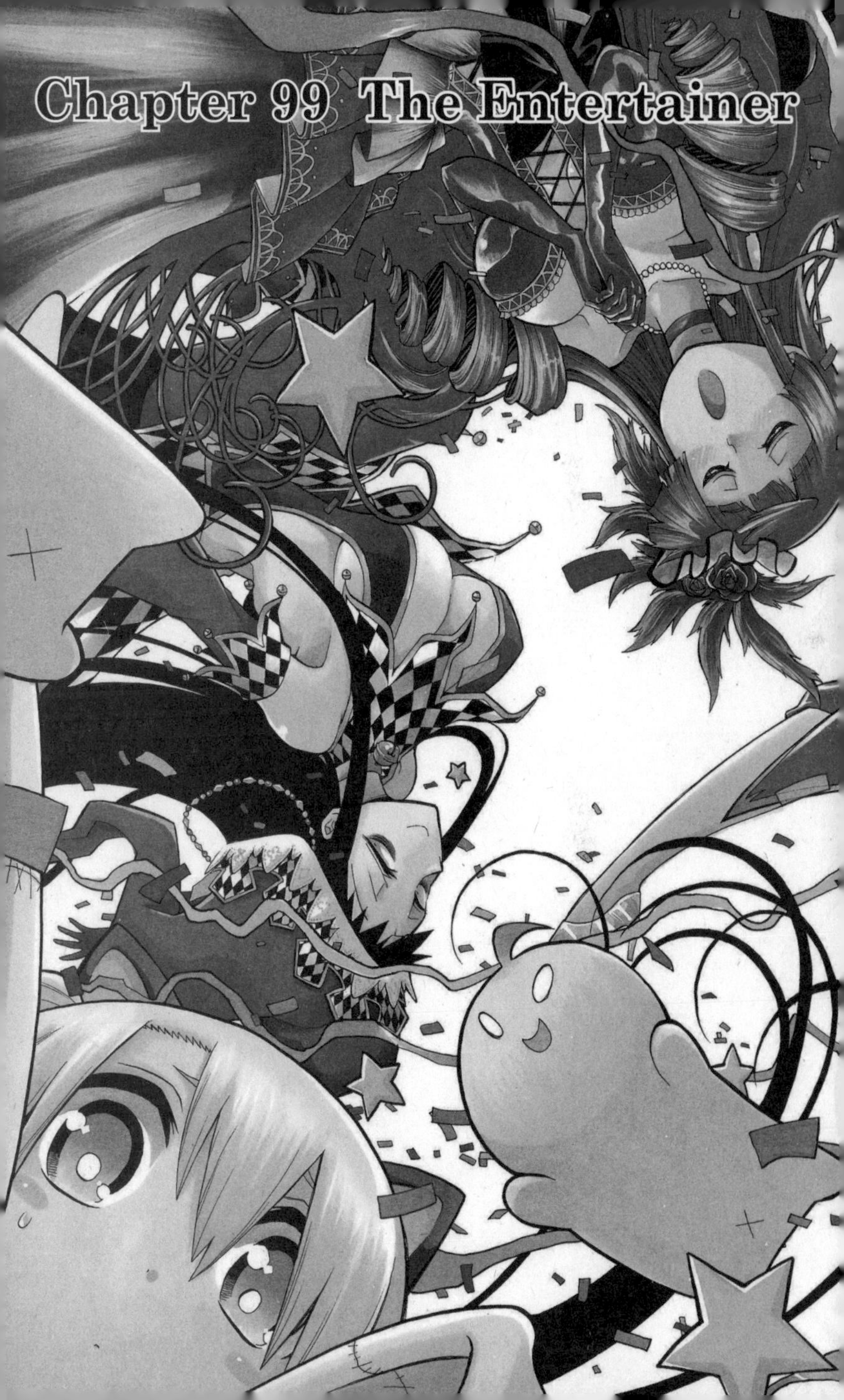

MURCIÉLAGO

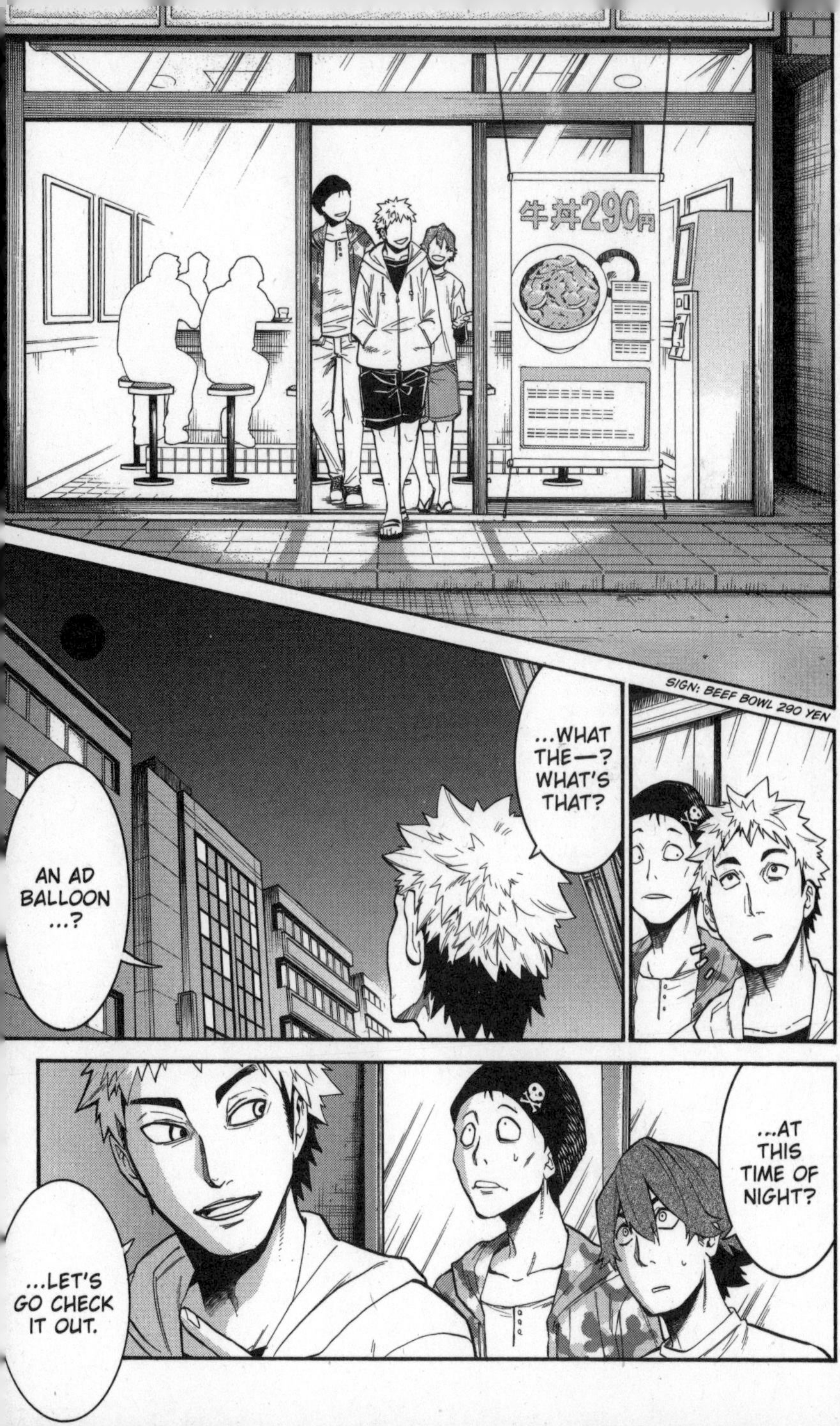
牛丼290円
SIGN: BEEF BOWL 290 YEN
...WHAT THE—? WHAT'S THAT?
AN AD BALLOON ...?
...AT THIS TIME OF NIGHT?
...LET'S GO CHECK IT OUT.

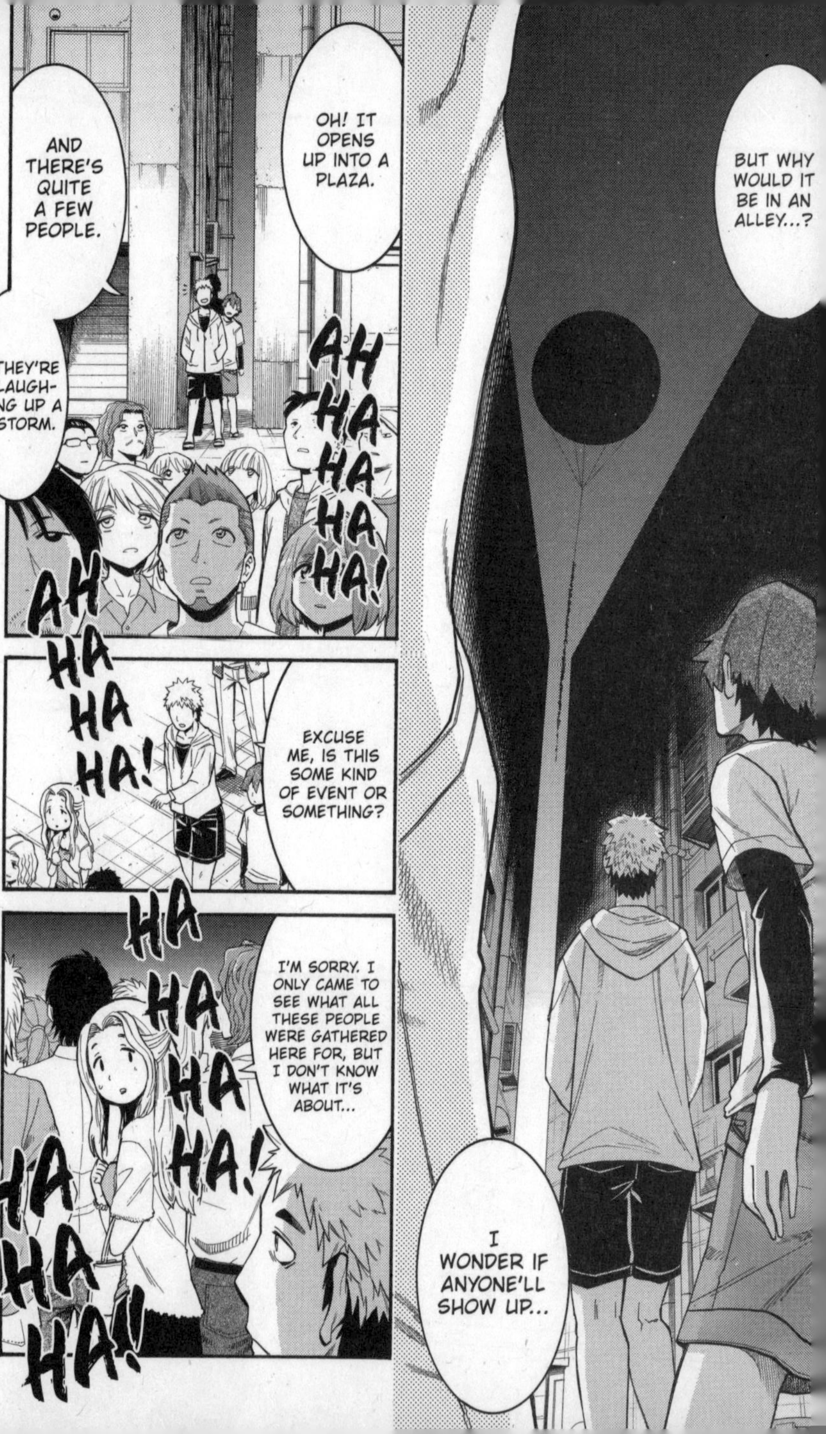
BUT WHY WOULD IT BE IN AN ALLEY...?
I WONDER IF ANYONE'LL SHOW UP...
OH! IT OPENS UP INTO A PLAZA.
AND THERE'S QUITE A FEW PEOPLE.
THEY'RE LAUGH-ING UP A STORM.
AH HA HA HA HA!
AH HA HA HA HA!
EXCUSE ME, IS THIS SOME KIND OF EVENT OR SOMETHING?
I'M SORRY. I ONLY CAME TO SEE WHAT ALL THESE PEOPLE WERE GATHERED HERE FOR, BUT I DON'T KNOW WHAT IT'S ABOUT...
HA HA HA HA HA!
HA HA HA HA!

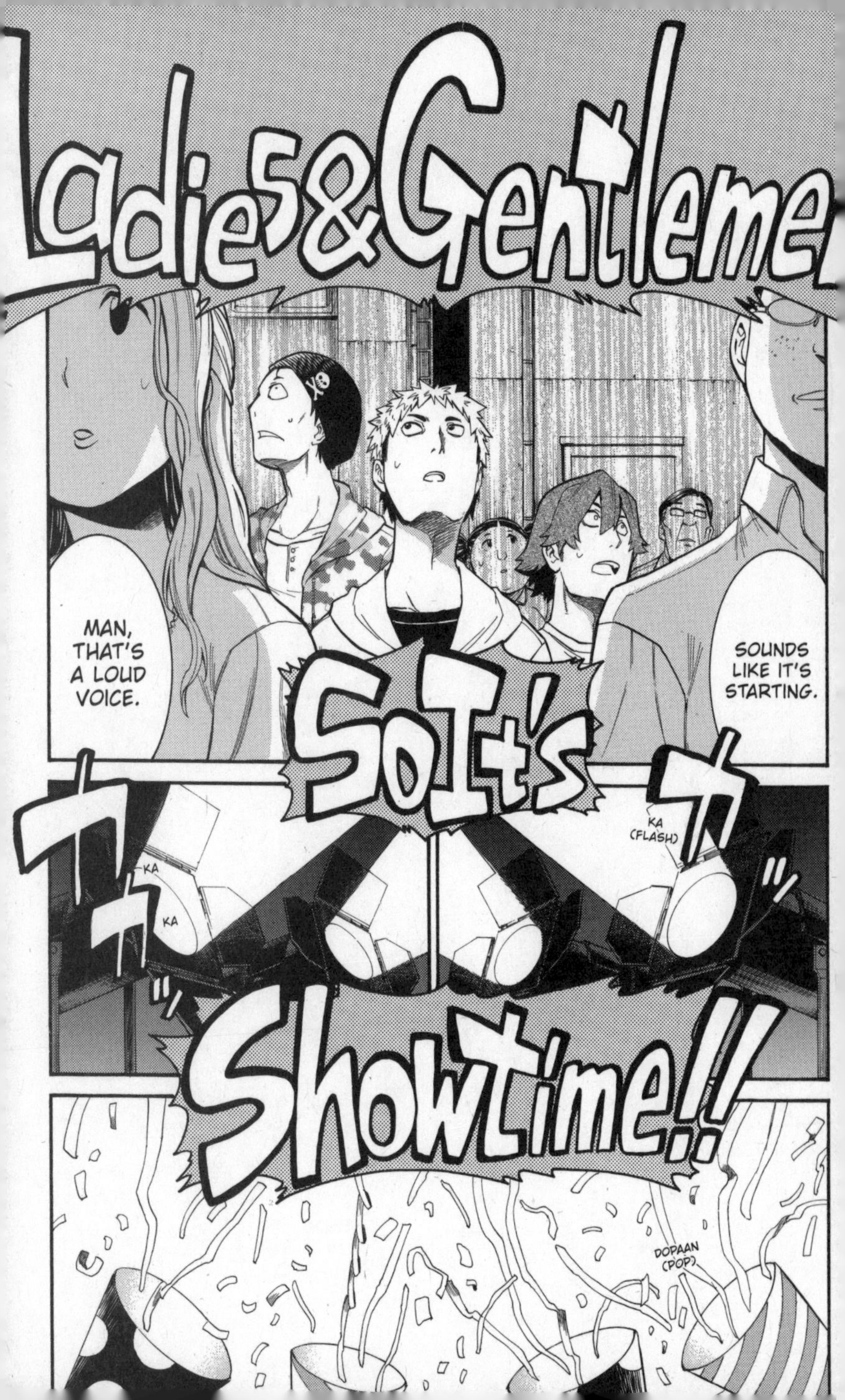
Ladies & Gentleme
SOUNDS LIKE IT'S STARTING.
MAN, THAT'S A LOUD VOICE.
So It's
KA (FLASH)
KA
KA
Showtime!!
DOPAAN (POP)

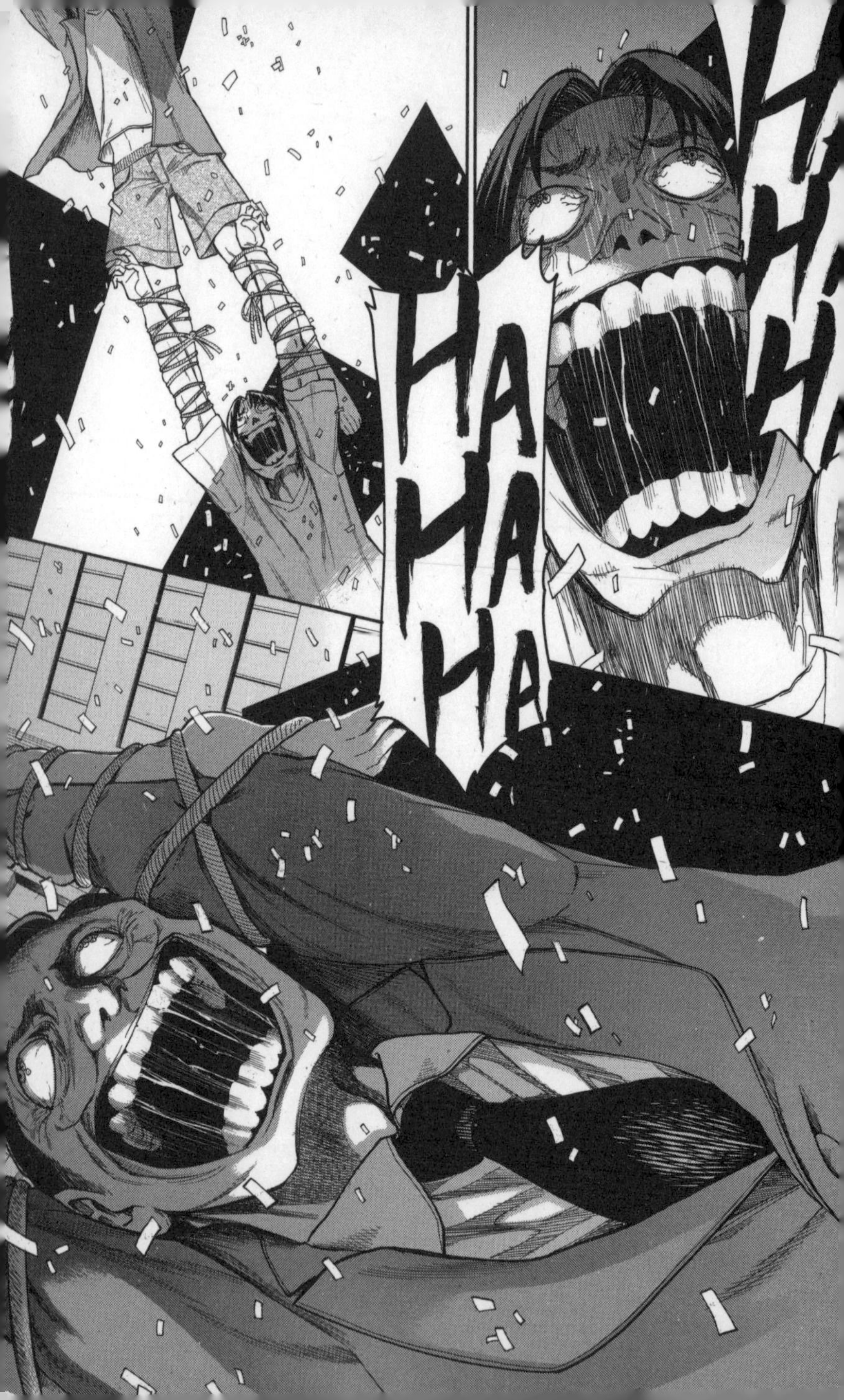

HA
HA
HA
HA

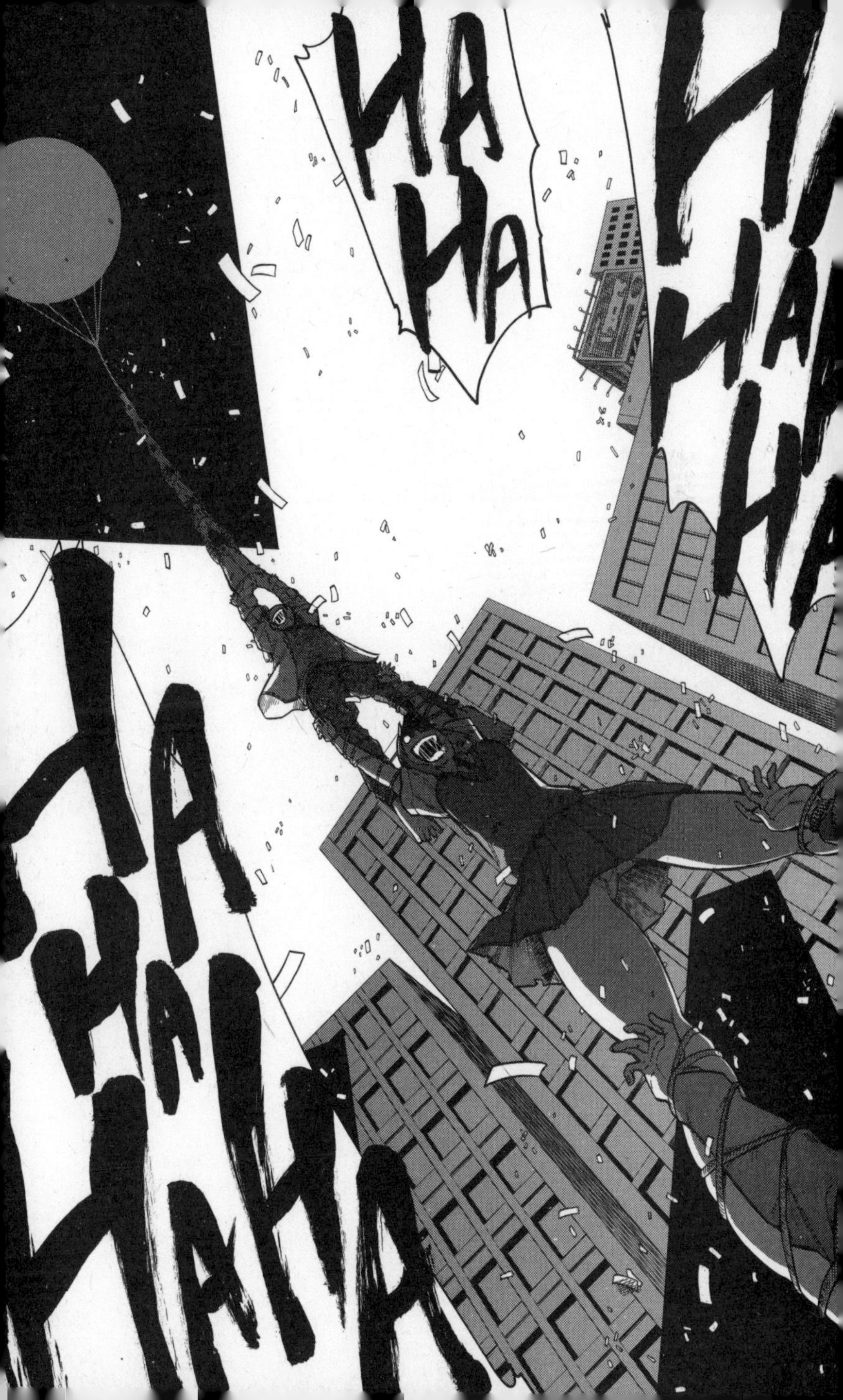
HA HA HA
HA HA HA HA

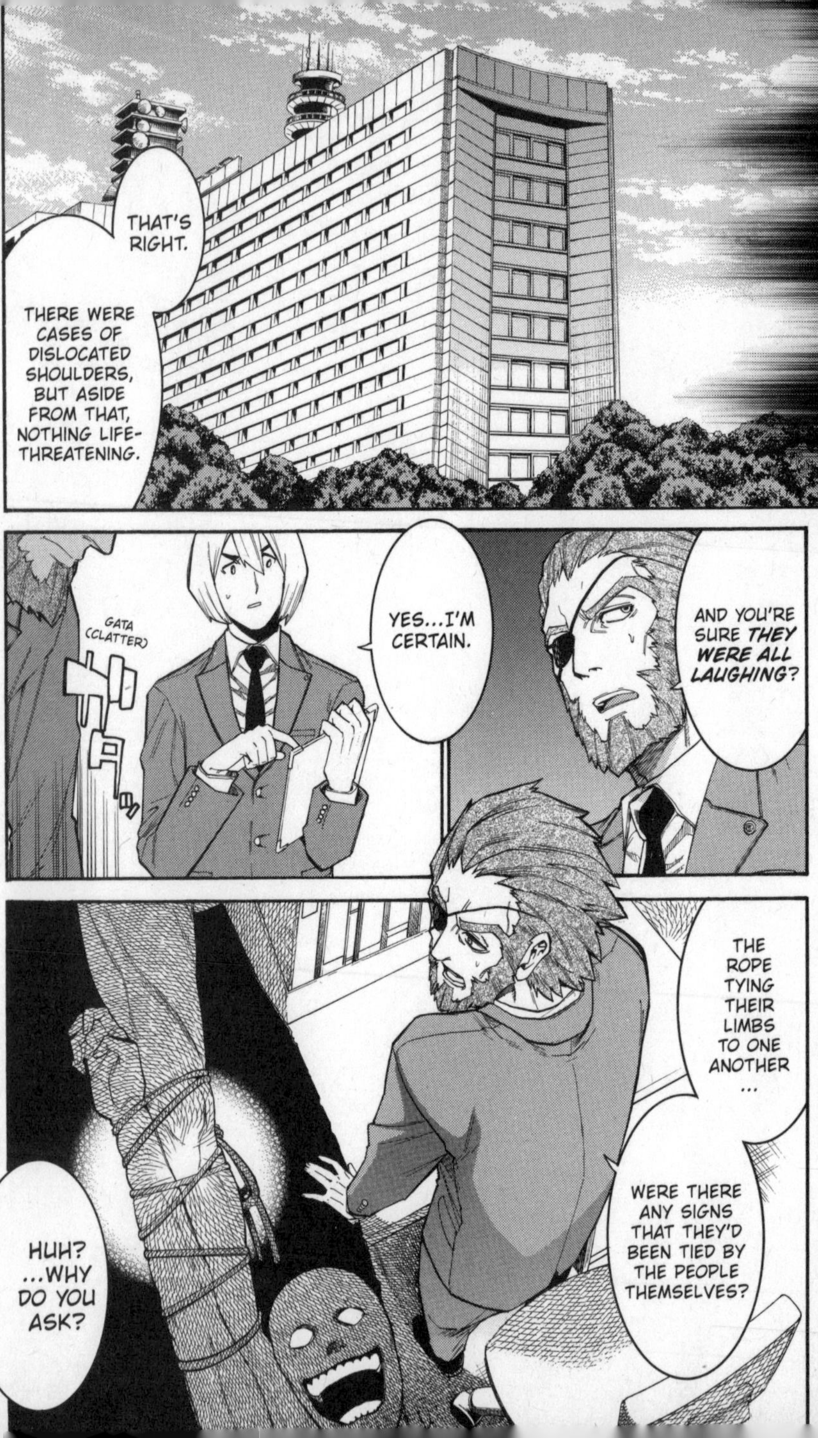
THAT'S RIGHT.
THERE WERE CASES OF DISLOCATED SHOULDERS, BUT ASIDE FROM THAT, NOTHING LIFE-THREATENING.
AND YOU'RE SURE *THEY WERE ALL LAUGHING*?
YES...I'M CERTAIN.
GATA (CLATTER)
THE ROPE TYING THEIR LIMBS TO ONE ANOTHER ...
WERE THERE ANY SIGNS THAT THEY'D BEEN TIED BY THE PEOPLE THEMSELVES?
HUH? ...WHY DO YOU ASK?

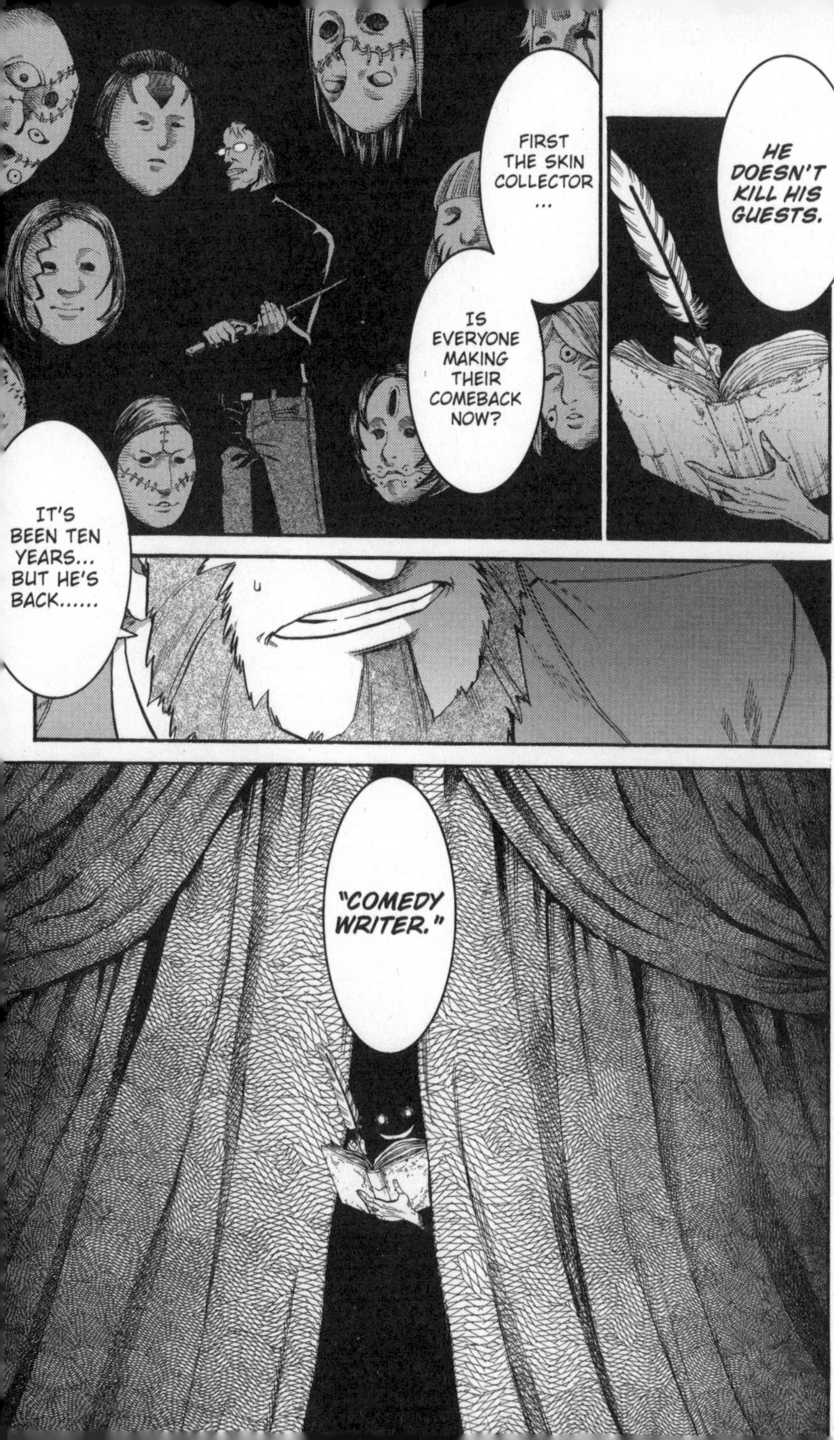
HE DOESN'T KILL HIS GUESTS.
FIRST THE SKIN COLLECTOR ...
IS EVERYONE MAKING THEIR COMEBACK NOW?
IT'S BEEN TEN YEARS... BUT HE'S BACK......
"COMEDY WRITER."

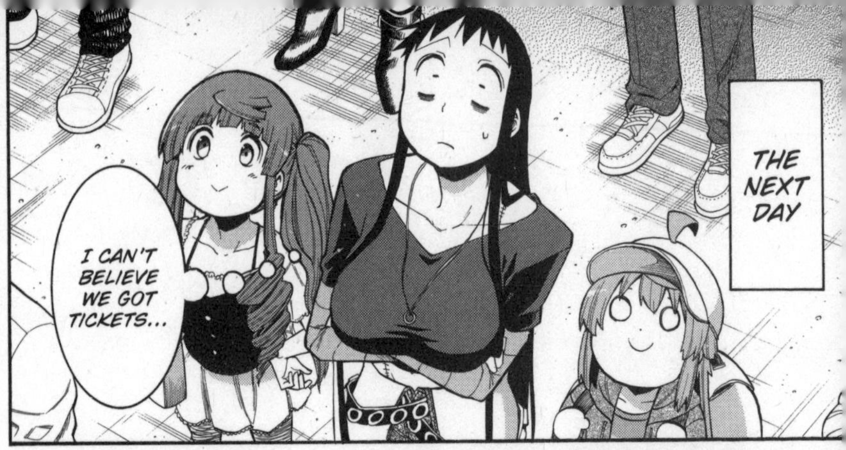
THE NEXT DAY
I CAN'T BELIEVE WE GOT TICKETS...
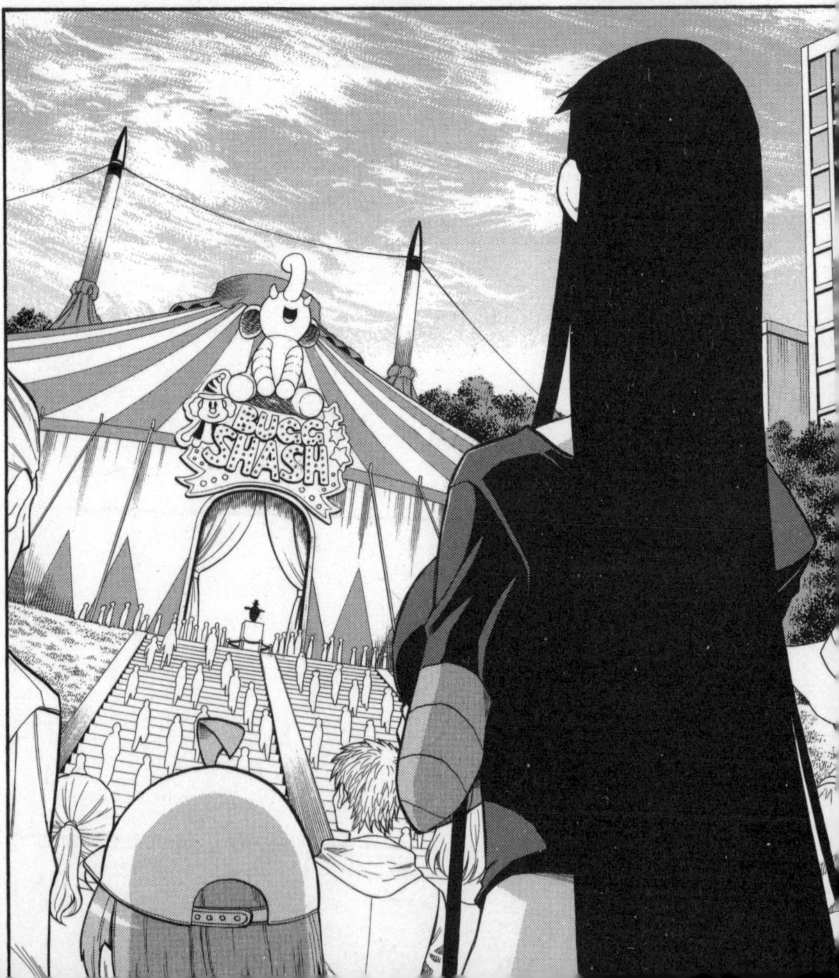
BUGG SHASH

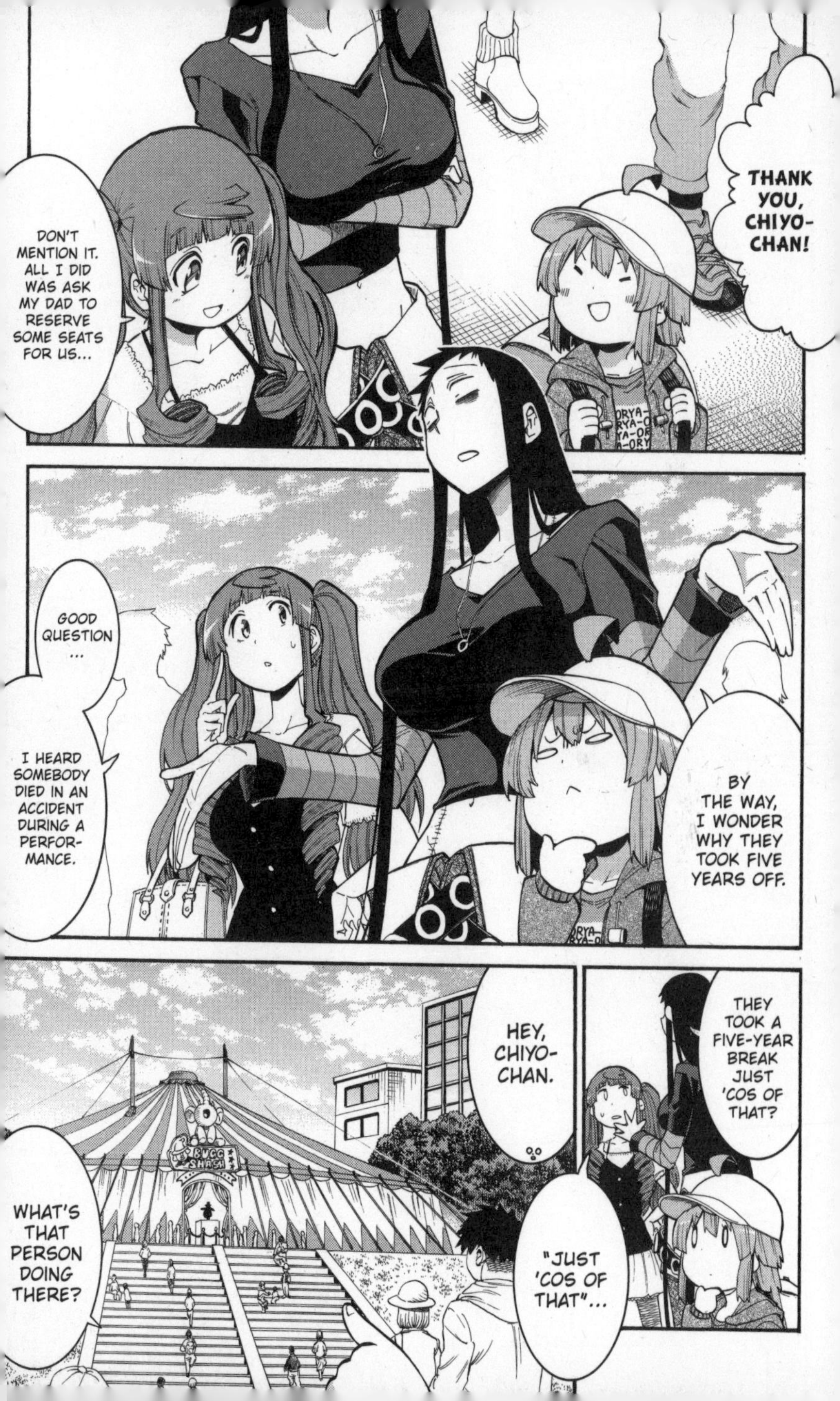
THANK YOU, CHIYO-CHAN!
DON'T MENTION IT. ALL I DID WAS ASK MY DAD TO RESERVE SOME SEATS FOR US...
BY THE WAY, I WONDER WHY THEY TOOK FIVE YEARS OFF.
GOOD QUESTION...
I HEARD SOMEBODY DIED IN AN ACCIDENT DURING A PERFORMANCE.
THEY TOOK A FIVE-YEAR BREAK JUST 'COS OF THAT?
"JUST 'COS OF THAT"...
HEY, CHIYO-CHAN.
WHAT'S THAT PERSON DOING THERE?

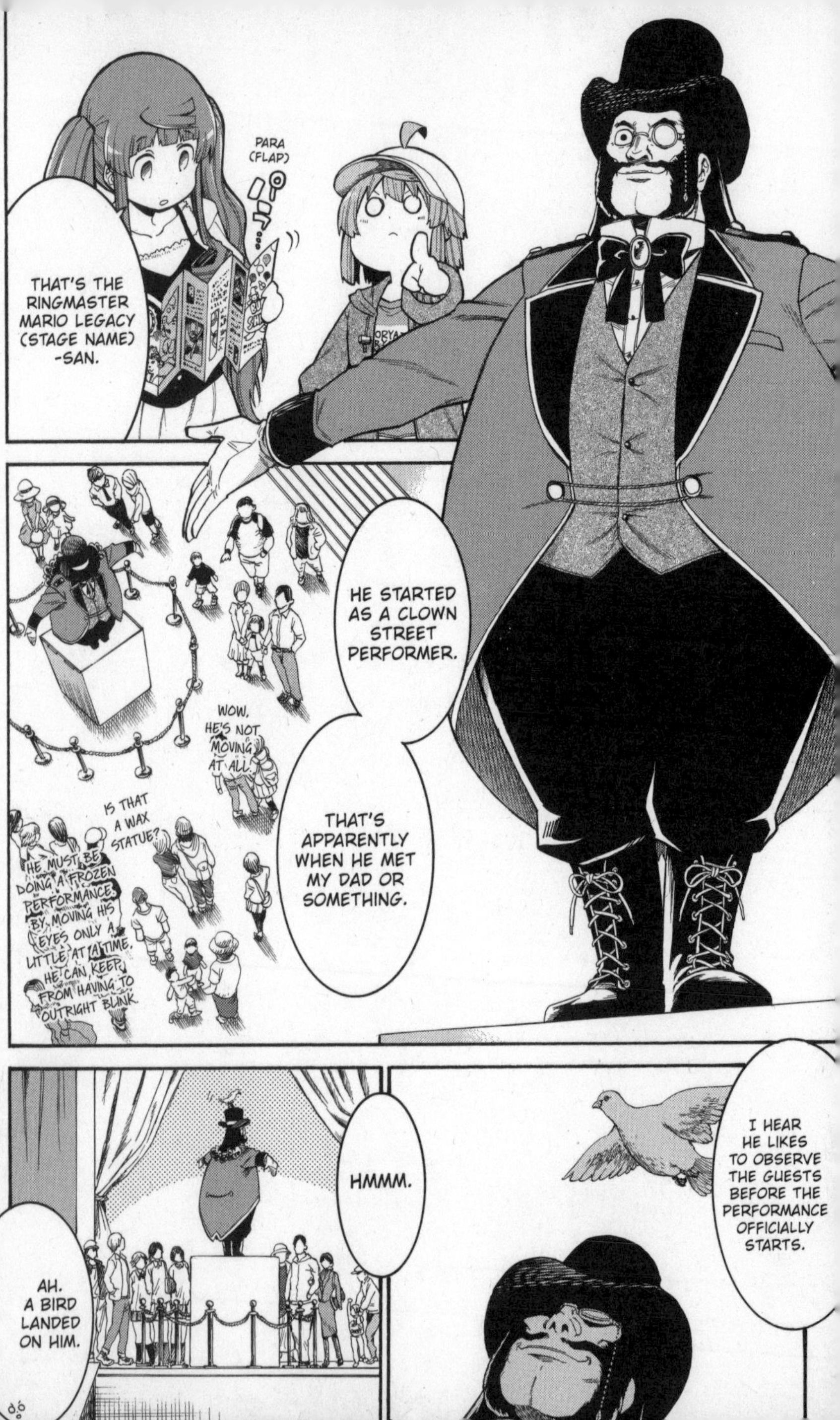
PARA (FLAP)
THAT'S THE RINGMASTER MARIO LEGACY (STAGE NAME) -SAN.
HE STARTED AS A CLOWN STREET PERFORMER.
THAT'S APPARENTLY WHEN HE MET MY DAD OR SOMETHING.
WOW, HE'S NOT MOVING AT ALL.
IS THAT A WAX STATUE?
HE MUST BE DOING A FROZEN PERFORMANCE. BY MOVING HIS EYES ONLY A LITTLE AT A TIME, HE CAN KEEP FROM HAVING TO OUTRIGHT BLINK.
I HEAR HE LIKES TO OBSERVE THE GUESTS BEFORE THE PERFORMANCE OFFICIALLY STARTS.
HMMM.
AH. A BIRD LANDED ON HIM.

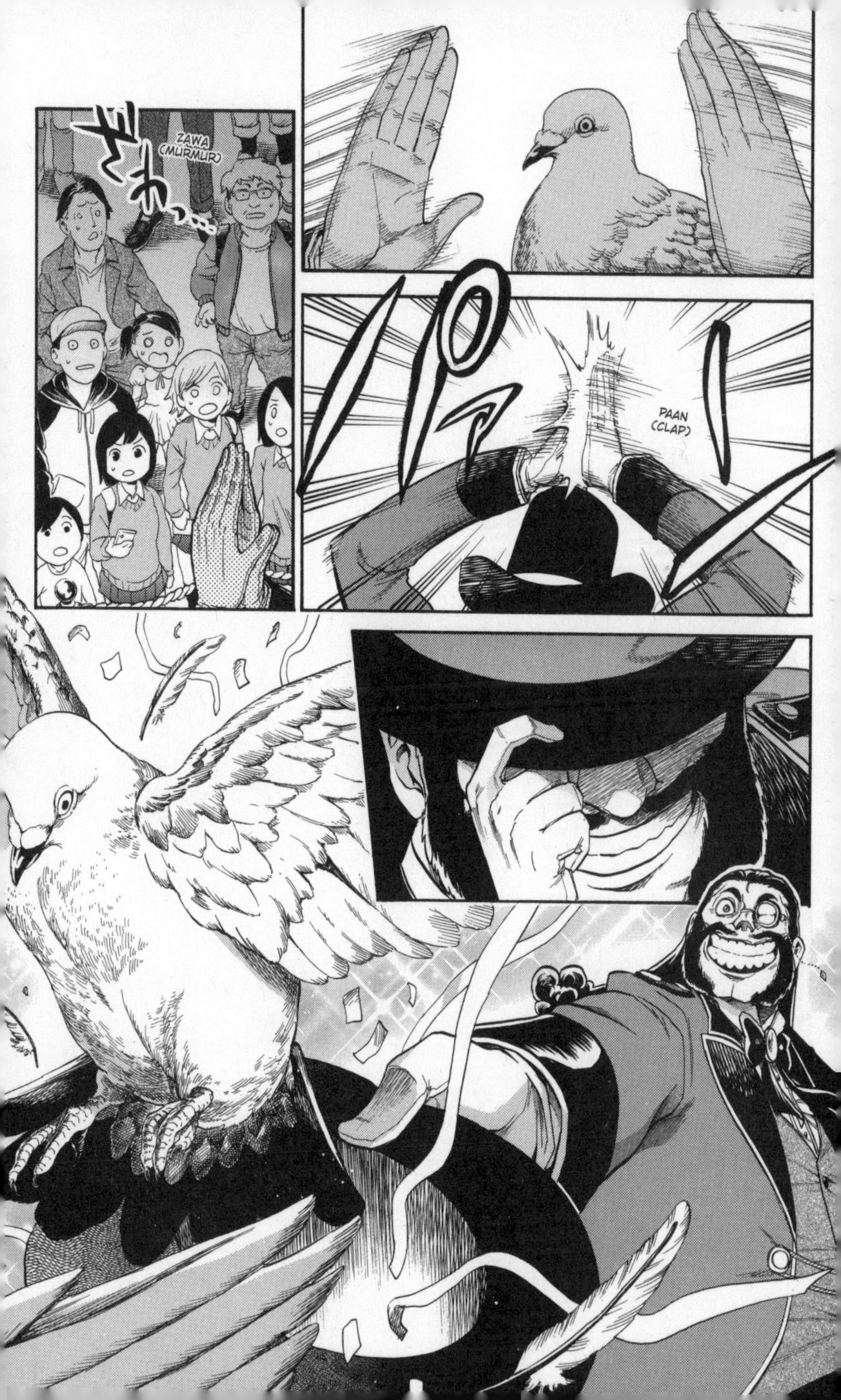
PAAN
(CLAP)
ZAWA
(MURMUR)

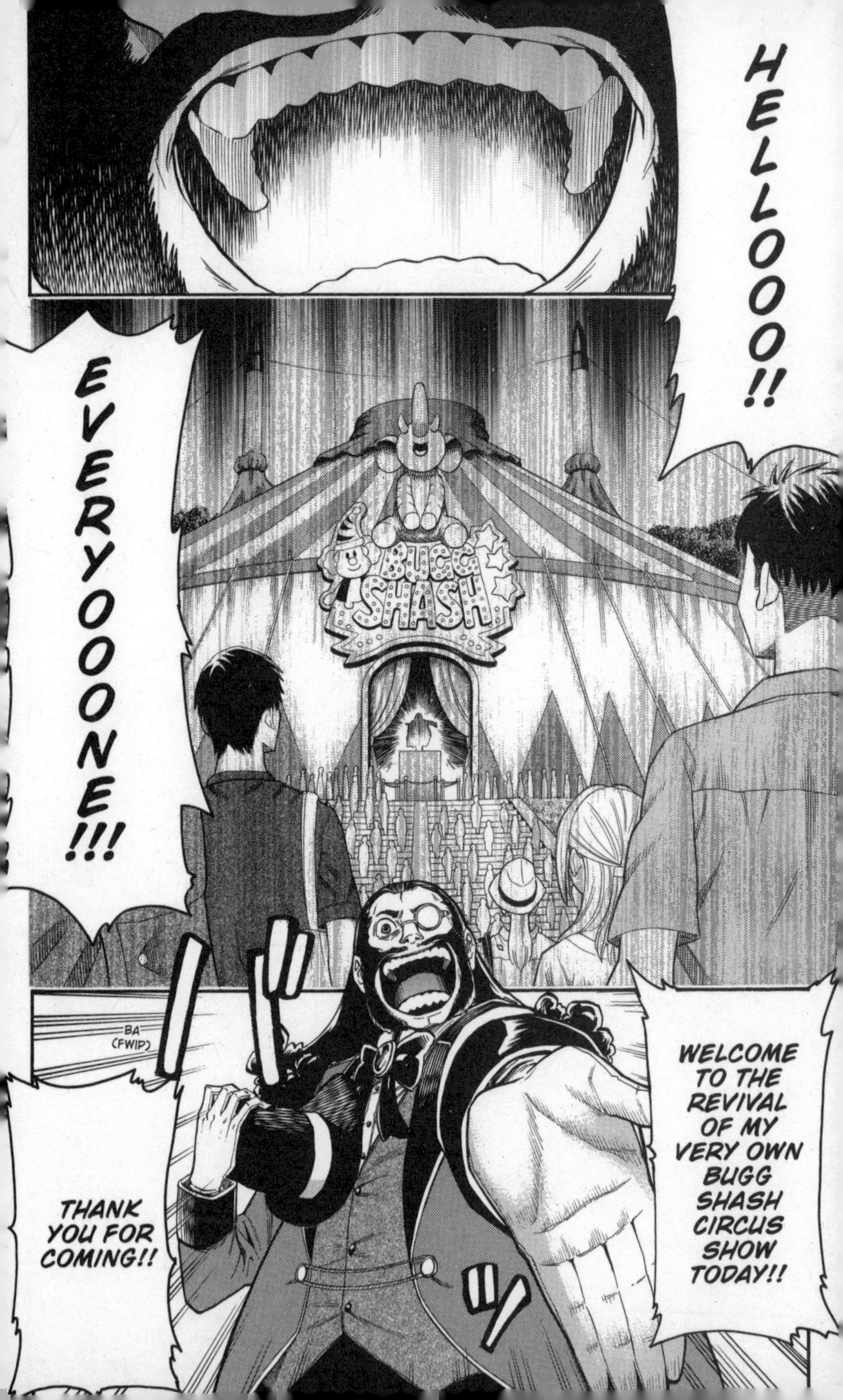
HELLOOOO!!
EVERYOOOONE!!!
BA (FWIP)
WELCOME TO THE REVIVAL OF MY VERY OWN BUGG SHASH CIRCUS SHOW TODAY!!
THANK YOU FOR COMING!!
BUGG SHASH

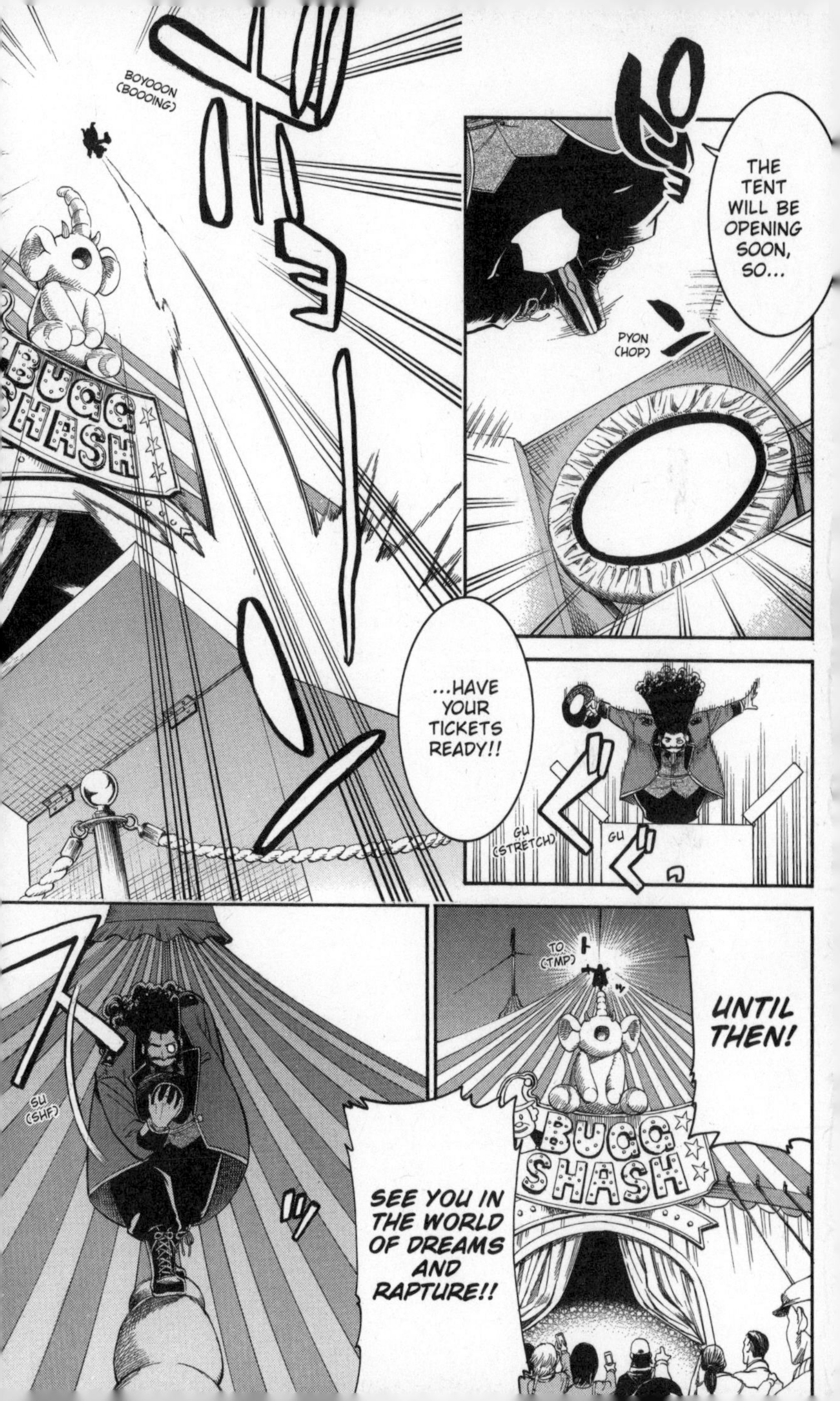
THE TENT WILL BE OPENING SOON, SO...
PYON (HOP)
GU (STRETCH)
GU
...HAVE YOUR TICKETS READY!!
BOYOON (BOOING)
BUGG SHASH
TO (TMP)
UNTIL THEN!
BUGG SHASH
SEE YOU IN THE WORLD OF DREAMS AND RAPTURE!!
SU (SHF)

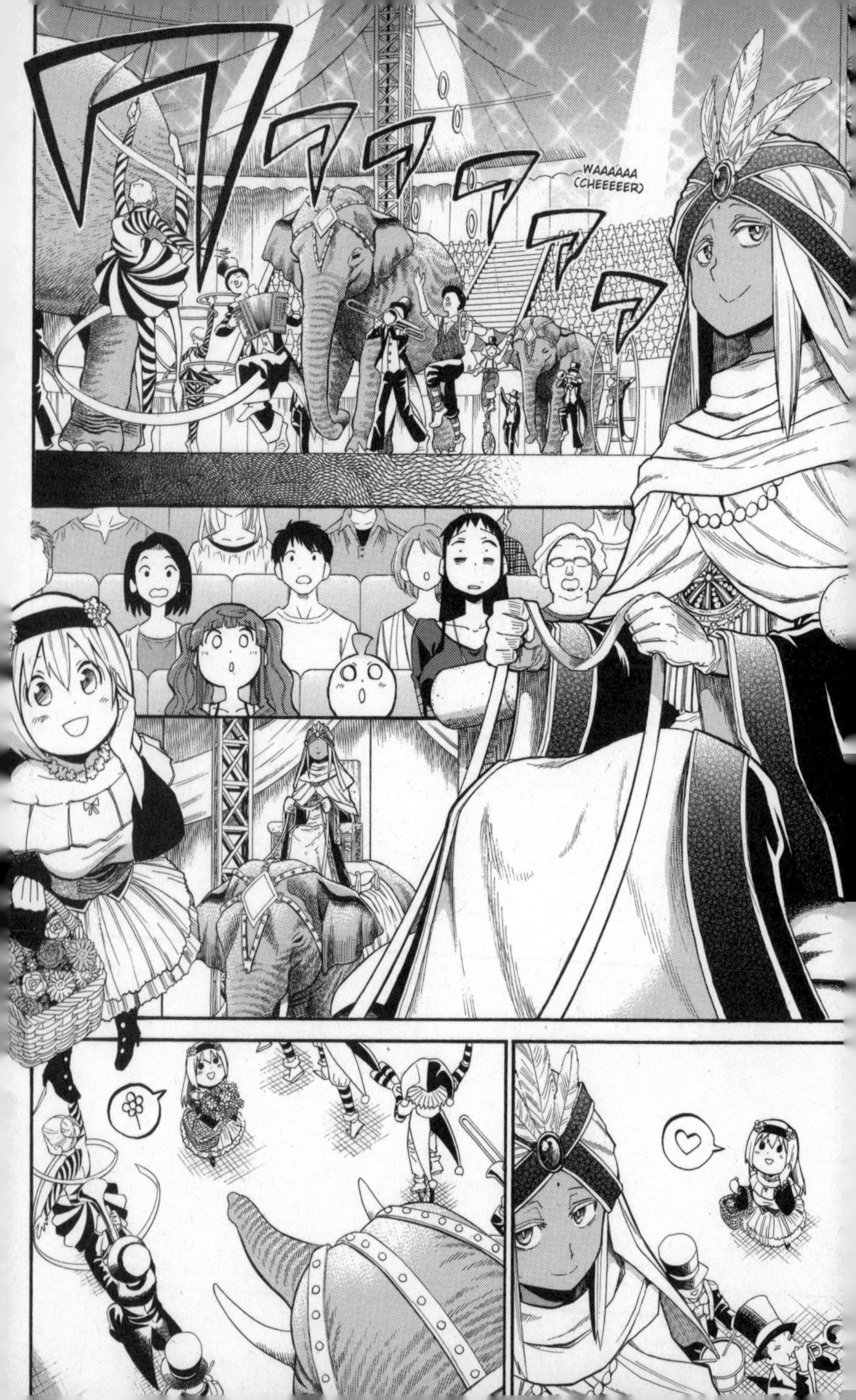
WAAAAAA
(CHEEEEER)

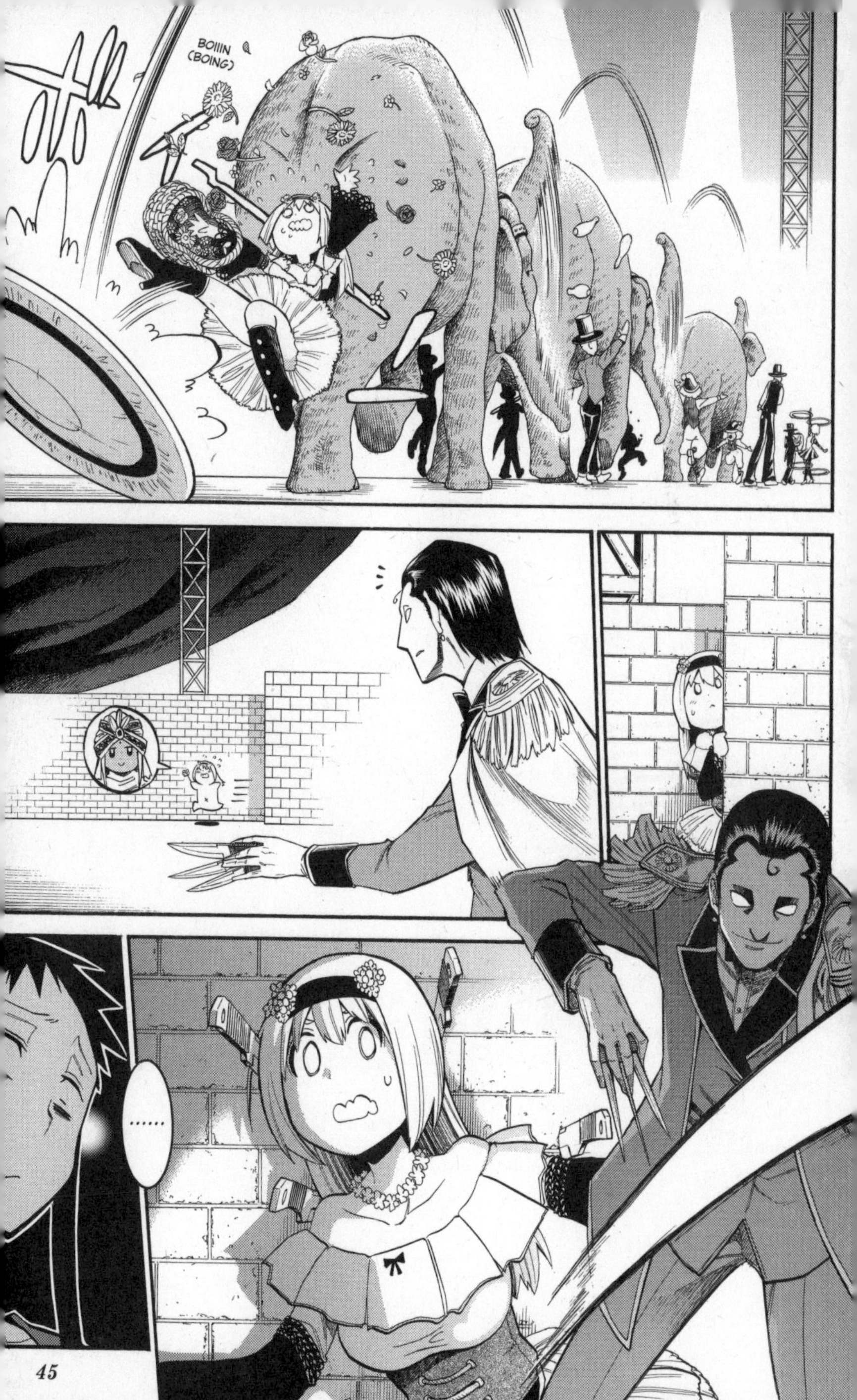
BOIIIN
(BOING)
......

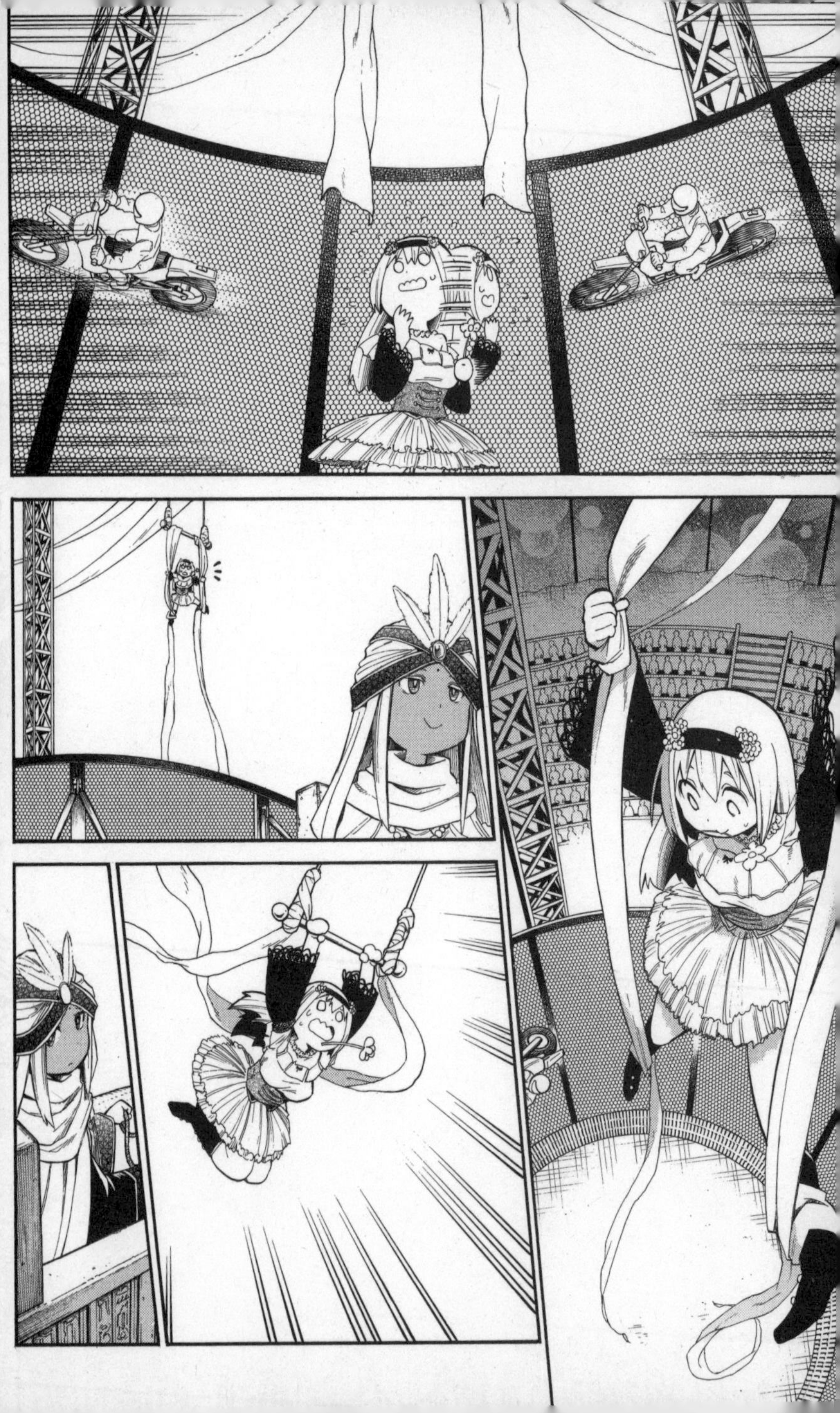

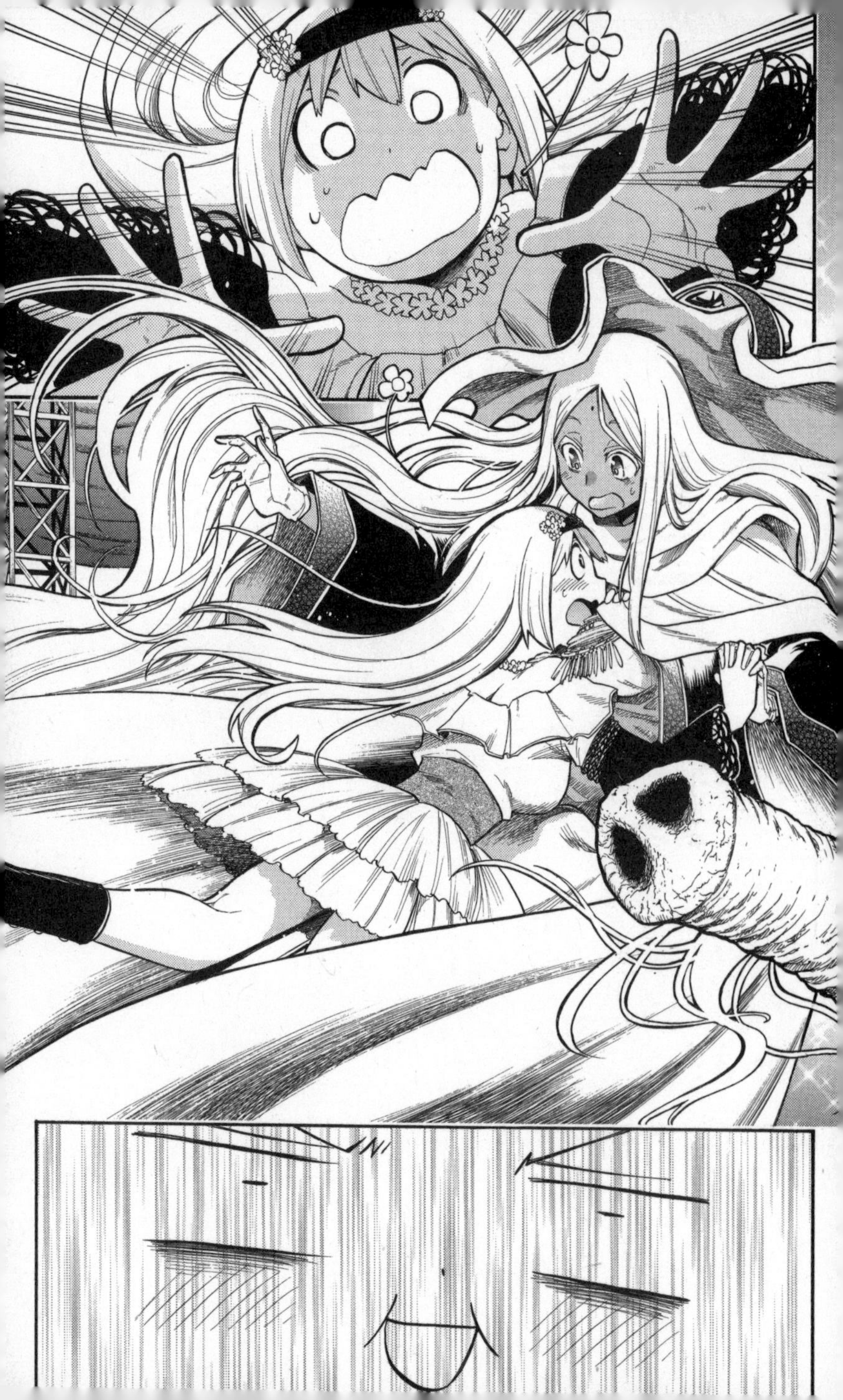

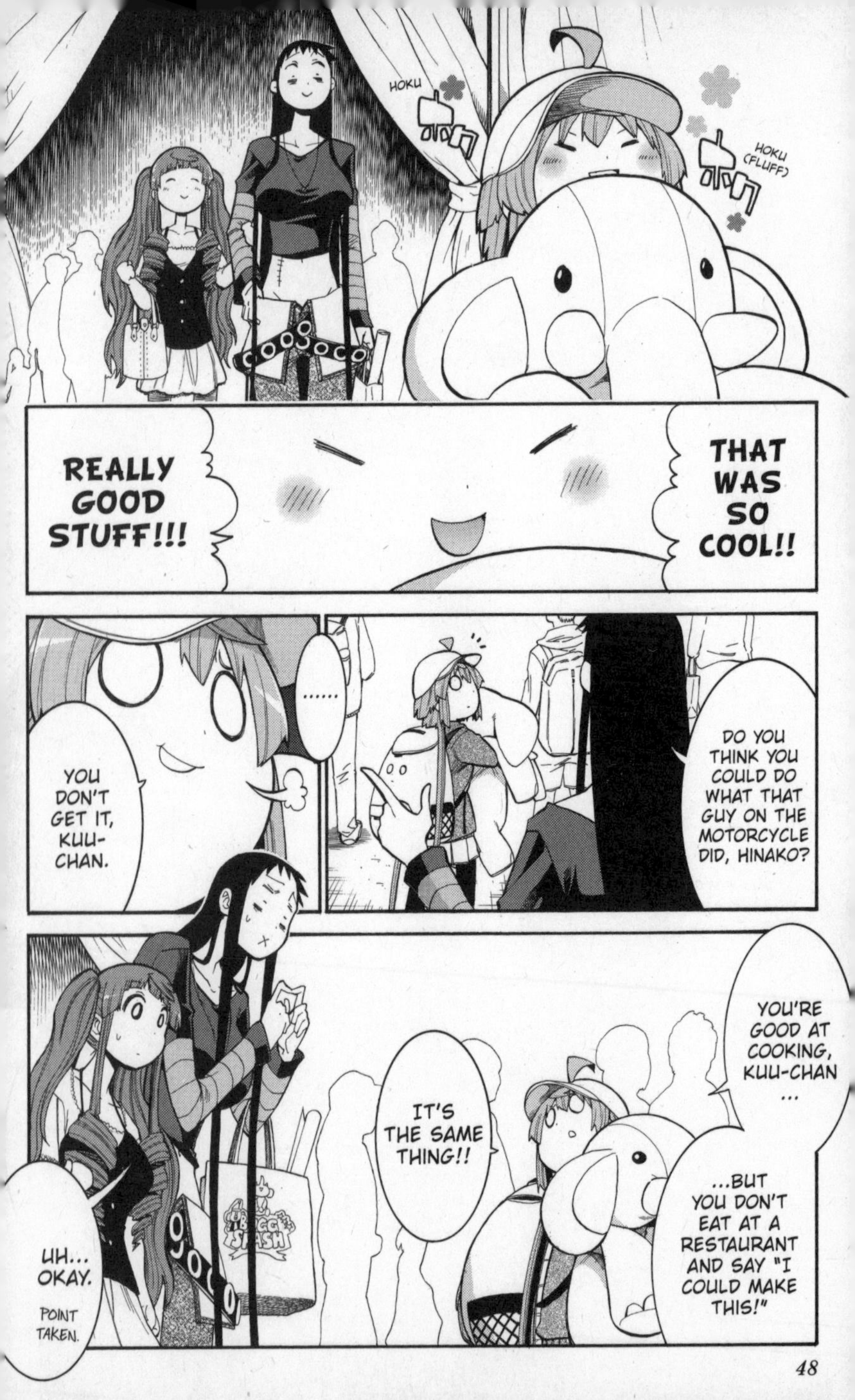
HOKU
HOKU (FLUFF)
THAT WAS SO COOL!!
REALLY GOOD STUFF!!!
DO YOU THINK YOU COULD DO WHAT THAT GUY ON THE MOTORCYCLE DID, HINAKO?
......
YOU DON'T GET IT, KUU-CHAN.
YOU'RE GOOD AT COOKING, KUU-CHAN ...
...BUT YOU DON'T EAT AT A RESTAURANT AND SAY "I COULD MAKE THIS!"
IT'S THE SAME THING!!
UH... OKAY.
POINT TAKEN.

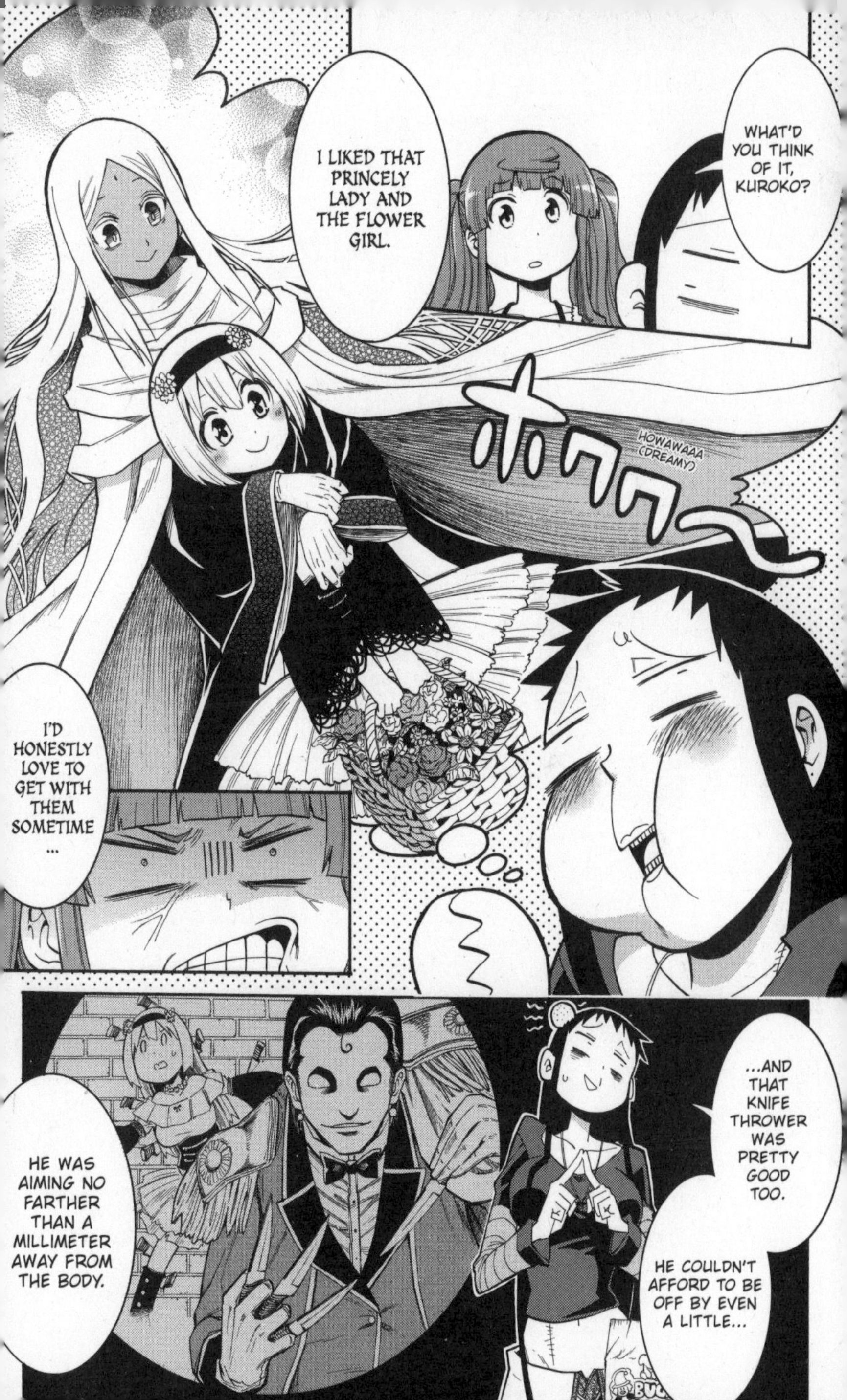
WHAT'D YOU THINK OF IT, KUROKO?
I LIKED THAT PRINCELY LADY AND THE FLOWER GIRL.
HOWAWAAA (DREAMY)
I'D HONESTLY LOVE TO GET WITH THEM SOMETIME ...
...AND THAT KNIFE THROWER WAS PRETTY GOOD TOO.
HE COULDN'T AFFORD TO BE OFF BY EVEN A LITTLE...
HE WAS AIMING NO FARTHER THAN A MILLIMETER AWAY FROM THE BODY.

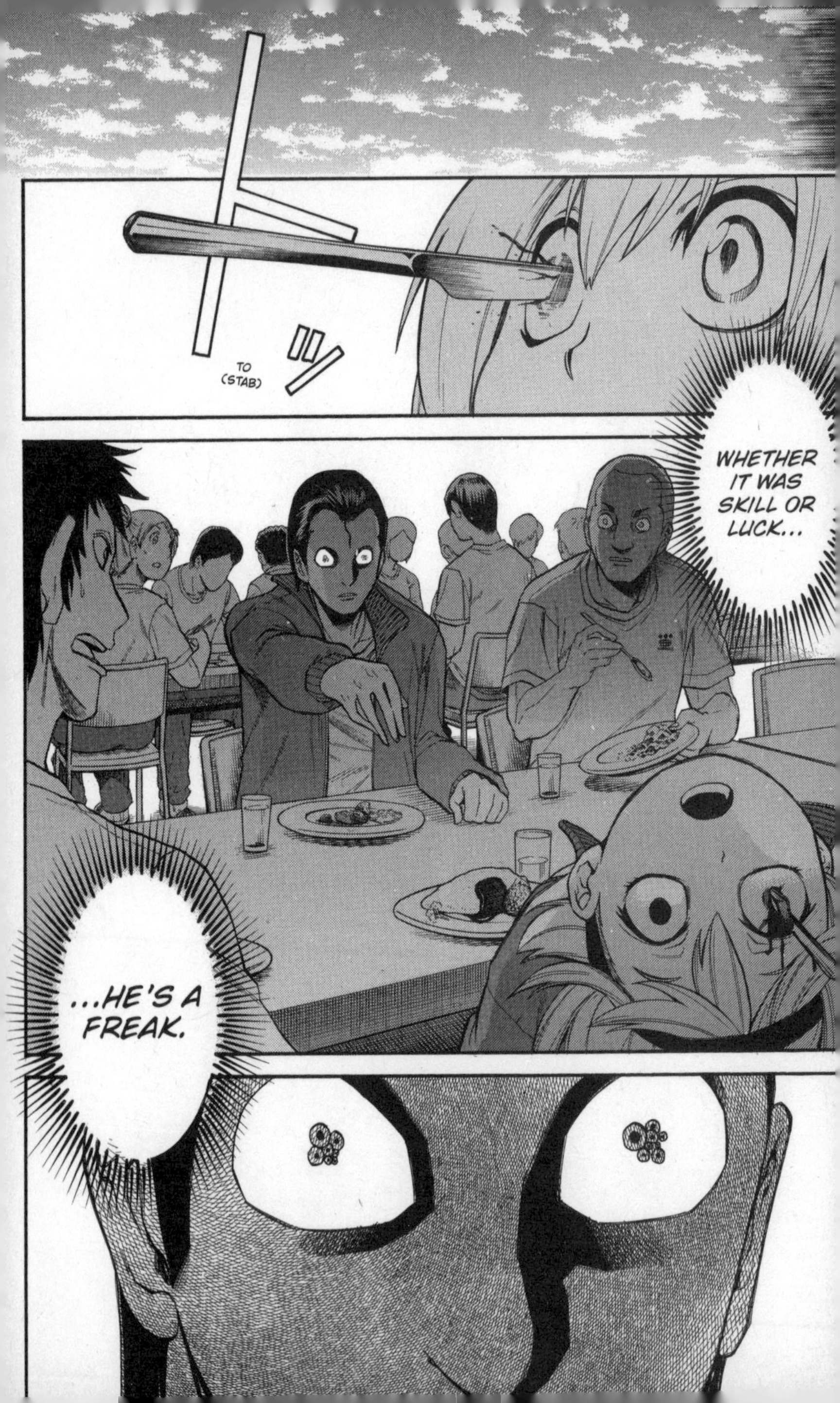
TO
(STAB)
WHETHER IT WAS SKILL OR LUCK...
...HE'S A FREAK.

MURCIÉLAGO

MURCIÉLAGO

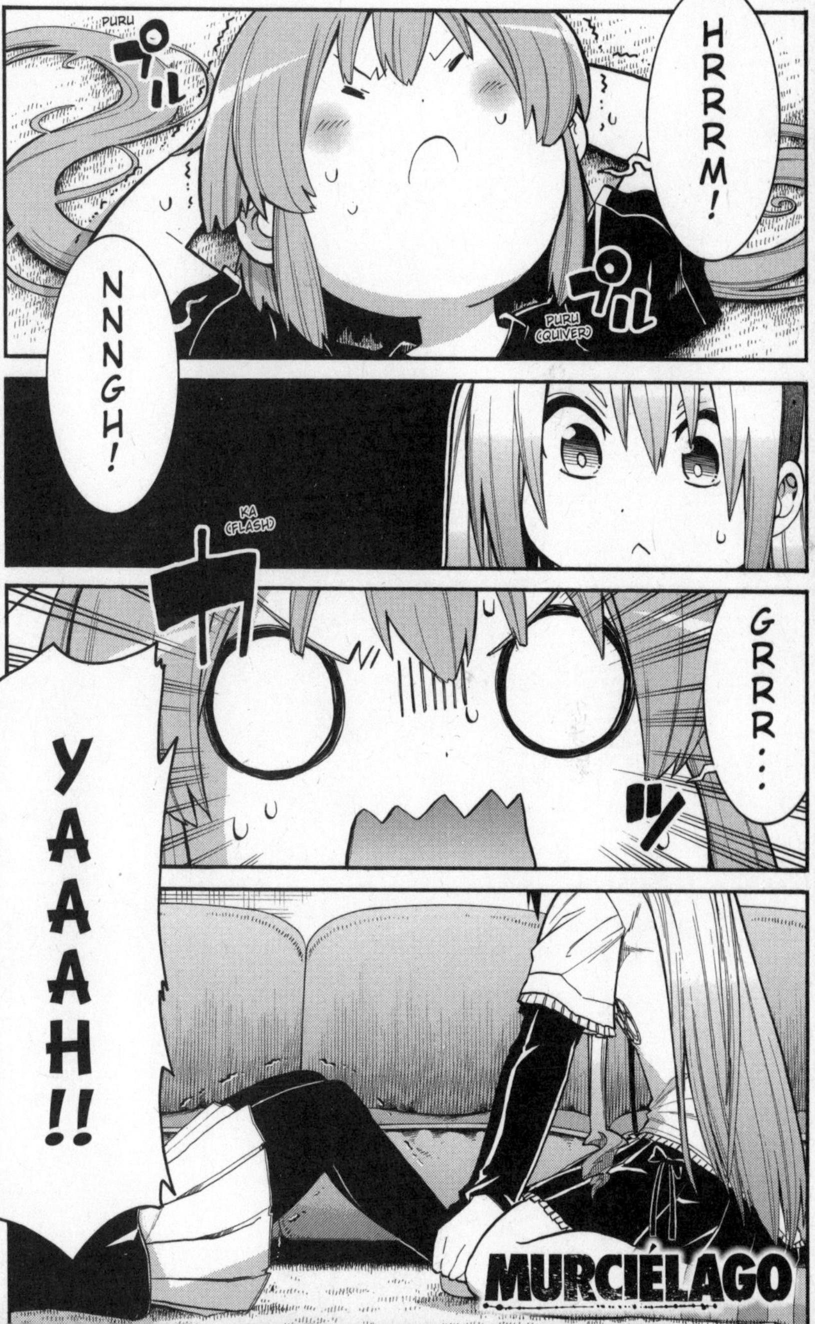
HRRRM!
PURU
PURU (QUIVER)
NNNGH!
KA (FLASH)
GRRR...
YAAAH!!
MURCIÉLAGO

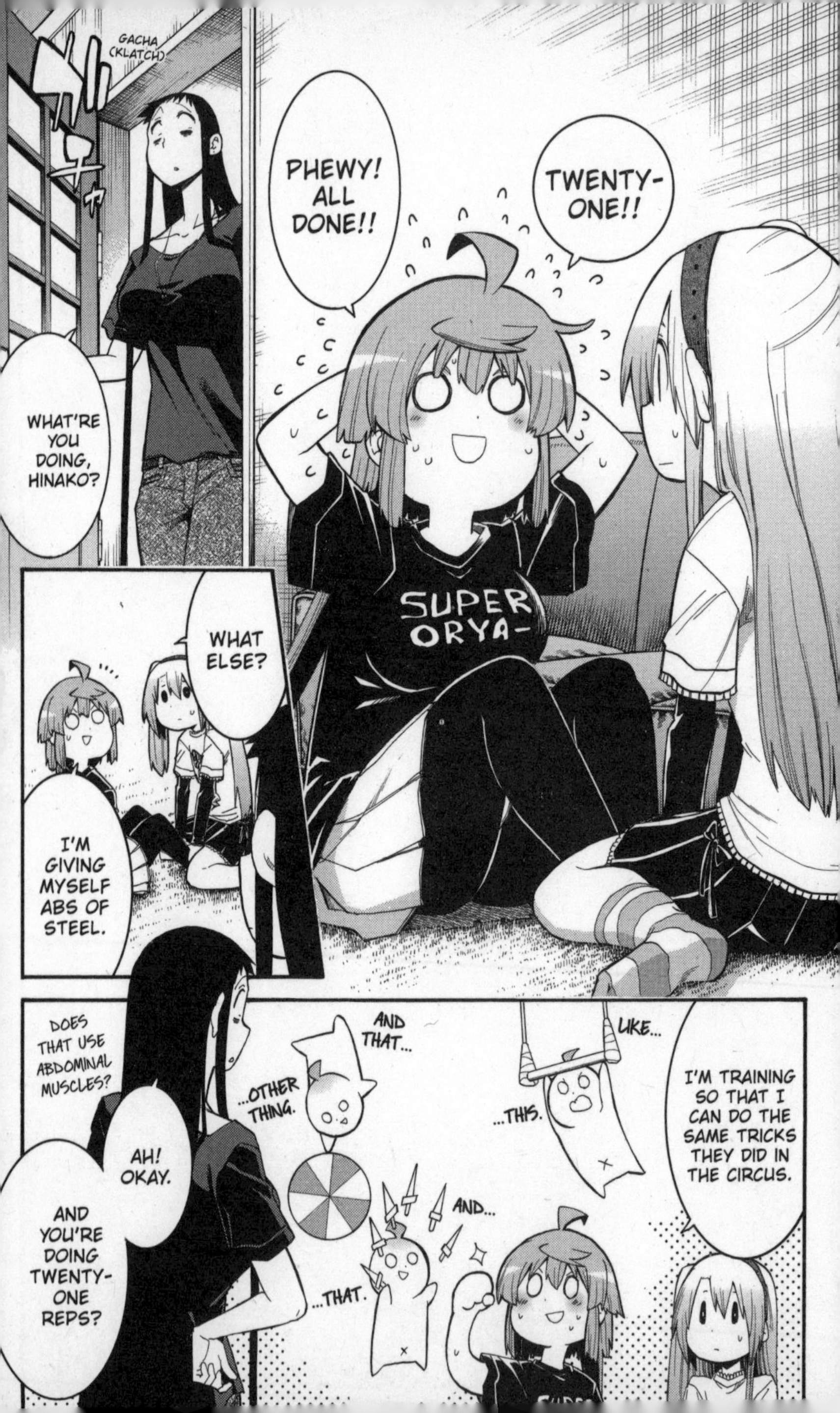
TWENTY-ONE!!
PHEWY! ALL DONE!!
SUPER ORYA-
GACHA (KLATCH)
WHAT'RE YOU DOING, HINAKO?
WHAT ELSE?
I'M GIVING MYSELF ABS OF STEEL.
I'M TRAINING SO THAT I CAN DO THE SAME TRICKS THEY DID IN THE CIRCUS.
LIKE...
...THIS.
AND THAT...
...OTHER THING.
AND...
...THAT.
DOES THAT USE ABDOMINAL MUSCLES?
AH! OKAY.
AND YOU'RE DOING TWENTY-ONE REPS?

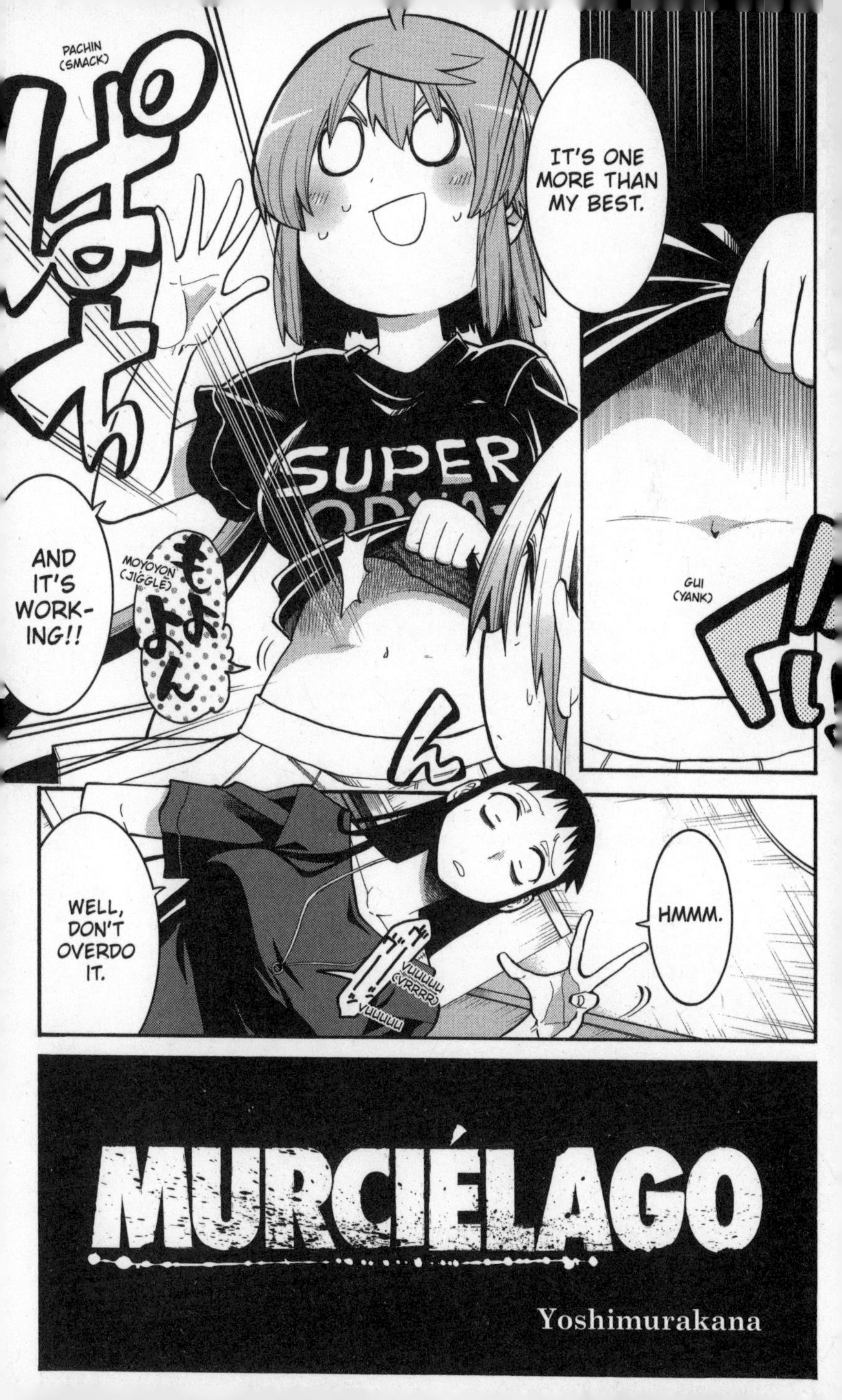
GUI (YANK)
IT'S ONE MORE THAN MY BEST.
PACHIN (SMACK)
SUPER
AND IT'S WORKING!!
MOYOYON (JIGGLE)
HMMM.
VUUUUU (VRRRR) VUUUUU
WELL, DON'T OVERDO IT.

# MURCIÉLAGO

Yoshimurakana

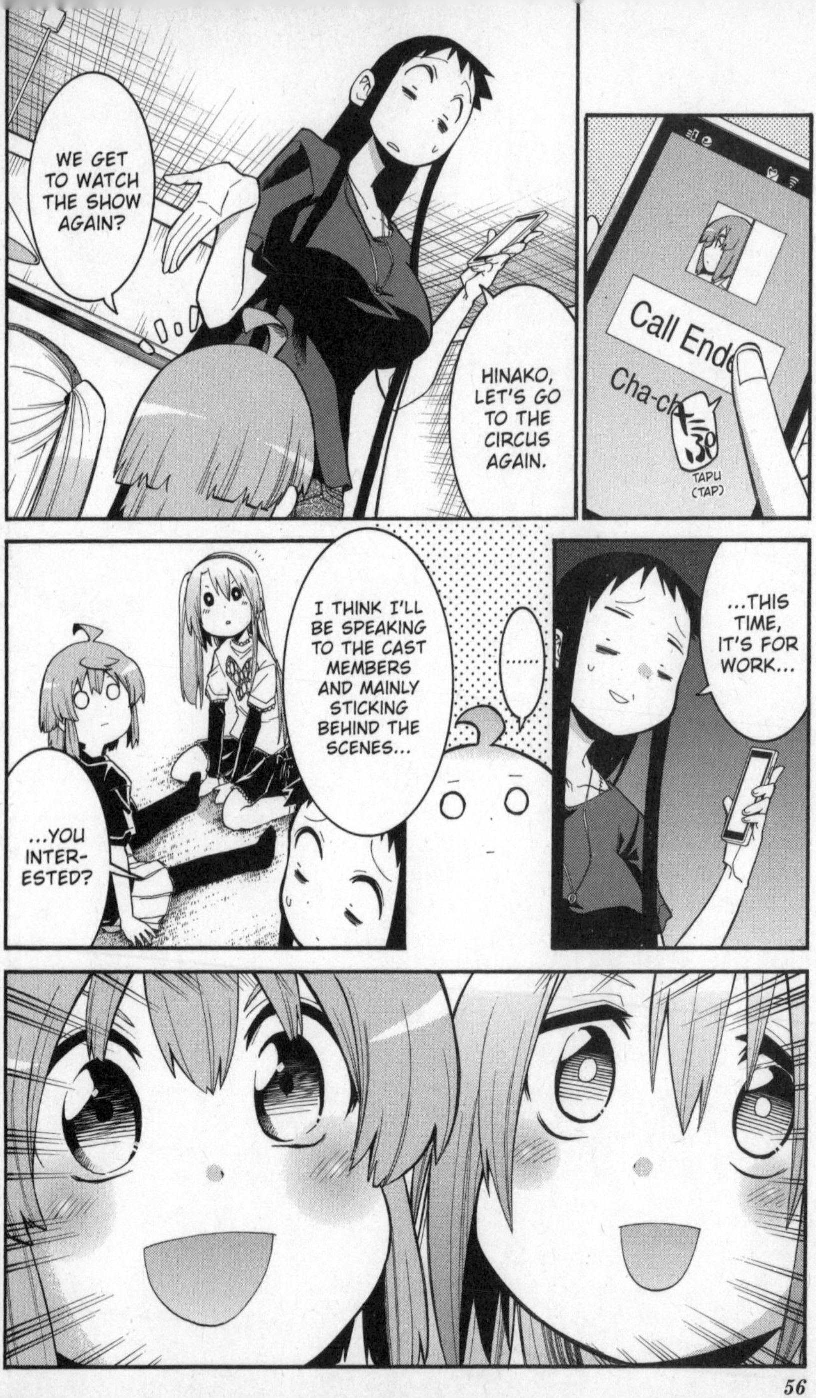

Call Ende
Cha-ch
TAPU (TAP)
HINAKO, LET'S GO TO THE CIRCUS AGAIN.
WE GET TO WATCH THE SHOW AGAIN?
...THIS TIME, IT'S FOR WORK...
......
I THINK I'LL BE SPEAKING TO THE CAST MEMBERS AND MAINLY STICKING BEHIND THE SCENES...
...YOU INTERESTED?

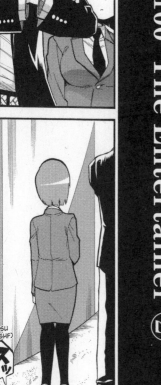

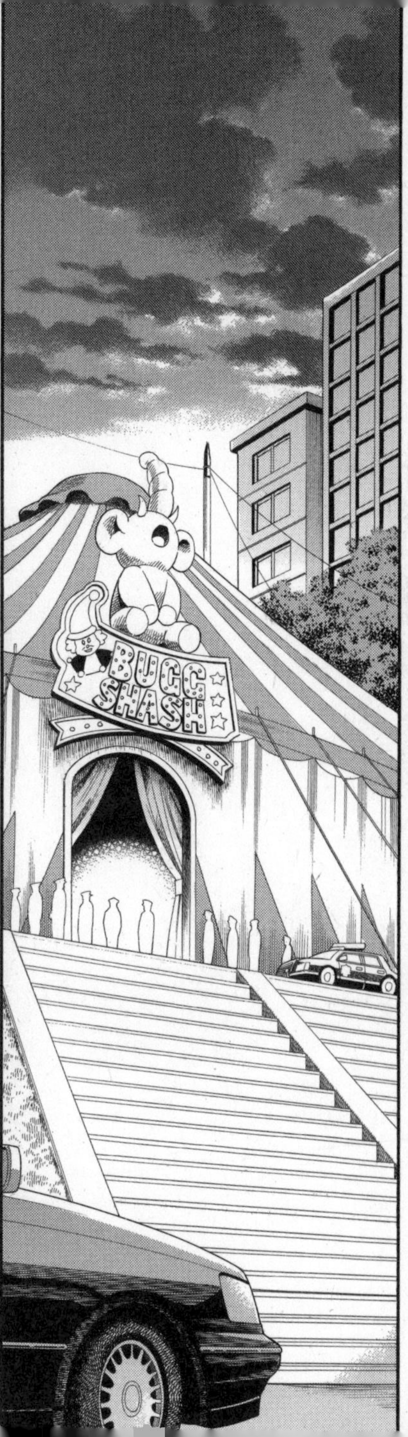
BUGG SHASH

# Chapter 100 The Entertainer ②

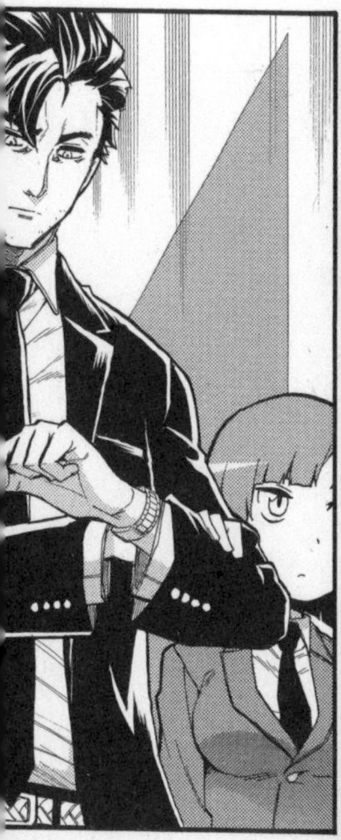

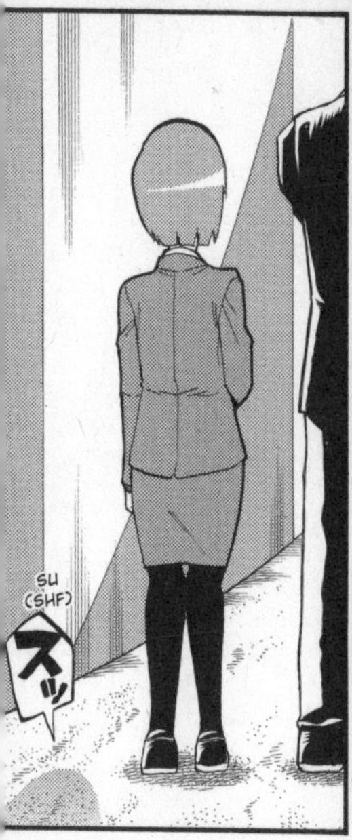
SU (SHF)
スッ

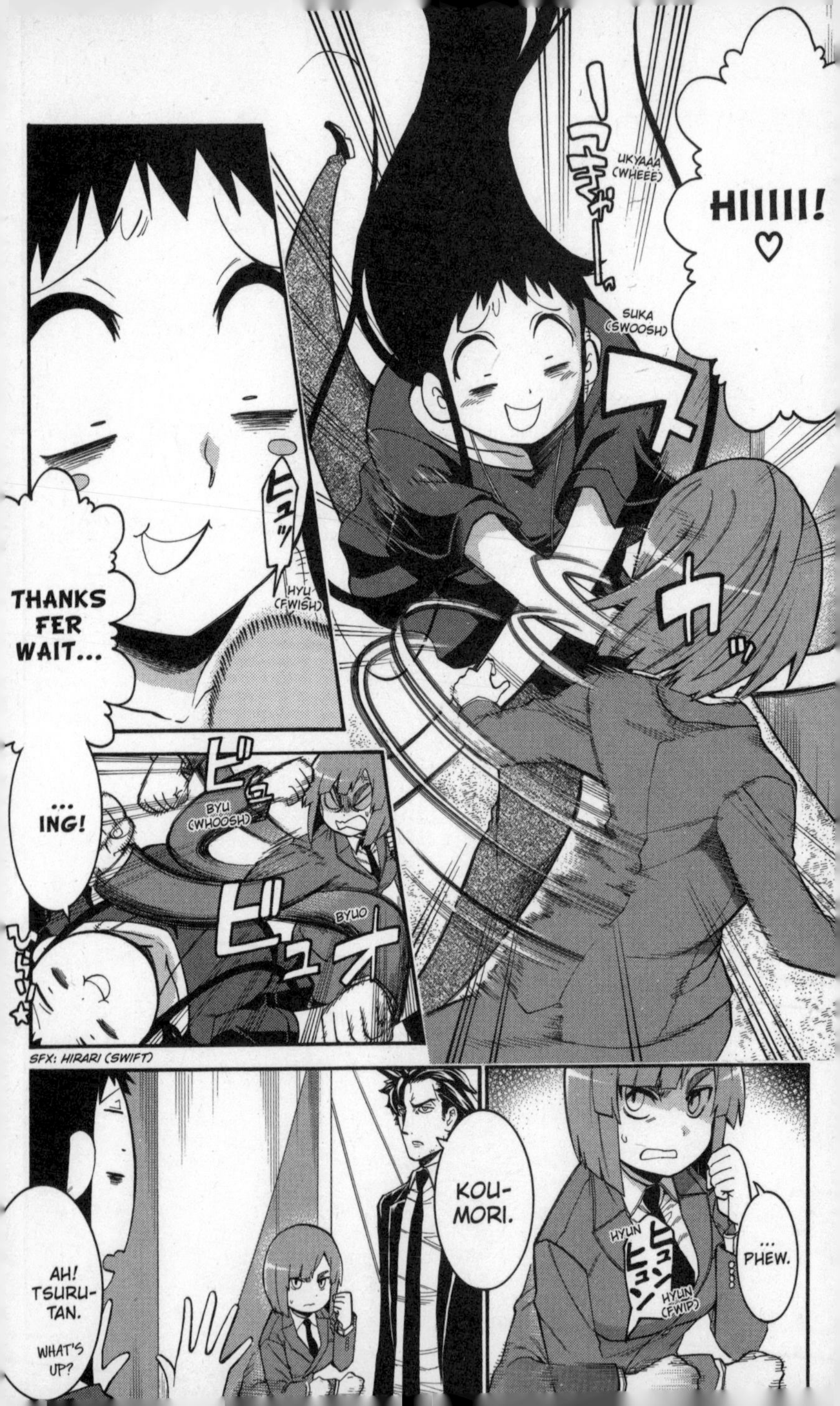
HIIIII! ♥
UKYAAA (WHEEE)
SUKA (SWOOSH)
THANKS FER WAIT...
HYU (FWISH)
...ING!
BYU (WHOOSH)
BYUO
SFX: HIRARI (SWIFT)
...PHEW.
HYUN
HYUN (FWIP)
KOU-MORI.
AH! TSURU-TAN.
WHAT'S UP?

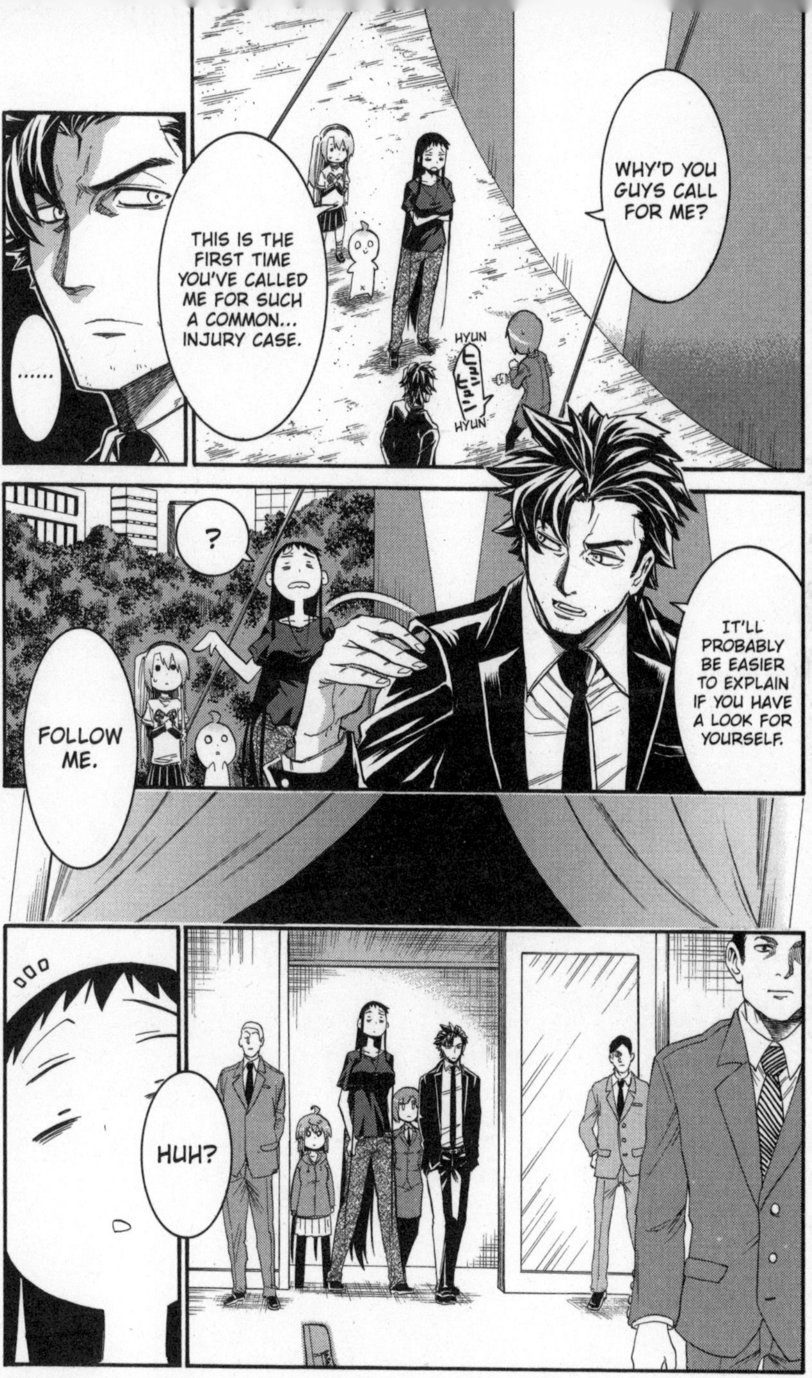
WHY'D YOU GUYS CALL FOR ME?
THIS IS THE FIRST TIME YOU'VE CALLED ME FOR SUCH A COMMON... INJURY CASE.
HYUN
HYUN
......
IT'LL PROBABLY BE EASIER TO EXPLAIN IF YOU HAVE A LOOK FOR YOURSELF.
?
FOLLOW ME.
HUH?

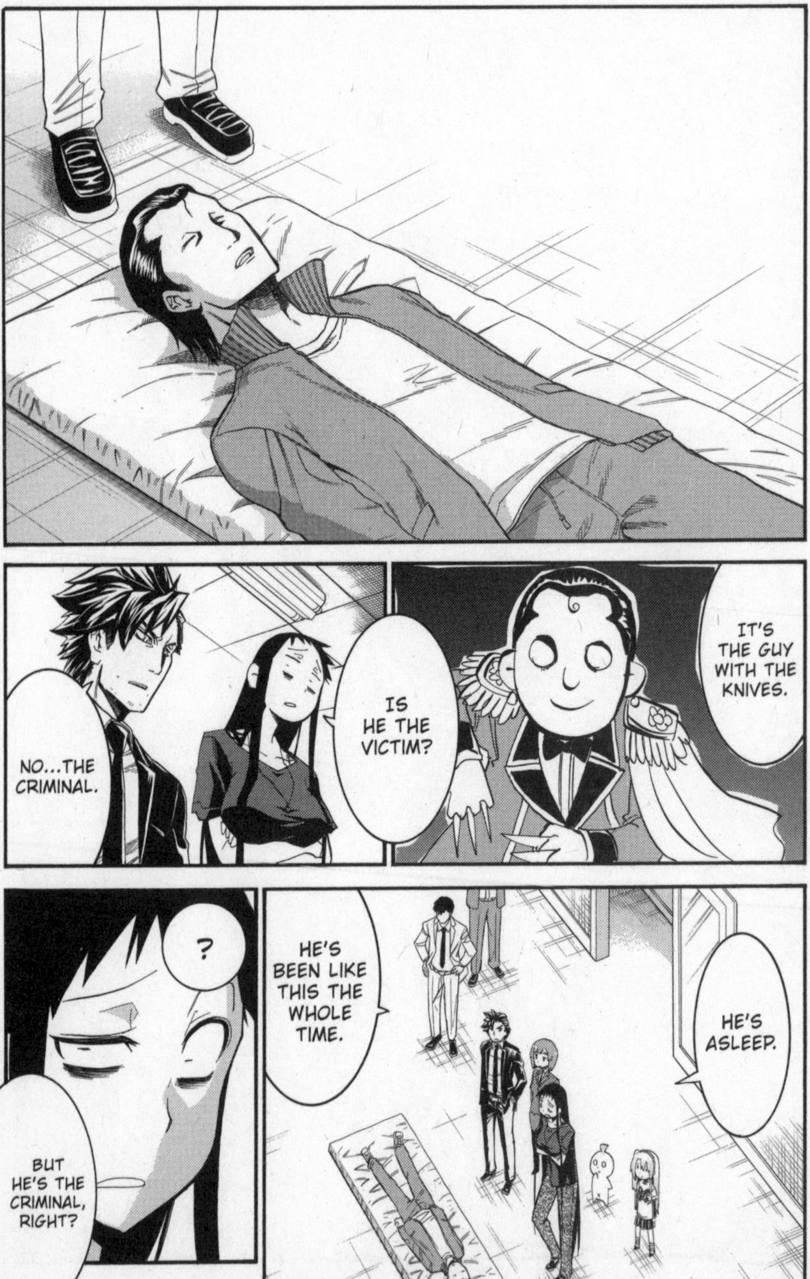
IT'S THE GUY WITH THE KNIVES.
IS HE THE VICTIM?
NO...THE CRIMINAL.
HE'S ASLEEP.
HE'S BEEN LIKE THIS THE WHOLE TIME.
?
BUT HE'S THE CRIMINAL, RIGHT?

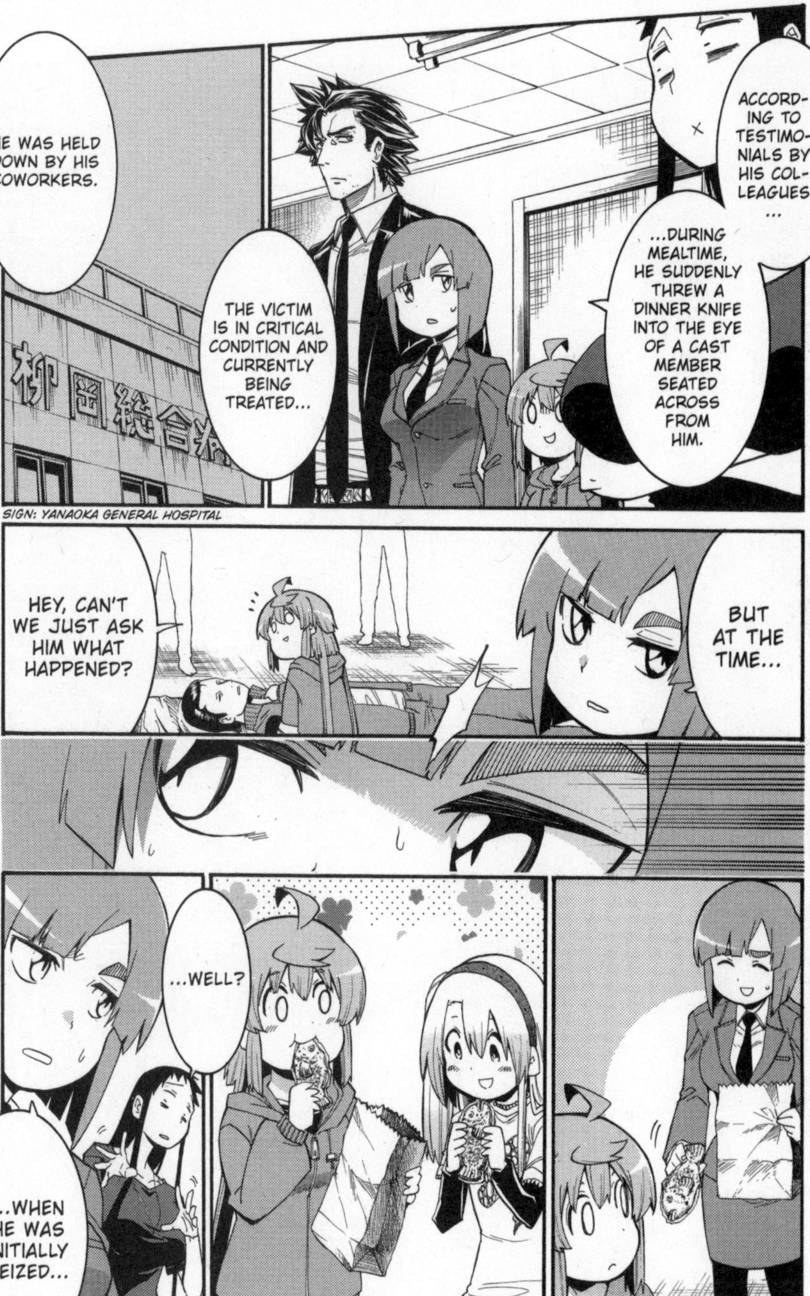
ACCORDING TO TESTIMONIALS BY HIS COLLEAGUES...
...DURING MEALTIME, HE SUDDENLY THREW A DINNER KNIFE INTO THE EYE OF A CAST MEMBER SEATED ACROSS FROM HIM.
THE VICTIM IS IN CRITICAL CONDITION AND CURRENTLY BEING TREATED...
HE WAS HELD DOWN BY HIS COWORKERS.
SIGN: YANAOKA GENERAL HOSPITAL
BUT AT THE TIME...
HEY, CAN'T WE JUST ASK HIM WHAT HAPPENED?
...WELL?
...WHEN HE WAS INITIALLY SEIZED...

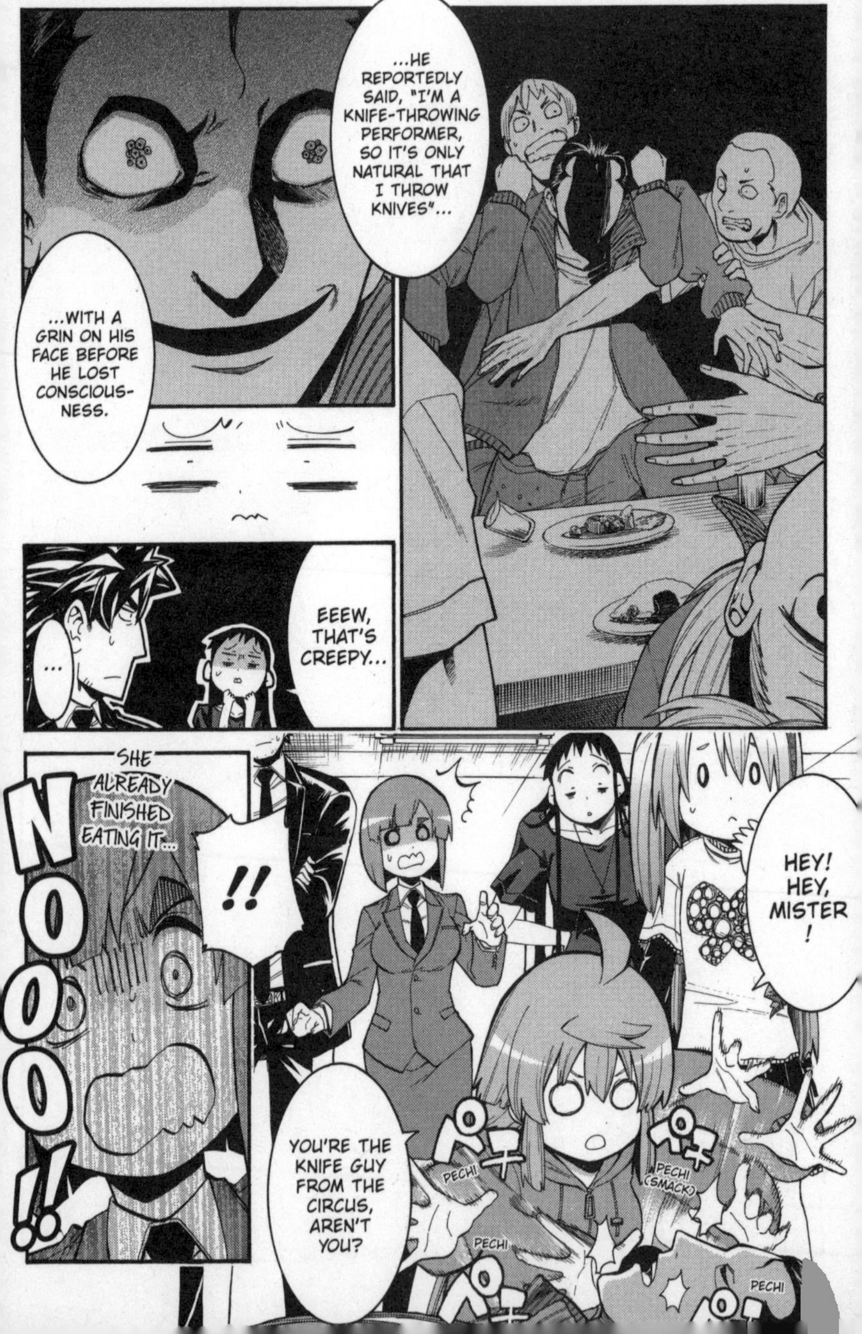

...HE REPORTEDLY SAID, "I'M A KNIFE-THROWING PERFORMER, SO IT'S ONLY NATURAL THAT I THROW KNIVES"...
...WITH A GRIN ON HIS FACE BEFORE HE LOST CONSCIOUS-NESS.
EEEW, THAT'S CREEPY...
...
HEY! HEY, MISTER!
YOU'RE THE KNIFE GUY FROM THE CIRCUS, AREN'T YOU?
PECHI (SMACK)
PECHI
PECHI
PECHI
!!
NOOO!!
SHE ALREADY FINISHED EATING IT...

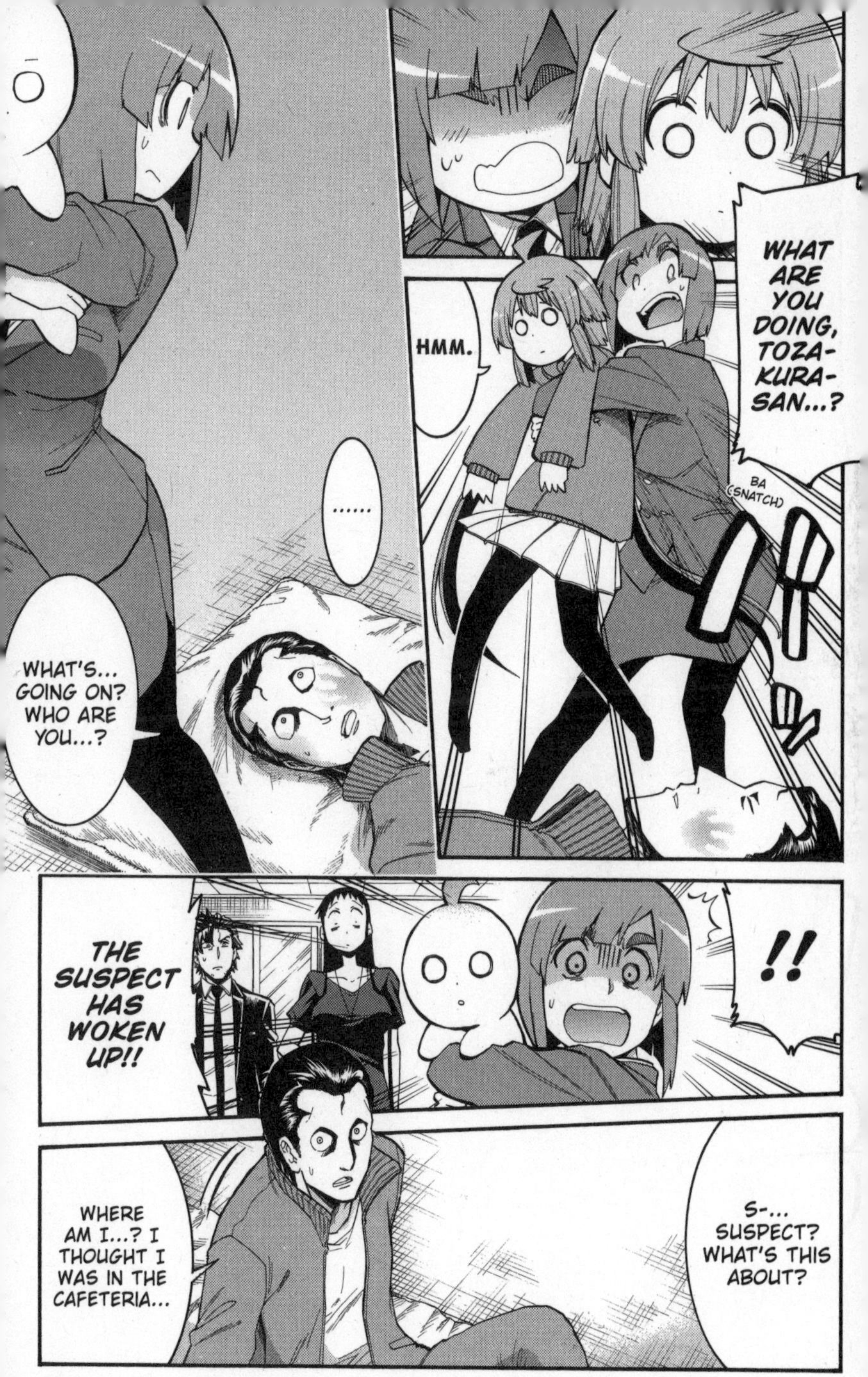
WHAT ARE YOU DOING, TOZAKURA-SAN...?
HMM.
BA (SNATCH)
......
WHAT'S... GOING ON? WHO ARE YOU...?
!!
THE SUSPECT HAS WOKEN UP!!
S-... SUSPECT? WHAT'S THIS ABOUT?
WHERE AM I...? I THOUGHT I WAS IN THE CAFETERIA...

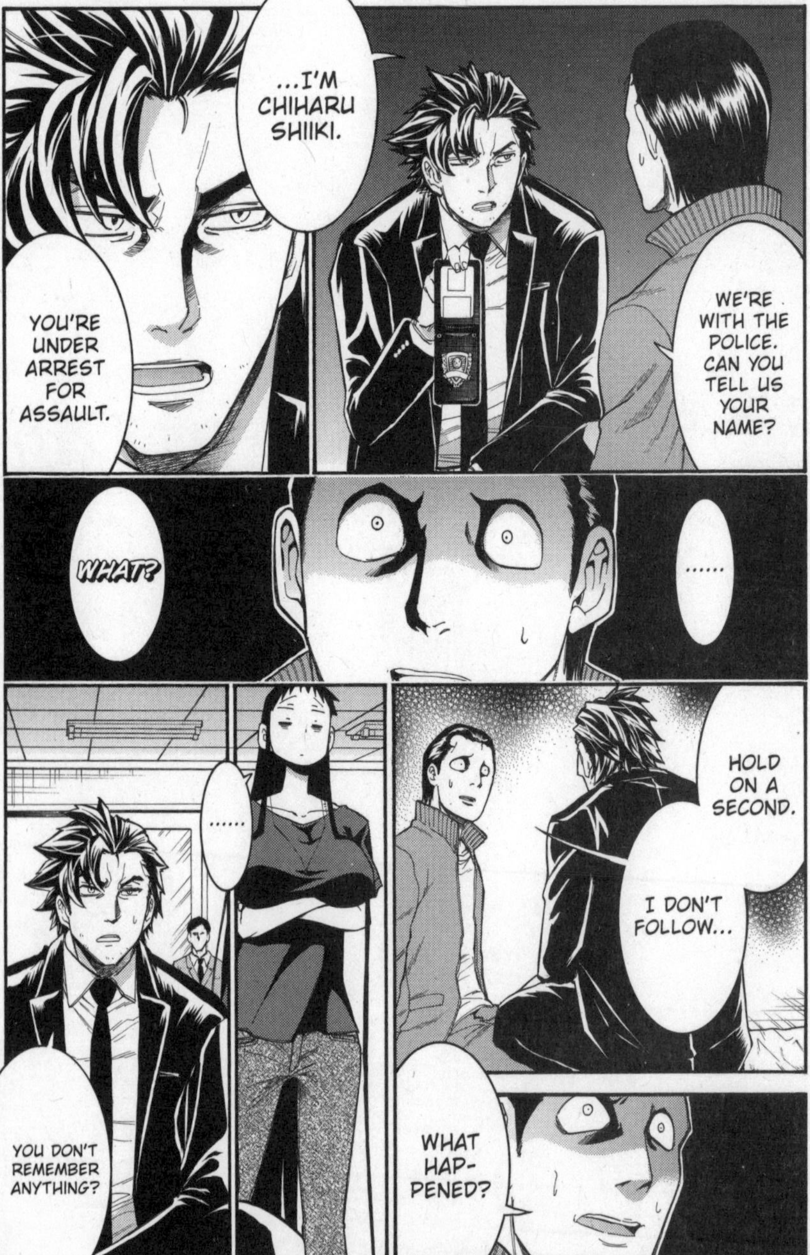
WE'RE WITH THE POLICE. CAN YOU TELL US YOUR NAME?
...I'M CHIHARU SHIIKI.
YOU'RE UNDER ARREST FOR ASSAULT.
......
WHAT?
HOLD ON A SECOND.
I DON'T FOLLOW...
WHAT HAP-PENED?
......
YOU DON'T REMEMBER ANYTHING?

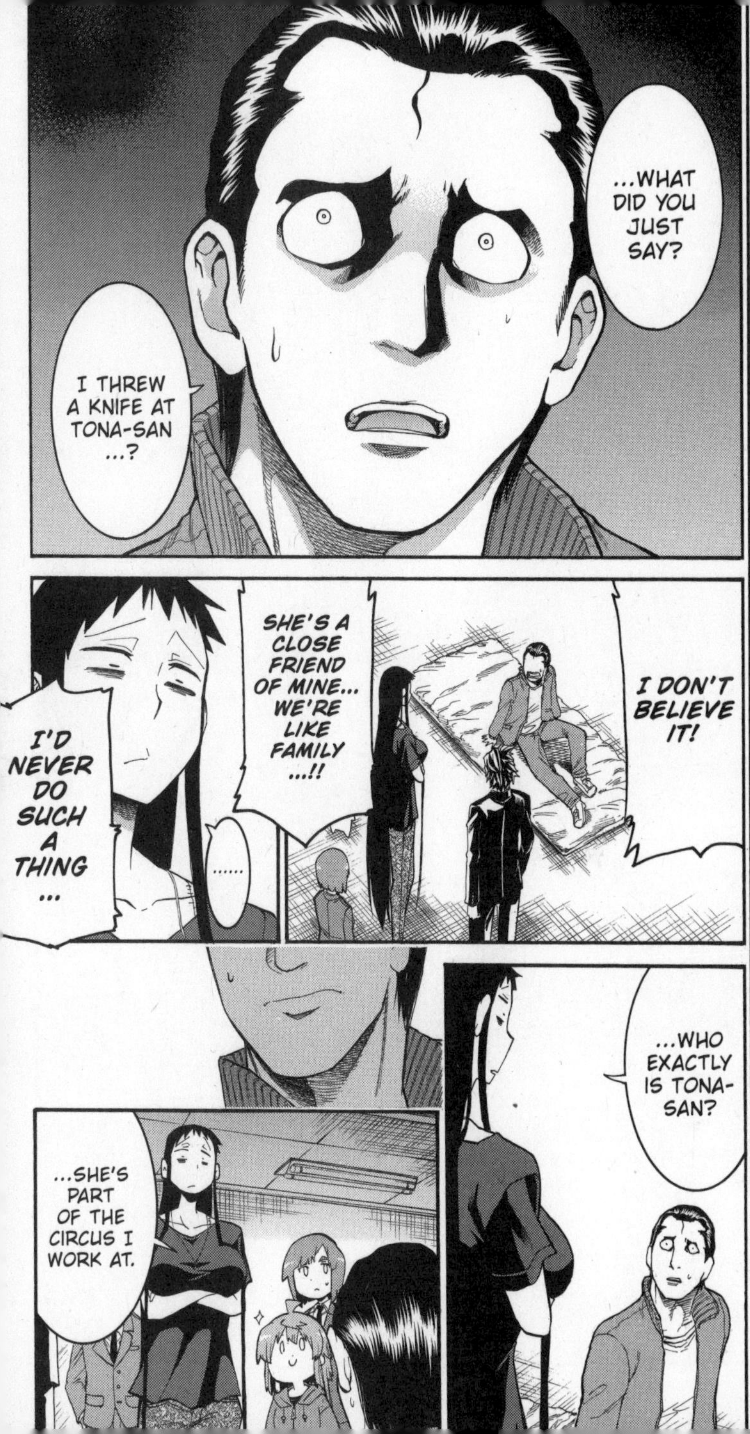
...WHAT DID YOU JUST SAY?
I THREW A KNIFE AT TONA-SAN ...?
I DON'T BELIEVE IT!
SHE'S A CLOSE FRIEND OF MINE... WE'RE LIKE FAMILY ...!!
I'D NEVER DO SUCH A THING ...
......
...WHO EXACTLY IS TONA-SAN?
...SHE'S PART OF THE CIRCUS I WORK AT.

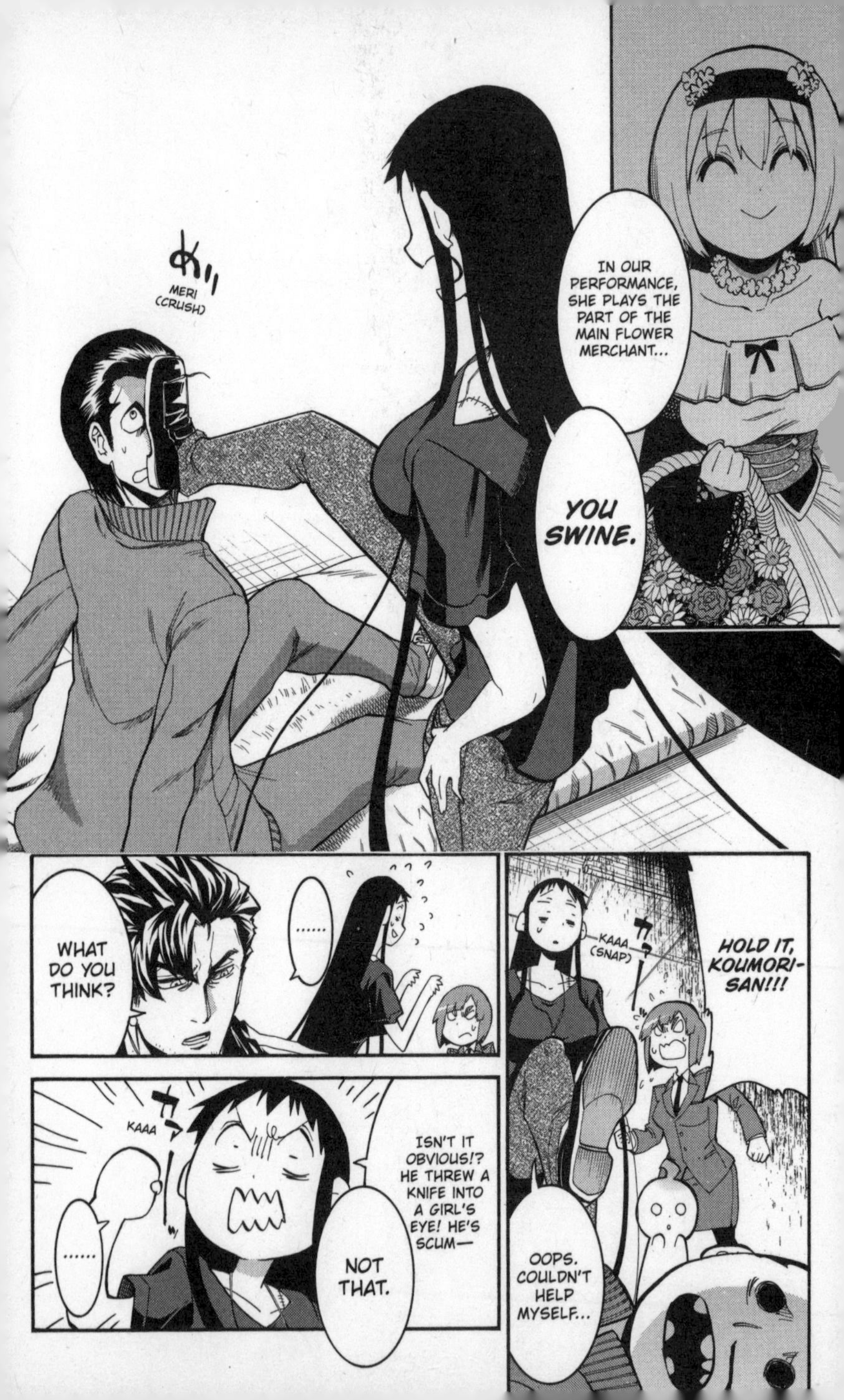
IN OUR PERFORMANCE, SHE PLAYS THE PART OF THE MAIN FLOWER MERCHANT...
YOU SWINE.
MERI (CRUSH)
HOLD IT, KOUMORI-SAN!!!
KAAA (SNAP)
OOPS. COULDN'T HELP MYSELF...
......
WHAT DO YOU THINK?
ISN'T IT OBVIOUS!? HE THREW A KNIFE INTO A GIRL'S EYE! HE'S SCUM—
NOT THAT.
KAAA
......

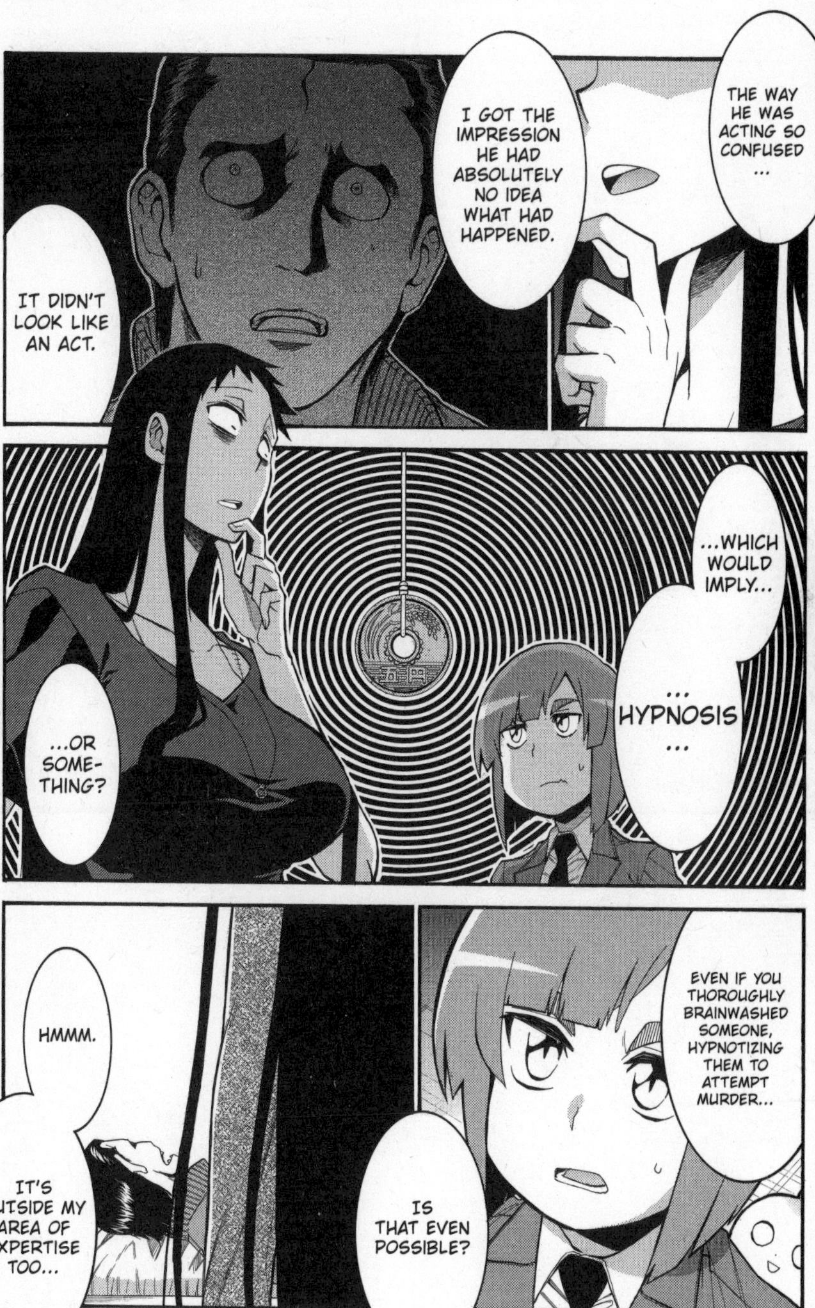
THE WAY HE WAS ACTING SO CONFUSED...
I GOT THE IMPRESSION HE HAD ABSOLUTELY NO IDEA WHAT HAD HAPPENED.
IT DIDN'T LOOK LIKE AN ACT.
...WHICH WOULD IMPLY...
... HYPNOSIS ...
...OR SOMETHING?
EVEN IF YOU THOROUGHLY BRAINWASHED SOMEONE, HYPNOTIZING THEM TO ATTEMPT MURDER...
IS THAT EVEN POSSIBLE?
HMMM.
IT'S OUTSIDE MY AREA OF EXPERTISE TOO...

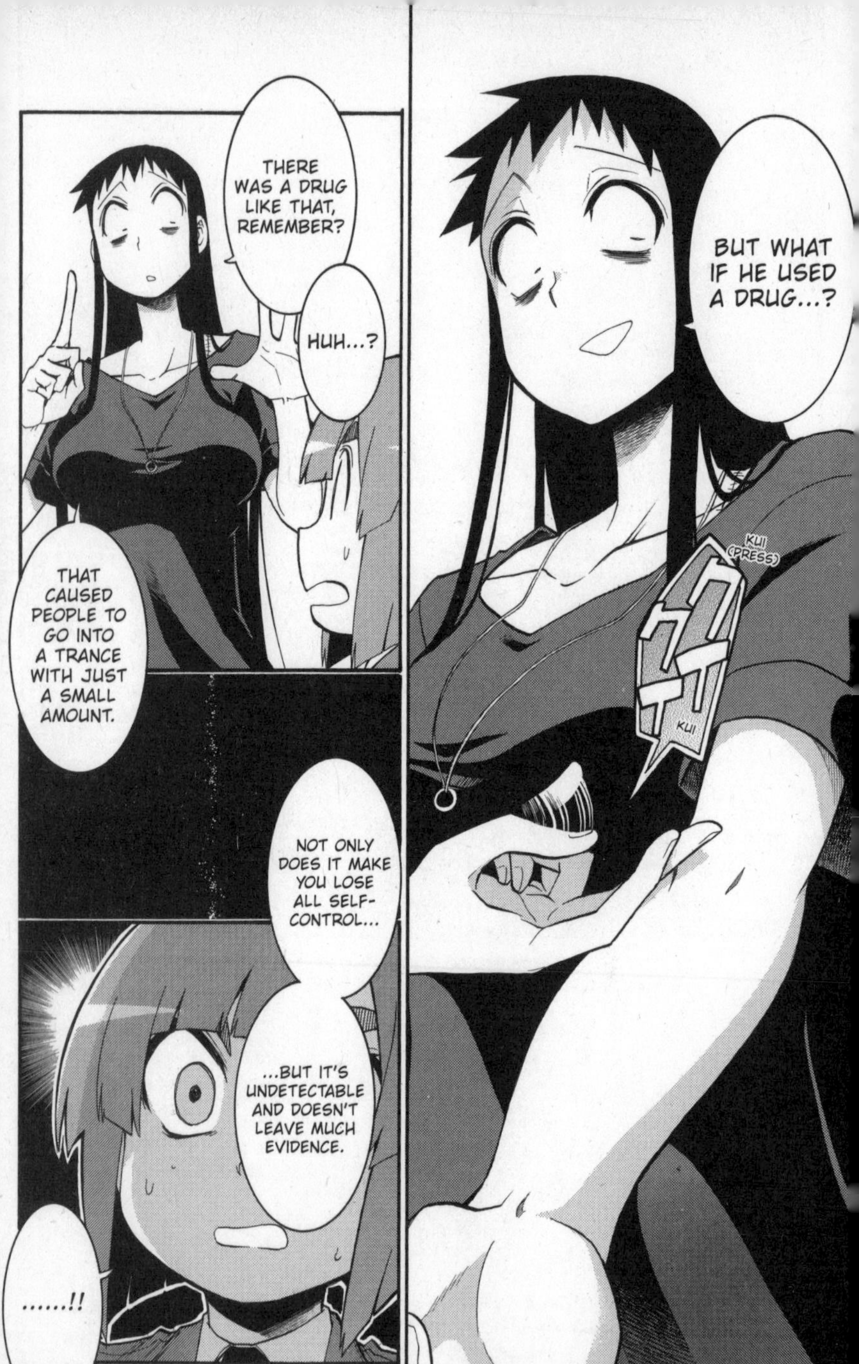
BUT WHAT IF HE USED A DRUG...?
KUI (PRESS)
KUI
THERE WAS A DRUG LIKE THAT, REMEMBER?
HUH...?
THAT CAUSED PEOPLE TO GO INTO A TRANCE WITH JUST A SMALL AMOUNT.
NOT ONLY DOES IT MAKE YOU LOSE ALL SELF-CONTROL...
...BUT IT'S UNDETECTABLE AND DOESN'T LEAVE MUCH EVIDENCE.
......!!

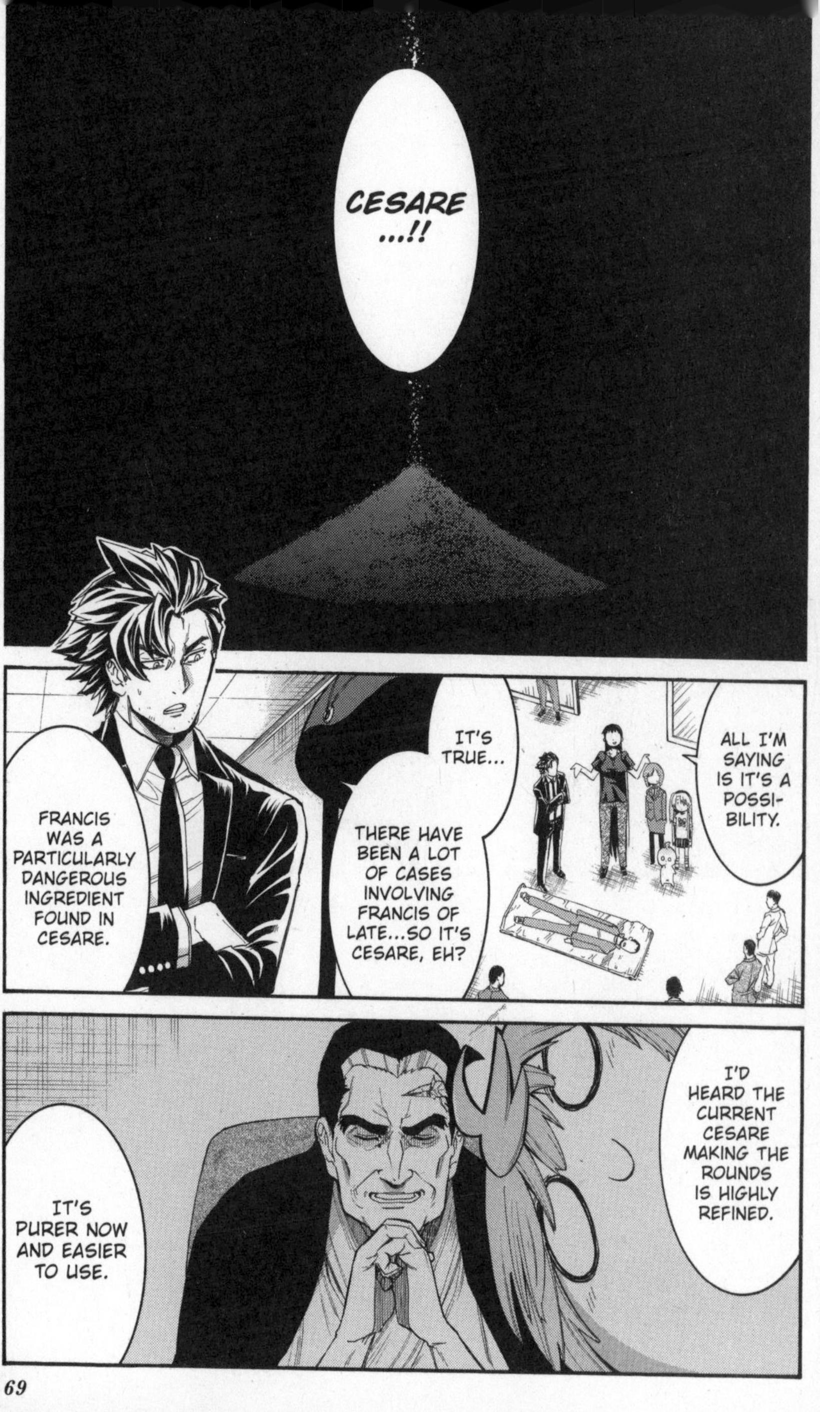
CESARE ...!!
ALL I'M SAYING IS IT'S A POSSIBILITY.
IT'S TRUE...
THERE HAVE BEEN A LOT OF CASES INVOLVING FRANCIS OF LATE...SO IT'S CESARE, EH?
FRANCIS WAS A PARTICULARLY DANGEROUS INGREDIENT FOUND IN CESARE.
I'D HEARD THE CURRENT CESARE MAKING THE ROUNDS IS HIGHLY REFINED.
IT'S PURER NOW AND EASIER TO USE.

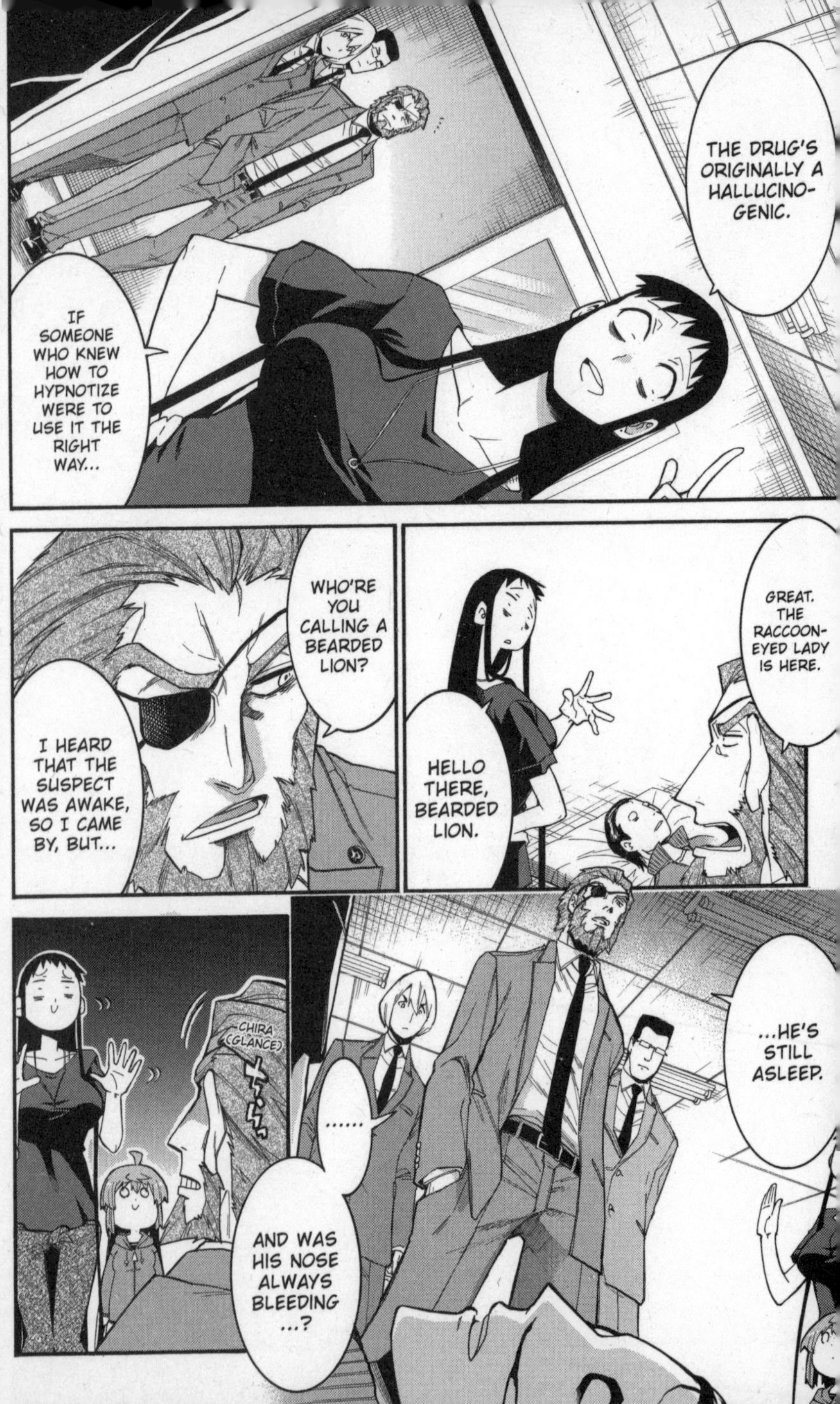
THE DRUG'S ORIGINALLY A HALLUCINO-GENIC.
IF SOMEONE WHO KNEW HOW TO HYPNOTIZE WERE TO USE IT THE RIGHT WAY...
GREAT. THE RACCOON-EYED LADY IS HERE.
HELLO THERE, BEARDED LION.
WHO'RE YOU CALLING A BEARDED LION?
I HEARD THAT THE SUSPECT WAS AWAKE, SO I CAME BY, BUT...
...HE'S STILL ASLEEP.
......
CHIRA (GLANCE)
AND WAS HIS NOSE ALWAYS BLEEDING ...?

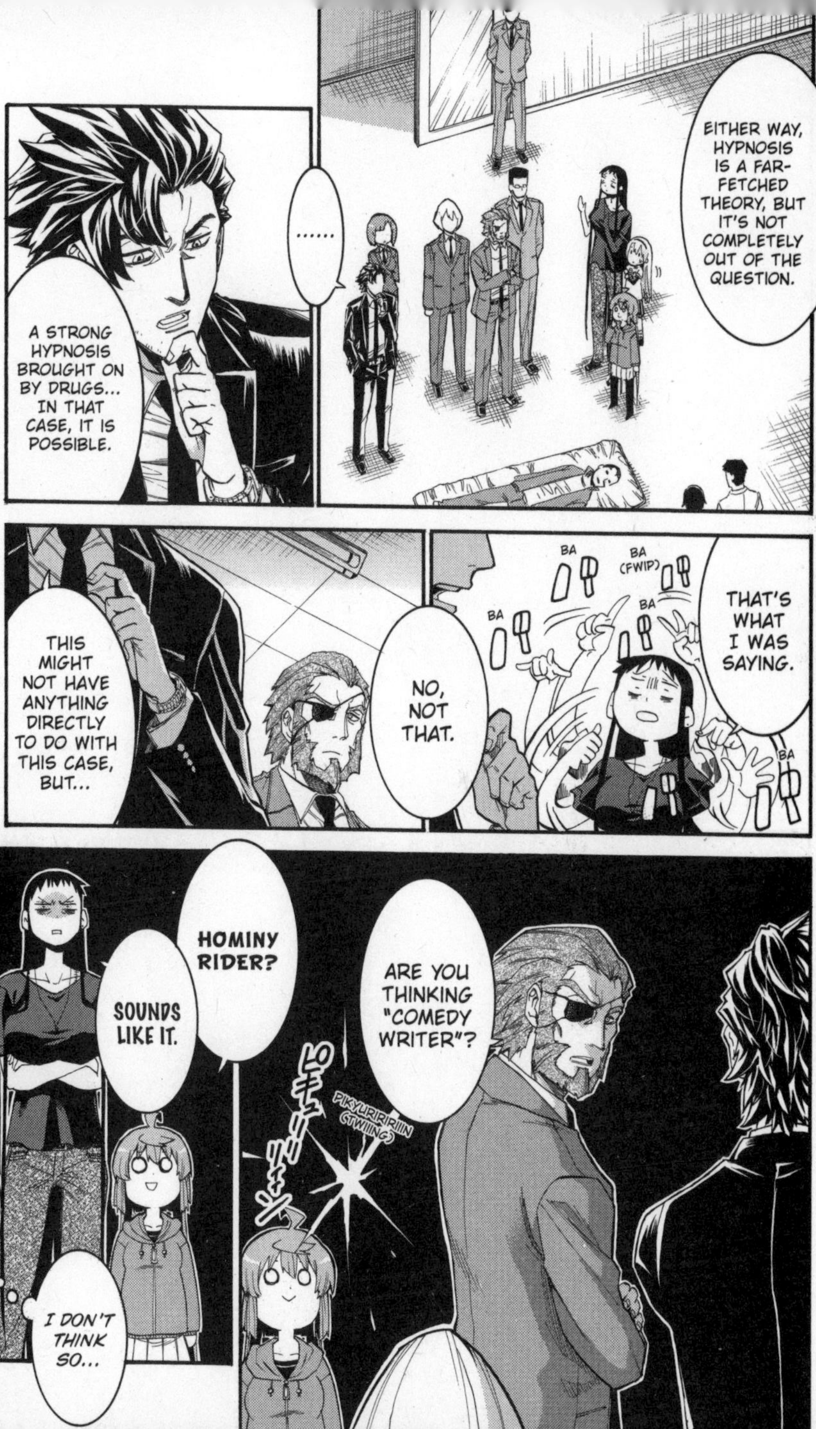
EITHER WAY, HYPNOSIS IS A FAR-FETCHED THEORY, BUT IT'S NOT COMPLETELY OUT OF THE QUESTION.
......
A STRONG HYPNOSIS BROUGHT ON BY DRUGS... IN THAT CASE, IT IS POSSIBLE.
THAT'S WHAT I WAS SAYING.
BA
BA (FWIP)
BA
BA
BA
NO, NOT THAT.
THIS MIGHT NOT HAVE ANYTHING DIRECTLY TO DO WITH THIS CASE, BUT...
ARE YOU THINKING "COMEDY WRITER"?
PIKYURIRIRIIIN (TWIIING)
HOMINY RIDER?
SOUNDS LIKE IT.
I DON'T THINK SO...

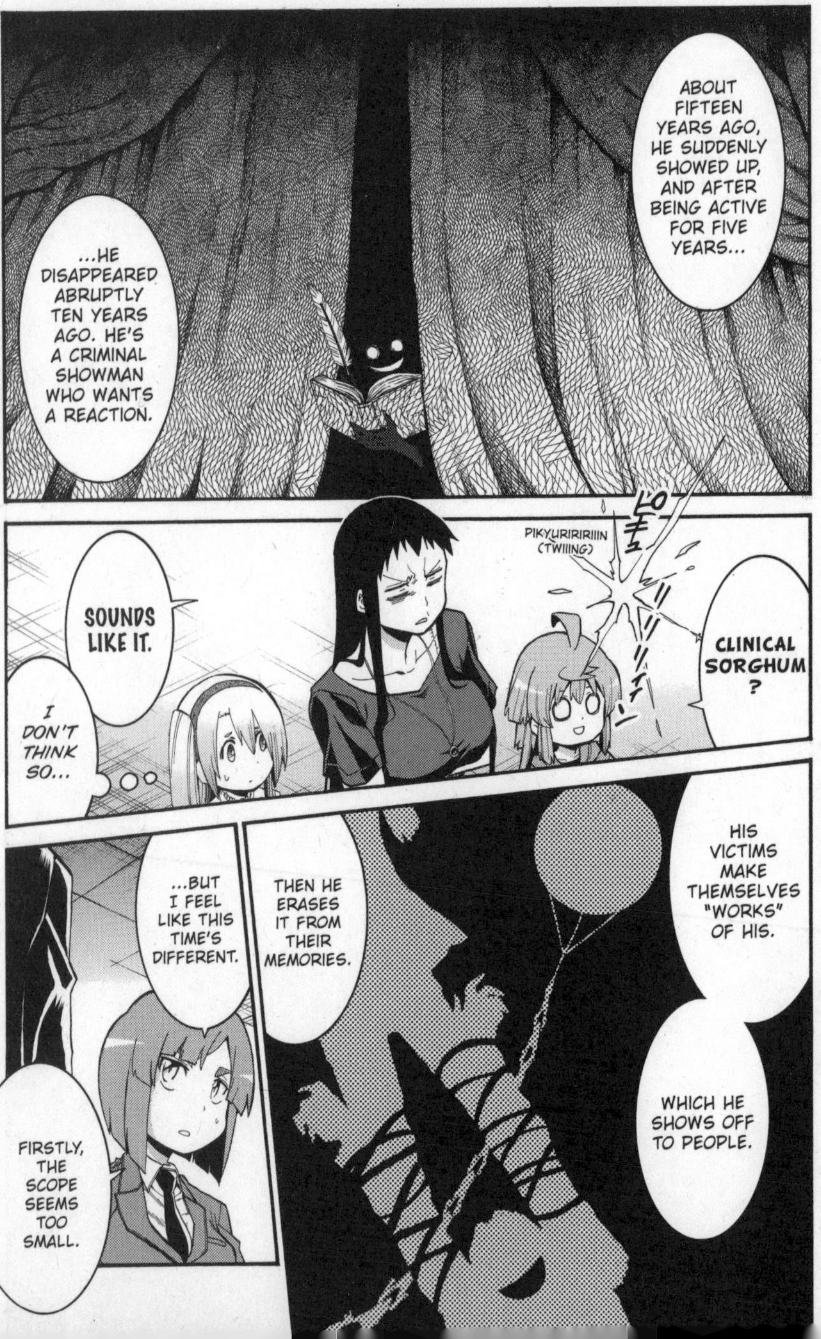
ABOUT FIFTEEN YEARS AGO, HE SUDDENLY SHOWED UP, AND AFTER BEING ACTIVE FOR FIVE YEARS...
...HE DISAPPEARED ABRUPTLY TEN YEARS AGO. HE'S A CRIMINAL SHOWMAN WHO WANTS A REACTION.
CLINICAL SORGHUM?
PIKYURIRIRIIIN (TWIIING)
SOUNDS LIKE IT.
I DON'T THINK SO...
HIS VICTIMS MAKE THEMSELVES "WORKS" OF HIS.
WHICH HE SHOWS OFF TO PEOPLE.
THEN HE ERASES IT FROM THEIR MEMORIES.
...BUT I FEEL LIKE THIS TIME'S DIFFERENT.
FIRSTLY, THE SCOPE SEEMS TOO SMALL.

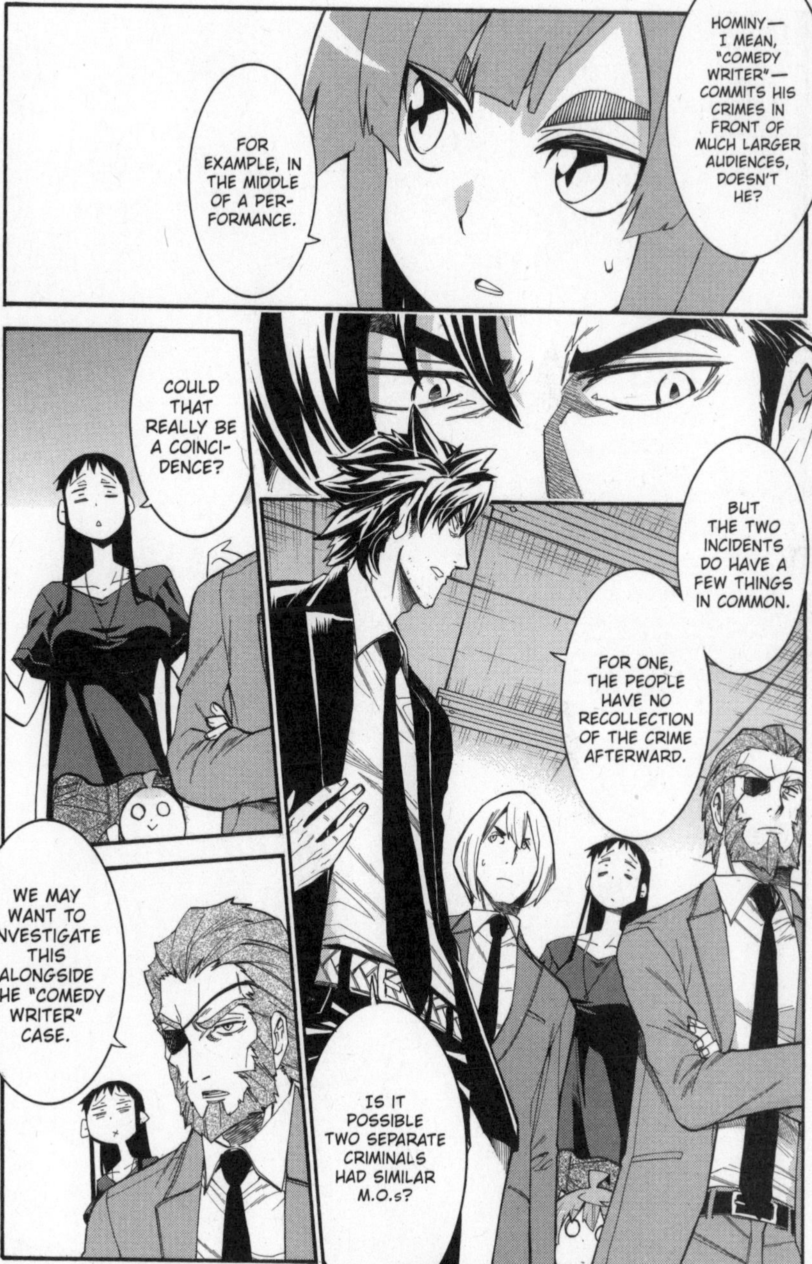

HOMINY— I MEAN, "COMEDY WRITER"— COMMITS HIS CRIMES IN FRONT OF MUCH LARGER AUDIENCES, DOESN'T HE?
FOR EXAMPLE, IN THE MIDDLE OF A PER-FORMANCE.
COULD THAT REALLY BE A COINCI-DENCE?
BUT THE TWO INCIDENTS DO HAVE A FEW THINGS IN COMMON.
FOR ONE, THE PEOPLE HAVE NO RECOLLECTION OF THE CRIME AFTERWARD.
IS IT POSSIBLE TWO SEPARATE CRIMINALS HAD SIMILAR M.O.s?
WE MAY WANT TO INVESTIGATE THIS ALONGSIDE THE "COMEDY WRITER" CASE.

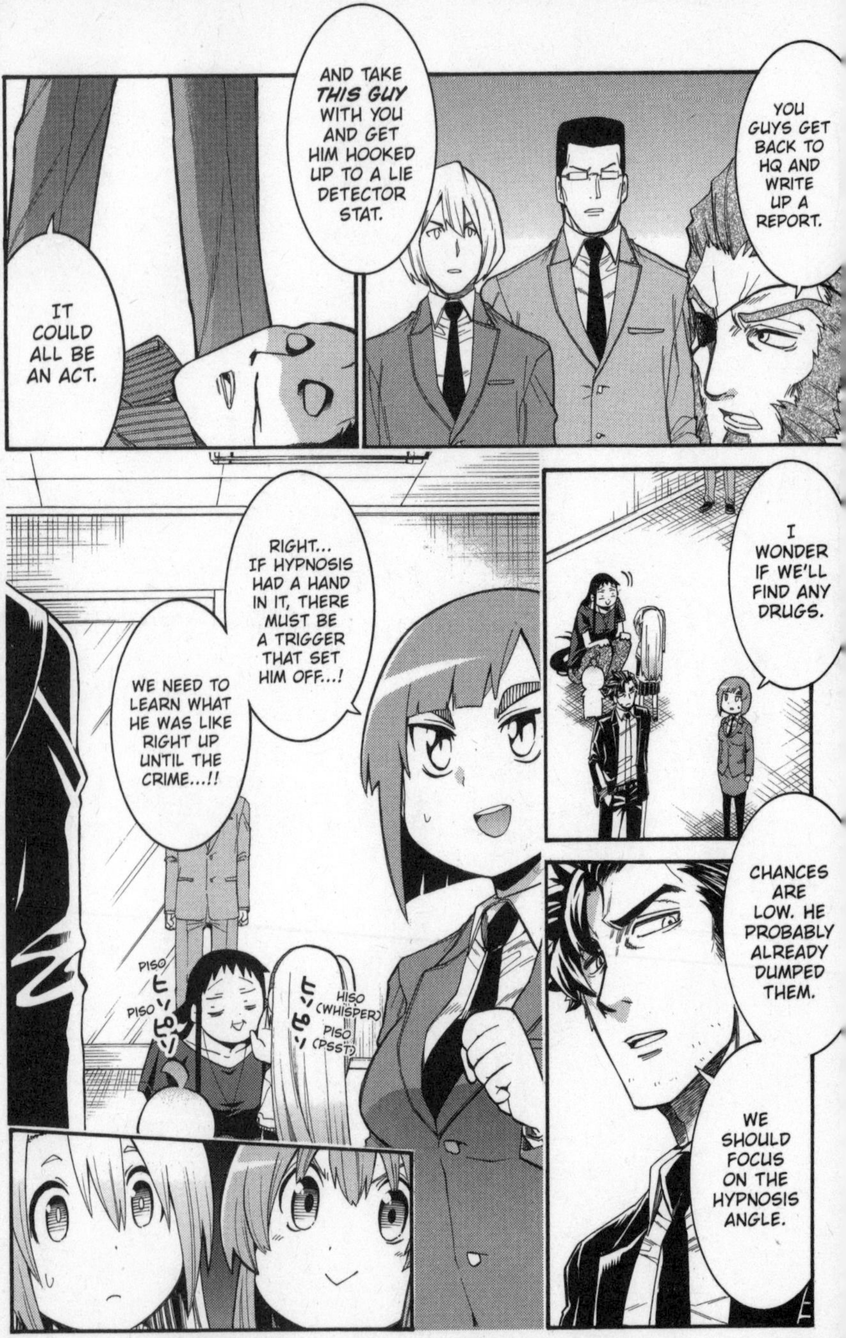

YOU GUYS GET BACK TO HQ AND WRITE UP A REPORT.
AND TAKE *THIS GUY* WITH YOU AND GET HIM HOOKED UP TO A LIE DETECTOR STAT.
IT COULD ALL BE AN ACT.
I WONDER IF WE'LL FIND ANY DRUGS.
CHANCES ARE LOW. HE PROBABLY ALREADY DUMPED THEM.
WE SHOULD FOCUS ON THE HYPNOSIS ANGLE.
RIGHT... IF HYPNOSIS HAD A HAND IN IT, THERE MUST BE A TRIGGER THAT SET HIM OFF...!
WE NEED TO LEARN WHAT HE WAS LIKE RIGHT UP UNTIL THE CRIME...!!
HISO (WHISPER) PISO (PSST)
PISO PISO

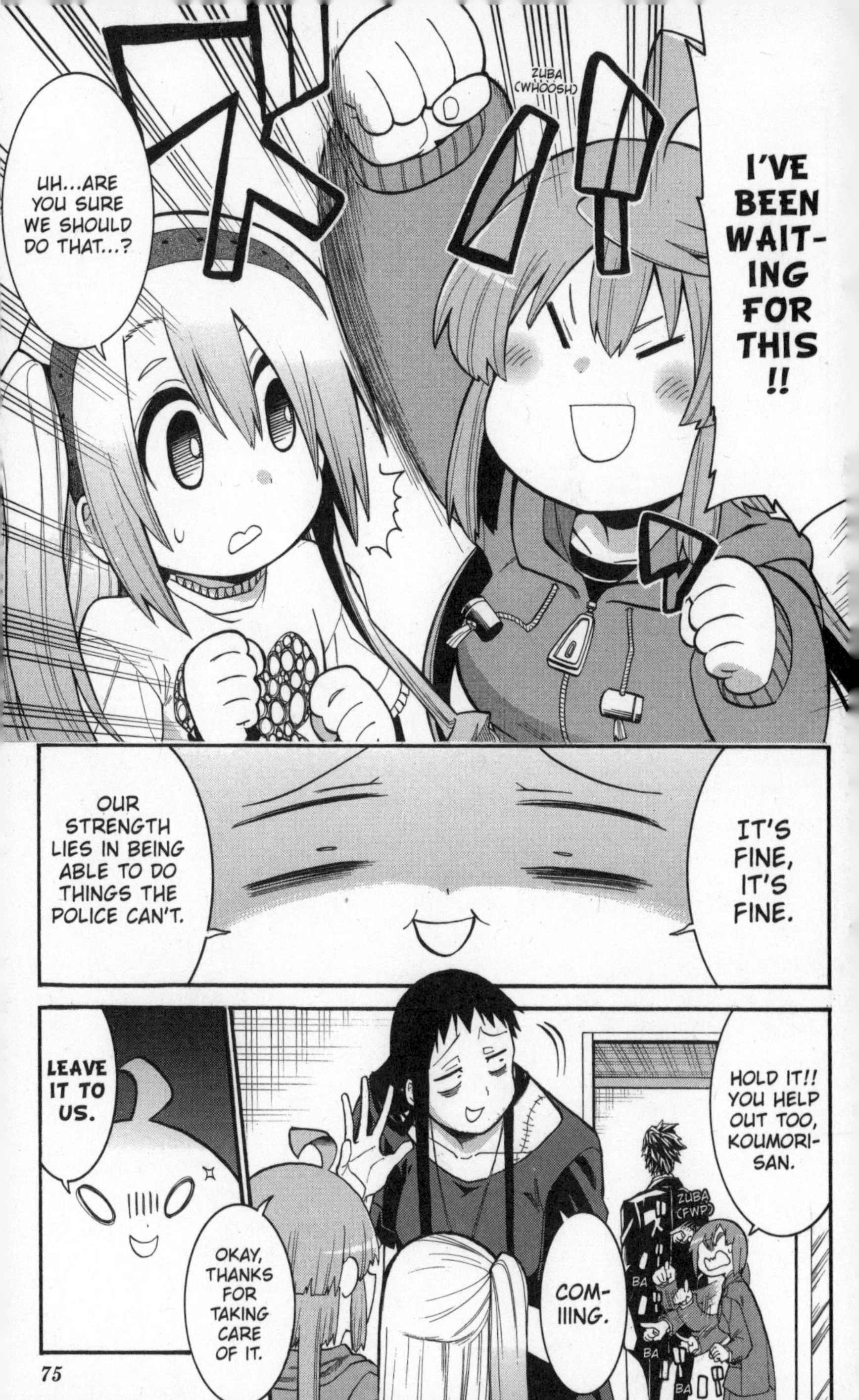
I'VE BEEN WAIT-ING FOR THIS!!
ZUBA (WHOOSH)
UH...ARE YOU SURE WE SHOULD DO THAT...?
IT'S FINE, IT'S FINE.
OUR STRENGTH LIES IN BEING ABLE TO DO THINGS THE POLICE CAN'T.
HOLD IT!! YOU HELP OUT TOO, KOUMORI-SAN.
ZUBA (FWP)
BA
BA
BA
BA
COM-IIING.
OKAY, THANKS FOR TAKING CARE OF IT.
LEAVE IT TO US.

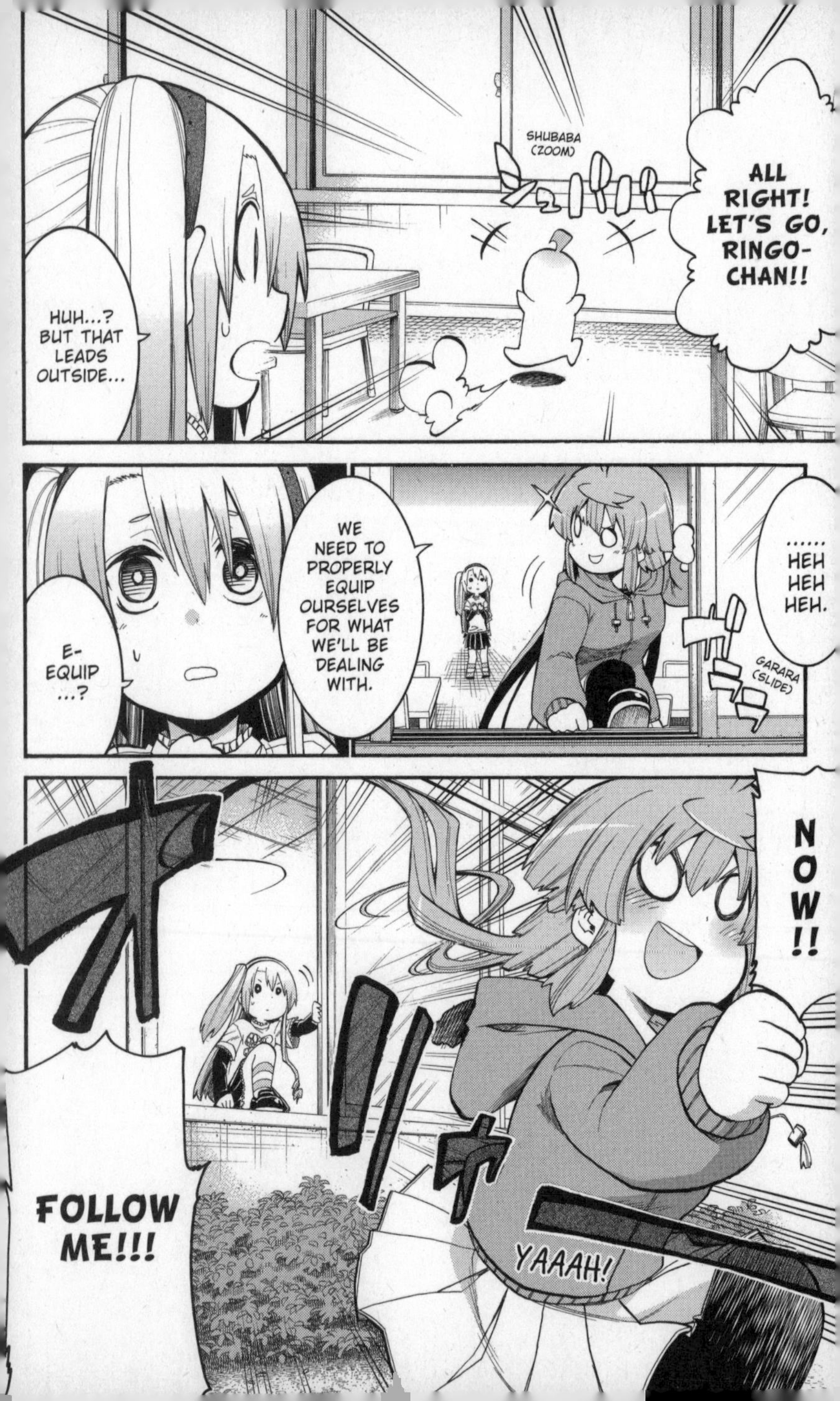
ALL RIGHT! LET'S GO, RINGO-CHAN!!
SHUBABA (ZOOM)
HUH...? BUT THAT LEADS OUTSIDE...
......HEH HEH HEH.
GARARA (SLIDE)
WE NEED TO PROPERLY EQUIP OURSELVES FOR WHAT WE'LL BE DEALING WITH.
E-EQUIP...?
NOW!!
YAAAH!
FOLLOW ME!!!

MURCIÉLAGO

MURCIÉLAGO

......
HINAKO-SAN...

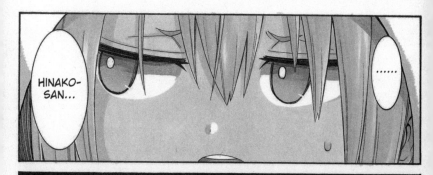

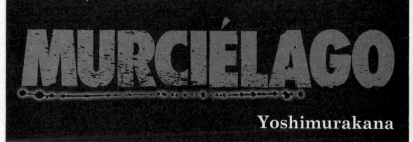

# MURCIÉLAGO

Yoshimurakana

YES...
...RINGO-SHI?

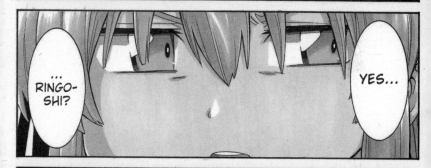

## Chapter 101
## The Entertainer ③

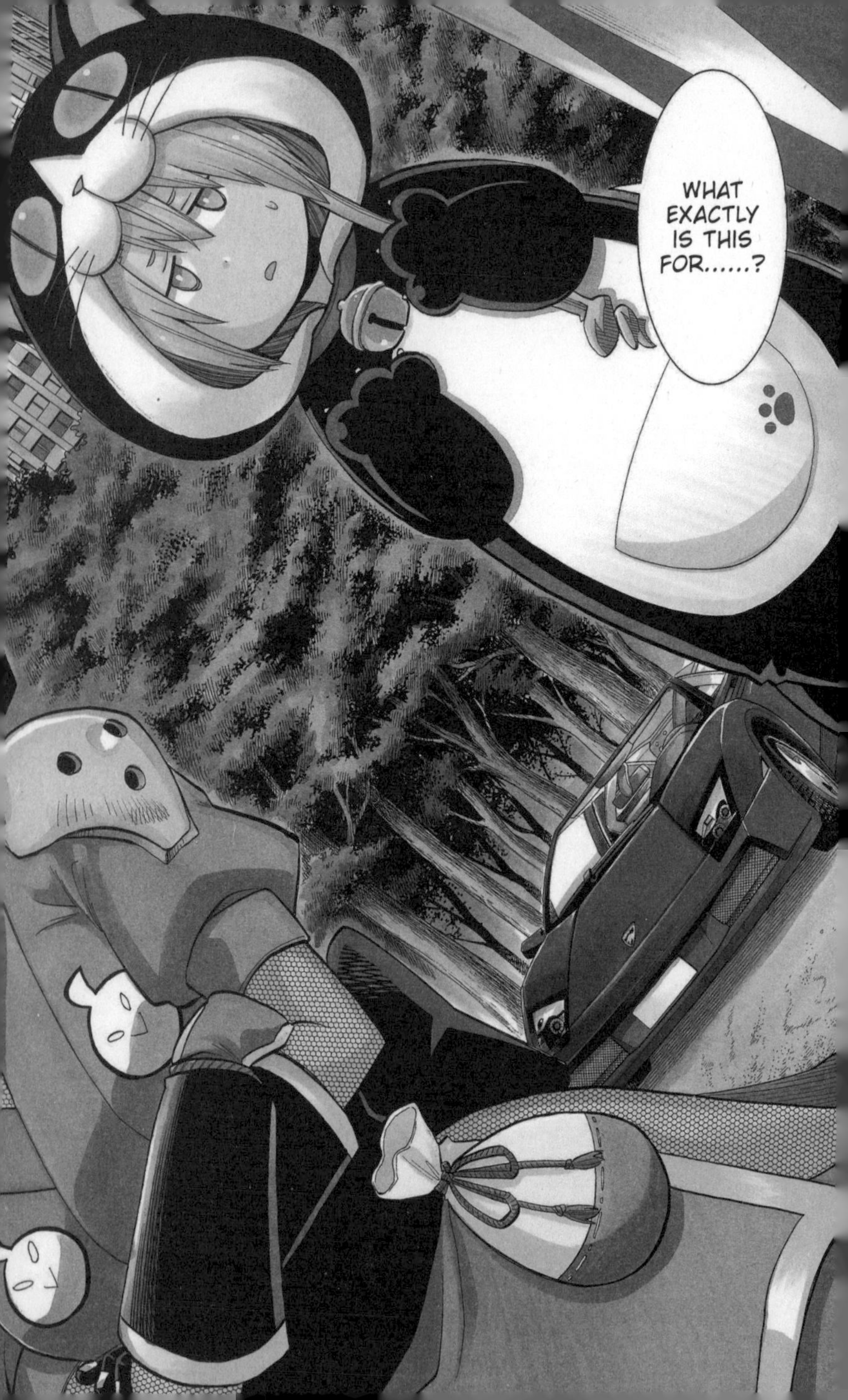
WHAT EXACTLY IS THIS FOR......?

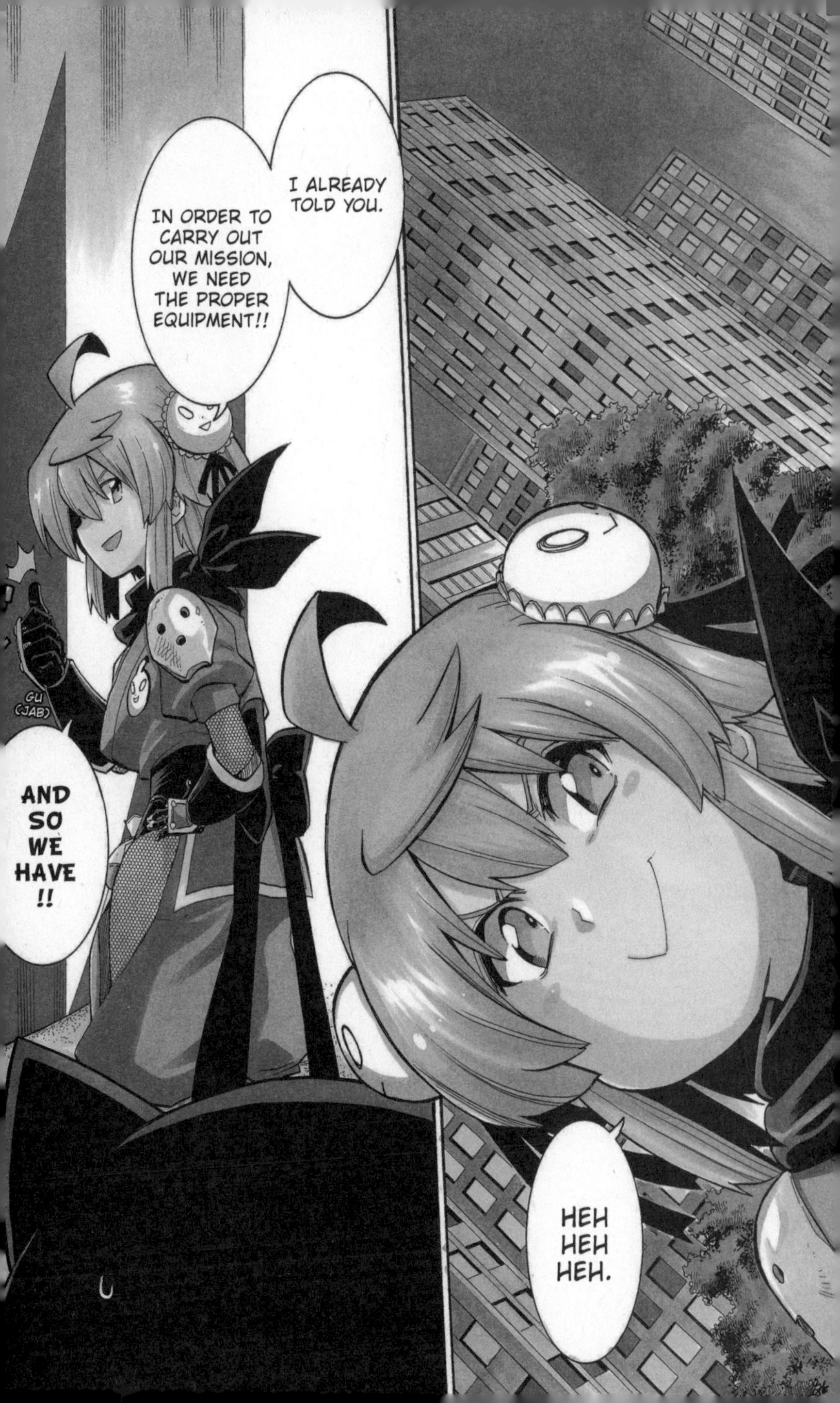
HEH HEH HEH.
I ALREADY TOLD YOU.
IN ORDER TO CARRY OUT OUR MISSION, WE NEED THE PROPER EQUIPMENT!!
GU (JAB)
AND SO WE HAVE!!

MURCIÉLAGO

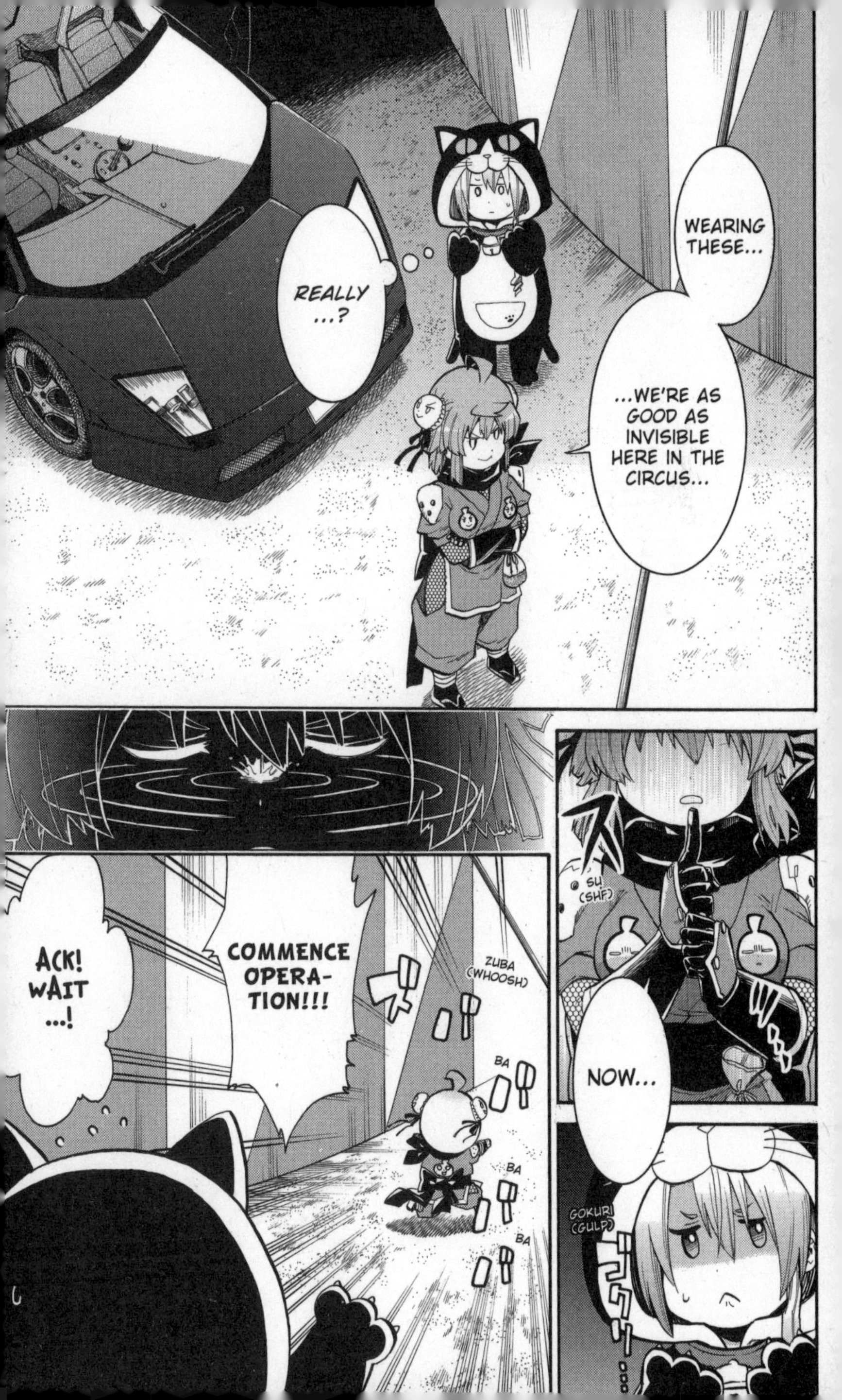
WEARING THESE...
...WE'RE AS GOOD AS INVISIBLE HERE IN THE CIRCUS...
REALLY ...?
SU (SHF)
NOW...
GOKURI (GULP)
COMMENCE OPERATION!!!
ZUBA (WHOOSH)
BA
BA
BA
ACK! WAIT ...!

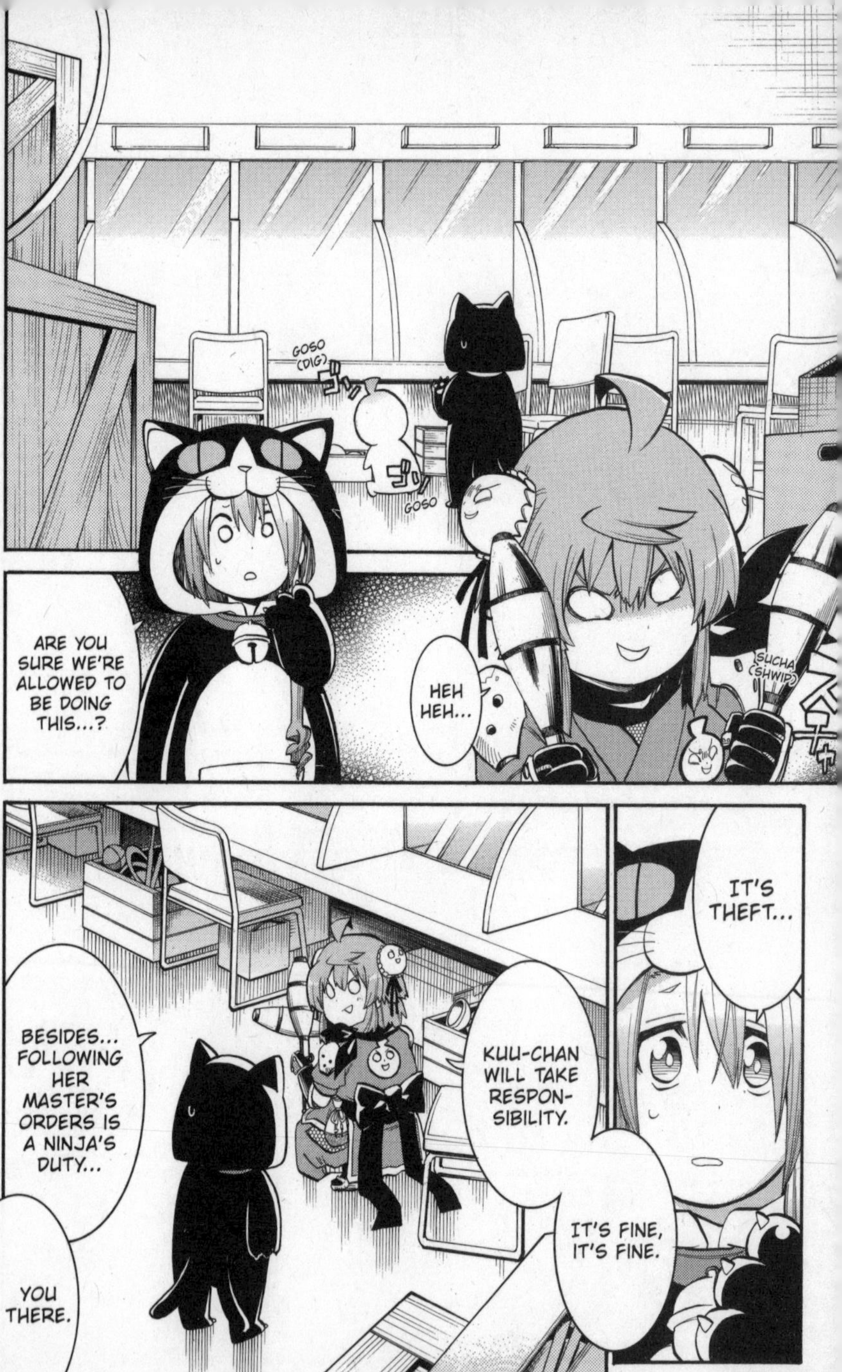
GOSO (DIG)
GOSO
ARE YOU SURE WE'RE ALLOWED TO BE DOING THIS...?
HEH HEH...
SUCHA (SHWIP)
IT'S THEFT...
KUU-CHAN WILL TAKE RESPON-SIBILITY.
IT'S FINE, IT'S FINE.
BESIDES... FOLLOWING HER MASTER'S ORDERS IS A NINJA'S DUTY...
YOU THERE.

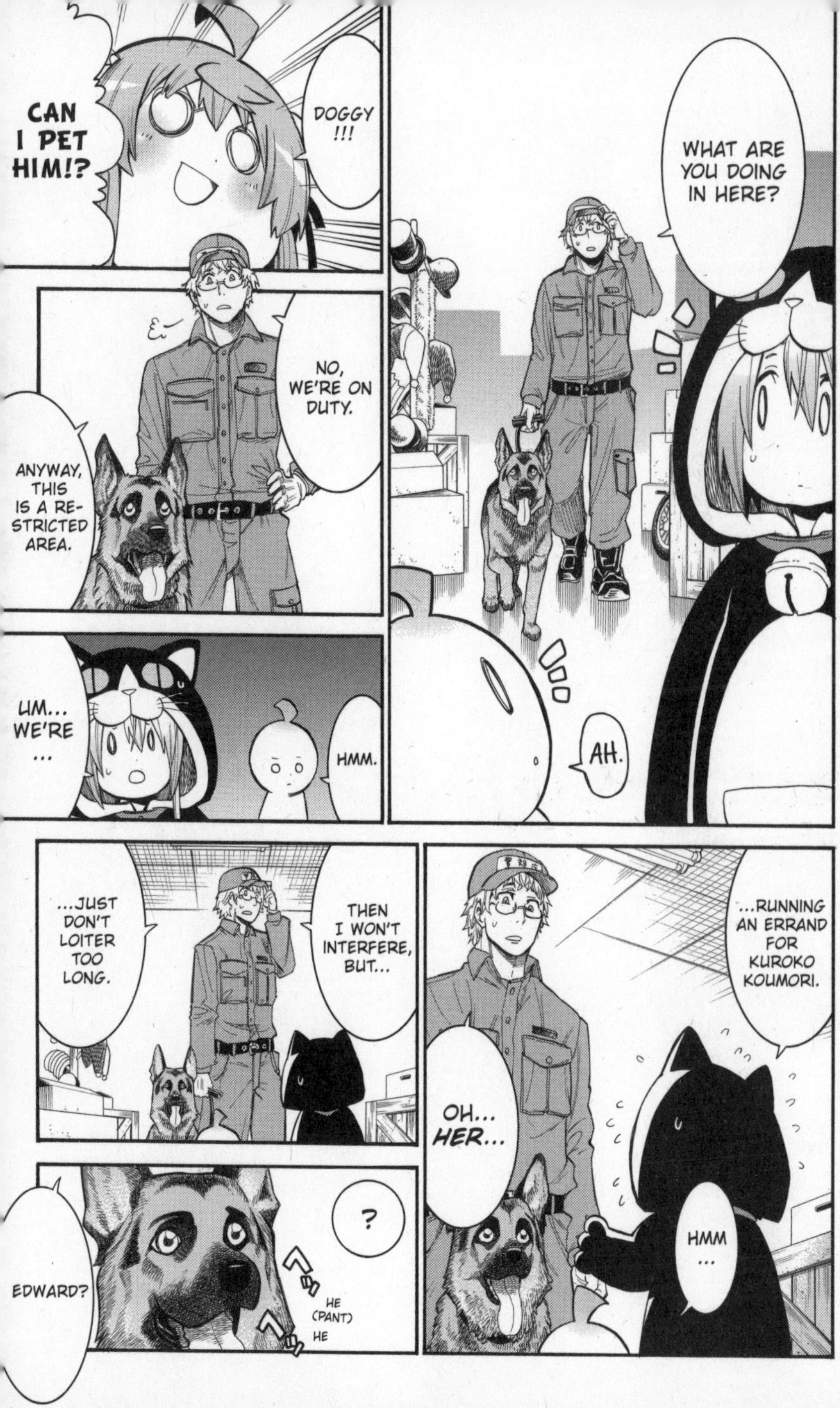
WHAT ARE YOU DOING IN HERE?
AH.
DOGGY !!!
CAN I PET HIM!?
NO, WE'RE ON DUTY.
ANYWAY, THIS IS A RE-STRICTED AREA.
HMM.
UM... WE'RE ...
...RUNNING AN ERRAND FOR KUROKO KOUMORI.
OH... *HER*...
HMM ...
THEN I WON'T INTERFERE, BUT...
...JUST DON'T LOITER TOO LONG.
?
HE (PANT) HE
EDWARD?

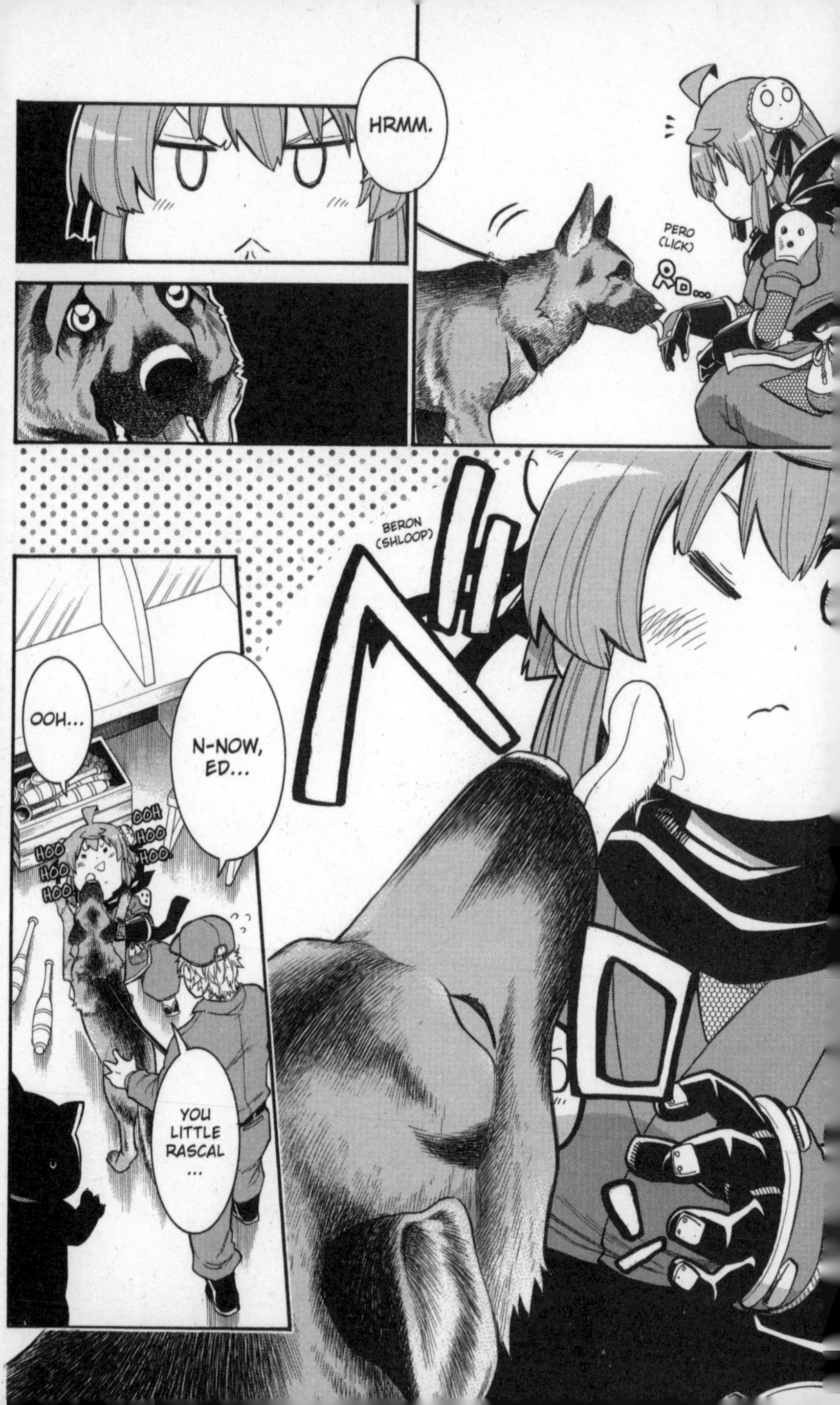
PERO
(LICK)
HRMM.
BERON
(SHLOOP)
N-NOW, ED...
OOH...
OOH HOO HOO.
HOO HOO HOO.
YOU LITTLE RASCAL
...

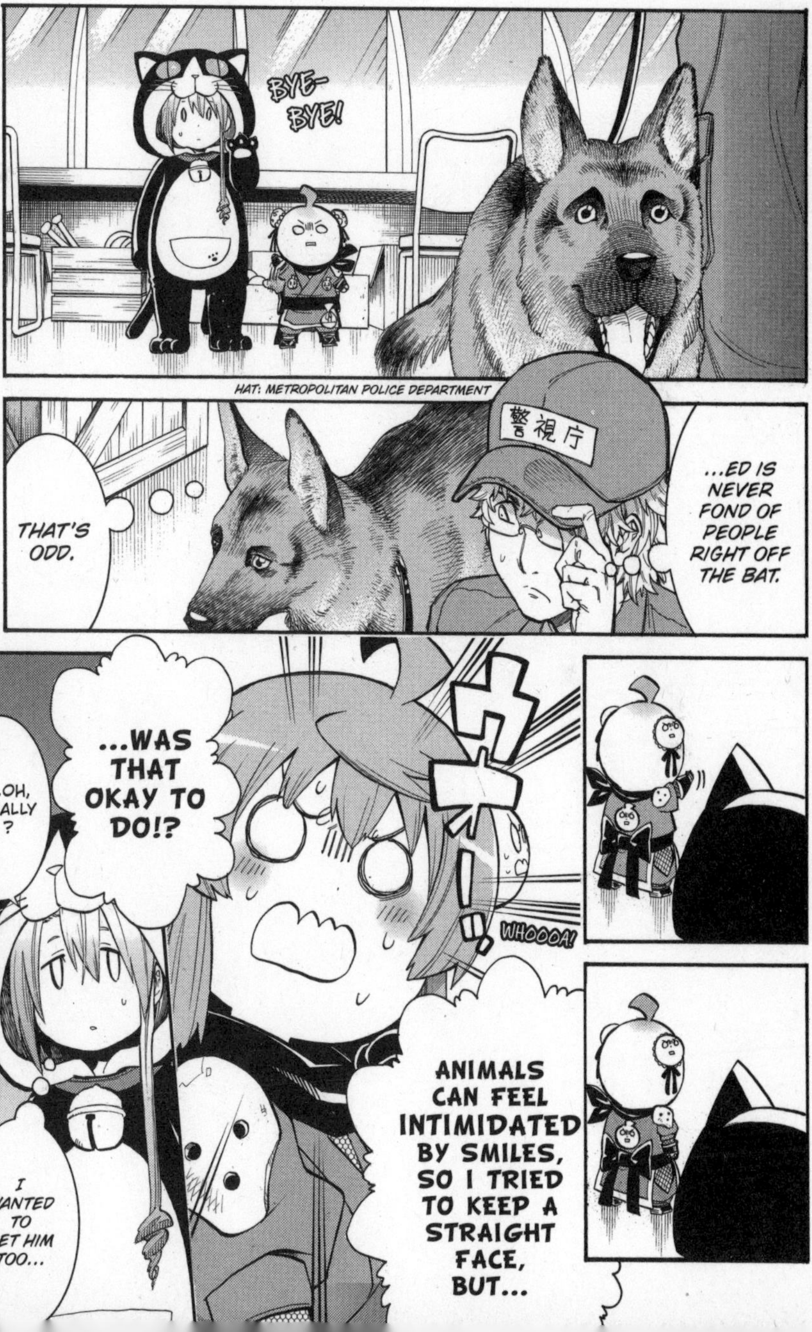
BYE-BYE!
HAT: METROPOLITAN POLICE DEPARTMENT
警視庁
...ED IS NEVER FOND OF PEOPLE RIGHT OFF THE BAT.
THAT'S ODD.
WHOOOA!
...WAS THAT OKAY TO DO!?
...OH, REALLY?
ANIMALS CAN FEEL INTIMIDATED BY SMILES, SO I TRIED TO KEEP A STRAIGHT FACE, BUT...
I WANTED TO PET HIM TOO...

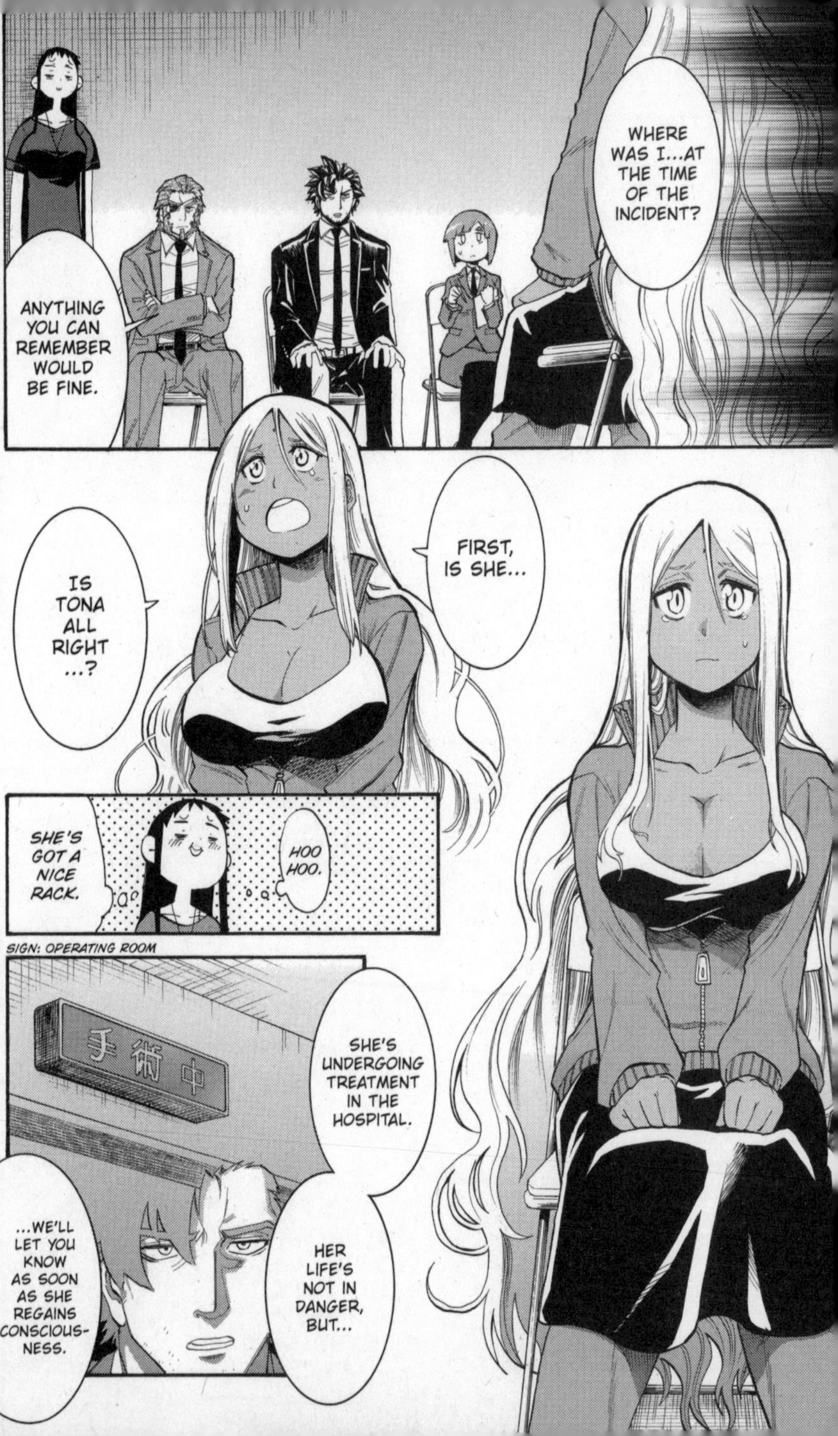
WHERE WAS I...AT THE TIME OF THE INCIDENT?
ANYTHING YOU CAN REMEMBER WOULD BE FINE.
FIRST, IS SHE...
IS TONA ALL RIGHT...?
HOO HOO.
SHE'S GOT A NICE RACK.
SIGN: OPERATING ROOM
手術中
SHE'S UNDERGOING TREATMENT IN THE HOSPITAL.
HER LIFE'S NOT IN DANGER, BUT...
...WE'LL LET YOU KNOW AS SOON AS SHE REGAINS CONSCIOUSNESS.

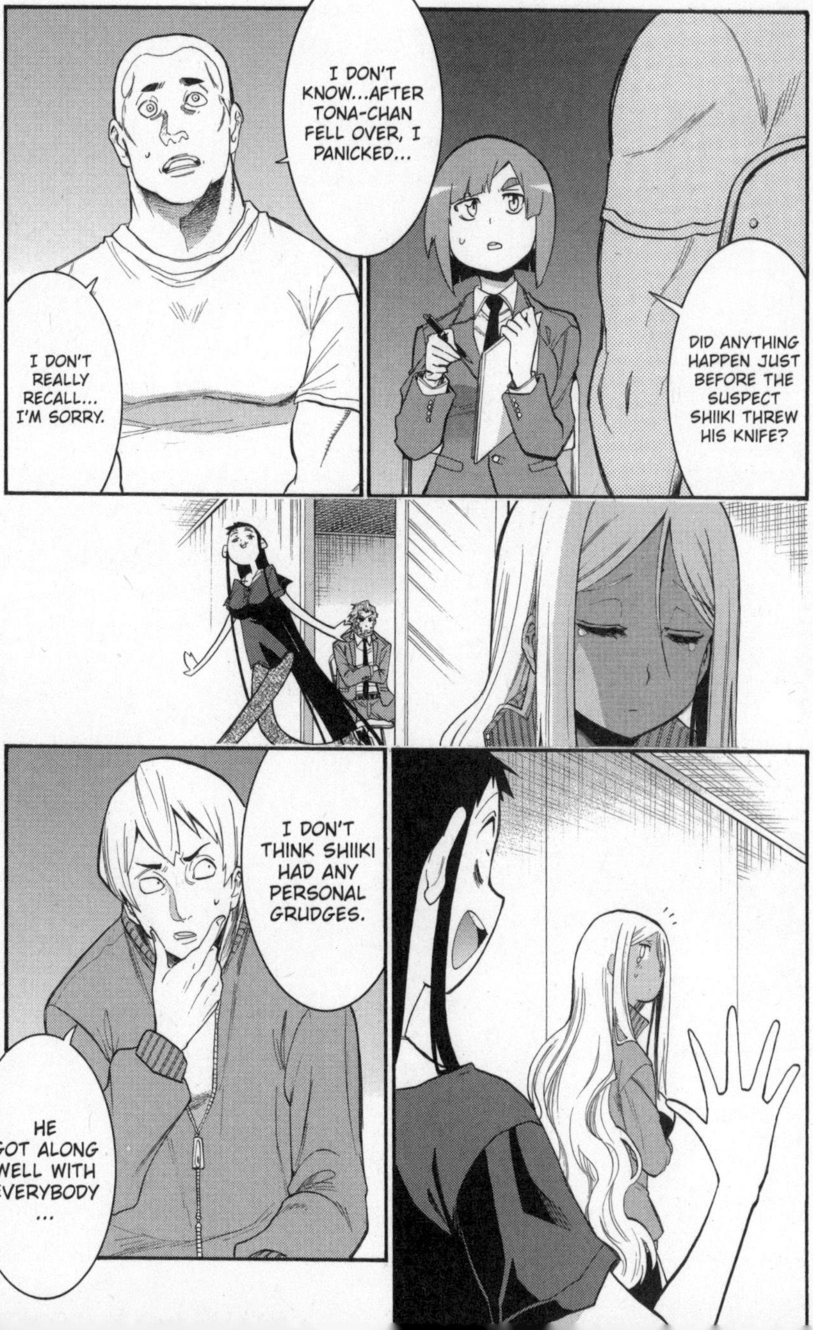
DID ANYTHING HAPPEN JUST BEFORE THE SUSPECT SHIIKI THREW HIS KNIFE?
I DON'T KNOW...AFTER TONA-CHAN FELL OVER, I PANICKED...
I DON'T REALLY RECALL... I'M SORRY.
I DON'T THINK SHIIKI HAD ANY PERSONAL GRUDGES.
HE GOT ALONG WELL WITH EVERYBODY ...

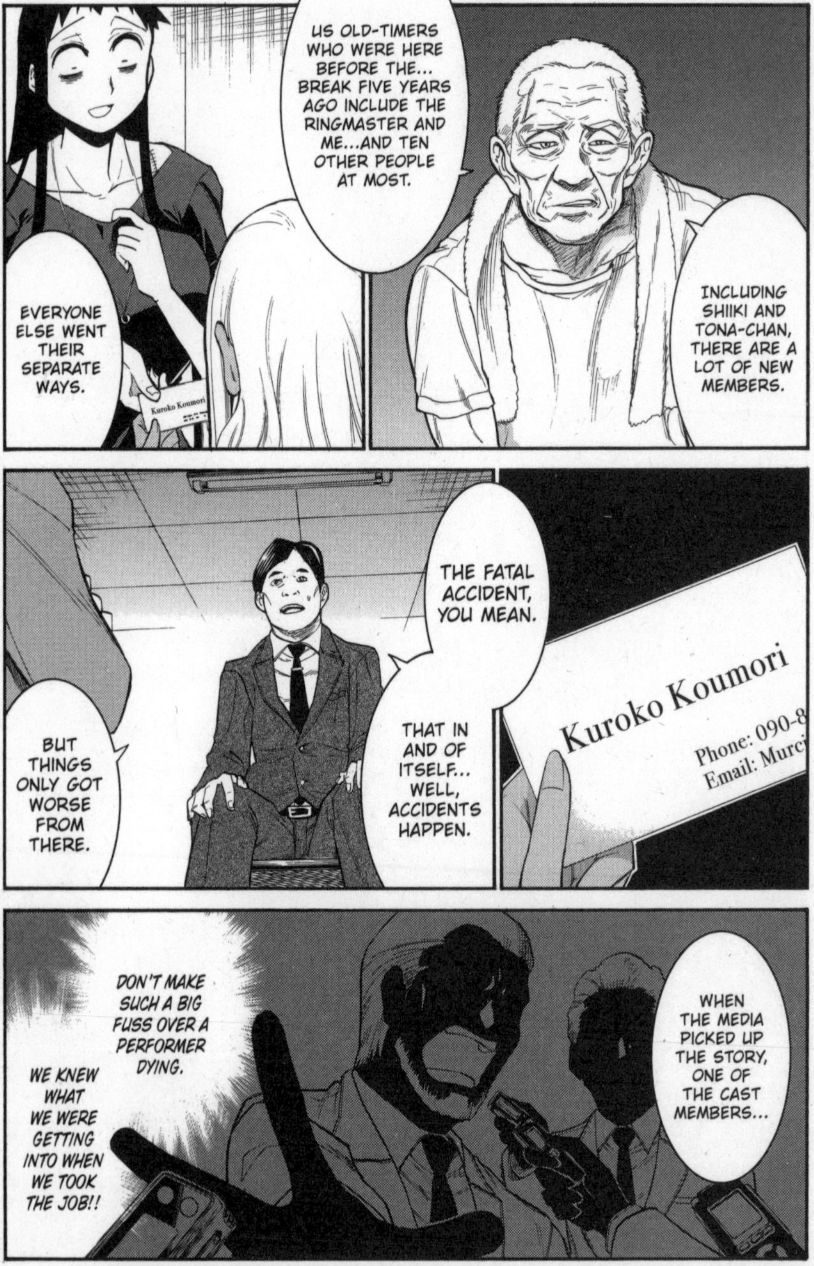
US OLD-TIMERS WHO WERE HERE BEFORE THE... BREAK FIVE YEARS AGO INCLUDE THE RINGMASTER AND ME...AND TEN OTHER PEOPLE AT MOST.
INCLUDING SHIIKI AND TONA-CHAN, THERE ARE A LOT OF NEW MEMBERS.
EVERYONE ELSE WENT THEIR SEPARATE WAYS.
Kuroko Koumori
Kuroko Koumori
Phone: 090-8
Email: Murc
THE FATAL ACCIDENT, YOU MEAN.
THAT IN AND OF ITSELF... WELL, ACCIDENTS HAPPEN.
BUT THINGS ONLY GOT WORSE FROM THERE.
WHEN THE MEDIA PICKED UP THE STORY, ONE OF THE CAST MEMBERS...
DON'T MAKE SUCH A BIG FUSS OVER A PERFORMER DYING.
WE KNEW WHAT WE WERE GETTING INTO WHEN WE TOOK THE JOB!!

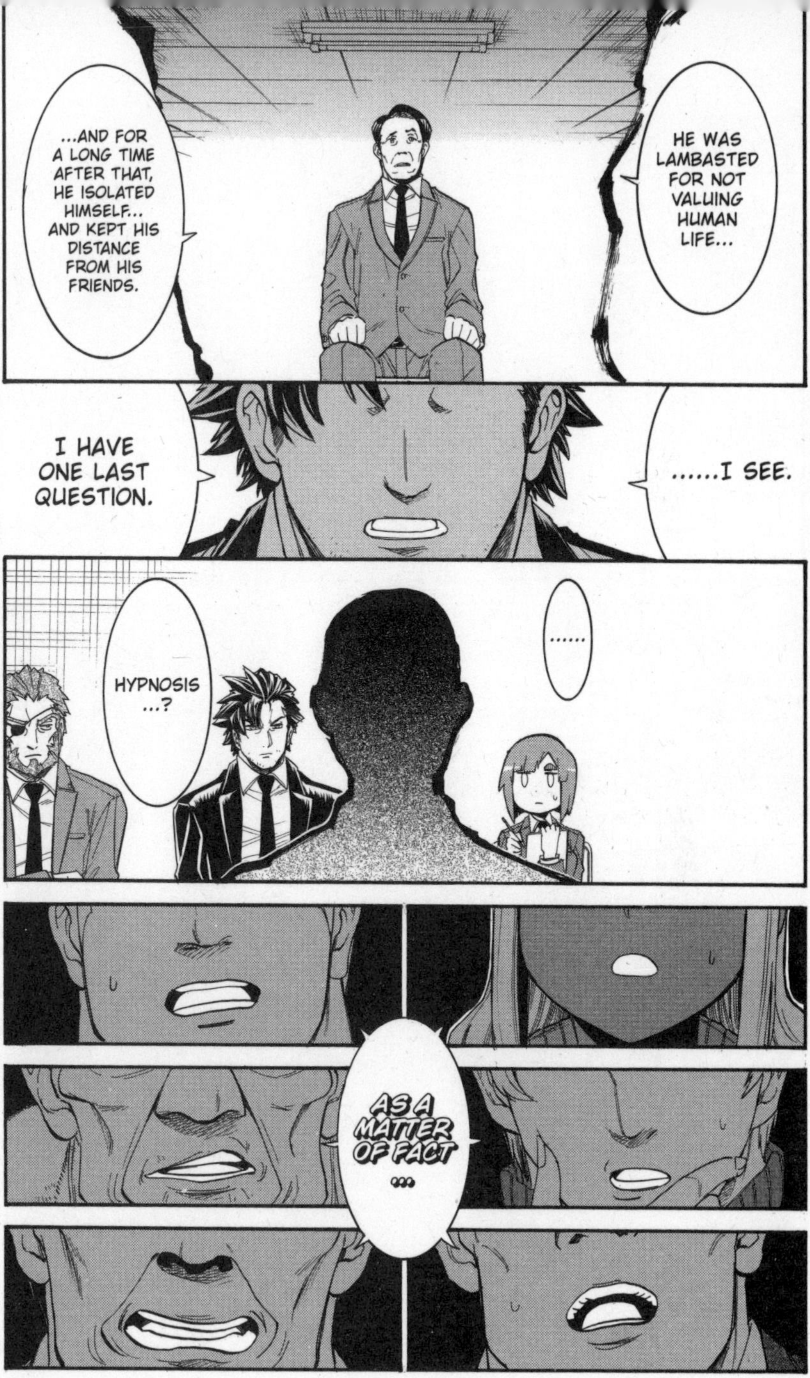
HE WAS LAMBASTED FOR NOT VALUING HUMAN LIFE...
...AND FOR A LONG TIME AFTER THAT, HE ISOLATED HIMSELF... AND KEPT HIS DISTANCE FROM HIS FRIENDS.
......I SEE.
I HAVE ONE LAST QUESTION.
......
HYPNOSIS ...?
AS A MATTER OF FACT ...

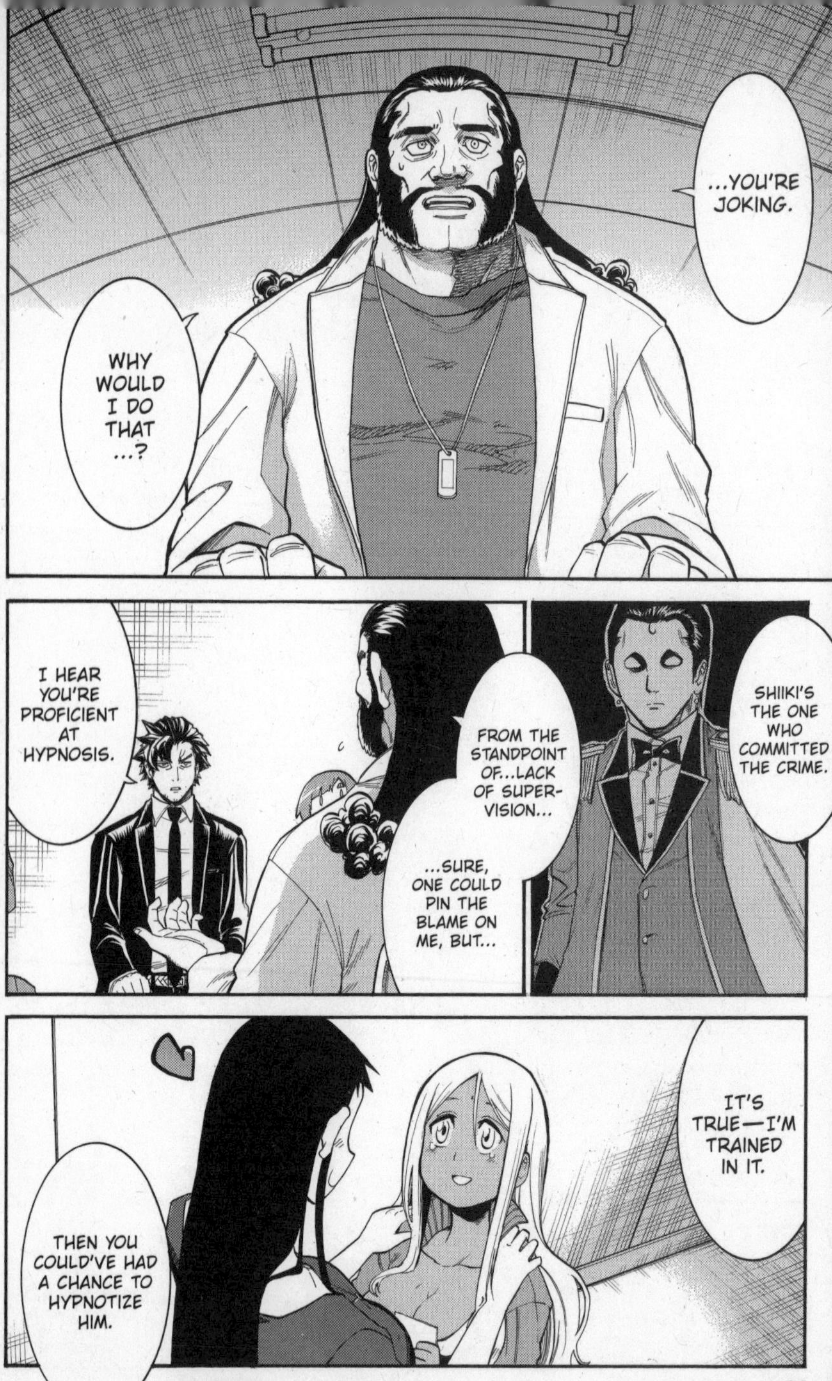
...YOU'RE JOKING.
WHY WOULD I DO THAT ...?
SHIIKI'S THE ONE WHO COMMITTED THE CRIME.
FROM THE STANDPOINT OF...LACK OF SUPER-VISION...
...SURE, ONE COULD PIN THE BLAME ON ME, BUT...
I HEAR YOU'RE PROFICIENT AT HYPNOSIS.
IT'S TRUE—I'M TRAINED IN IT.
THEN YOU COULD'VE HAD A CHANCE TO HYPNOTIZE HIM.

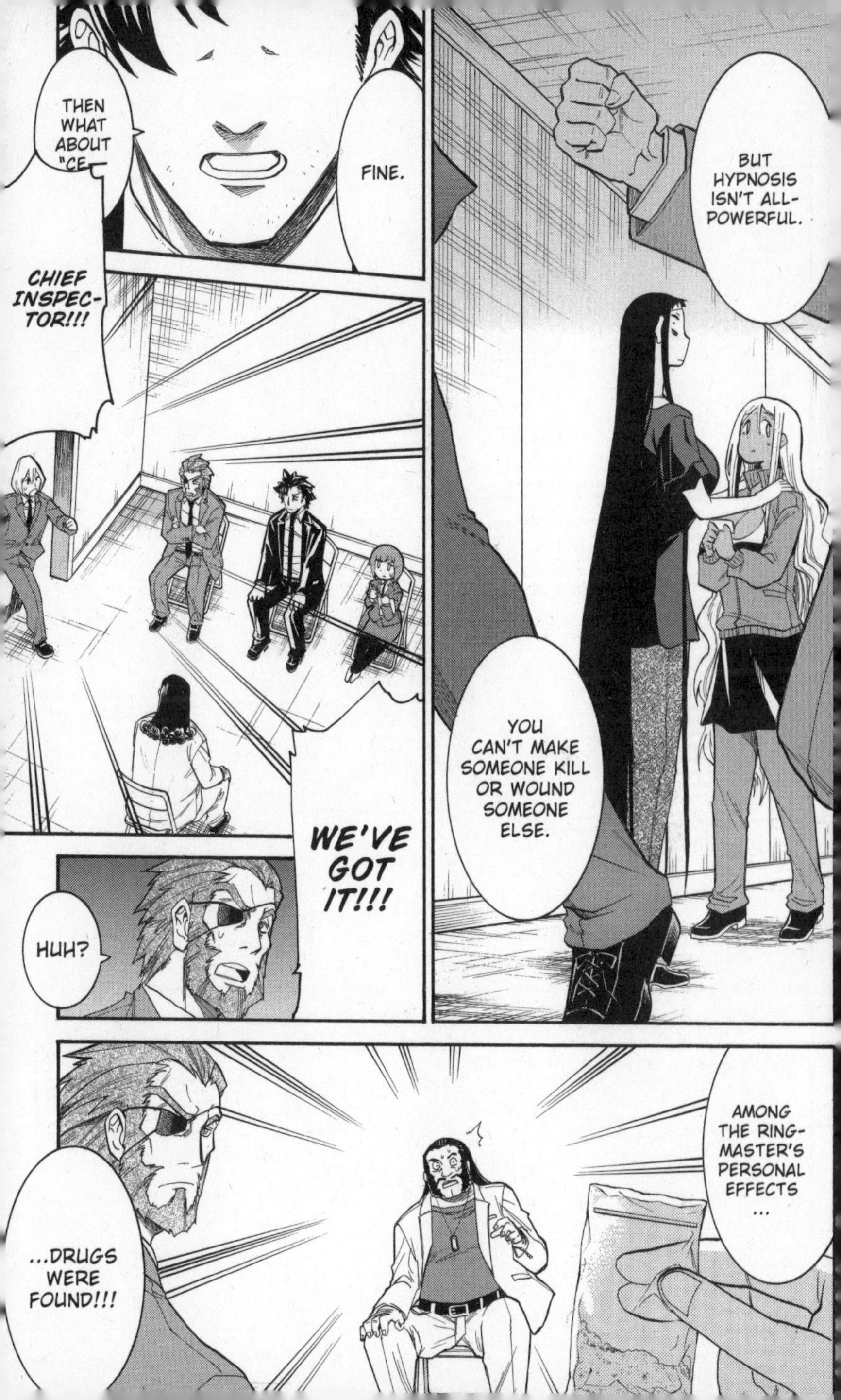
BUT HYPNOSIS ISN'T ALL-POWERFUL.
YOU CAN'T MAKE SOMEONE KILL OR WOUND SOMEONE ELSE.
FINE.
THEN WHAT ABOUT "CE—
CHIEF INSPECTOR!!!
WE'VE GOT IT!!!
HUH?
AMONG THE RING-MASTER'S PERSONAL EFFECTS ...
...DRUGS WERE FOUND!!!

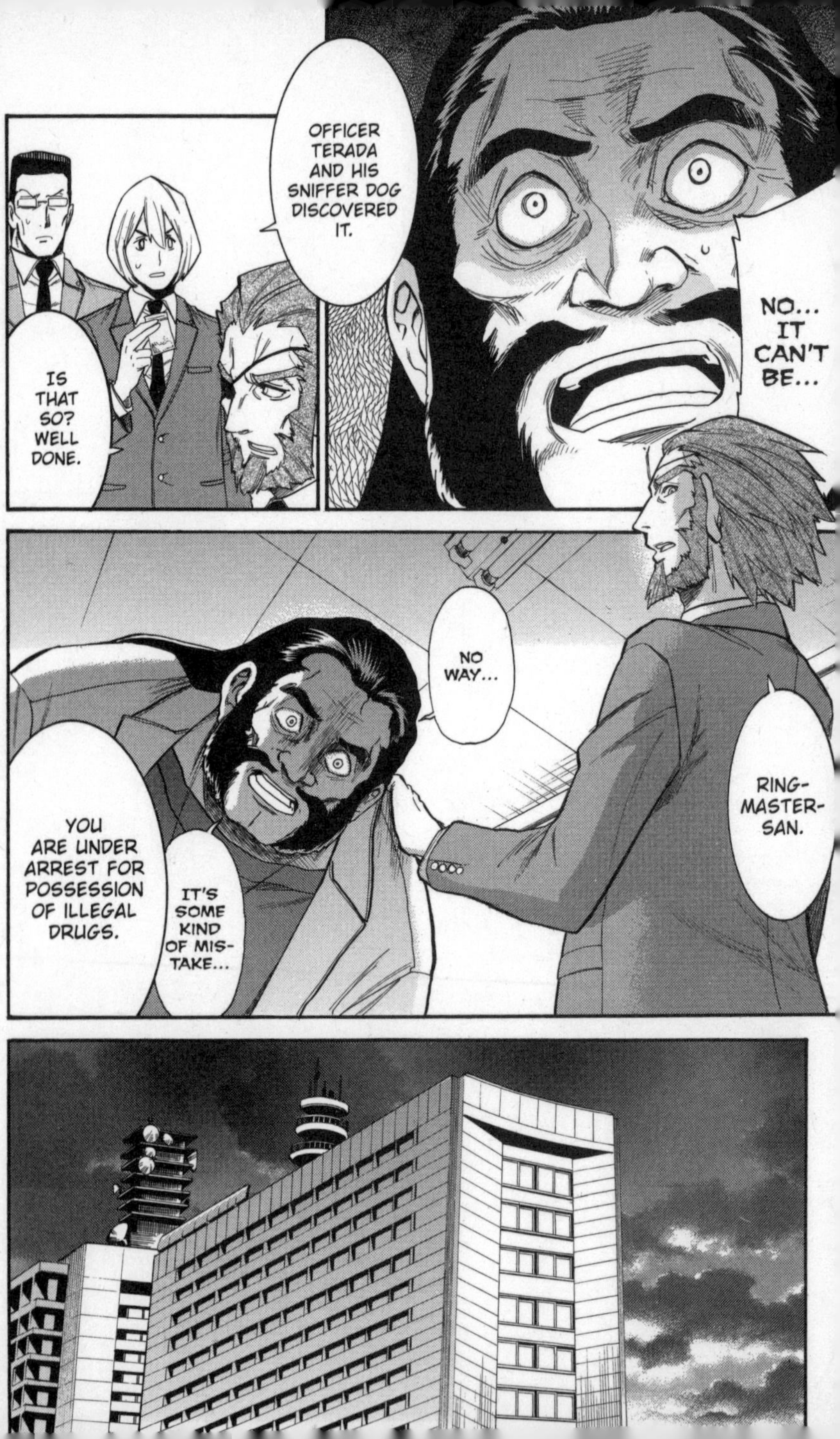
OFFICER TERADA AND HIS SNIFFER DOG DISCOVERED IT.
IS THAT SO? WELL DONE.
NO... IT CAN'T BE...
RING-MASTER-SAN.
NO WAY...
YOU ARE UNDER ARREST FOR POSSESSION OF ILLEGAL DRUGS.
IT'S SOME KIND OF MIS-TAKE...

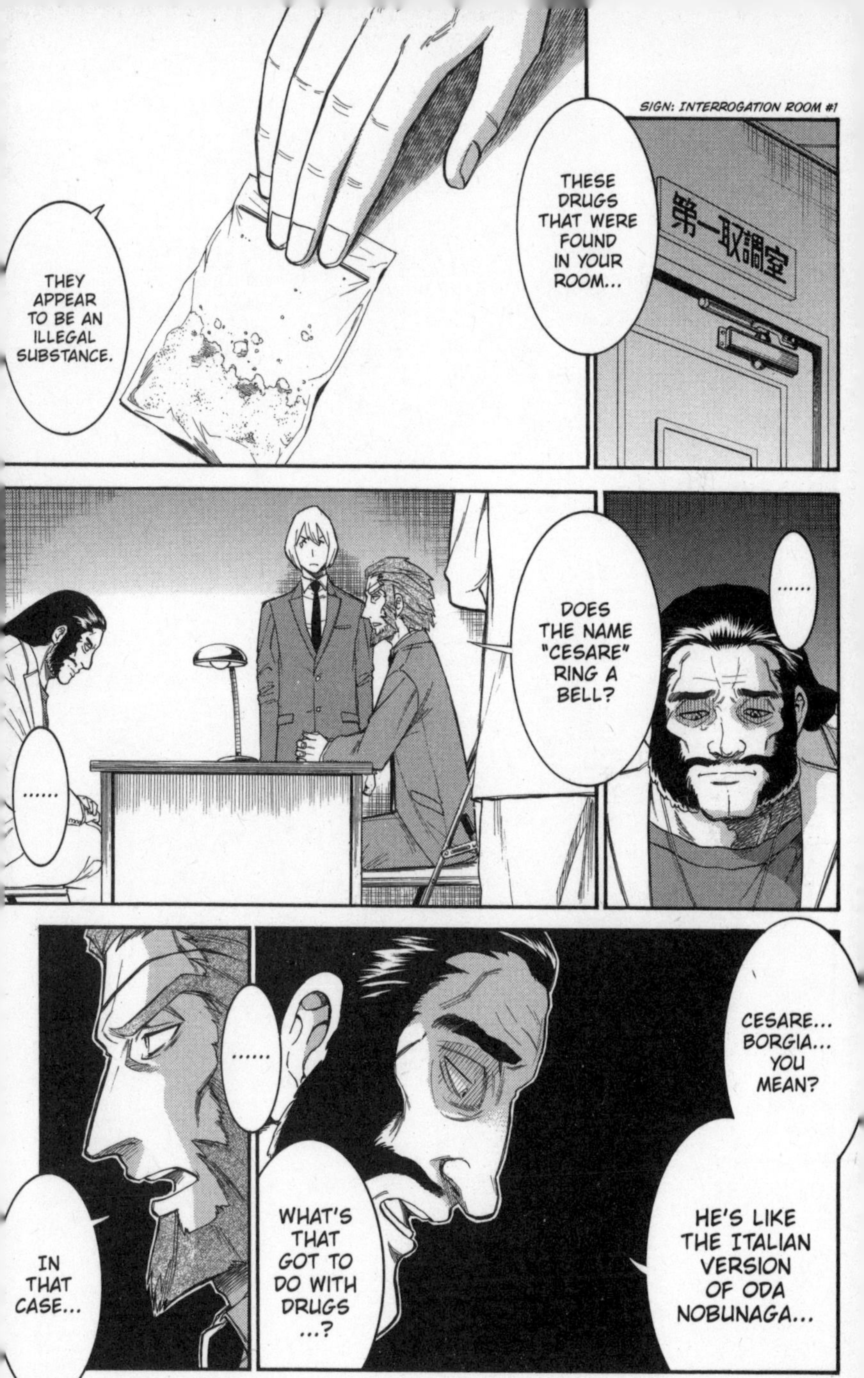
SIGN: INTERROGATION ROOM #1
第一取調室
THESE DRUGS THAT WERE FOUND IN YOUR ROOM...
THEY APPEAR TO BE AN ILLEGAL SUBSTANCE.
DOES THE NAME "CESARE" RING A BELL?
......
......
CESARE... BORGIA... YOU MEAN?
HE'S LIKE THE ITALIAN VERSION OF ODA NOBUNAGA...
WHAT'S THAT GOT TO DO WITH DRUGS ...?
......
IN THAT CASE...

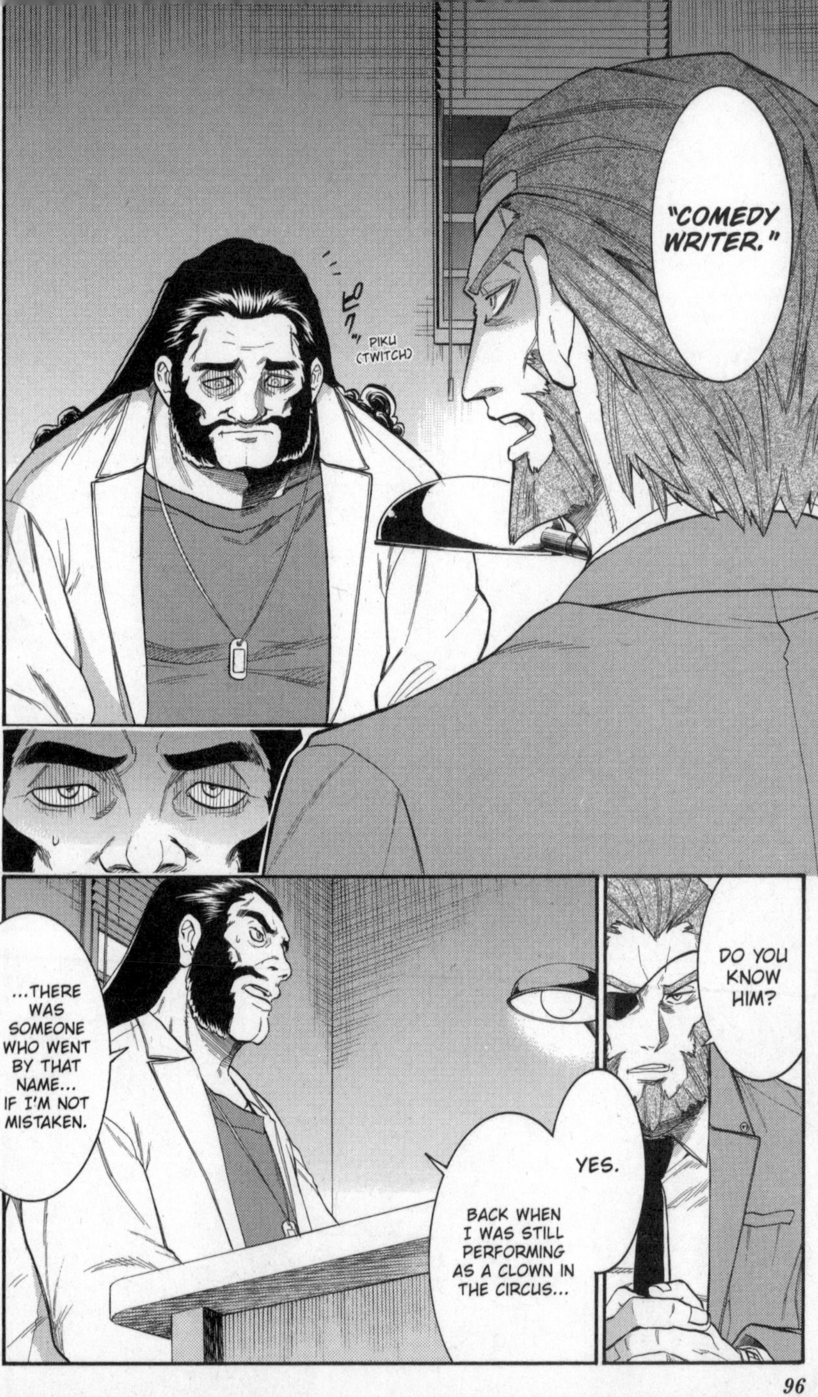
"COMEDY WRITER."
ピク PIKU (TWITCH)
DO YOU KNOW HIM?
YES.
BACK WHEN I WAS STILL PERFORMING AS A CLOWN IN THE CIRCUS...
...THERE WAS SOMEONE WHO WENT BY THAT NAME... IF I'M NOT MISTAKEN.

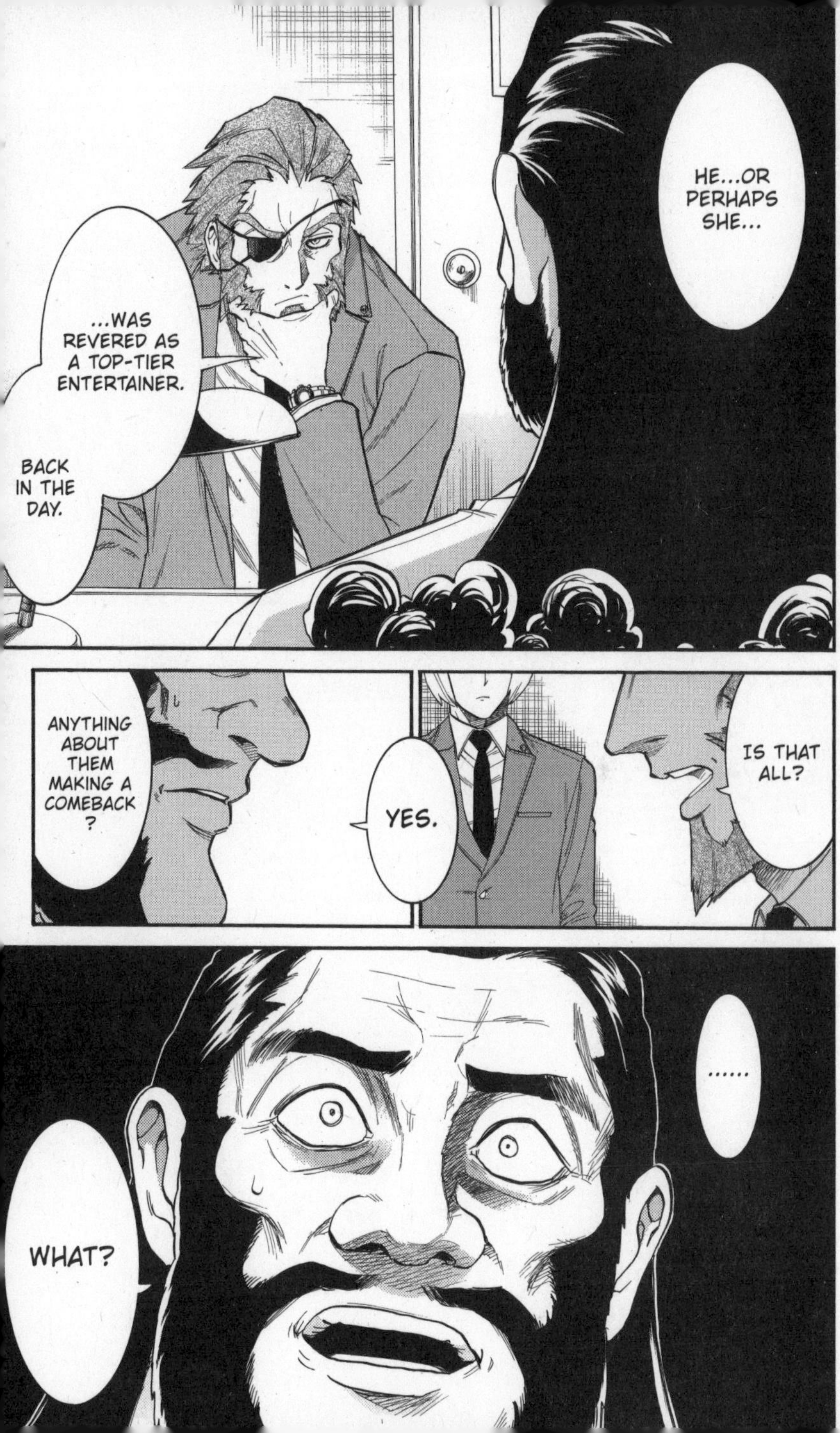
HE...OR PERHAPS SHE...
...WAS REVERED AS A TOP-TIER ENTERTAINER.
BACK IN THE DAY.
IS THAT ALL?
YES.
ANYTHING ABOUT THEM MAKING A COMEBACK?
......
WHAT?

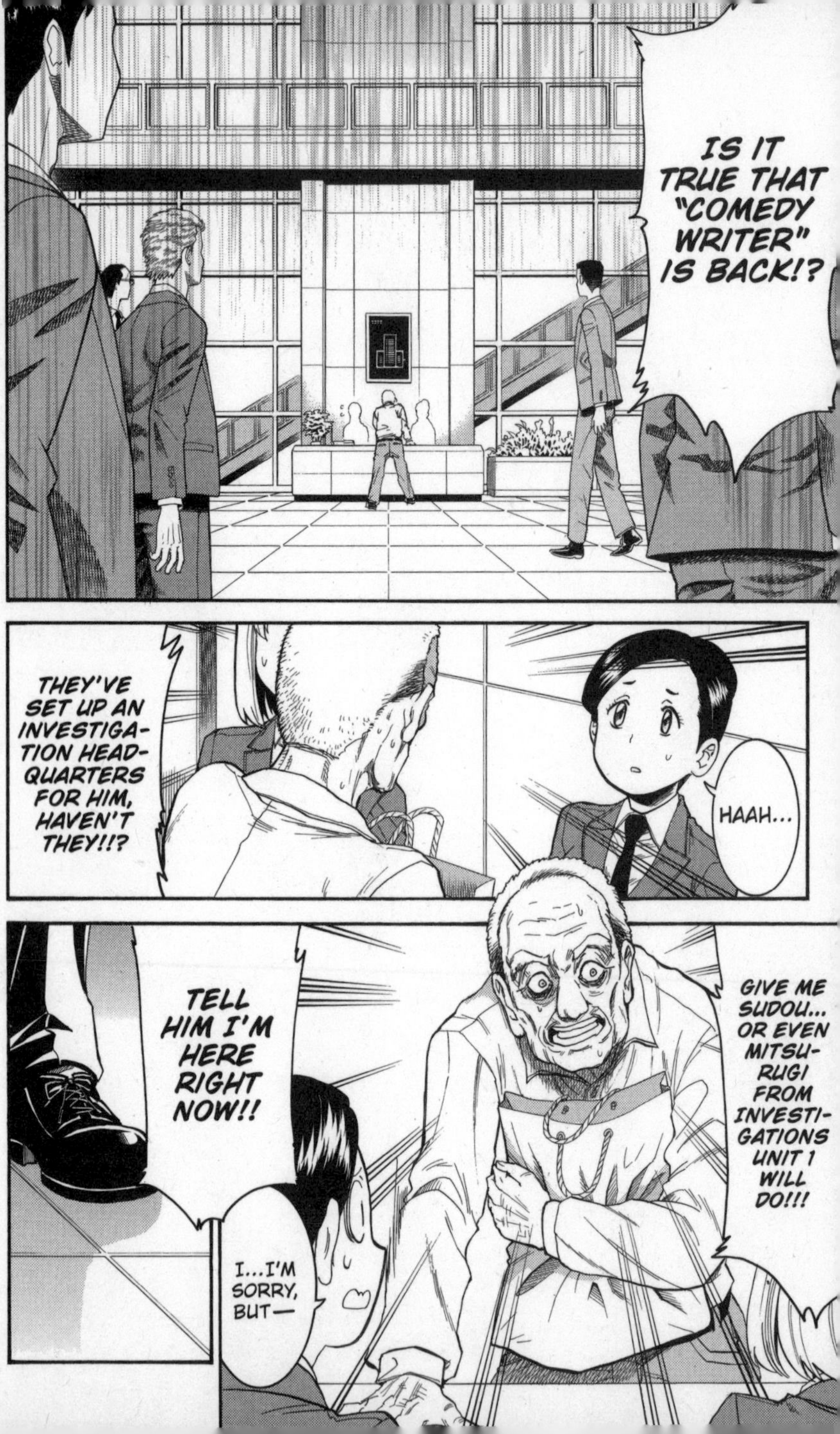
IS IT TRUE THAT "COMEDY WRITER" IS BACK!?
HAAH...
THEY'VE SET UP AN INVESTIGATION HEADQUARTERS FOR HIM, HAVEN'T THEY!!?
GIVE ME SUDOU... OR EVEN MITSURUGI FROM INVESTIGATIONS UNIT 1 WILL DO!!!
TELL HIM I'M HERE RIGHT NOW!!
I...I'M SORRY, BUT—

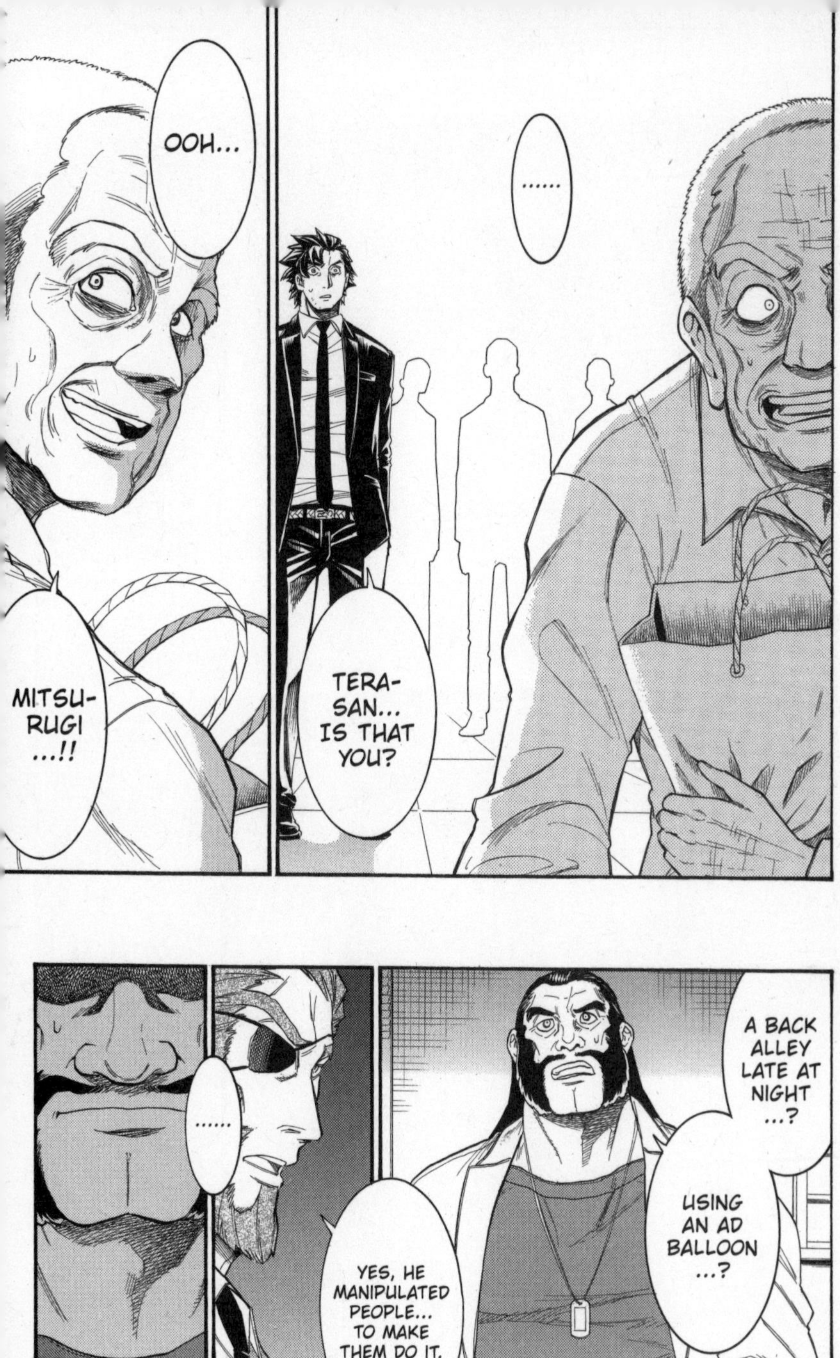
......
TERA-SAN... IS THAT YOU?
OOH...
MITSURUGI...!!
A BACK ALLEY LATE AT NIGHT...?
USING AN AD BALLOON...?
YES, HE MANIPULATED PEOPLE... TO MAKE THEM DO IT.
......

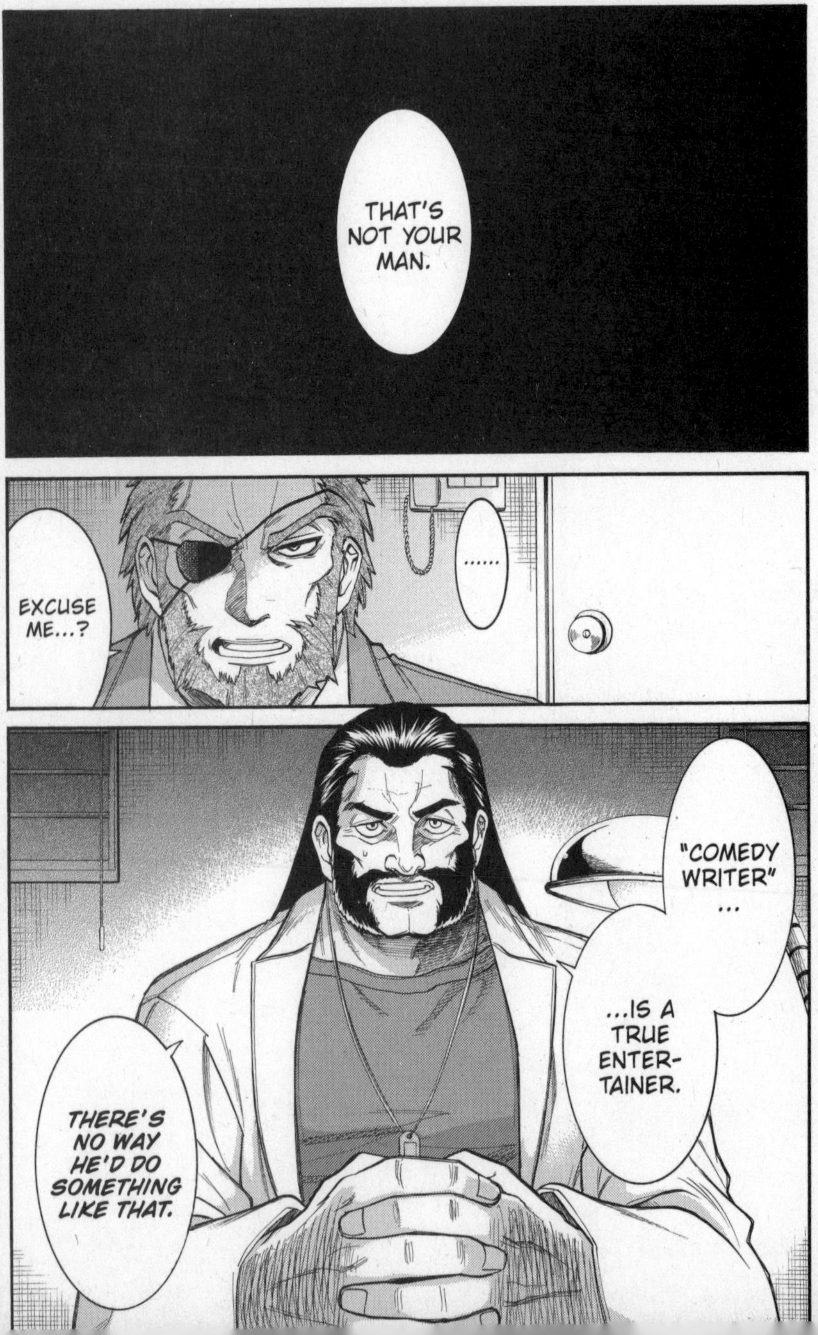
THAT'S NOT YOUR MAN.
......
EXCUSE ME...?
"COMEDY WRITER" ...
...IS A TRUE ENTER-TAINER.
THERE'S NO WAY HE'D DO SOMETHING LIKE THAT.

**MURCIÉLAGO**

**MURCIÉLAGO**

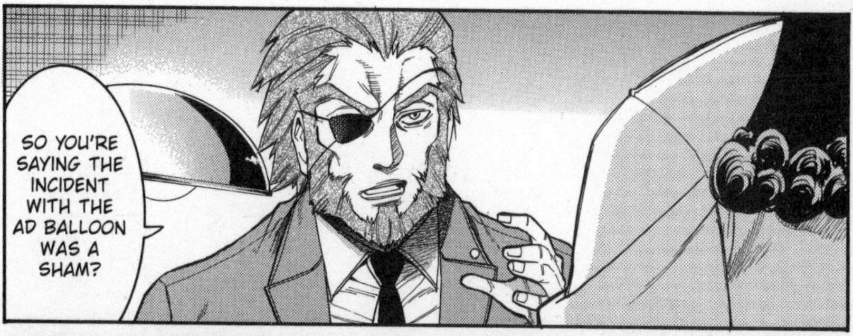
SO YOU'RE SAYING THE INCIDENT WITH THE AD BALLOON WAS A SHAM?

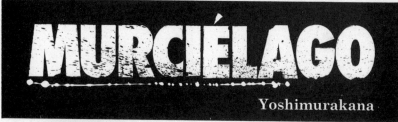

# MURCIÉLAGO

Yoshimurakana

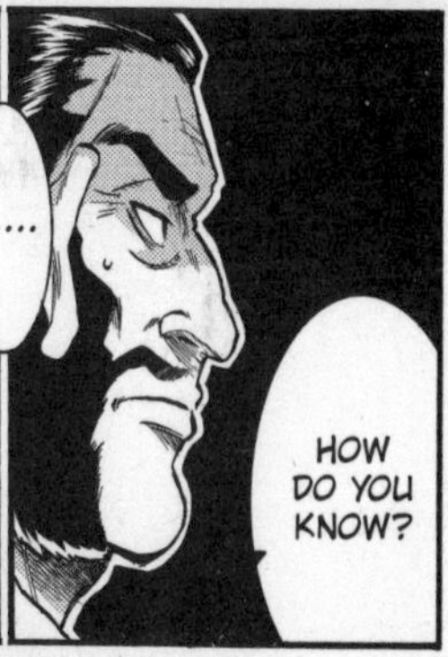
......
HOW DO YOU KNOW?

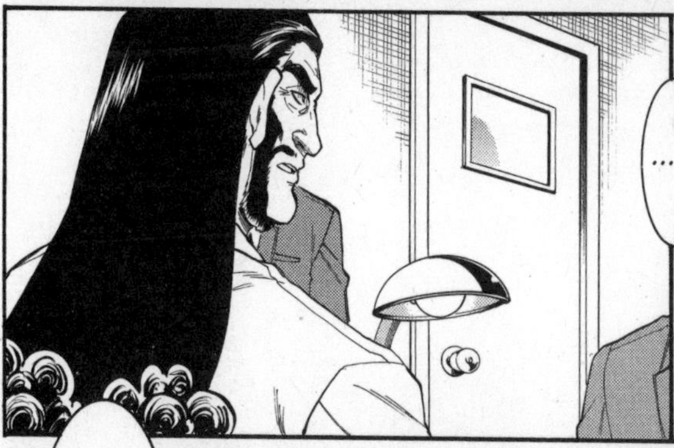

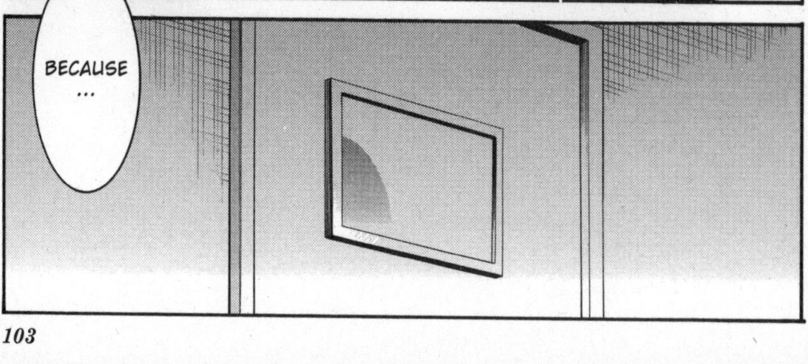
BECAUSE ...

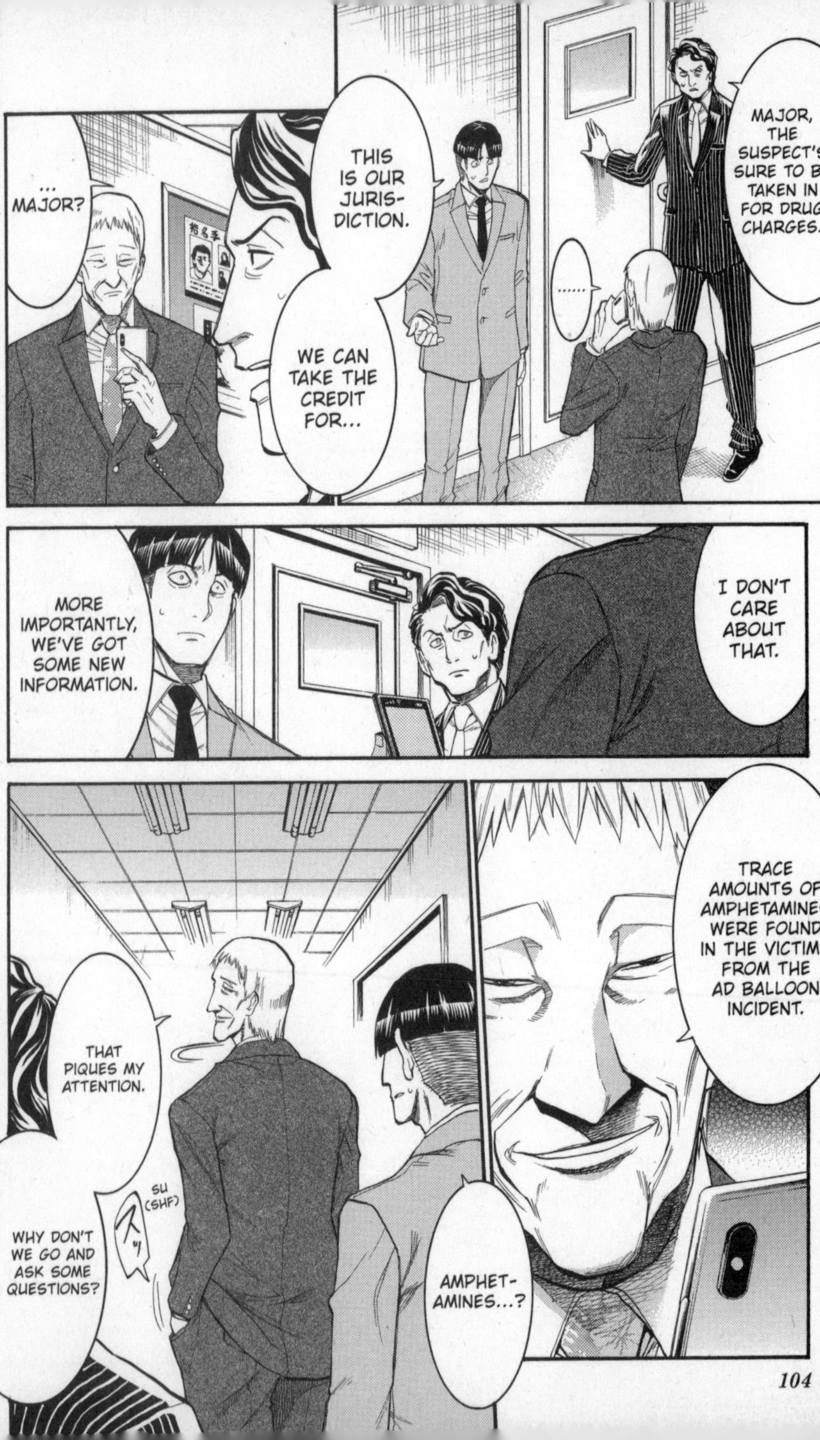
MAJOR, THE SUSPECT'S SURE TO BE TAKEN IN FOR DRUG CHARGES.
......
THIS IS OUR JURIS-DICTION.
WE CAN TAKE THE CREDIT FOR...
...MAJOR?
I DON'T CARE ABOUT THAT.
MORE IMPORTANTLY, WE'VE GOT SOME NEW INFORMATION.
TRACE AMOUNTS OF AMPHETAMINES WERE FOUND IN THE VICTIMS FROM THE AD BALLOON INCIDENT.
AMPHET-AMINES...?
THAT PIQUES MY ATTENTION.
SU (SHF)
WHY DON'T WE GO AND ASK SOME QUESTIONS?

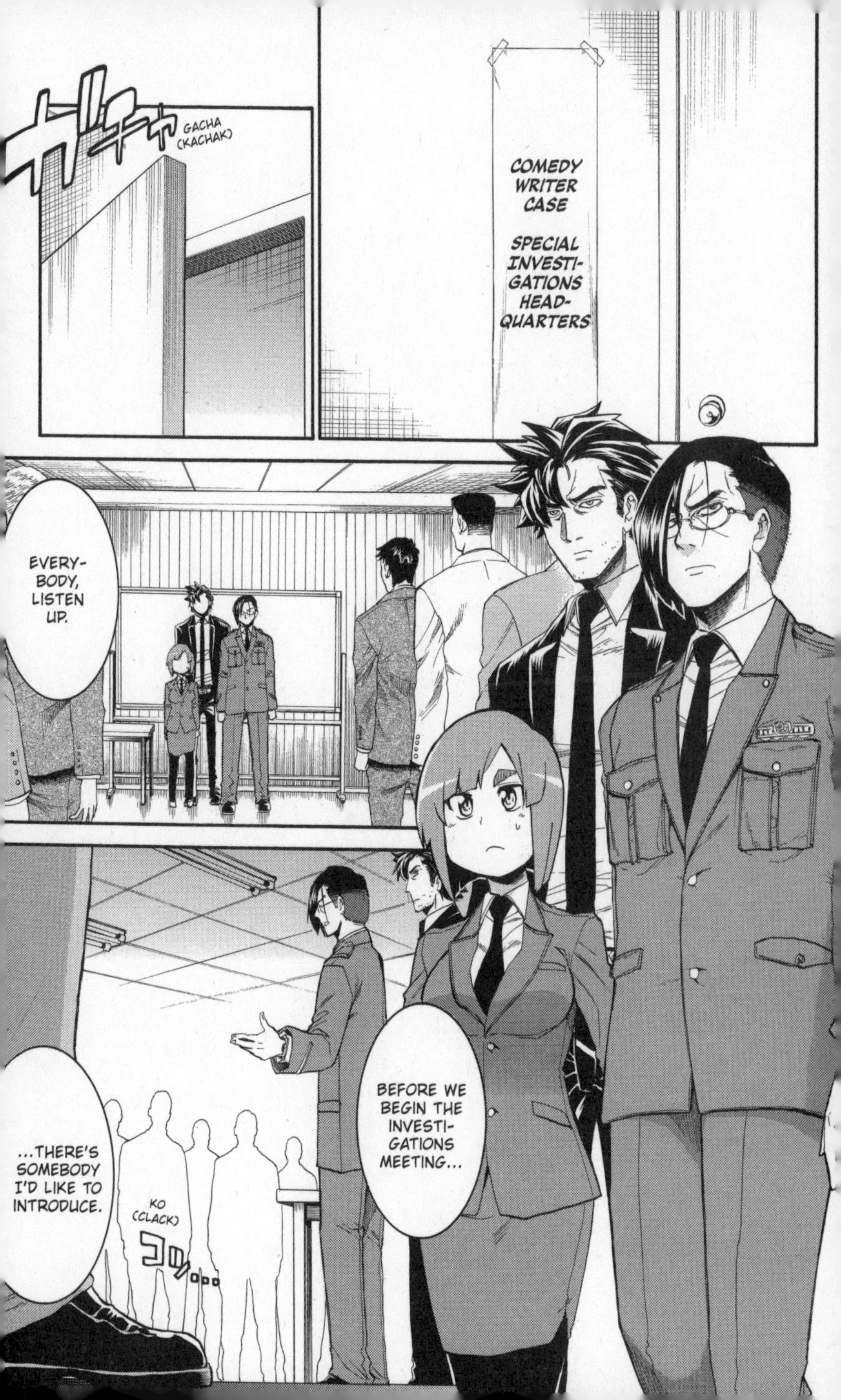

COMEDY WRITER CASE SPECIAL INVESTIGATIONS HEADQUARTERS
ガチャ
GACHA (KACHAK)
EVERYBODY, LISTEN UP.
BEFORE WE BEGIN THE INVESTIGATIONS MEETING...
...THERE'S SOMEBODY I'D LIKE TO INTRODUCE.
KO (CLACK)

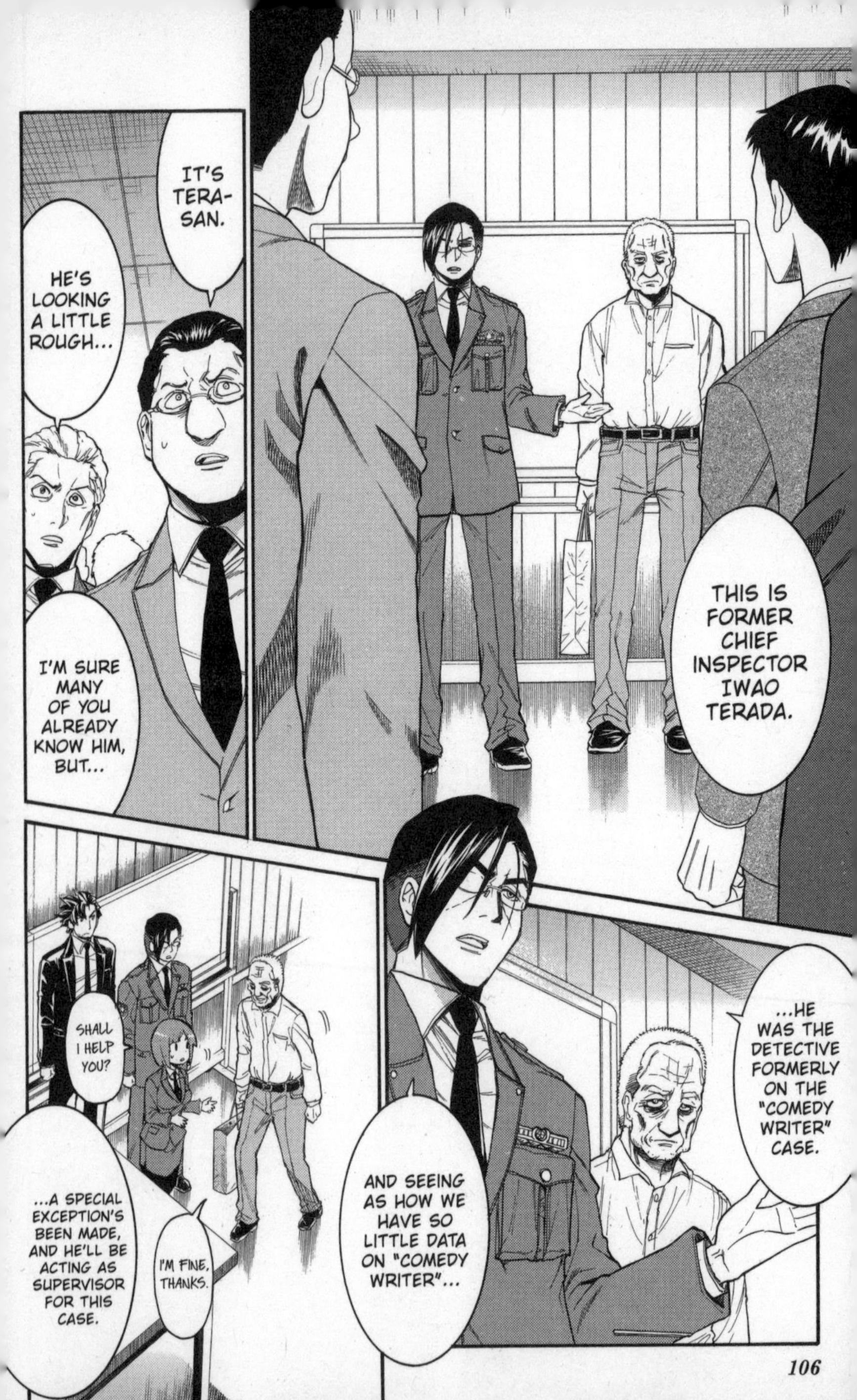
THIS IS FORMER CHIEF INSPECTOR IWAO TERADA.
IT'S TERA-SAN.
HE'S LOOKING A LITTLE ROUGH...
I'M SURE MANY OF YOU ALREADY KNOW HIM, BUT...
...HE WAS THE DETECTIVE FORMERLY ON THE "COMEDY WRITER" CASE.
AND SEEING AS HOW WE HAVE SO LITTLE DATA ON "COMEDY WRITER"...
SHALL I HELP YOU?
I'M FINE, THANKS.
...A SPECIAL EXCEPTION'S BEEN MADE, AND HE'LL BE ACTING AS SUPERVISOR FOR THIS CASE.

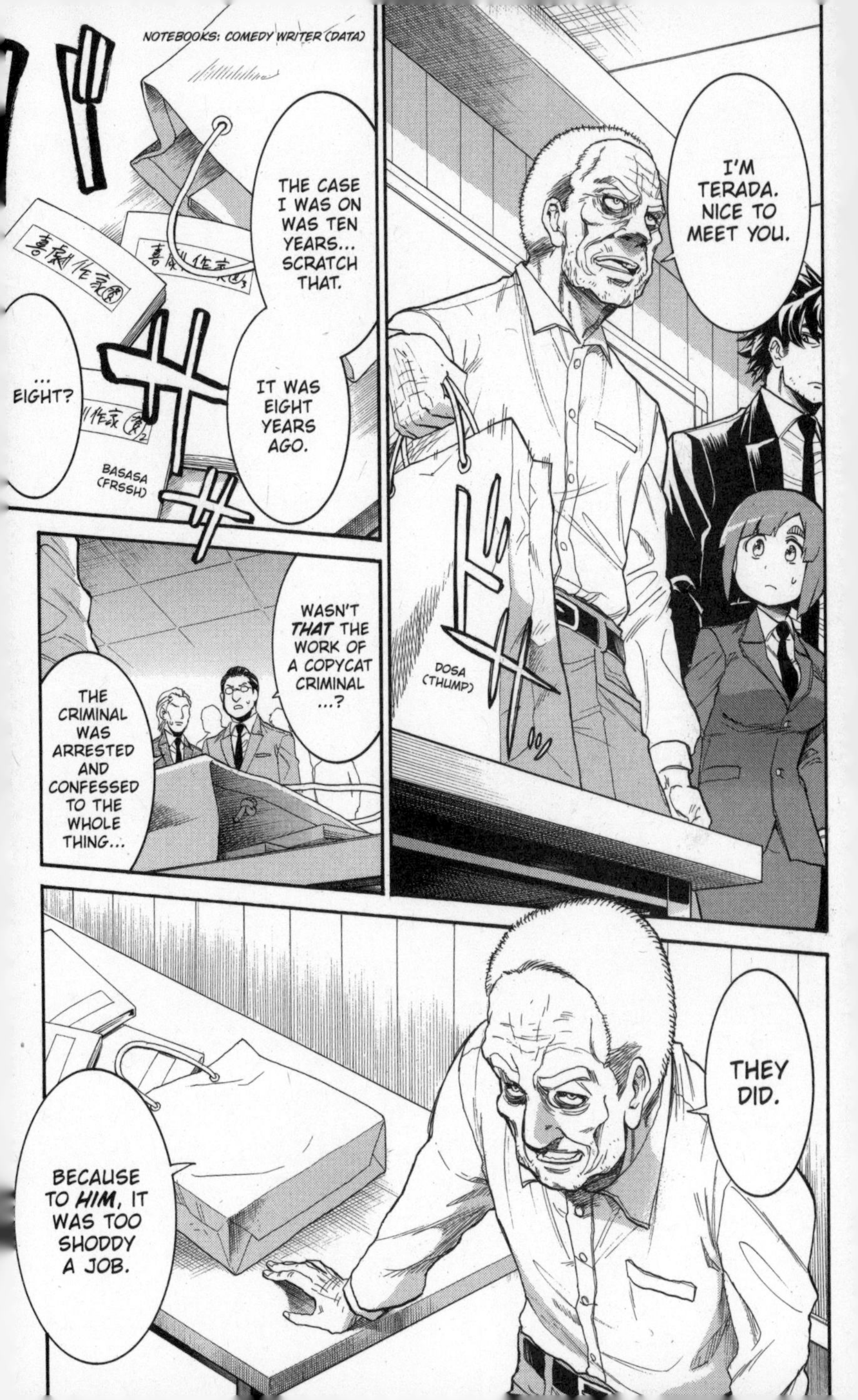
I'M TERADA. NICE TO MEET YOU.
DOSA (THUMP)
NOTEBOOKS: COMEDY WRITER (DATA)
THE CASE I WAS ON WAS TEN YEARS... SCRATCH THAT.
IT WAS EIGHT YEARS AGO.
BASASA (FRSSH)
... EIGHT?
WASN'T *THAT* THE WORK OF A COPYCAT CRIMINAL ...?
THE CRIMINAL WAS ARRESTED AND CONFESSED TO THE WHOLE THING...
THEY DID.
BECAUSE TO *HIM*, IT WAS TOO SHODDY A JOB.

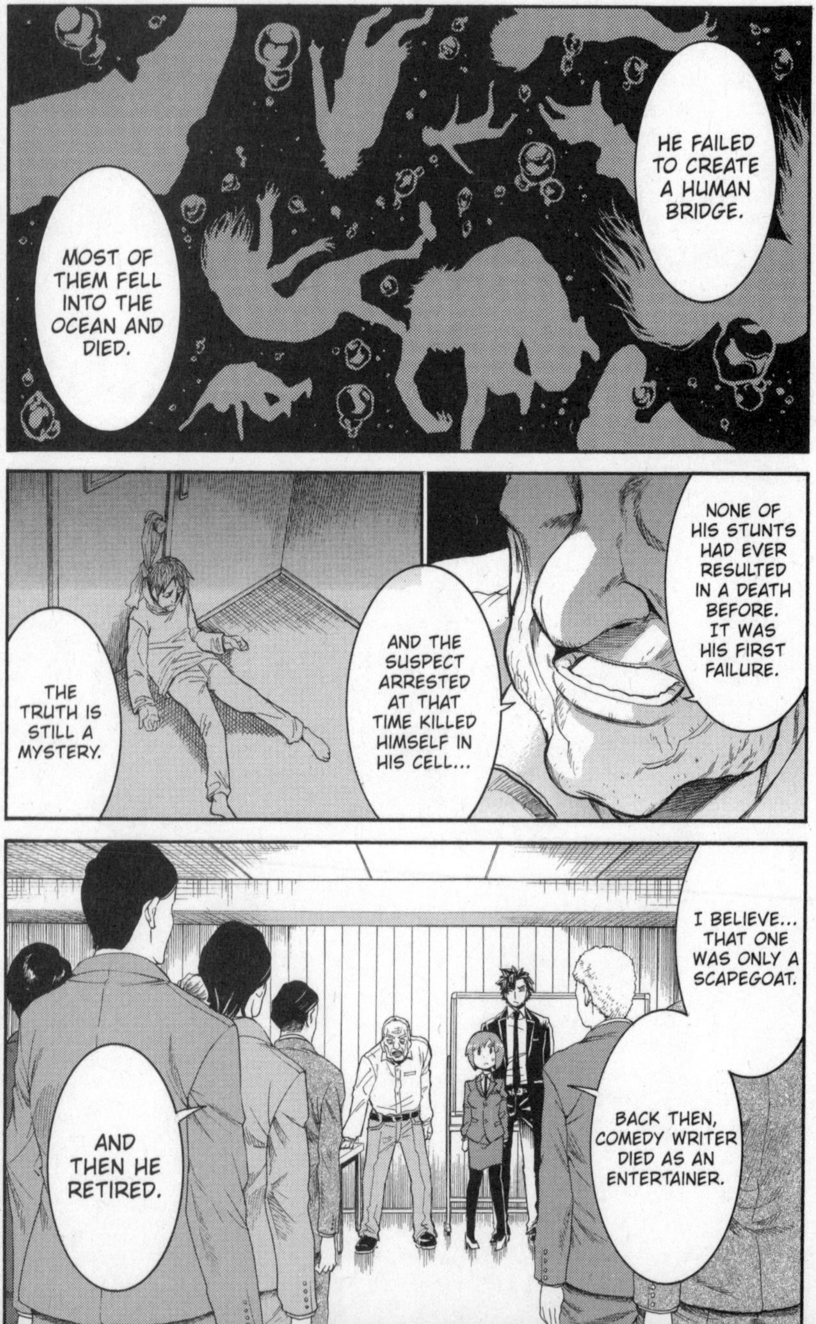
HE FAILED TO CREATE A HUMAN BRIDGE.
MOST OF THEM FELL INTO THE OCEAN AND DIED.
NONE OF HIS STUNTS HAD EVER RESULTED IN A DEATH BEFORE. IT WAS HIS FIRST FAILURE.
AND THE SUSPECT ARRESTED AT THAT TIME KILLED HIMSELF IN HIS CELL...
THE TRUTH IS STILL A MYSTERY.
I BELIEVE... THAT ONE WAS ONLY A SCAPEGOAT.
BACK THEN, COMEDY WRITER DIED AS AN ENTERTAINER.
AND THEN HE RETIRED.

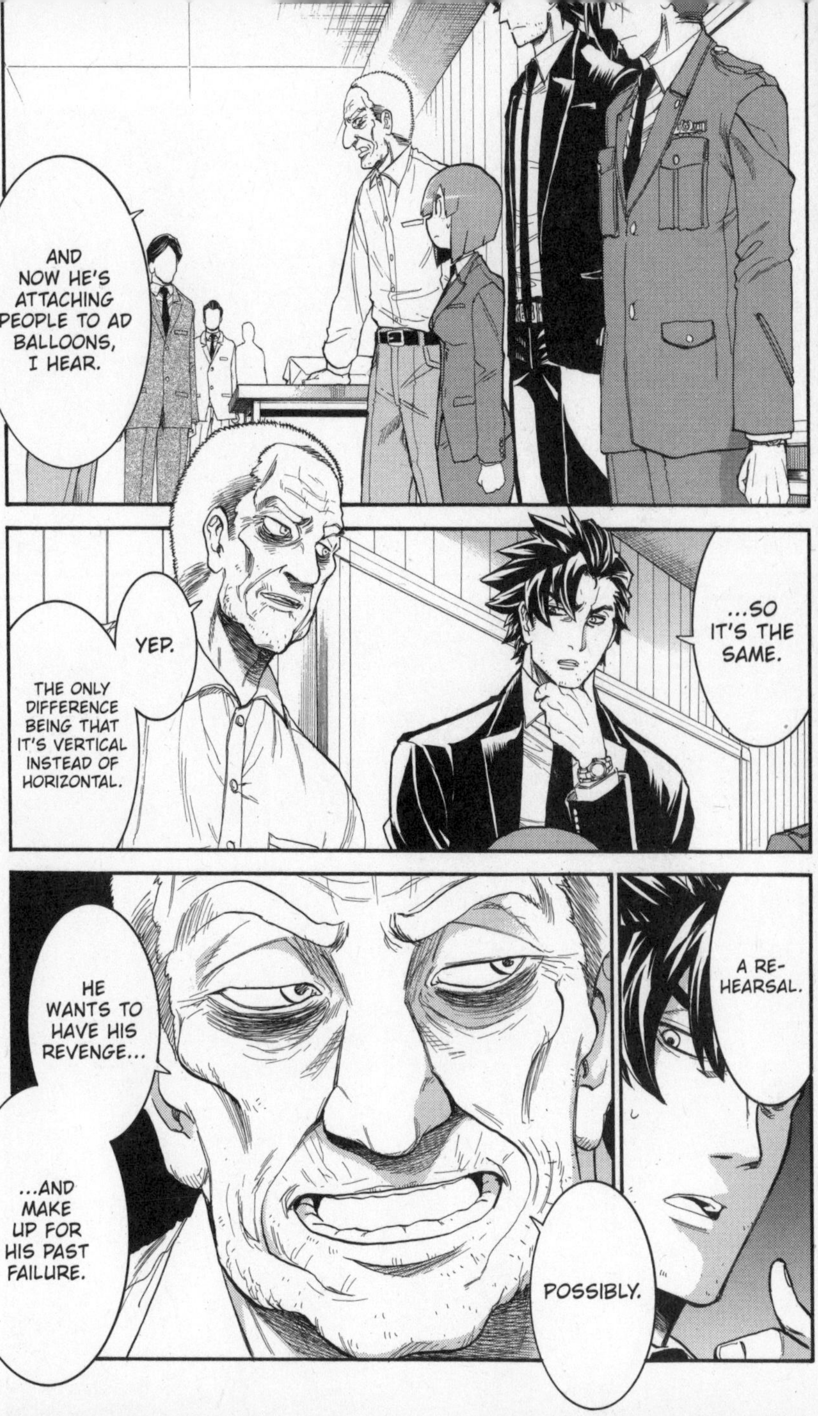
AND NOW HE'S ATTACHING PEOPLE TO AD BALLOONS, I HEAR.
...SO IT'S THE SAME.
YEP.
THE ONLY DIFFERENCE BEING THAT IT'S VERTICAL INSTEAD OF HORIZONTAL.
A RE-HEARSAL.
HE WANTS TO HAVE HIS REVENGE...
...AND MAKE UP FOR HIS PAST FAILURE.
POSSIBLY.

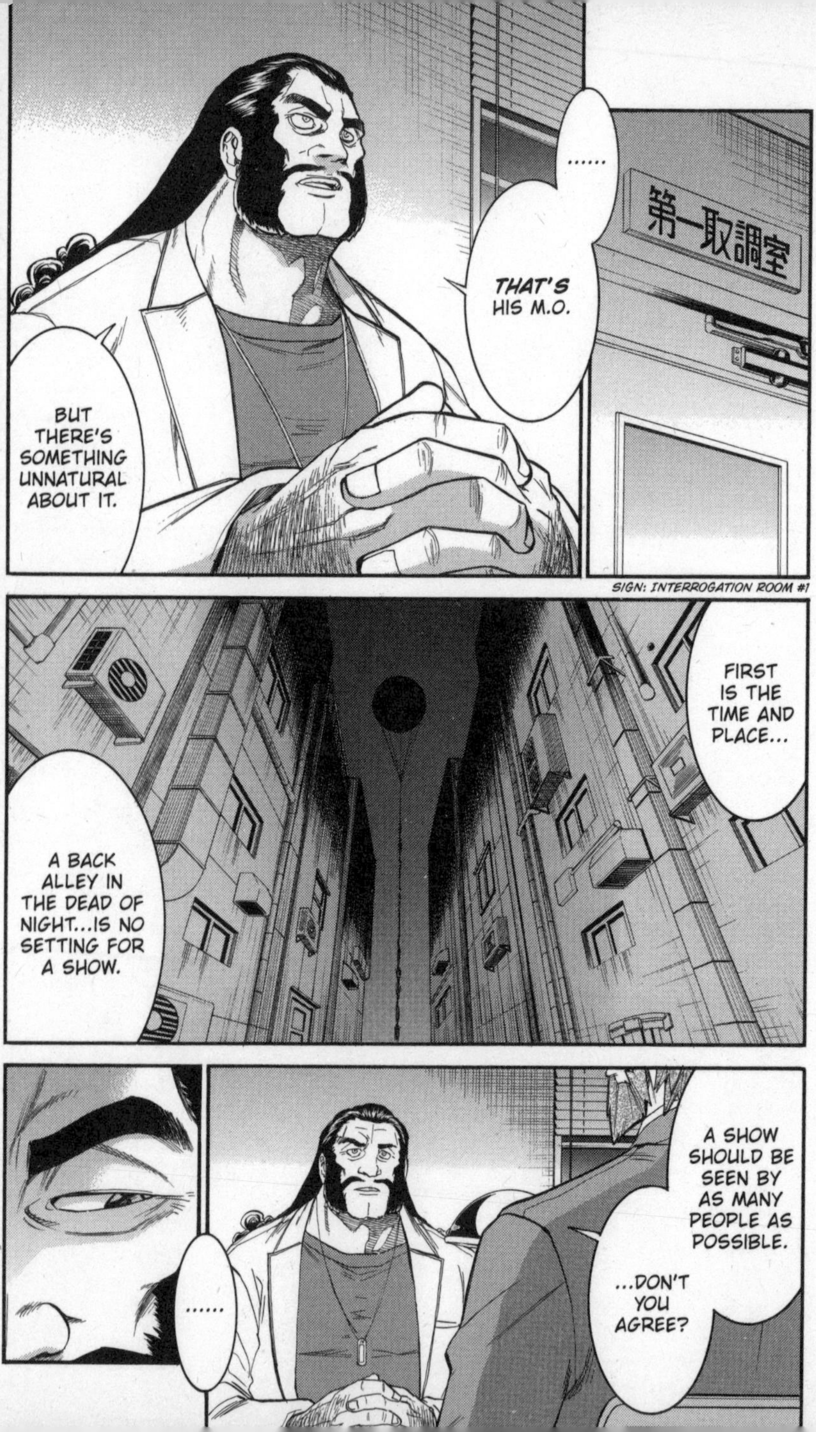
第一取調室
......
THAT'S HIS M.O.
BUT THERE'S SOMETHING UNNATURAL ABOUT IT.
SIGN: INTERROGATION ROOM #1
FIRST IS THE TIME AND PLACE...
A BACK ALLEY IN THE DEAD OF NIGHT...IS NO SETTING FOR A SHOW.
A SHOW SHOULD BE SEEN BY AS MANY PEOPLE AS POSSIBLE.
...DON'T YOU AGREE?
......

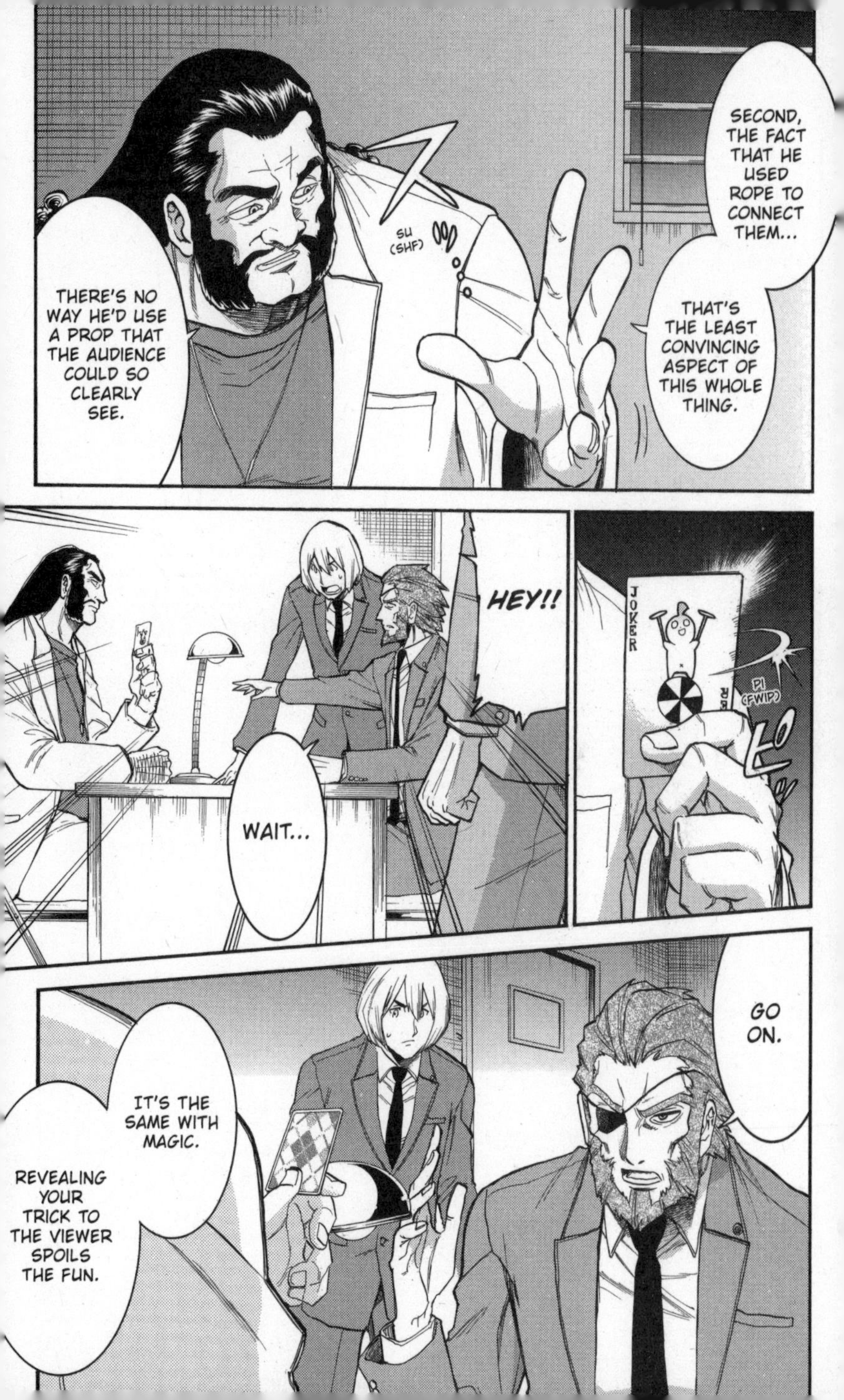
SECOND, THE FACT THAT HE USED ROPE TO CONNECT THEM...
THAT'S THE LEAST CONVINCING ASPECT OF THIS WHOLE THING.
SU (SHF)
THERE'S NO WAY HE'D USE A PROP THAT THE AUDIENCE COULD SO CLEARLY SEE.
JOKER
PI (FWIP)
HEY!!
WAIT...
GO ON.
IT'S THE SAME WITH MAGIC.
REVEALING YOUR TRICK TO THE VIEWER SPOILS THE FUN.

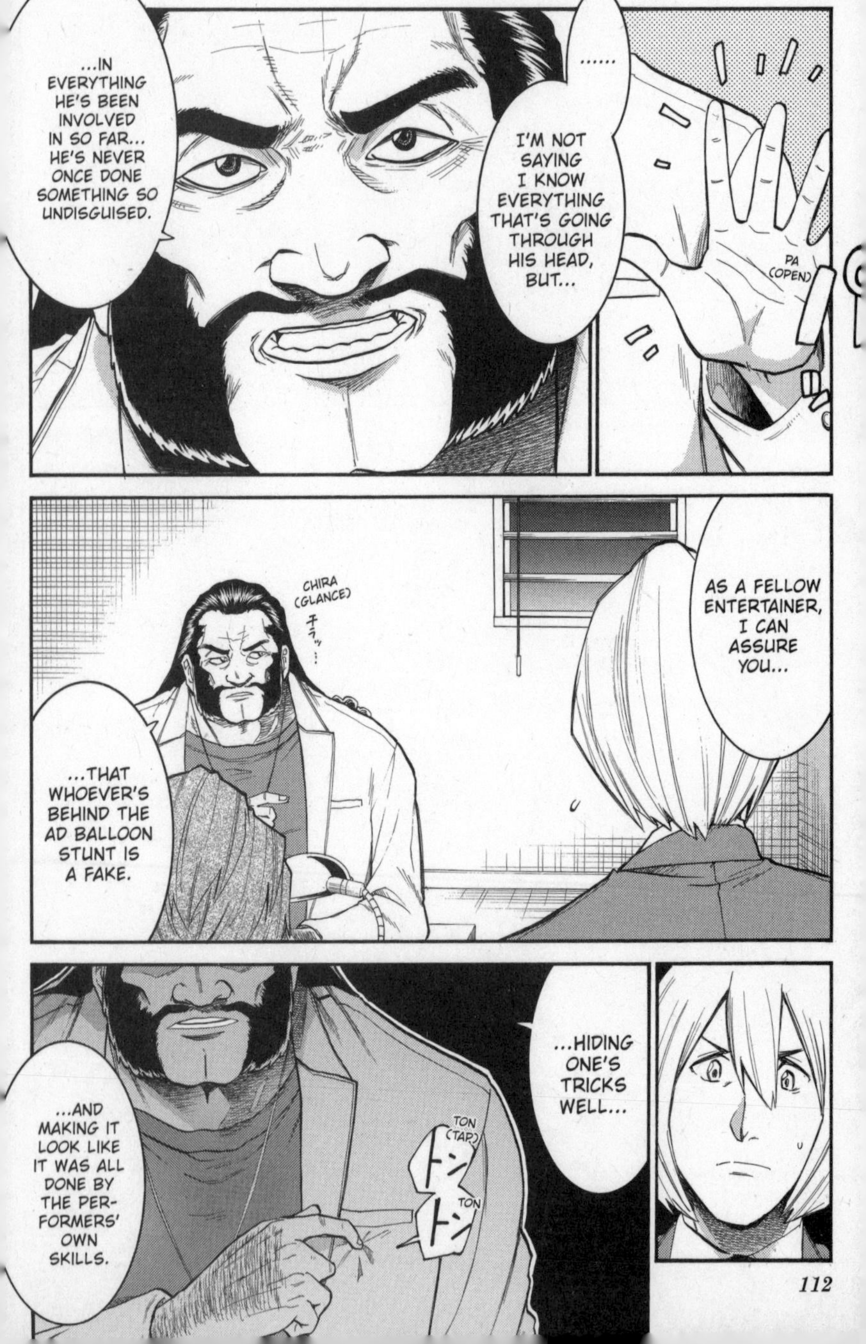
PA (OPEN)
......
I'M NOT SAYING I KNOW EVERYTHING THAT'S GOING THROUGH HIS HEAD, BUT...
...IN EVERYTHING HE'S BEEN INVOLVED IN SO FAR... HE'S NEVER ONCE DONE SOMETHING SO UNDISGUISED.
AS A FELLOW ENTERTAINER, I CAN ASSURE YOU...
CHIRA (GLANCE)
チラッ…
...THAT WHOEVER'S BEHIND THE AD BALLOON STUNT IS A FAKE.
...HIDING ONE'S TRICKS WELL...
...AND MAKING IT LOOK LIKE IT WAS ALL DONE BY THE PER-FORMERS' OWN SKILLS.
TON (TAP)
トン
TON
トン

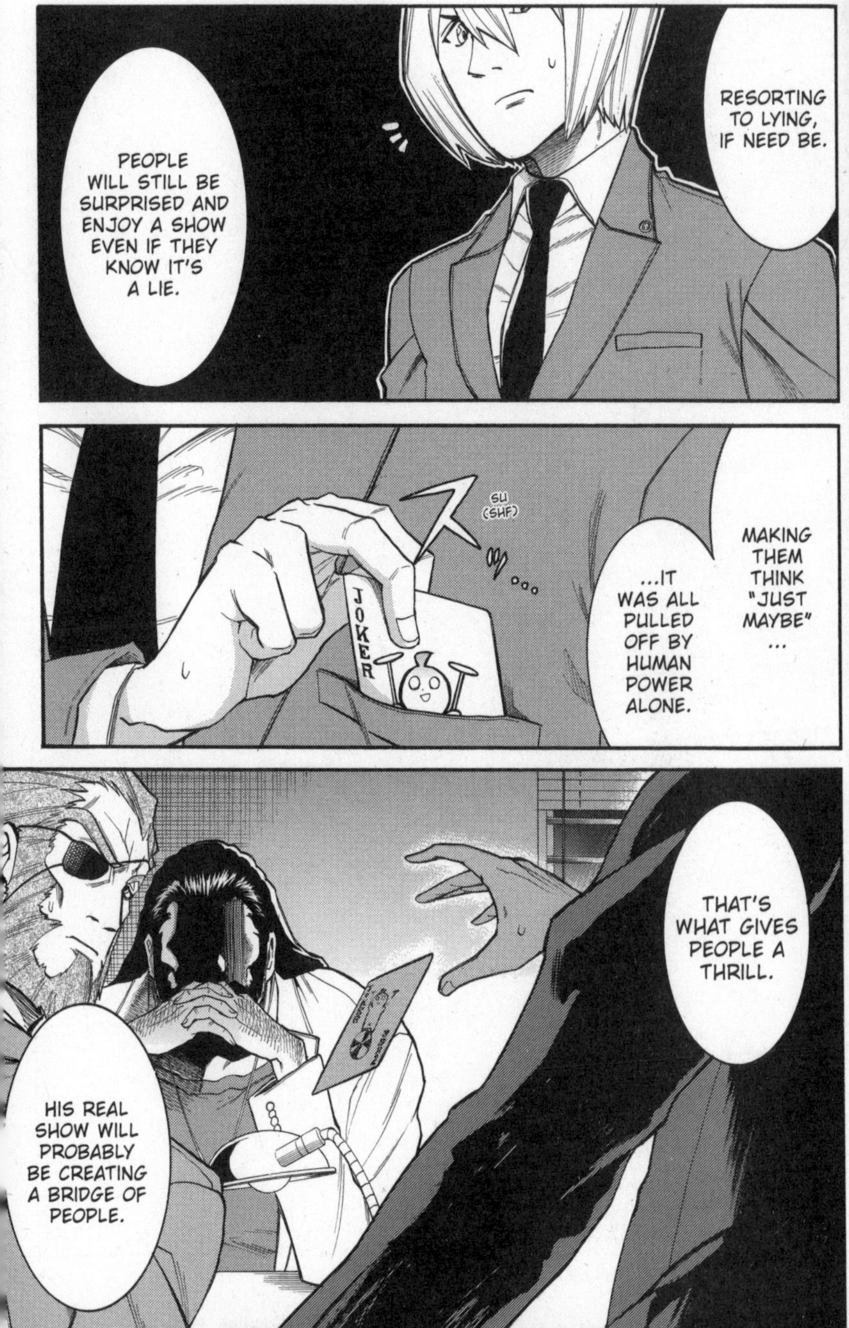
RESORTING TO LYING, IF NEED BE.
PEOPLE WILL STILL BE SURPRISED AND ENJOY A SHOW EVEN IF THEY KNOW IT'S A LIE.
MAKING THEM THINK "JUST MAYBE"...
...IT WAS ALL PULLED OFF BY HUMAN POWER ALONE.
SU (SHF)
JOKER
THAT'S WHAT GIVES PEOPLE A THRILL.
HIS REAL SHOW WILL PROBABLY BE CREATING A BRIDGE OF PEOPLE.

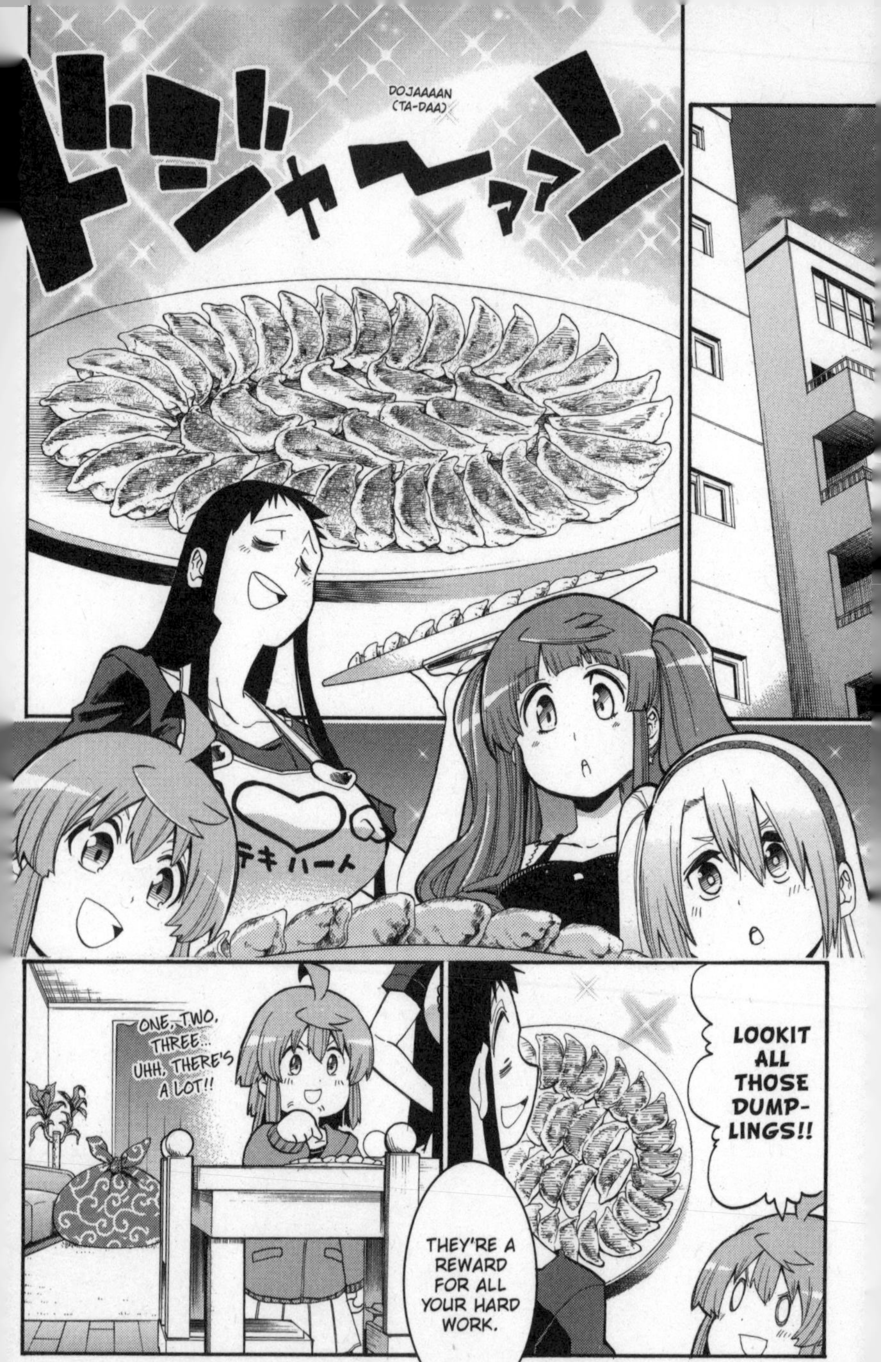
DOJAAAAN (TA-DAA)
LOOKIT ALL THOSE DUMP-LINGS!!
THEY'RE A REWARD FOR ALL YOUR HARD WORK.
ONE, TWO, THREE... UHH, THERE'S A LOT!!

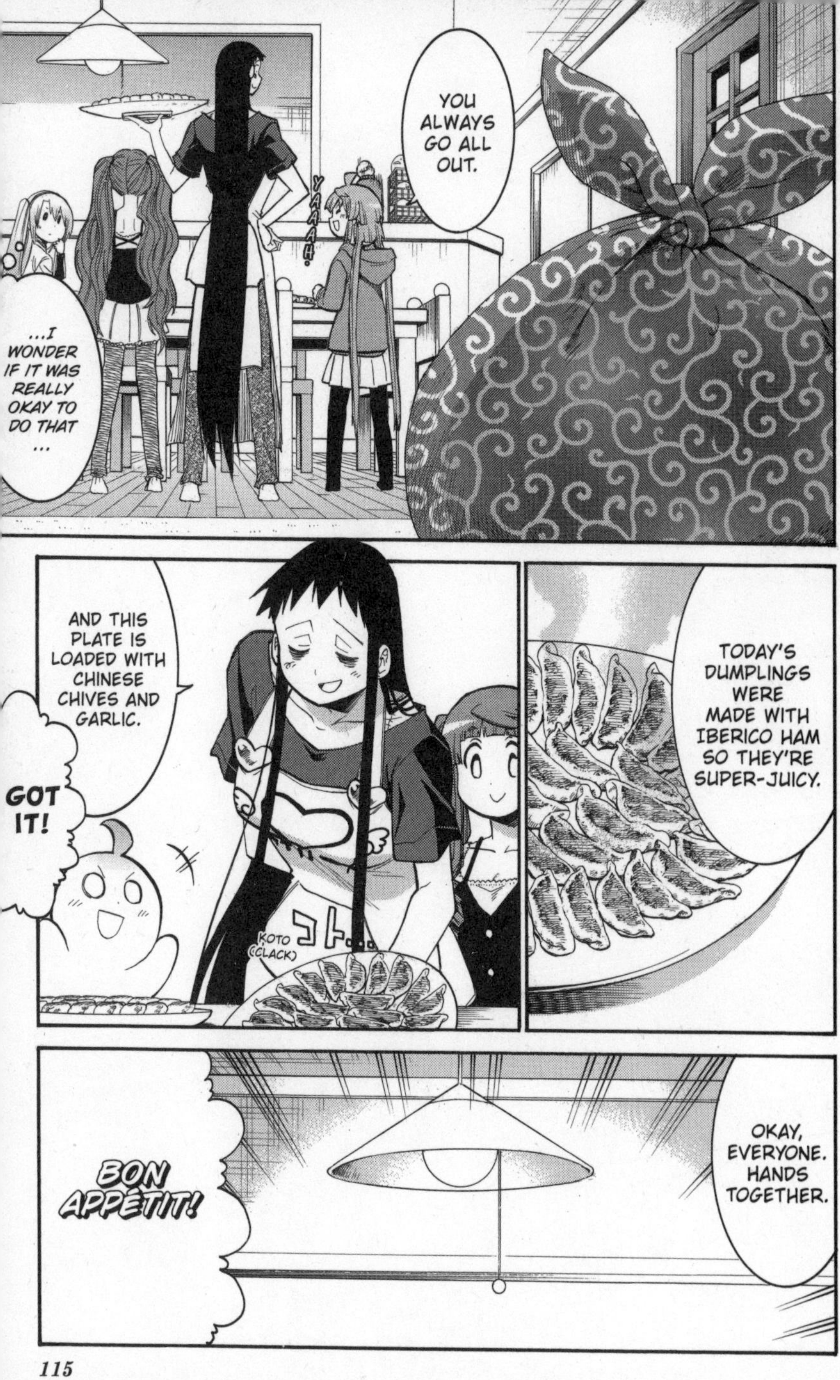
YOU ALWAYS GO ALL OUT.
YAAAAH.
...I WONDER IF IT WAS REALLY OKAY TO DO THAT ...
TODAY'S DUMPLINGS WERE MADE WITH IBERICO HAM SO THEY'RE SUPER-JUICY.
AND THIS PLATE IS LOADED WITH CHINESE CHIVES AND GARLIC.
KOTO (CLACK)
GOT IT!
OKAY, EVERYONE. HANDS TOGETHER.
BON APPÉTIT!

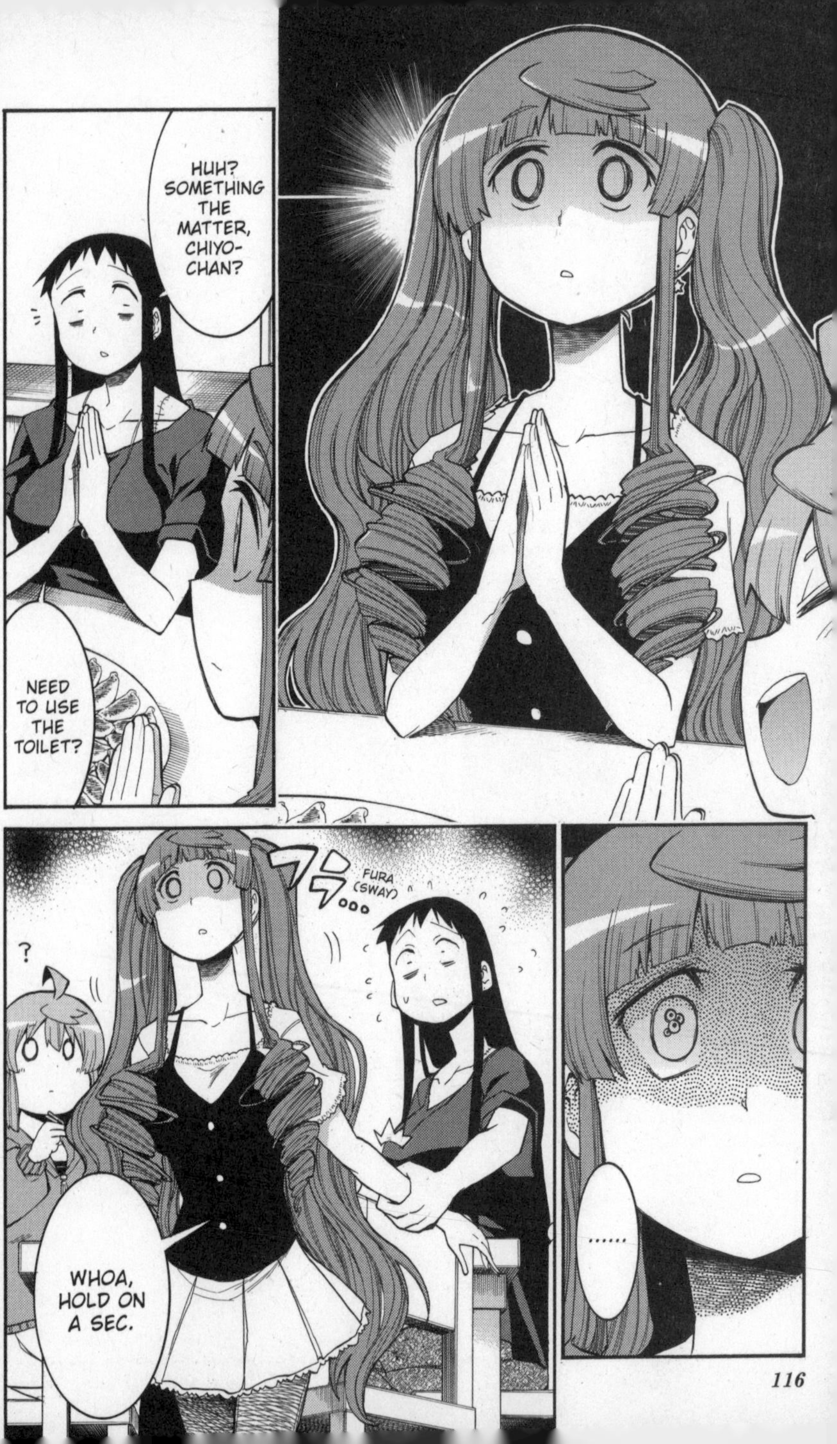
HUH? SOMETHING THE MATTER, CHIYO-CHAN?
NEED TO USE THE TOILET?
......
FURA (SWAY)
?
WHOA, HOLD ON A SEC.

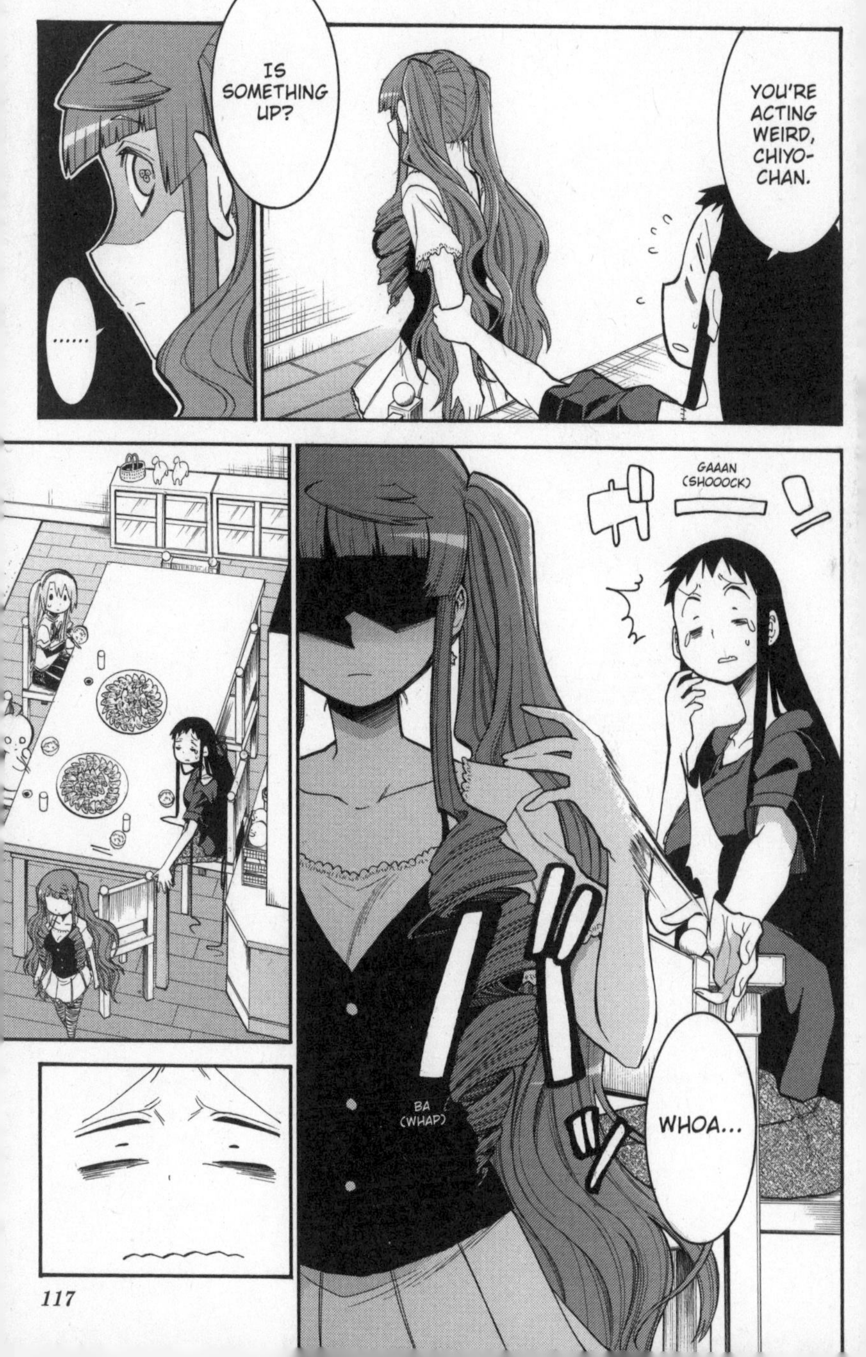

YOU'RE ACTING WEIRD, CHIYO-CHAN.
IS SOMETHING UP?
......
GAAAN (SHOOOCK)
WHOA...
BA (WHAP)

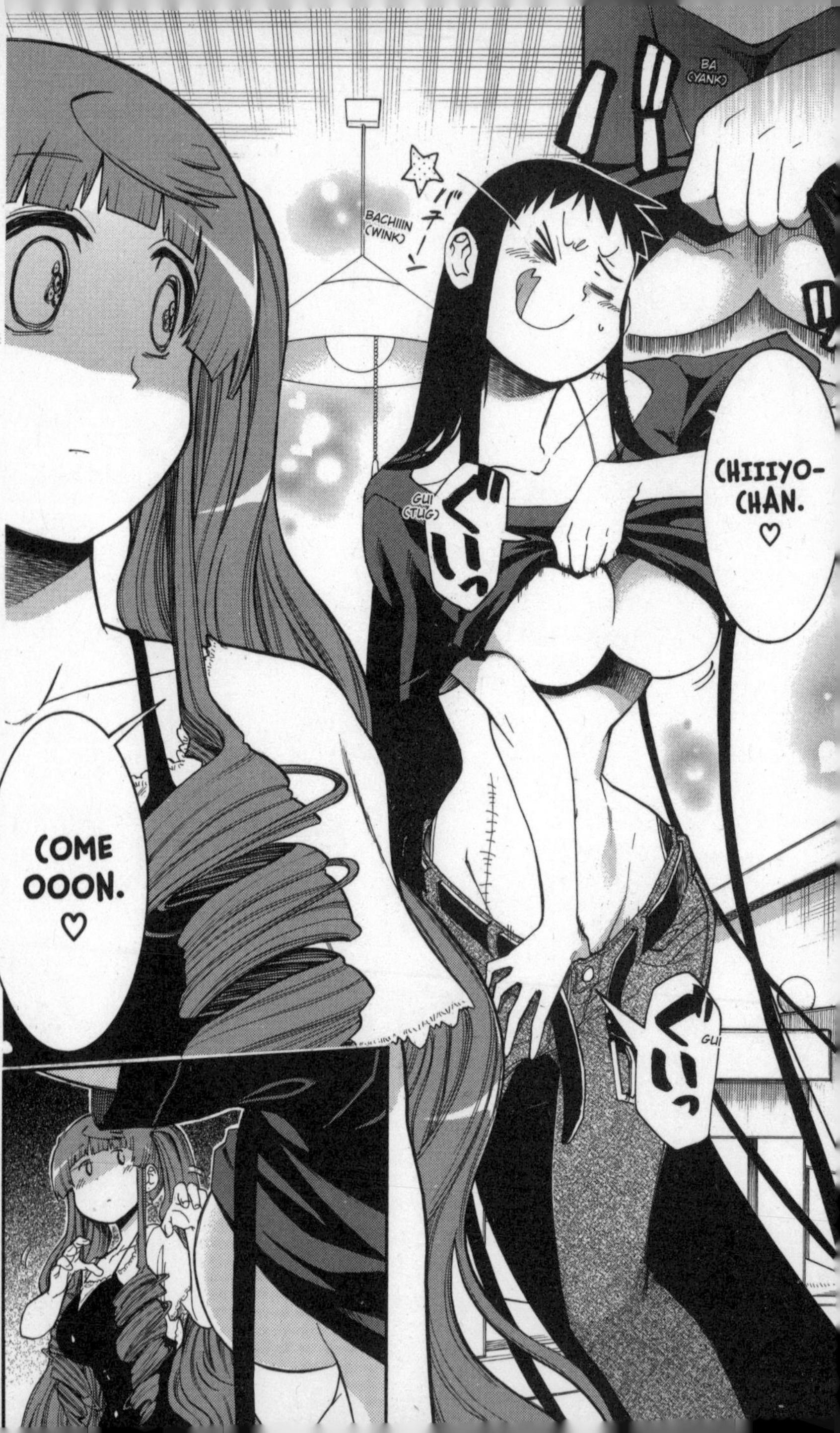
BA (YANK)
CHIIIYO-CHAN. ♡
BACHIIIN (WINK)
GUI (TUG)
COME OOON. ♡
GUI

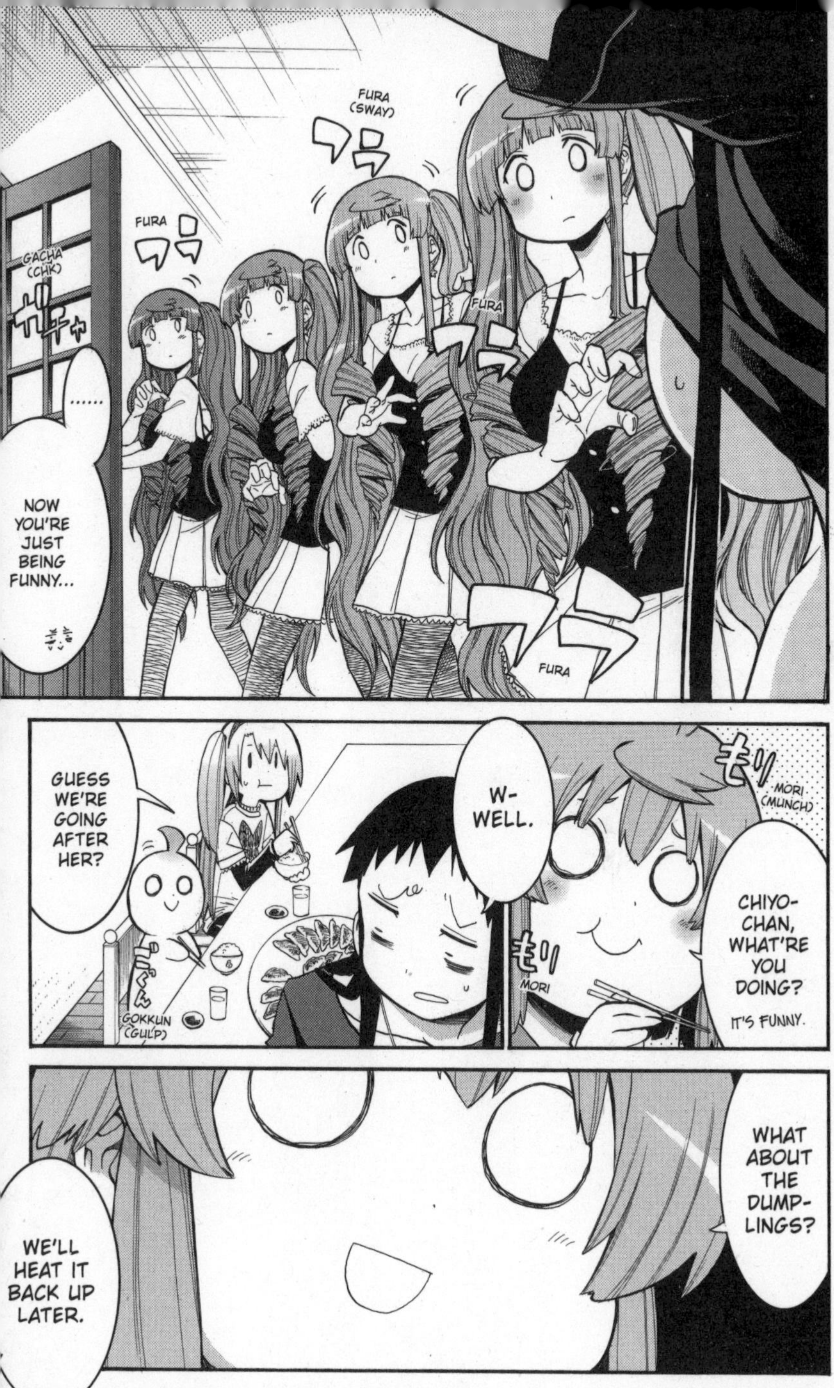

FURA (SWAY)
FURA
FURA
FURA
GACHA (CHK)
......
NOW YOU'RE JUST BEING FUNNY...
MORI (MUNCH)
CHIYO-CHAN, WHAT'RE YOU DOING?
IT'S FUNNY.
MORI
W-WELL.
GUESS WE'RE GOING AFTER HER?
GOKKUN (GULP)
WHAT ABOUT THE DUMPLINGS?
WE'LL HEAT IT BACK UP LATER.

NAKOTO BRIDGE 7:55 P.M.

ざわ
ZAWA

ざわ
ZAWA

ざわ
ZAWA (MURMUR)

WOW, THAT'S A LOT OF PEOPLE.

HEY, KUU-CHAN. WHAT'S THAT?

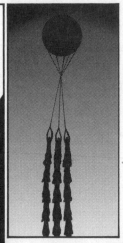

AN AD BALLOON...?

FURA (SWAY)

フラ

FURA

I WONDER IF IT'S LIKE THAT OTHER ONE. THEN THIS HUGE CROWD OF PEOPLE......

120

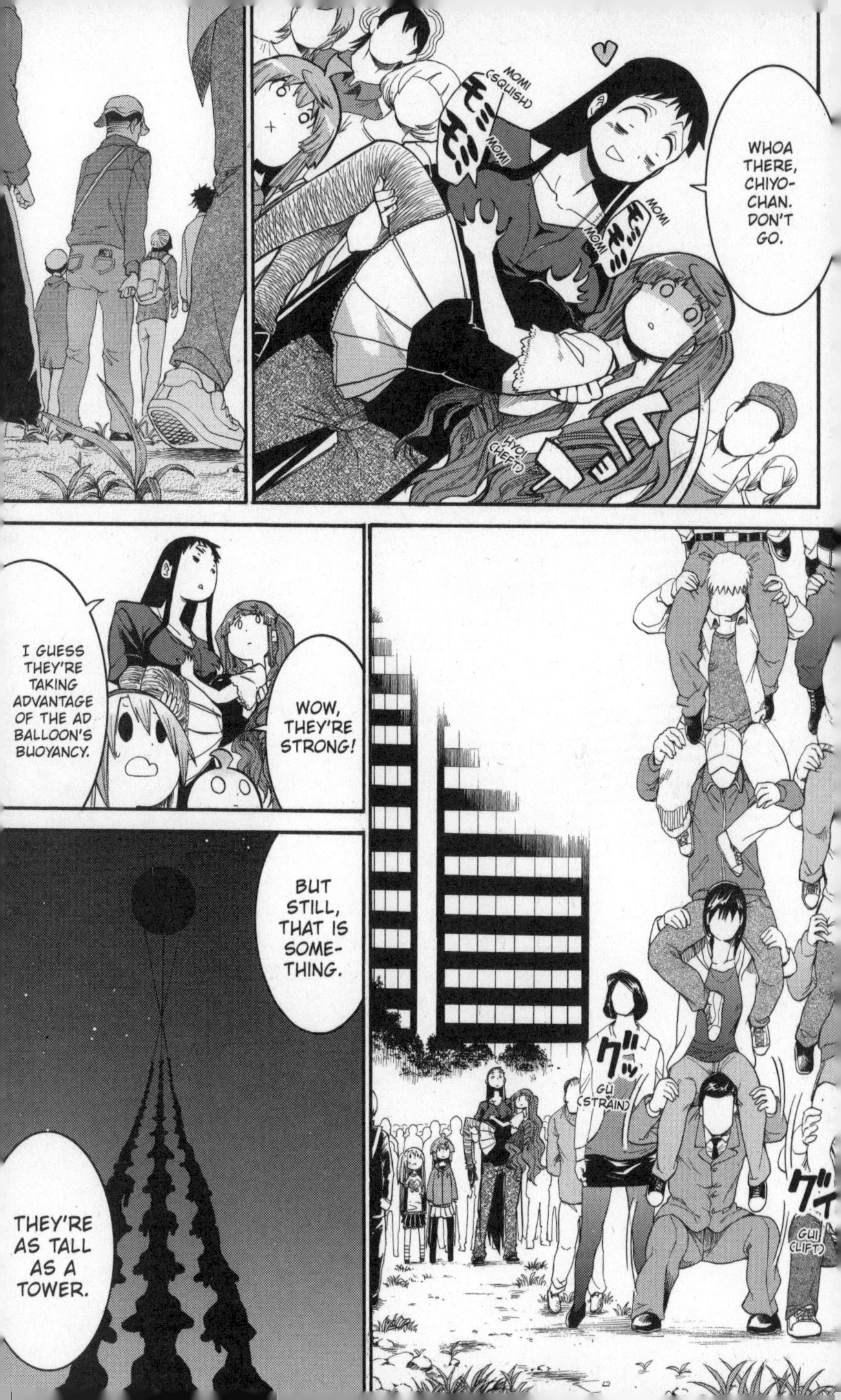
WHOA THERE, CHIYO-CHAN. DON'T GO.
MOMI (SQUISH)
MOMI
MOMI
MOMI
HYOI (HEFT)
GÜ (STRAIN)
GUI (LIFT)
WOW, THEY'RE STRONG!
I GUESS THEY'RE TAKING ADVANTAGE OF THE AD BALLOON'S BUOYANCY.
BUT STILL, THAT IS SOME-THING.
THEY'RE AS TALL AS A TOWER.

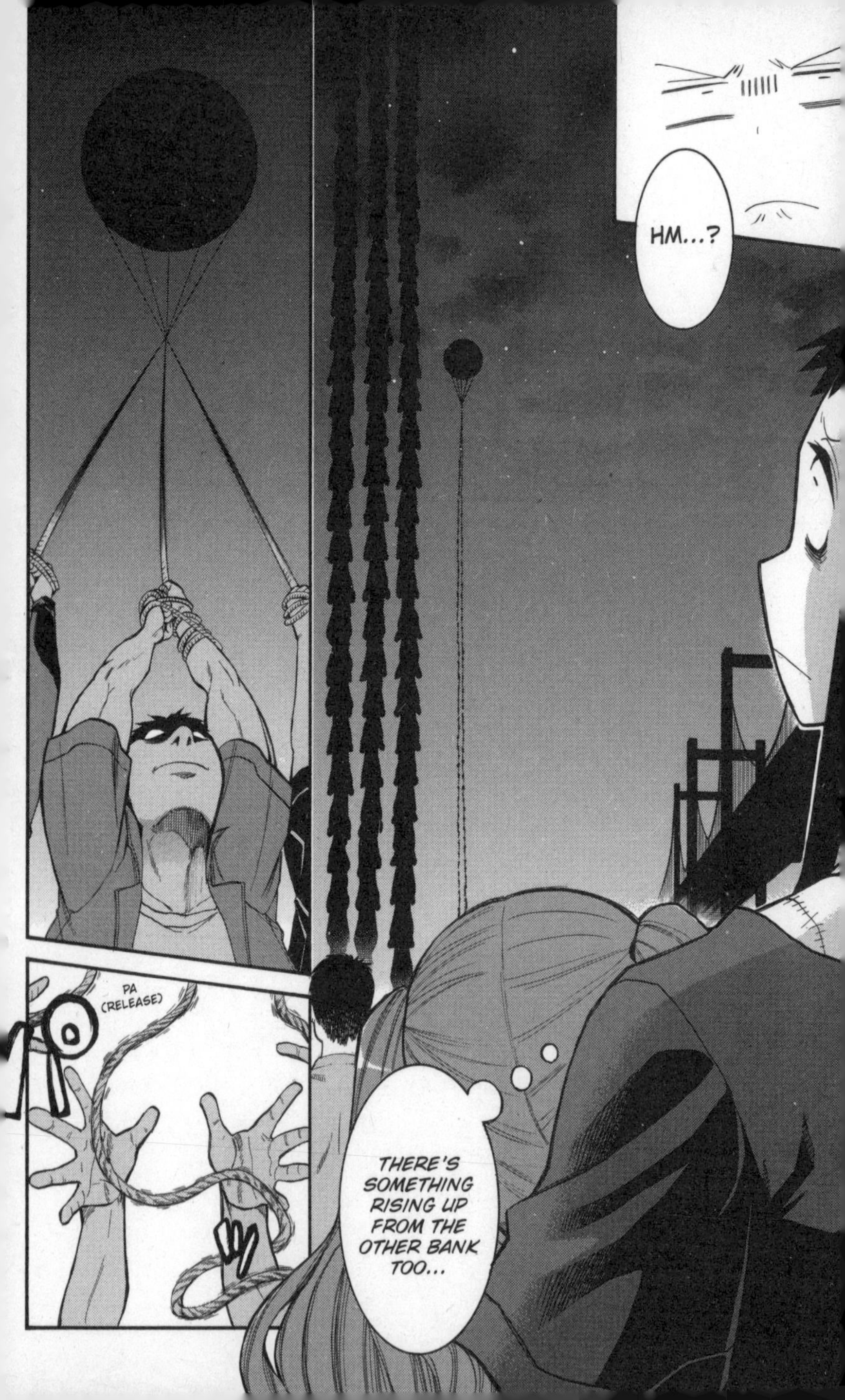
HM...?
THERE'S SOMETHING RISING UP FROM THE OTHER BANK TOO...
PA (RELEASE)

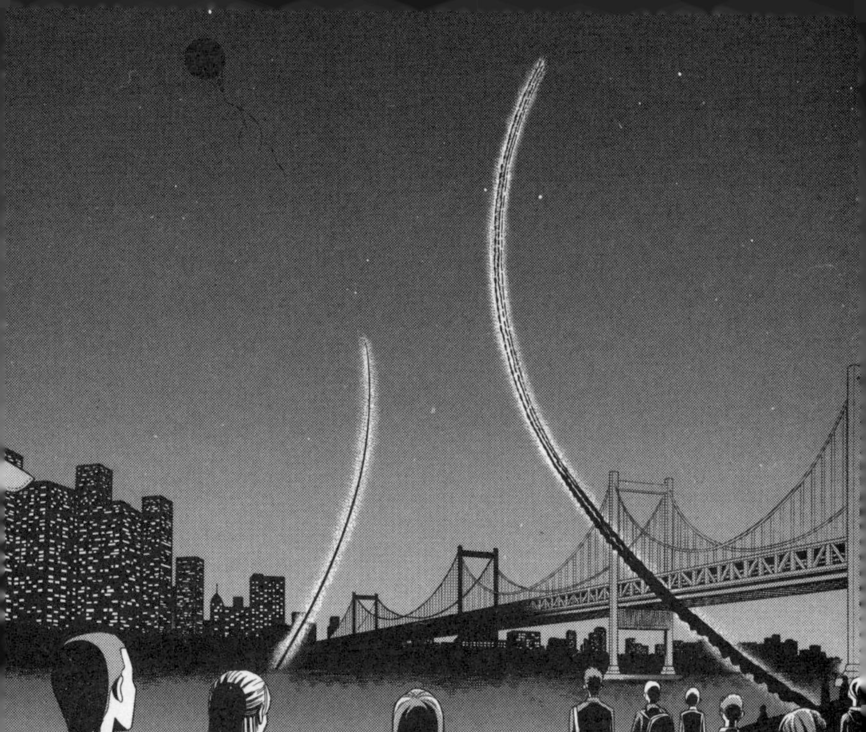

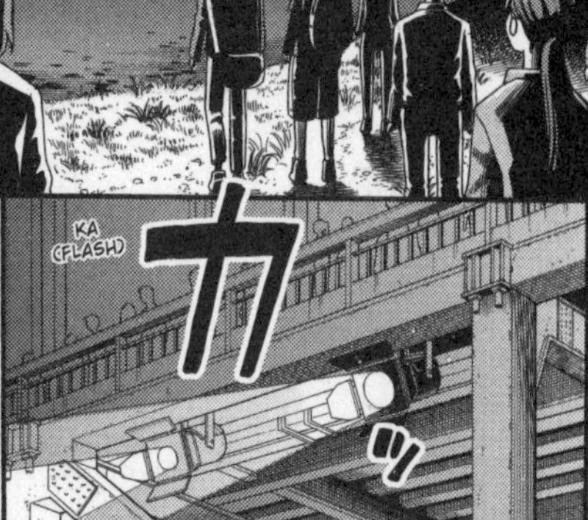
カッ
KA
(FLASH)

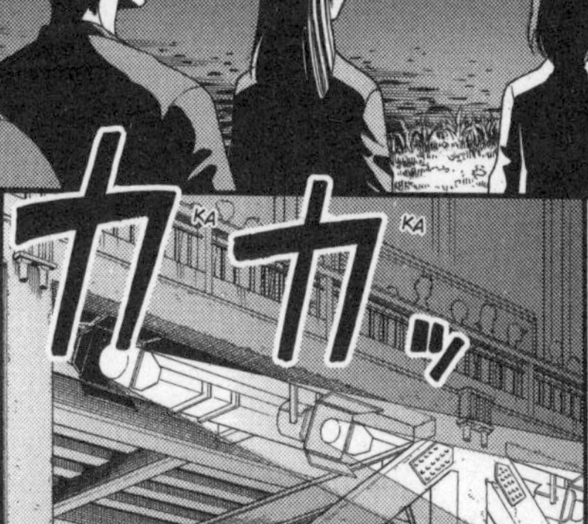
カカッ
KA
KA

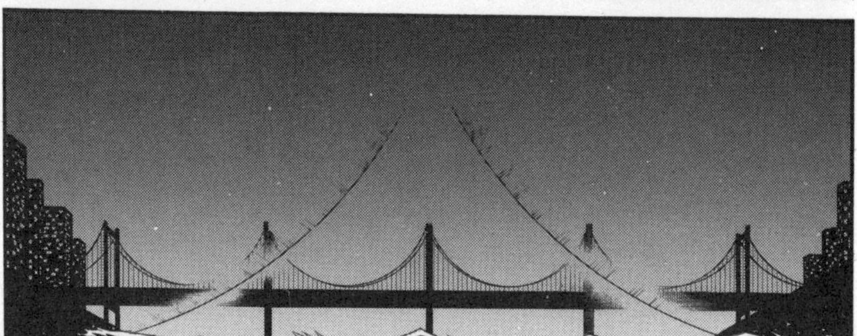

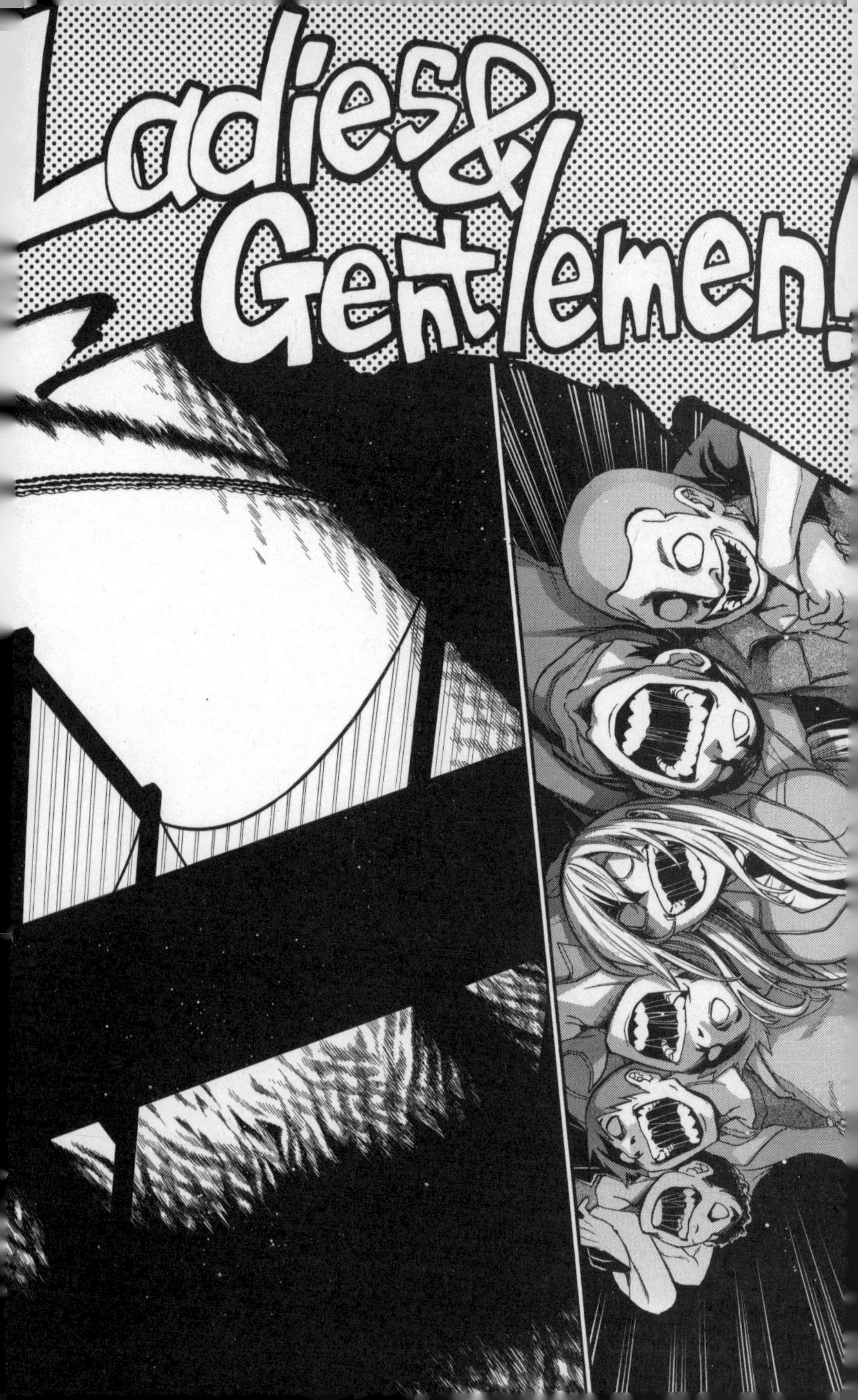
Ladies & Gentlemen!

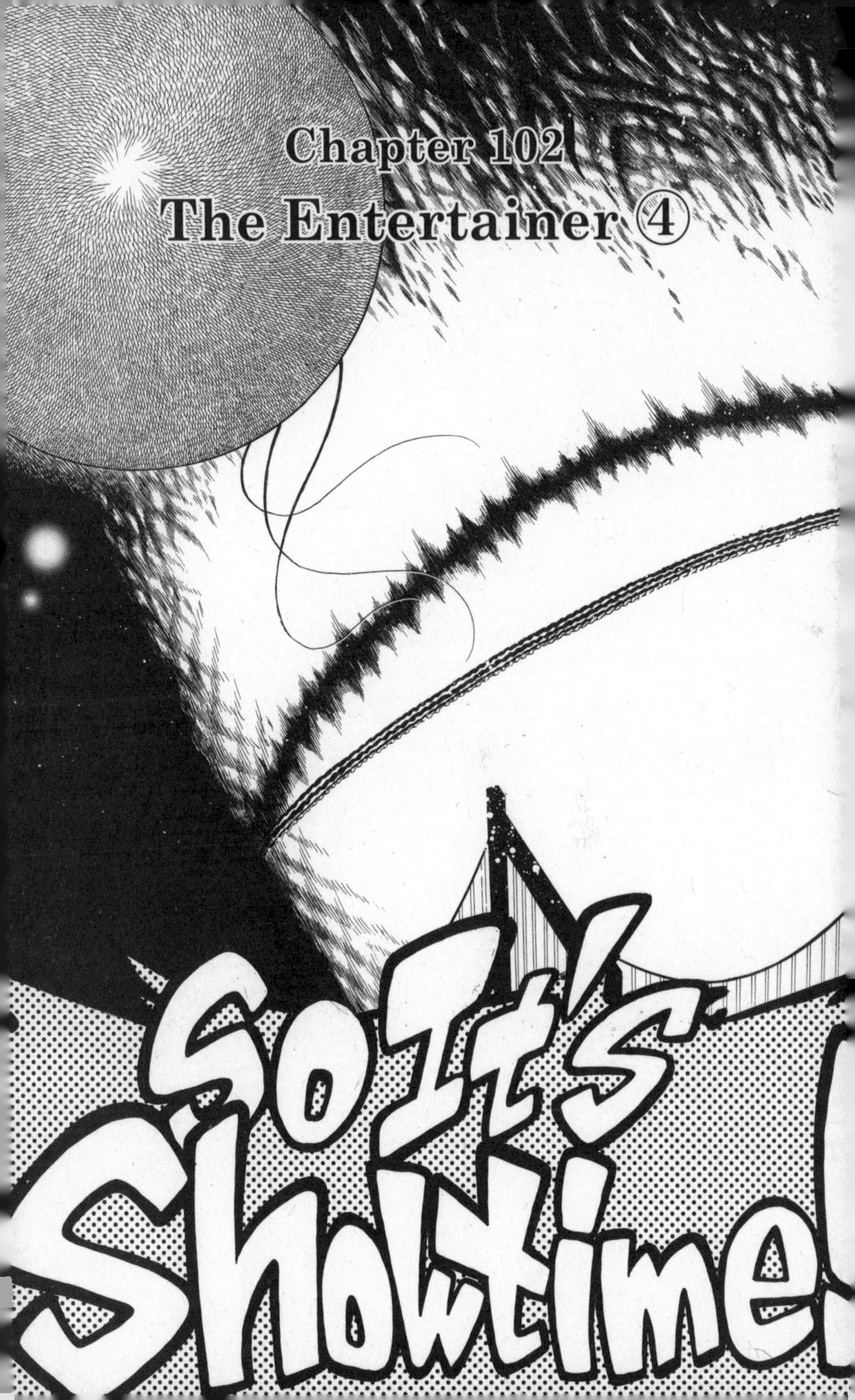
Chapter 102
The Entertainer ④
So It's Showtime!

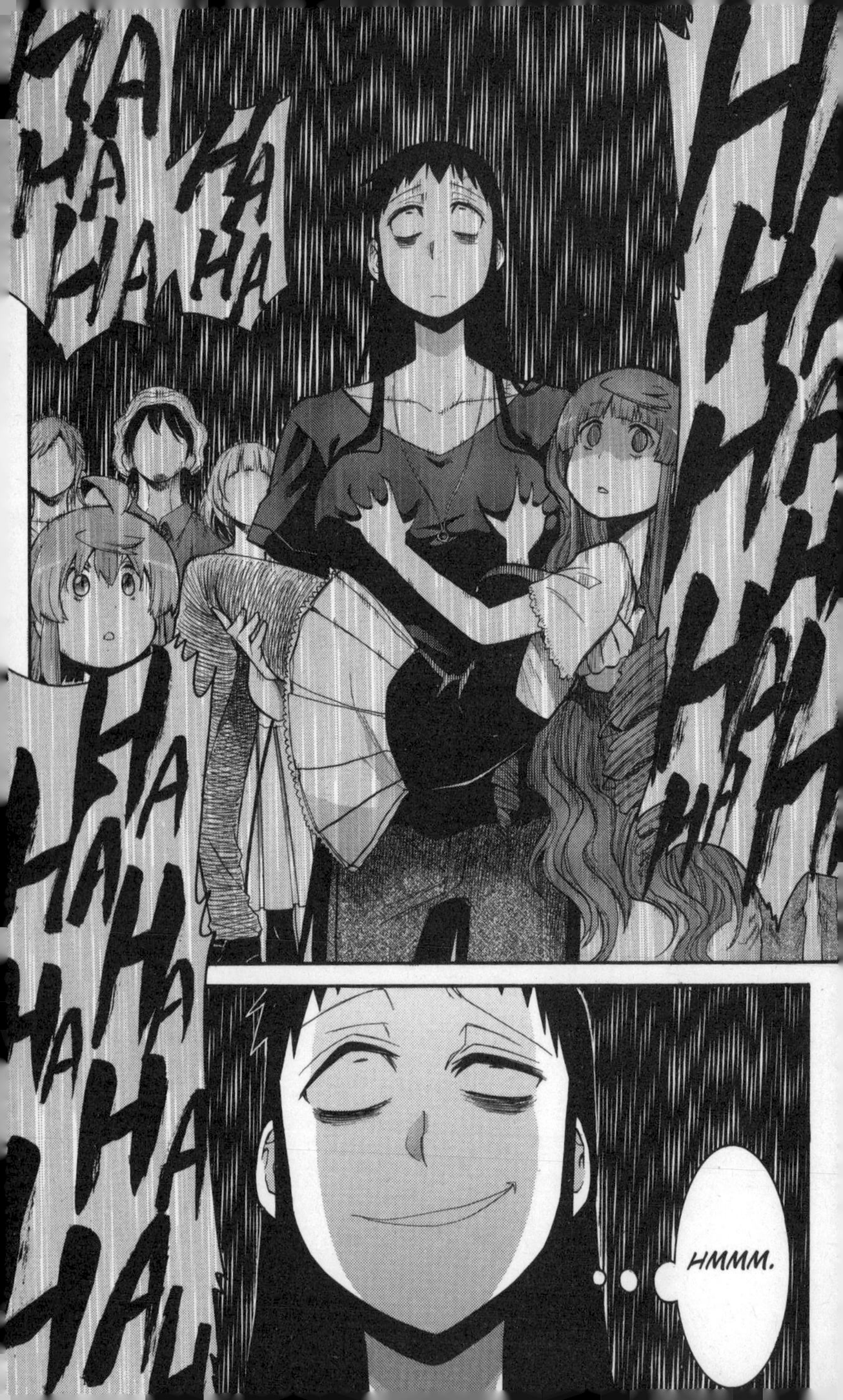
HAHAHAHAHAHA
HAHAHAHAHA
HAHAHAHAHAHA
HMMM.

**MURCIÉLAGO**

MURCIÉLAGO

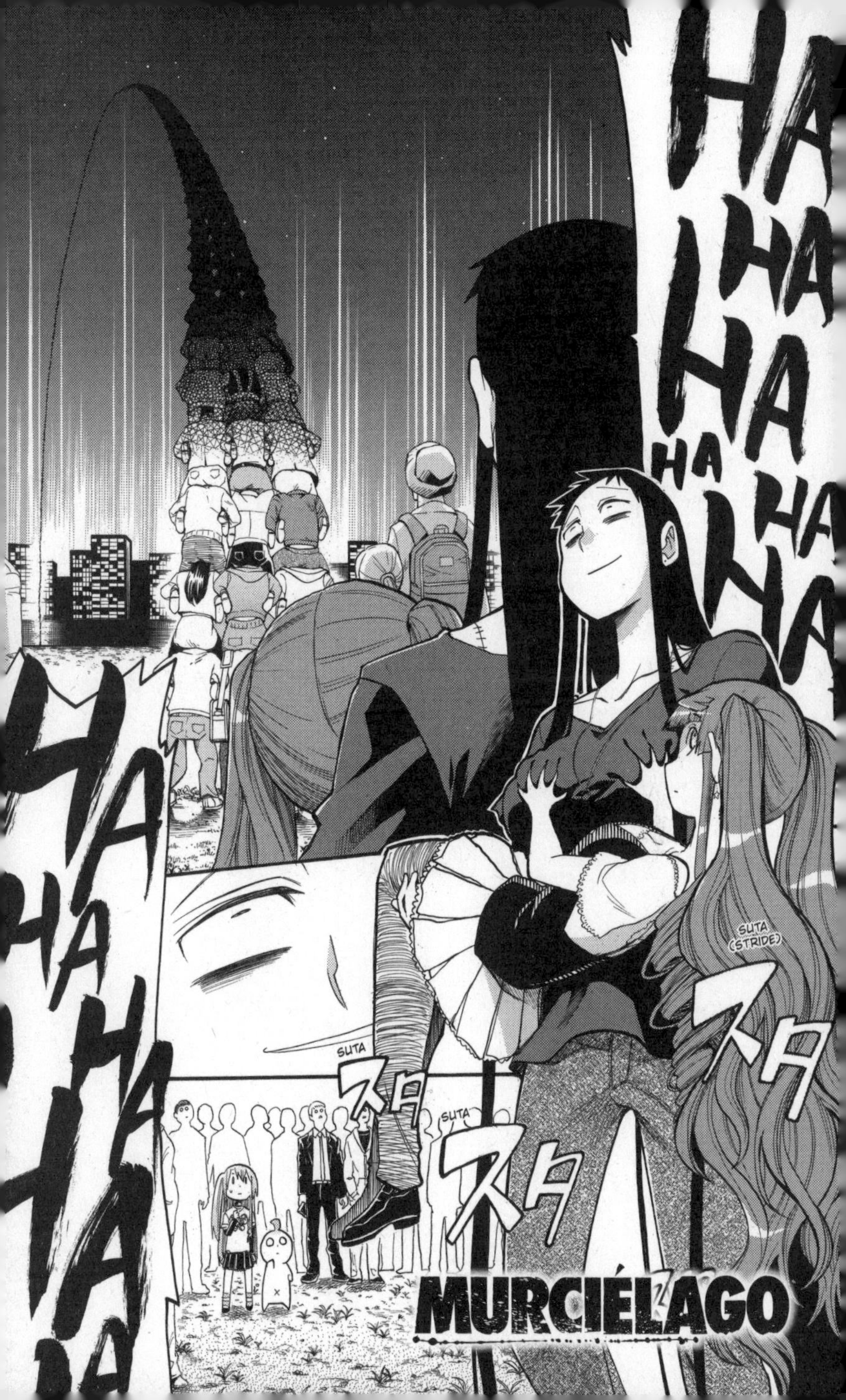
HAHAHAHAHAHAHA
HAHAHAHAHA
SUTA (STRIDE)
スタ
SUTA
スタ
SUTA
スタ
MURCIÉLAGO

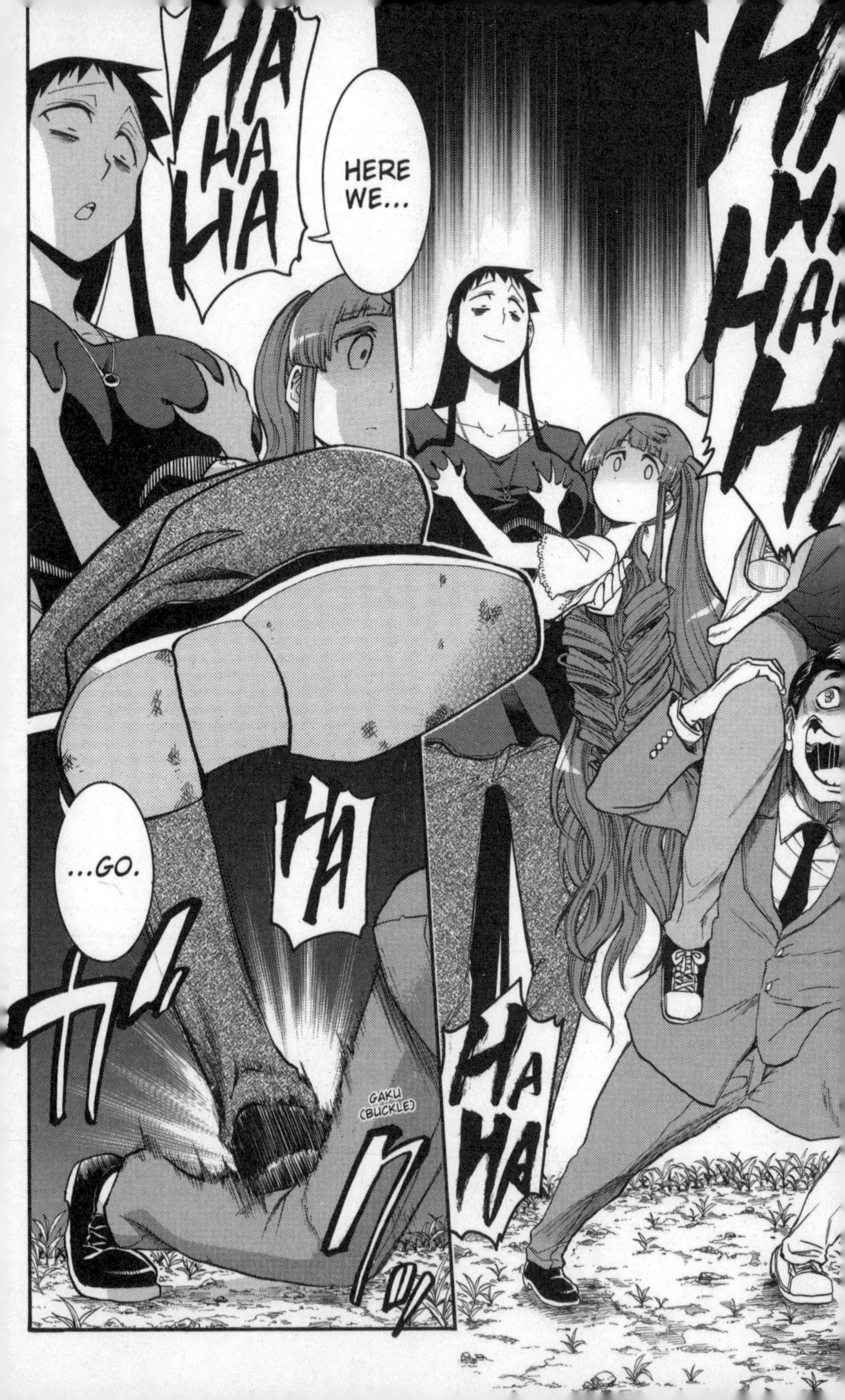
HA HA HA
HERE WE...
HA HA
HA
...GO.
GAKU (BUCKLE)

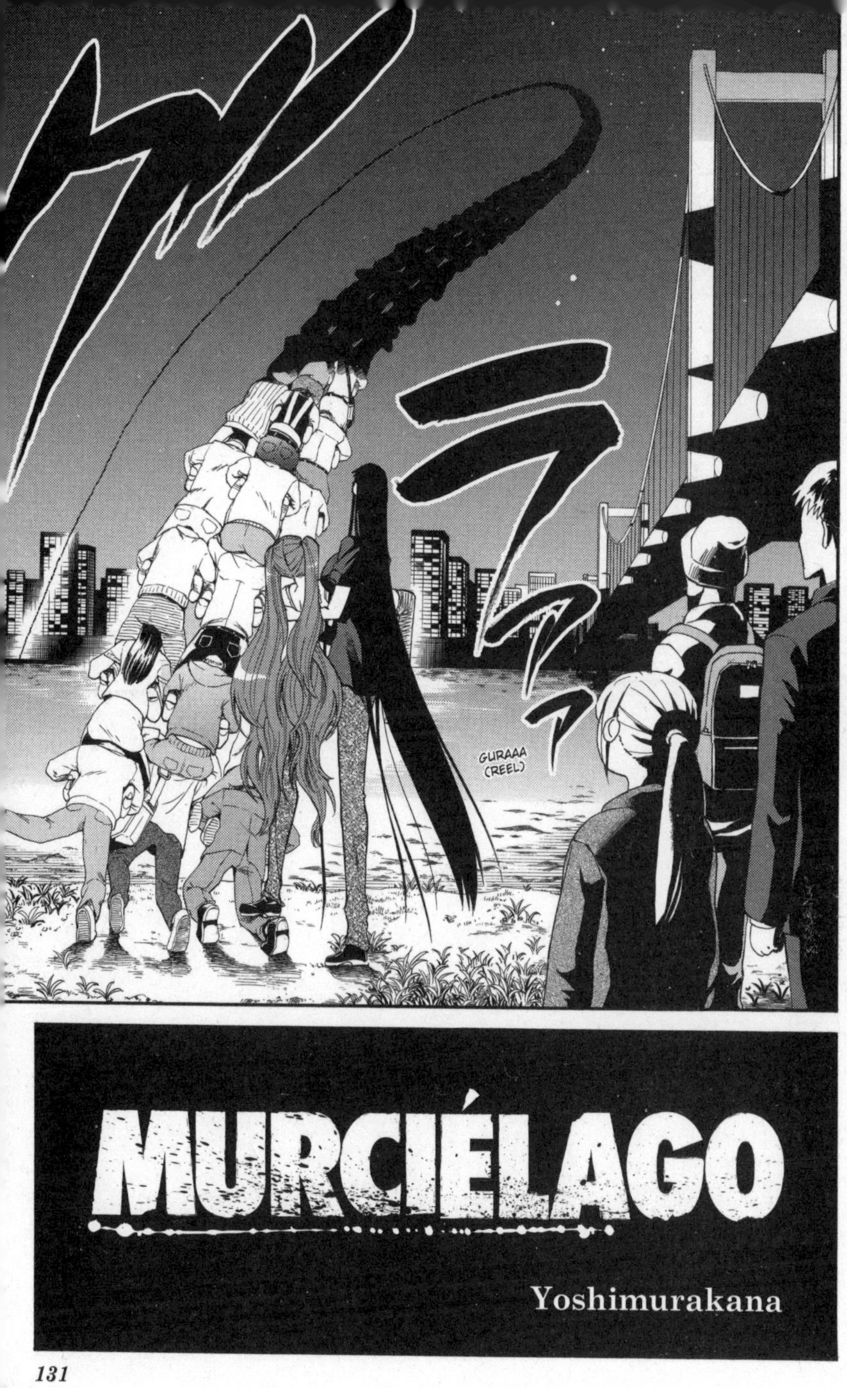
GURAAA
(REEL)

# MURCIÉLAGO

Yoshimurakana

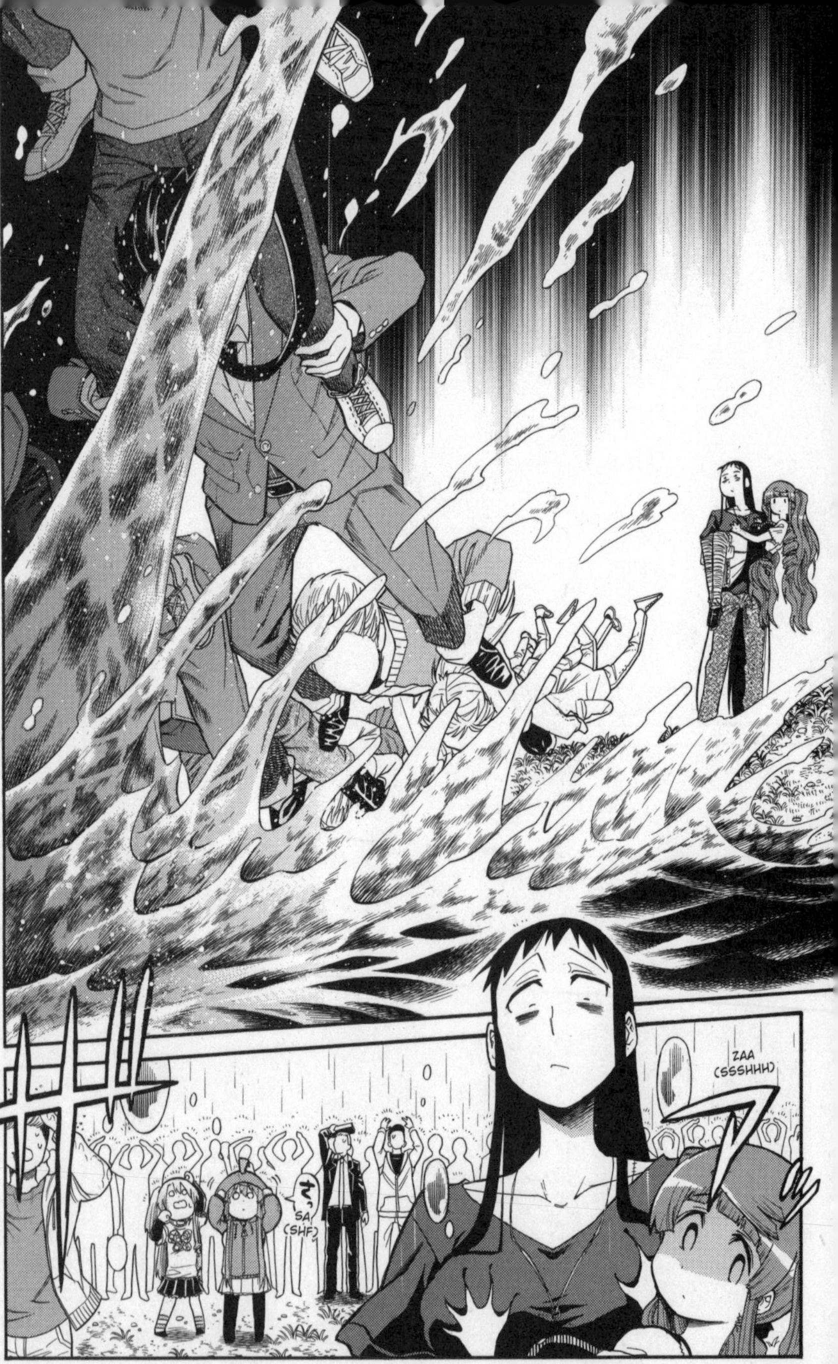
ZAA
(SSSHHH)
SA
(SHF)

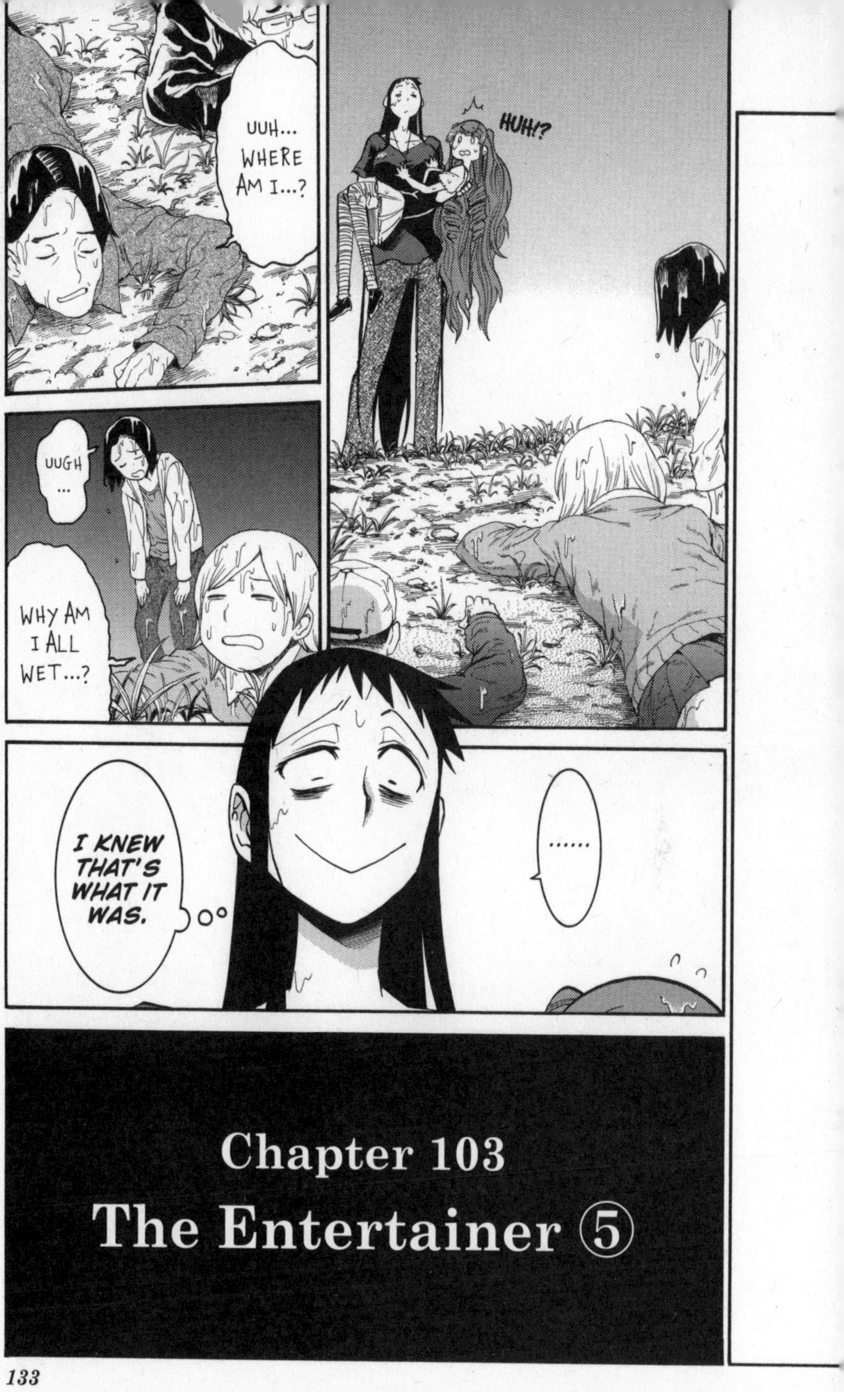
HUH!?
UUH... WHERE AM I...?
UUGH...
WHY AM I ALL WET...?
......
I KNEW THAT'S WHAT IT WAS.

# Chapter 103
## The Entertainer ⑤

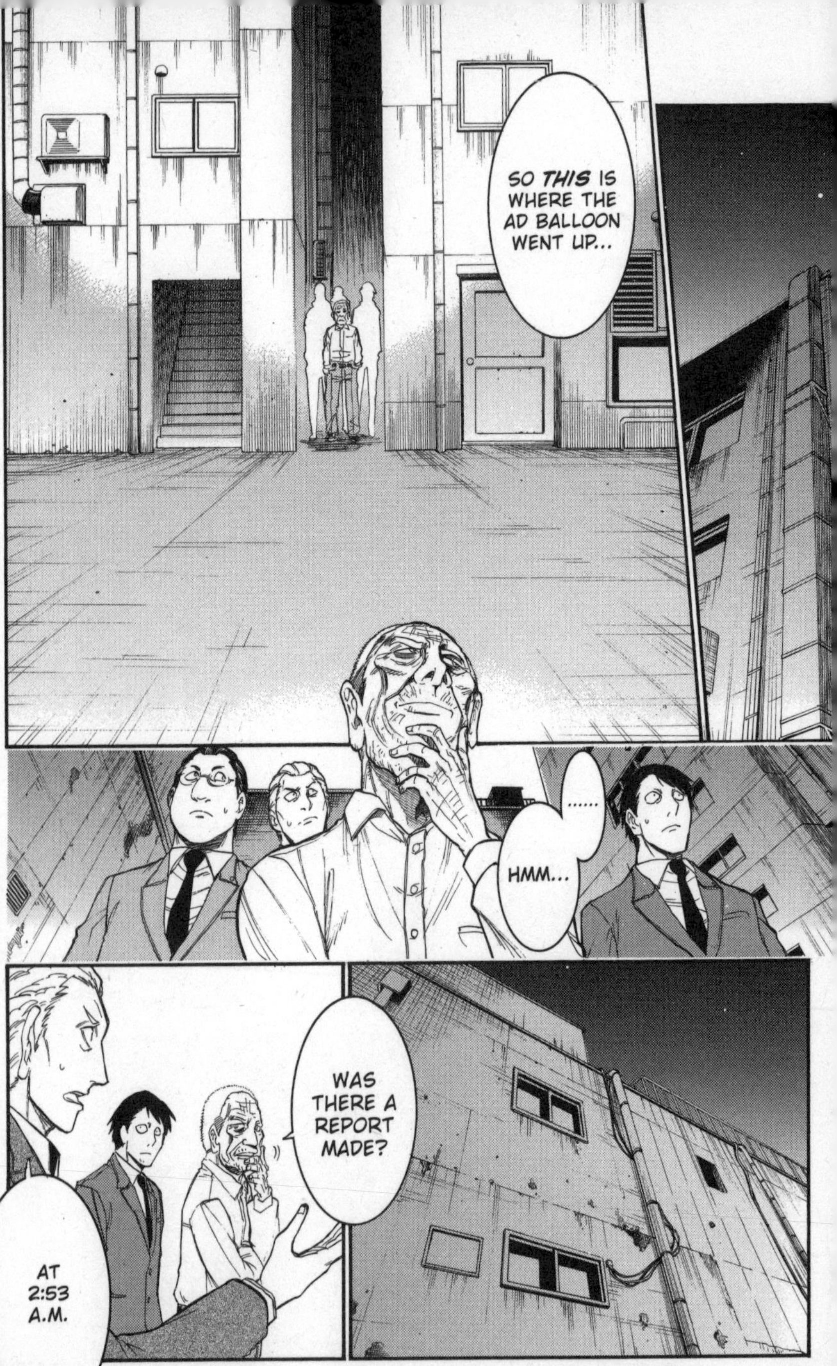
SO *THIS* IS WHERE THE AD BALLOON WENT UP...
......
HMM...
WAS THERE A REPORT MADE?
AT 2:53 A.M.

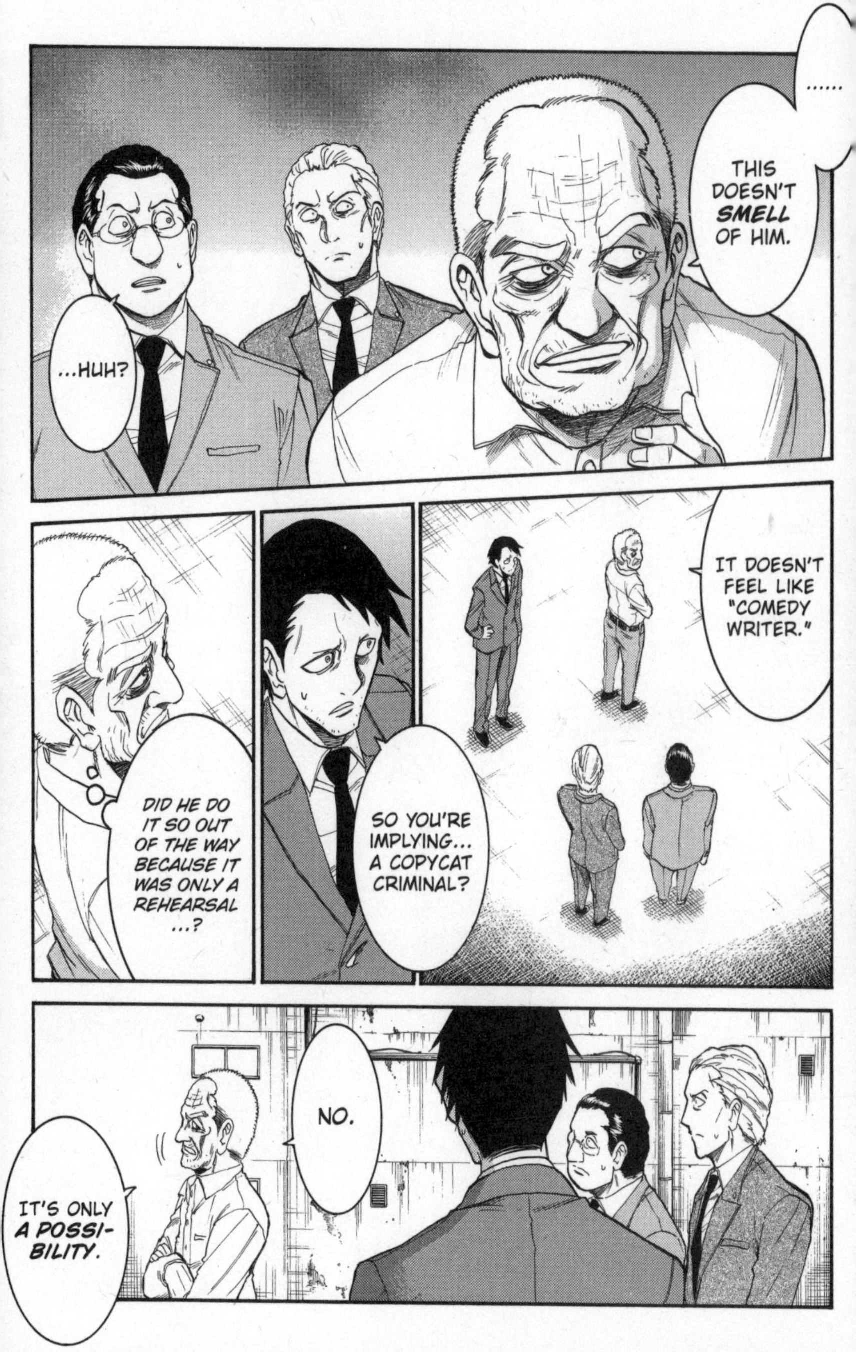
......
THIS DOESN'T **SMELL** OF HIM.
...HUH?
IT DOESN'T FEEL LIKE "COMEDY WRITER."
SO YOU'RE IMPLYING... A COPYCAT CRIMINAL?
*DID HE DO IT SO OUT OF THE WAY BECAUSE IT WAS ONLY A REHEARSAL...?*
NO.
IT'S ONLY ***A POSSIBILITY.***

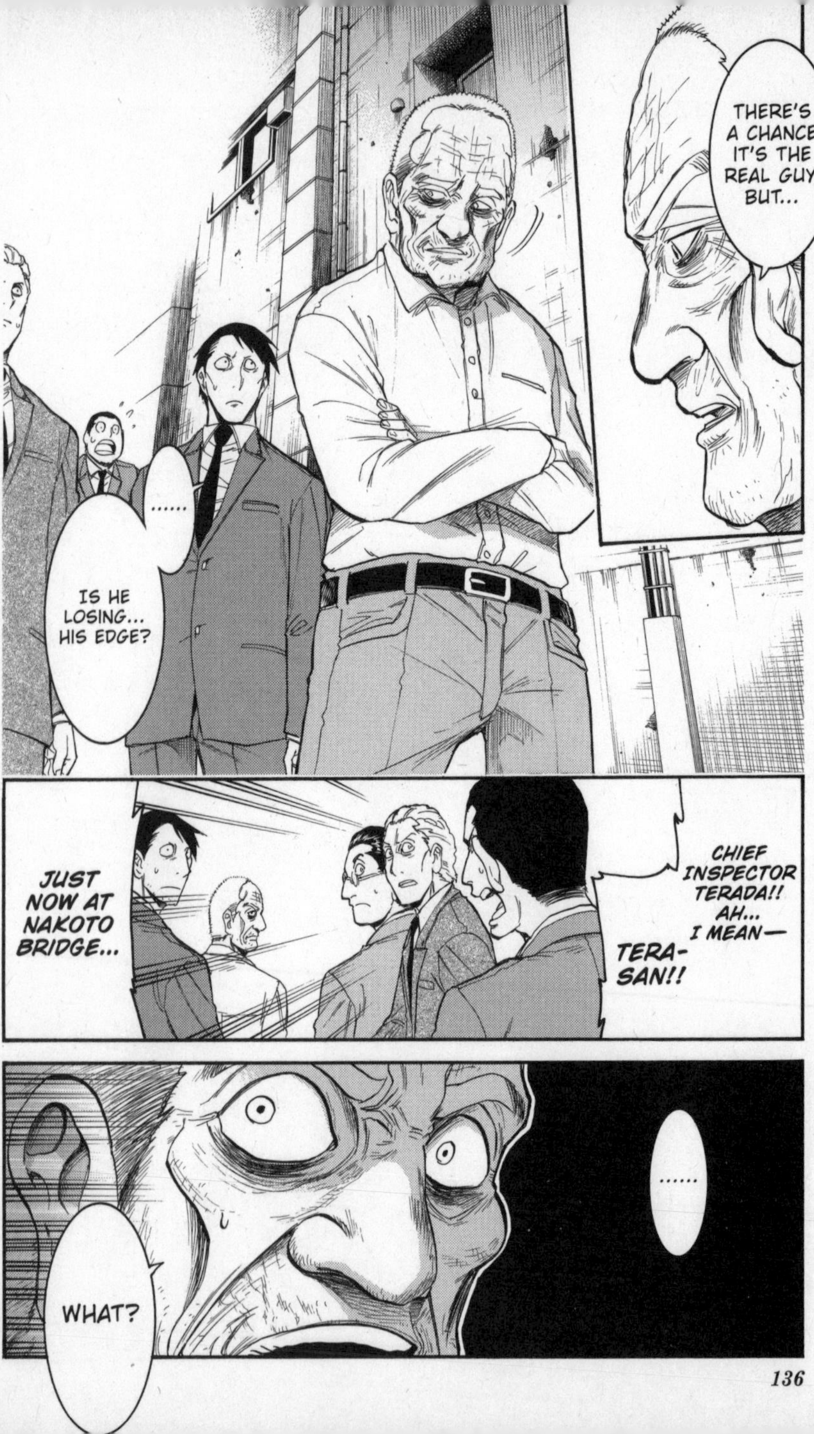
THERE'S A CHANCE IT'S THE REAL GUY, BUT...
......
IS HE LOSING... HIS EDGE?
CHIEF INSPECTOR TERADA!! AH... I MEAN—
TERA-SAN!!
JUST NOW AT NAKOTO BRIDGE...
......
WHAT?

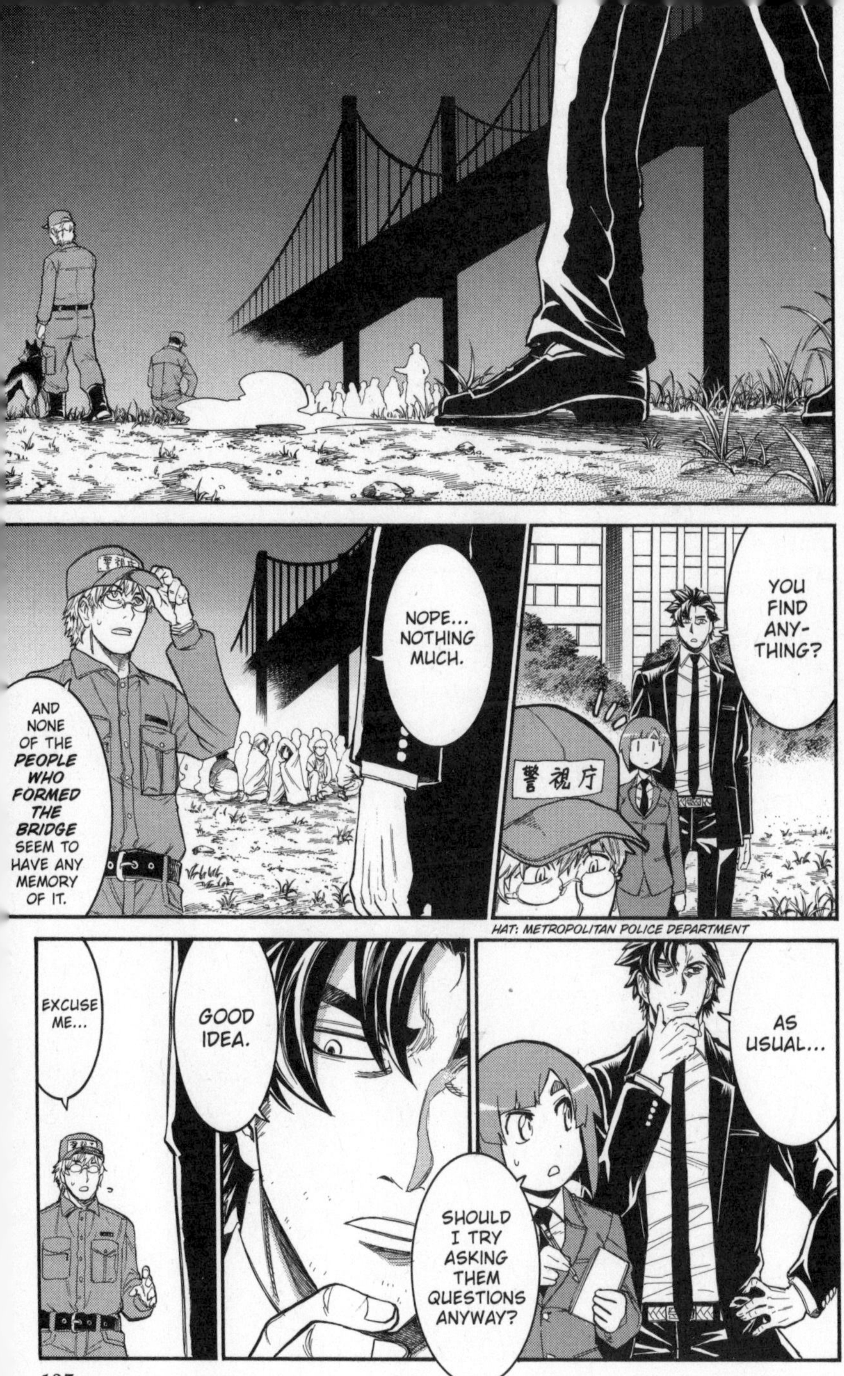
YOU FIND ANYTHING?
NOPE... NOTHING MUCH.
AND NONE OF THE ***PEOPLE WHO FORMED THE BRIDGE*** SEEM TO HAVE ANY MEMORY OF IT.
警視庁
HAT: METROPOLITAN POLICE DEPARTMENT
AS USUAL...
SHOULD I TRY ASKING THEM QUESTIONS ANYWAY?
GOOD IDEA.
EXCUSE ME...

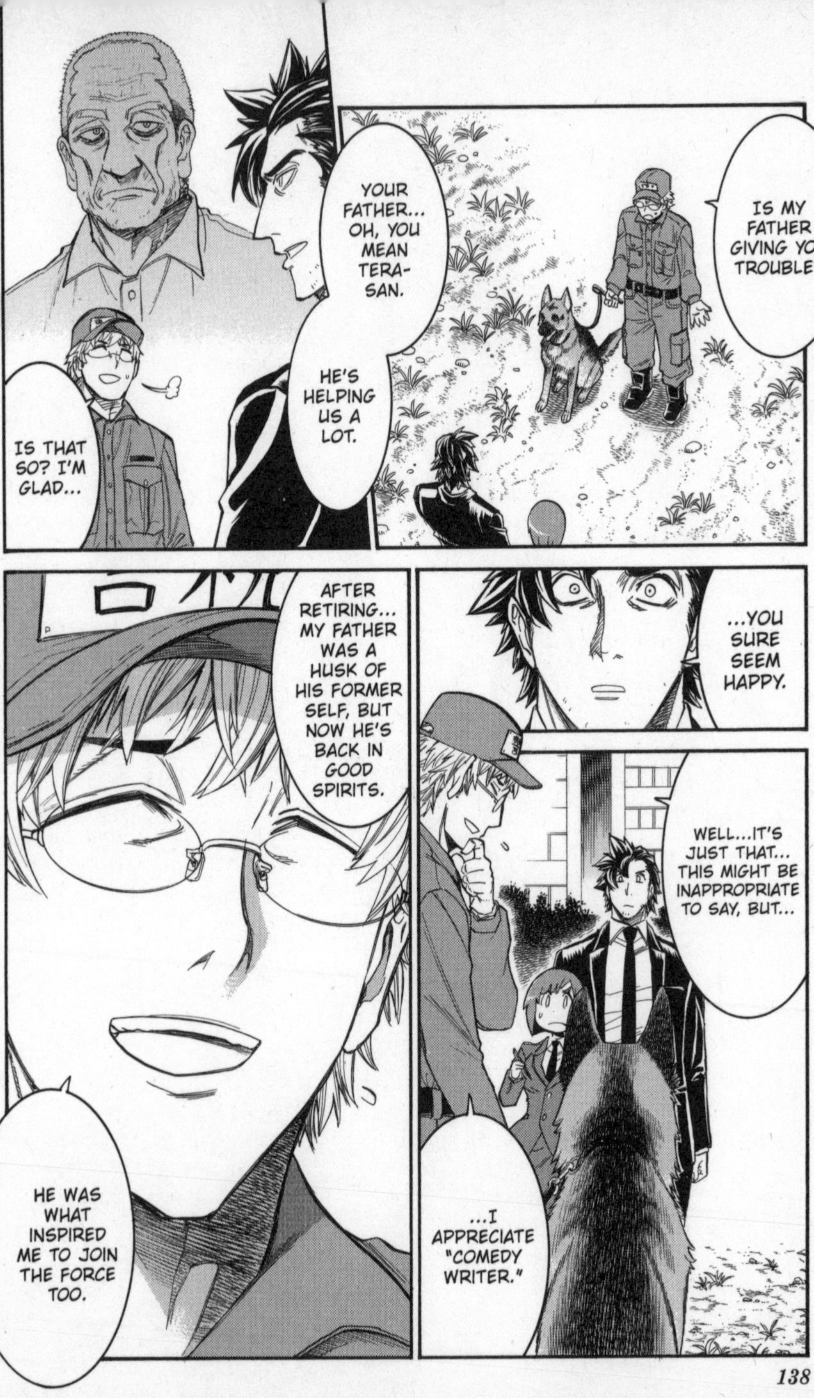
IS MY FATHER GIVING YOU TROUBLE?
YOUR FATHER... OH, YOU MEAN TERA-SAN.
HE'S HELPING US A LOT.
IS THAT SO? I'M GLAD...
...YOU SURE SEEM HAPPY.
WELL...IT'S JUST THAT... THIS MIGHT BE INAPPROPRIATE TO SAY, BUT...
...I APPRECIATE "COMEDY WRITER."
AFTER RETIRING... MY FATHER WAS A HUSK OF HIS FORMER SELF, BUT NOW HE'S BACK IN GOOD SPIRITS.
HE WAS WHAT INSPIRED ME TO JOIN THE FORCE TOO.

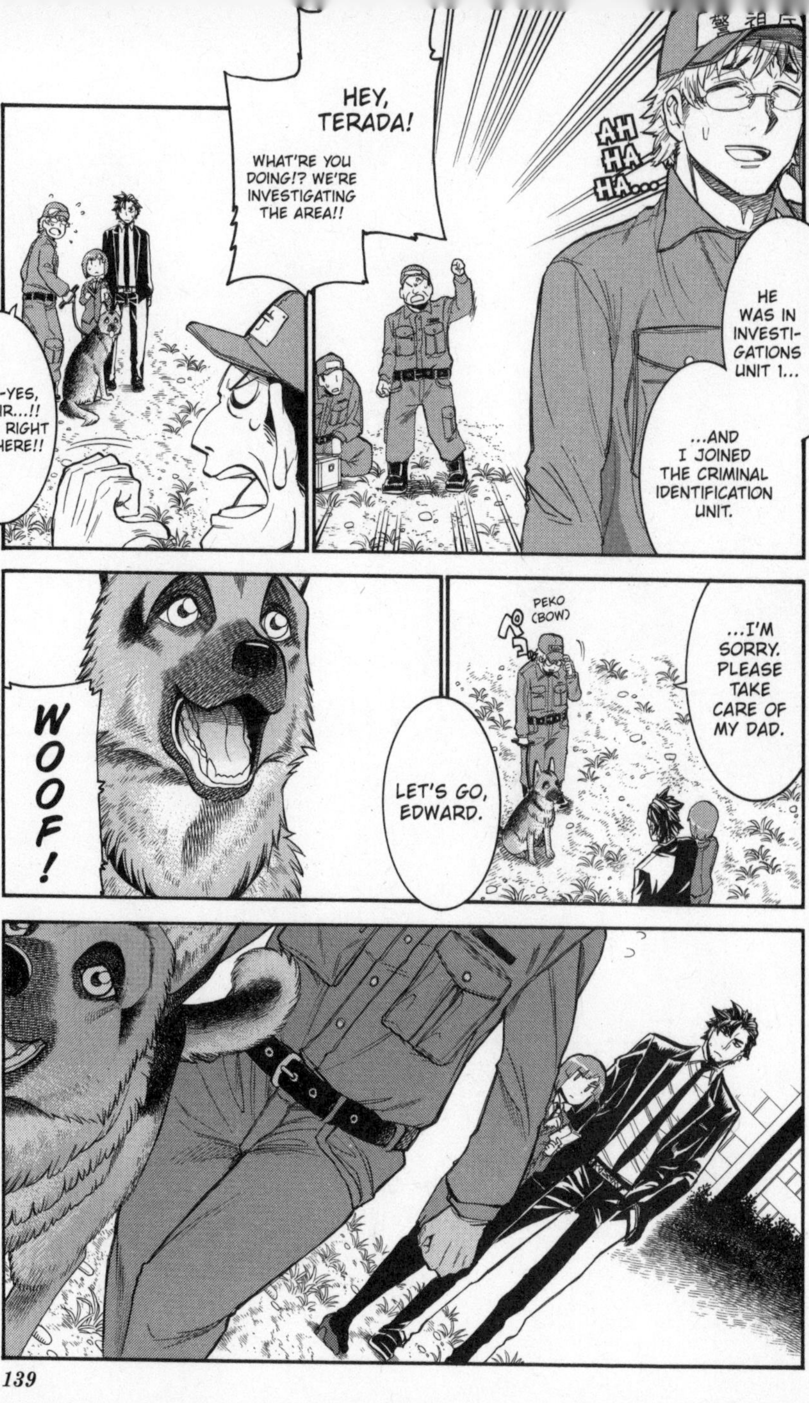
AH HA HA...
HE WAS IN INVESTIGATIONS UNIT 1...
...AND I JOINED THE CRIMINAL IDENTIFICATION UNIT.
HEY, TERADA!
WHAT'RE YOU DOING!? WE'RE INVESTIGATING THE AREA!!
Y-YES, SIR...!! BE RIGHT THERE!!
...I'M SORRY. PLEASE TAKE CARE OF MY DAD.
PEKO (BOW)
LET'S GO, EDWARD.
WOOF!

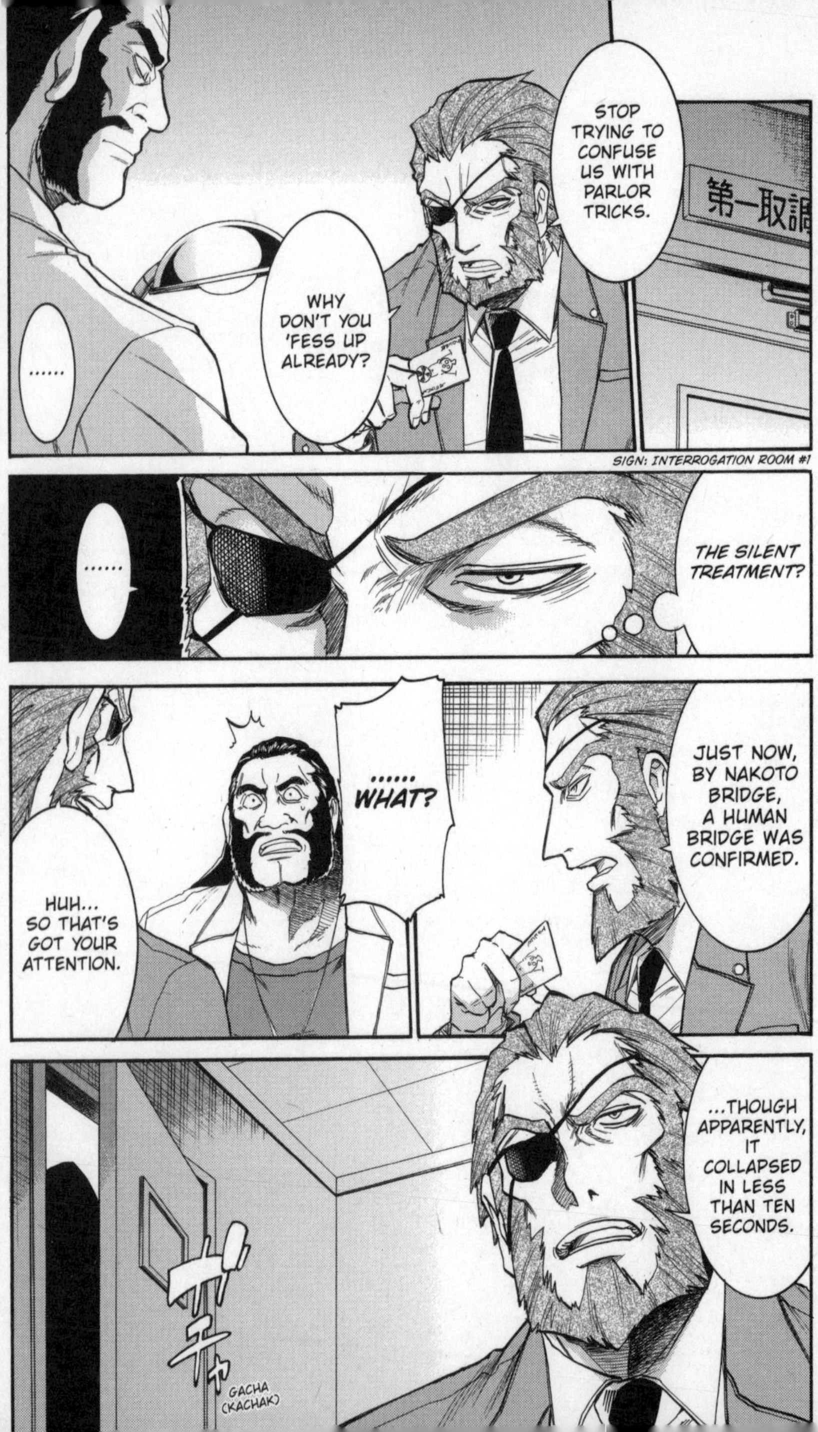
STOP TRYING TO CONFUSE US WITH PARLOR TRICKS.
第一取調
WHY DON'T YOU 'FESS UP ALREADY?
......
SIGN: INTERROGATION ROOM #1
THE SILENT TREATMENT?
......
JUST NOW, BY NAKOTO BRIDGE, A HUMAN BRIDGE WAS CONFIRMED.
...... WHAT?
HUH... SO THAT'S GOT YOUR ATTENTION.
...THOUGH APPARENTLY, IT COLLAPSED IN LESS THAN TEN SECONDS.
ガチャ
GACHA (KACHAK)

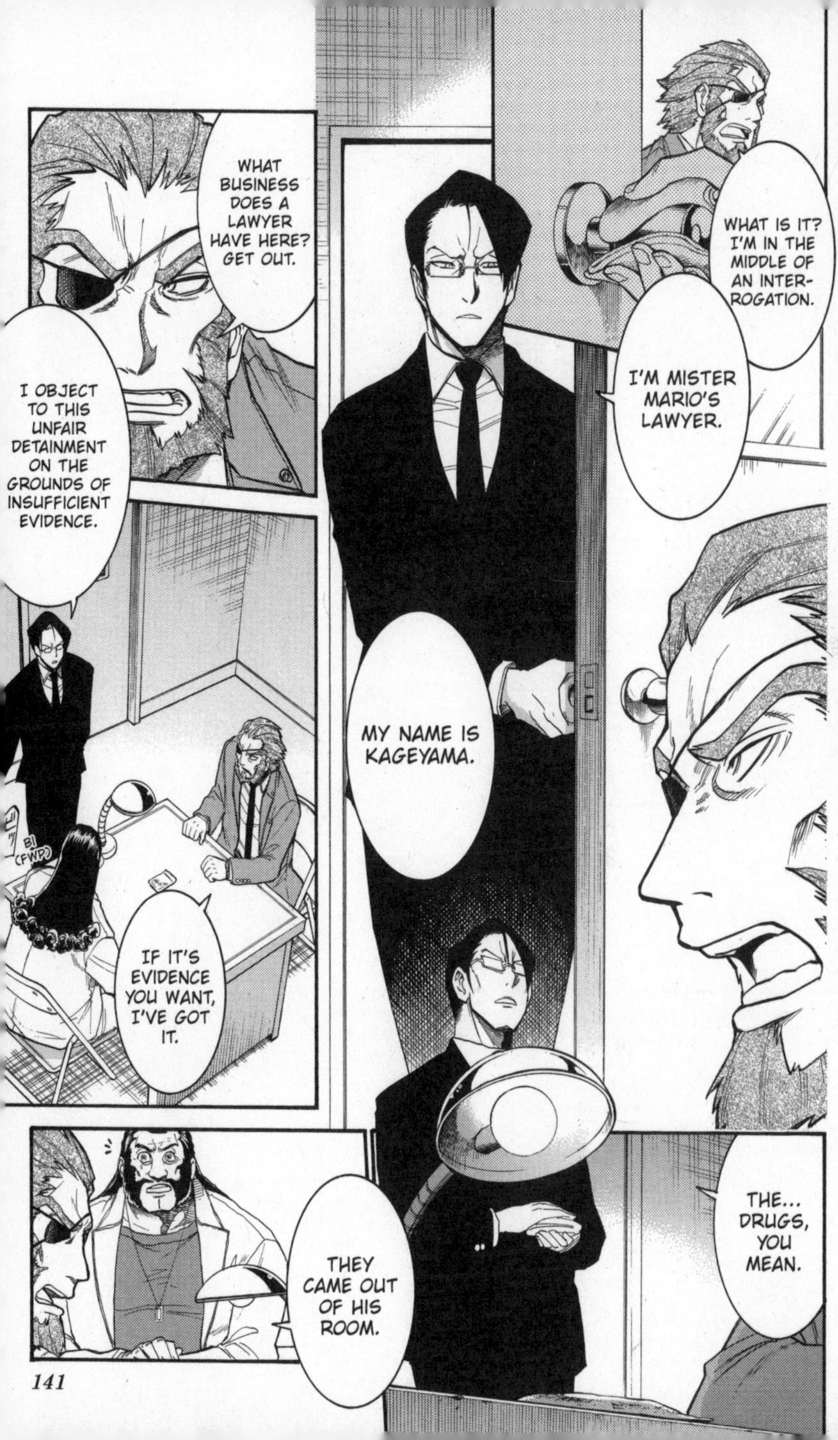
WHAT IS IT? I'M IN THE MIDDLE OF AN INTER-ROGATION.
I'M MISTER MARIO'S LAWYER.
MY NAME IS KAGEYAMA.
WHAT BUSINESS DOES A LAWYER HAVE HERE? GET OUT.
I OBJECT TO THIS UNFAIR DETAINMENT ON THE GROUNDS OF INSUFFICIENT EVIDENCE.
BI (FWP)
IF IT'S EVIDENCE YOU WANT, I'VE GOT IT.
THE... DRUGS, YOU MEAN.
THEY CAME OUT OF HIS ROOM.

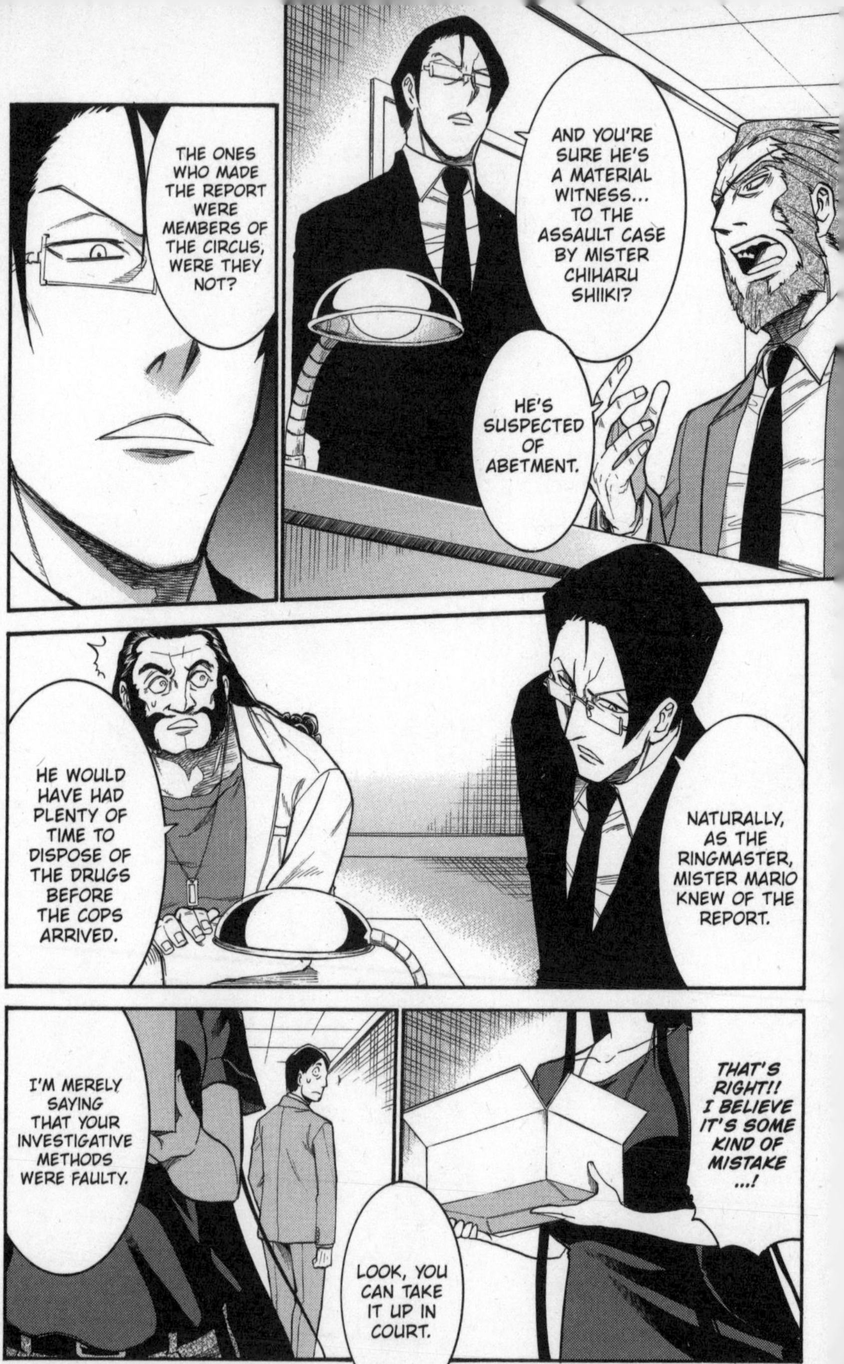
AND YOU'RE SURE HE'S A MATERIAL WITNESS... TO THE ASSAULT CASE BY MISTER CHIHARU SHIIKI?
HE'S SUSPECTED OF ABETMENT.
THE ONES WHO MADE THE REPORT WERE MEMBERS OF THE CIRCUS, WERE THEY NOT?
NATURALLY, AS THE RINGMASTER, MISTER MARIO KNEW OF THE REPORT.
HE WOULD HAVE HAD PLENTY OF TIME TO DISPOSE OF THE DRUGS BEFORE THE COPS ARRIVED.
THAT'S RIGHT!! I BELIEVE IT'S SOME KIND OF MISTAKE ...!
LOOK, YOU CAN TAKE IT UP IN COURT.
I'M MERELY SAYING THAT YOUR INVESTIGATIVE METHODS WERE FAULTY.

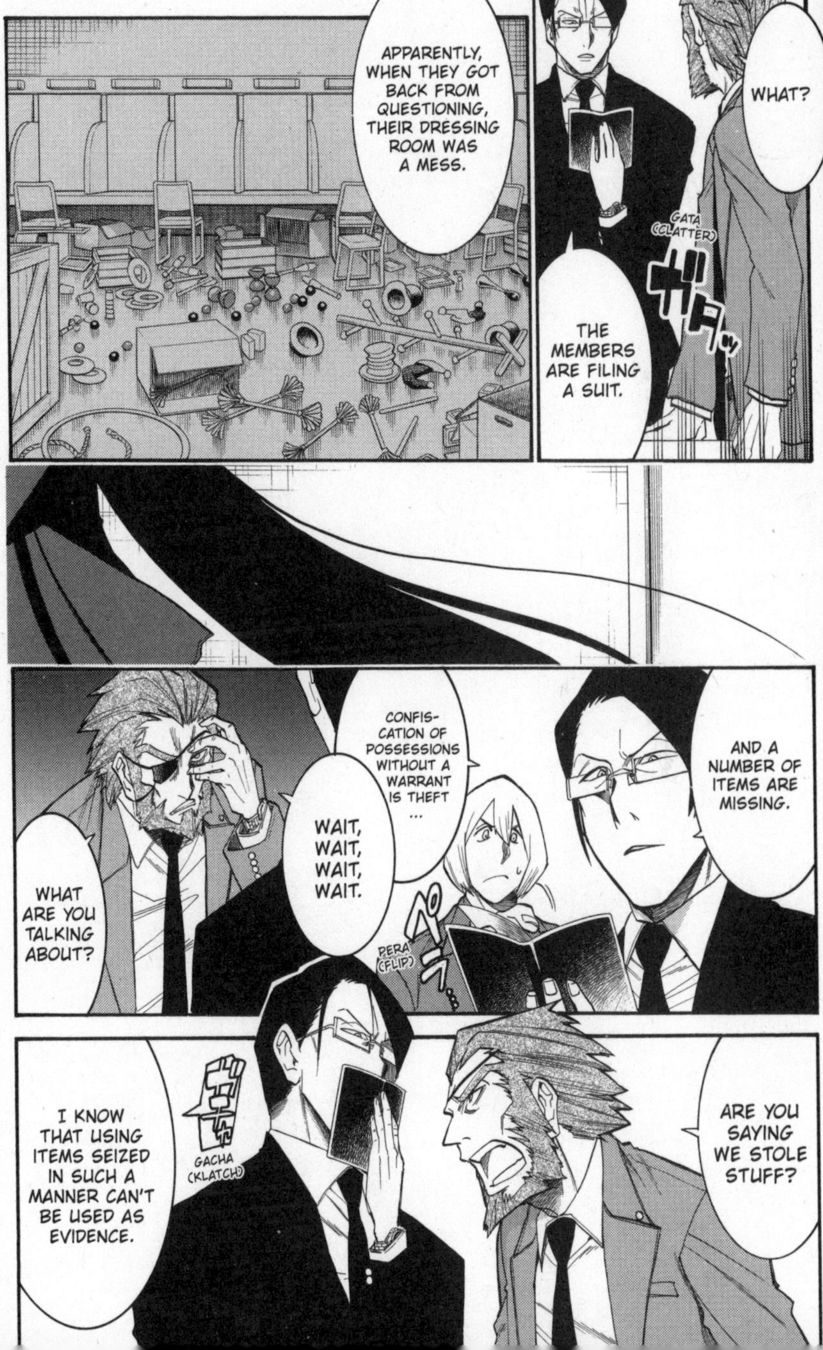
WHAT?
GATA (CLATTER)
THE MEMBERS ARE FILING A SUIT.
APPARENTLY, WHEN THEY GOT BACK FROM QUESTIONING, THEIR DRESSING ROOM WAS A MESS.
AND A NUMBER OF ITEMS ARE MISSING.
CONFISCATION OF POSSESSIONS WITHOUT A WARRANT IS THEFT ...
PERA (FLIP)
WAIT, WAIT, WAIT, WAIT.
WHAT ARE YOU TALKING ABOUT?
ARE YOU SAYING WE STOLE STUFF?
GACHA (KLATCH)
I KNOW THAT USING ITEMS SEIZED IN SUCH A MANNER CAN'T BE USED AS EVIDENCE.

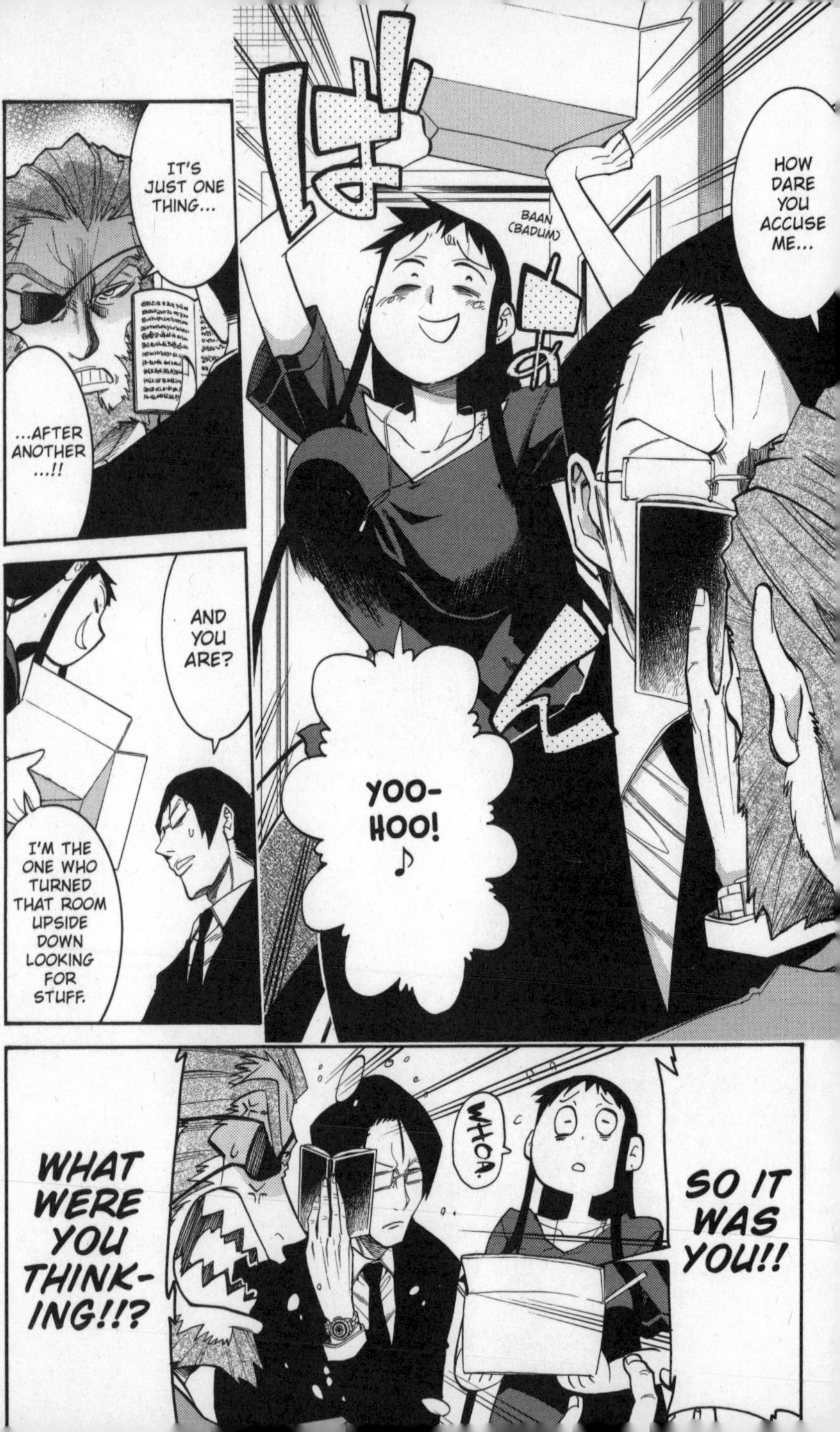
HOW DARE YOU ACCUSE ME...
BAAN (BADUM)
YOO-HOO! ♪
IT'S JUST ONE THING...
...AFTER ANOTHER ...!!
AND YOU ARE?
I'M THE ONE WHO TURNED THAT ROOM UPSIDE DOWN LOOKING FOR STUFF.
SO IT WAS YOU!!
WHOA.
WHAT WERE YOU THINK-ING!!?

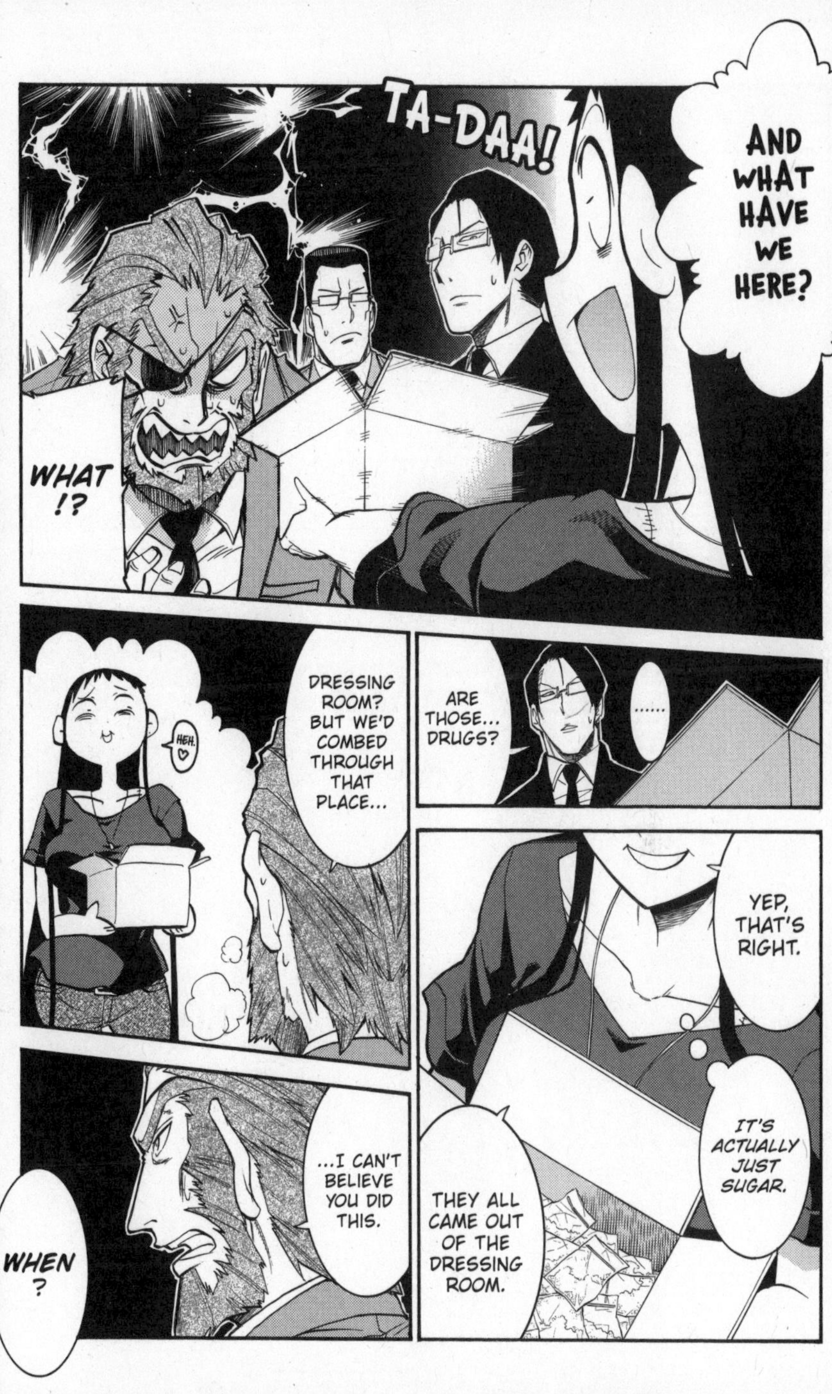
AND WHAT HAVE WE HERE?
TA-DAA!
WHAT !?
ARE THOSE... DRUGS?
......
YEP, THAT'S RIGHT.
IT'S ACTUALLY JUST SUGAR.
THEY ALL CAME OUT OF THE DRESSING ROOM.
HEH. ♥
DRESSING ROOM? BUT WE'D COMBED THROUGH THAT PLACE...
...I CAN'T BELIEVE YOU DID THIS.
WHEN ?

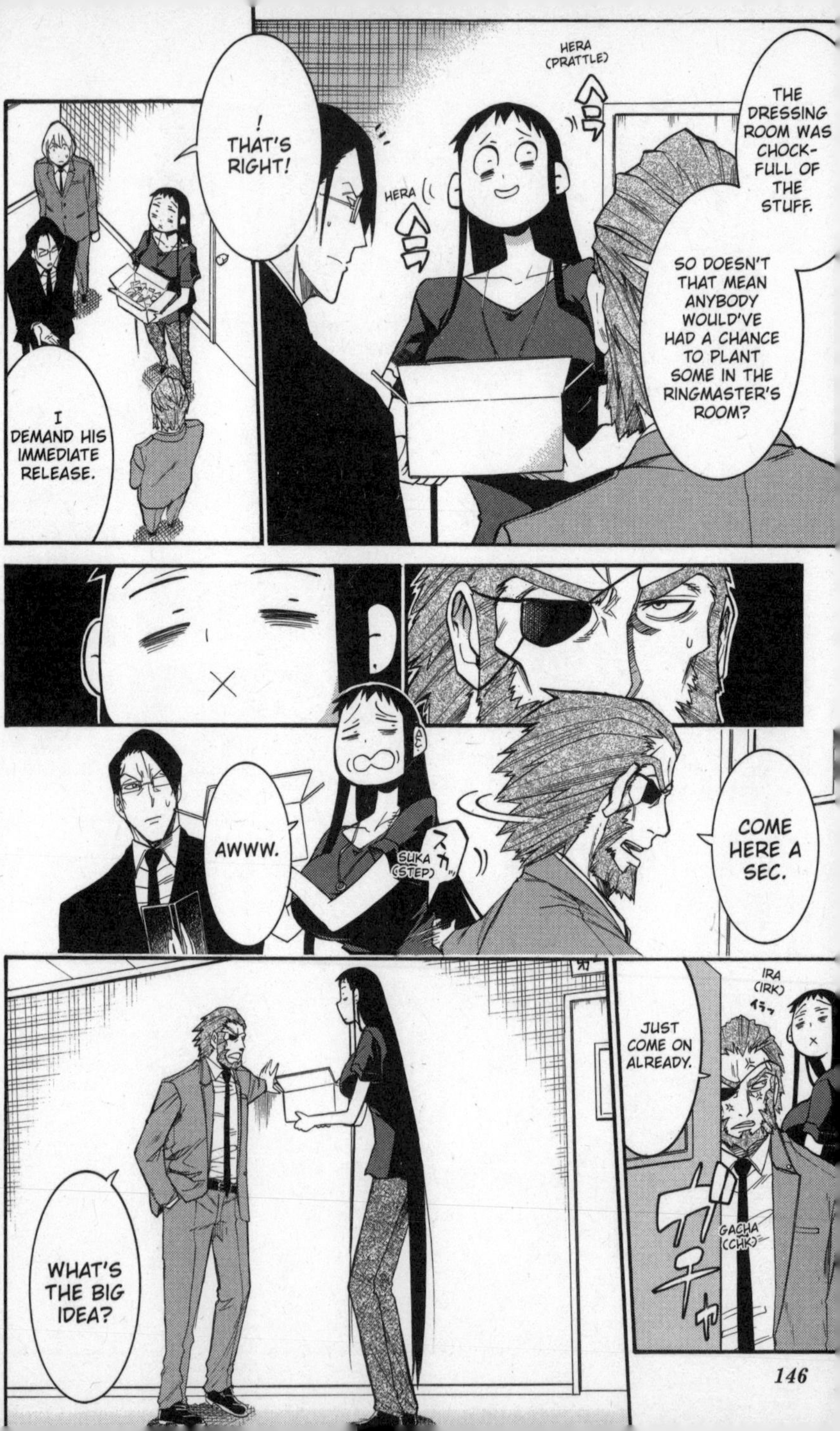
HERA (PRATTLE)
THE DRESSING ROOM WAS CHOCK-FULL OF THE STUFF.
SO DOESN'T THAT MEAN ANYBODY WOULD'VE HAD A CHANCE TO PLANT SOME IN THE RINGMASTER'S ROOM?
HERA
! THAT'S RIGHT!
I DEMAND HIS IMMEDIATE RELEASE.
COME HERE A SEC.
SUKA (STEP)
AWWW.
IRA (IRK)
JUST COME ON ALREADY.
GACHA (CHK)
WHAT'S THE BIG IDEA?

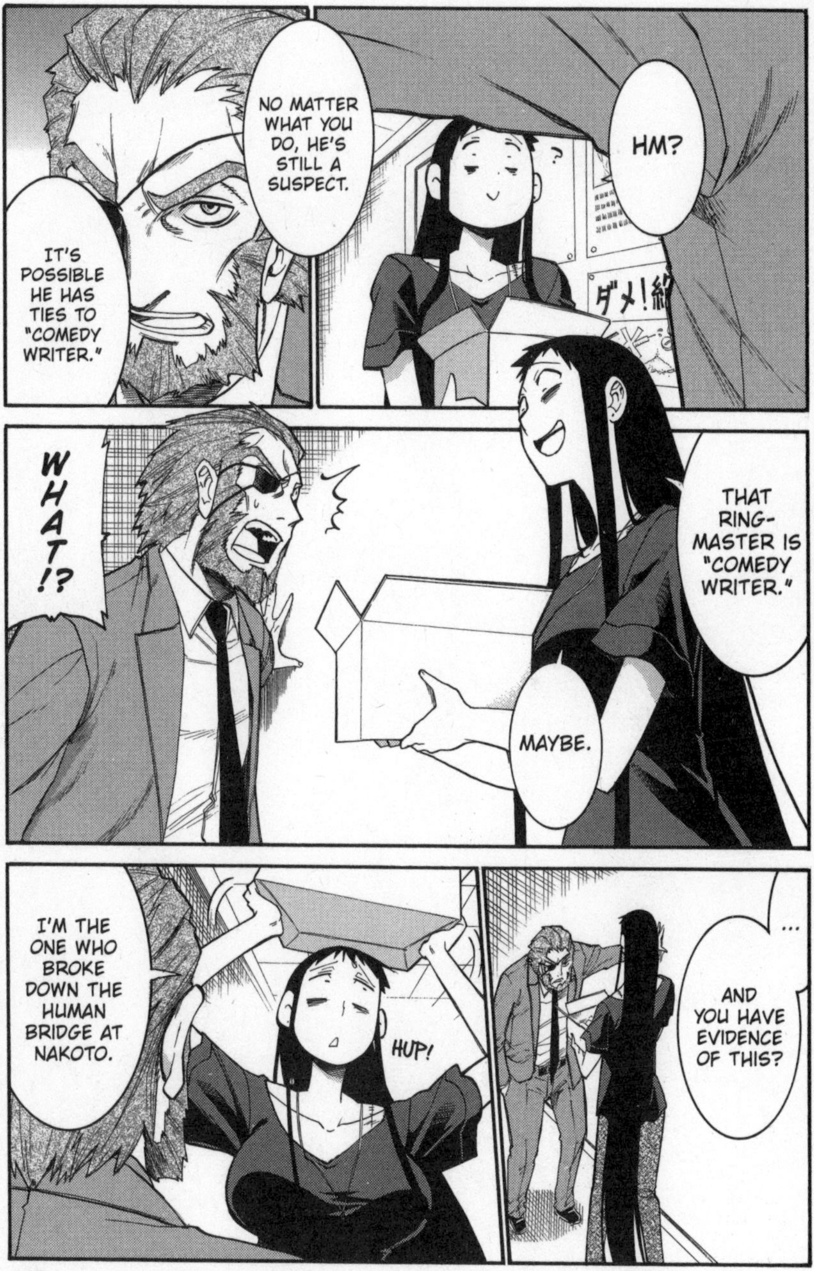
HM?
NO MATTER WHAT YOU DO, HE'S STILL A SUSPECT.
IT'S POSSIBLE HE HAS TIES TO "COMEDY WRITER."
THAT RING-MASTER IS "COMEDY WRITER."
WHAT!?
MAYBE.
...
AND YOU HAVE EVIDENCE OF THIS?
I'M THE ONE WHO BROKE DOWN THE HUMAN BRIDGE AT NAKOTO.
HUP!

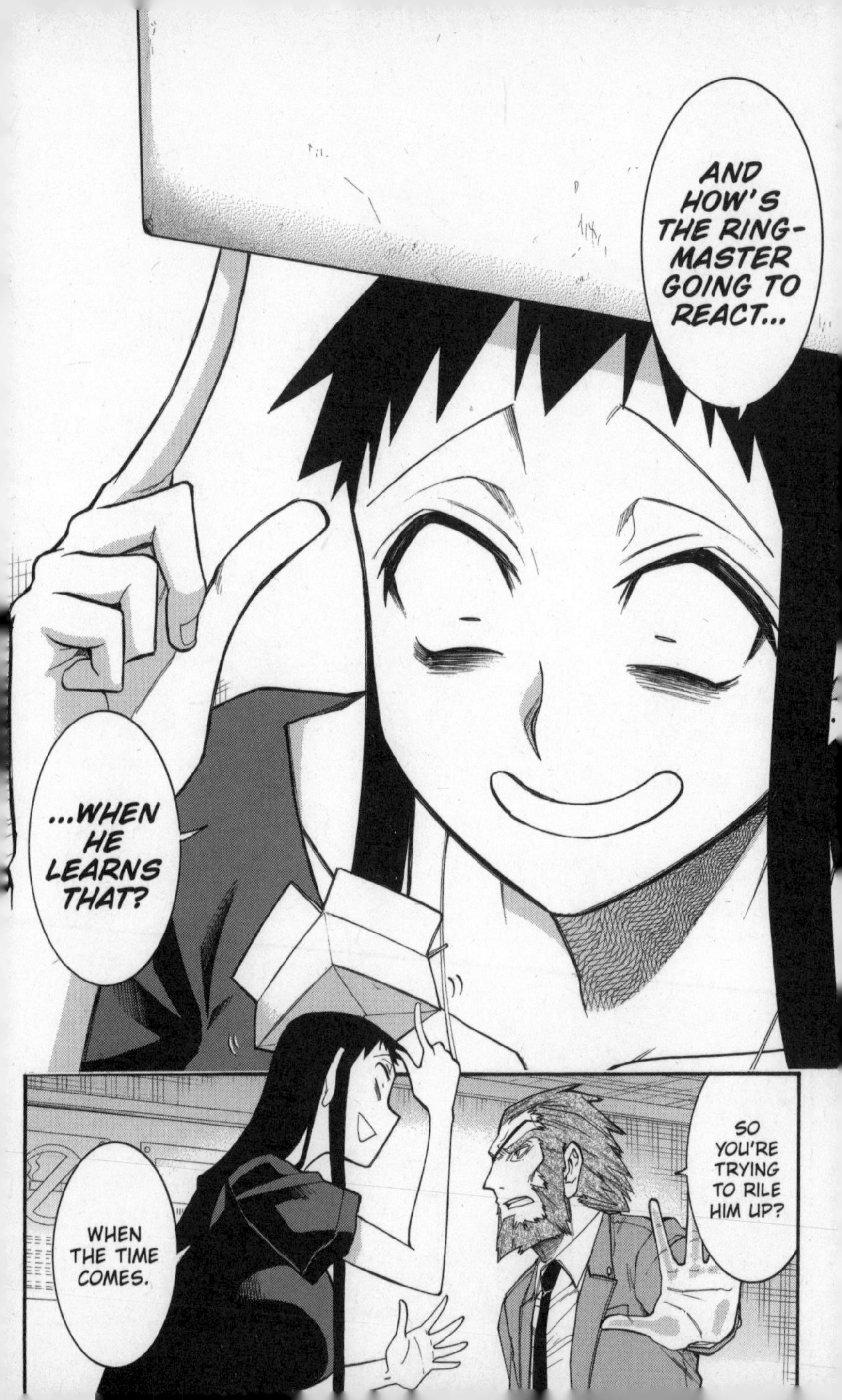
AND HOW'S THE RING-MASTER GOING TO REACT...
...WHEN HE LEARNS THAT?
SO YOU'RE TRYING TO RILE HIM UP?
WHEN THE TIME COMES.

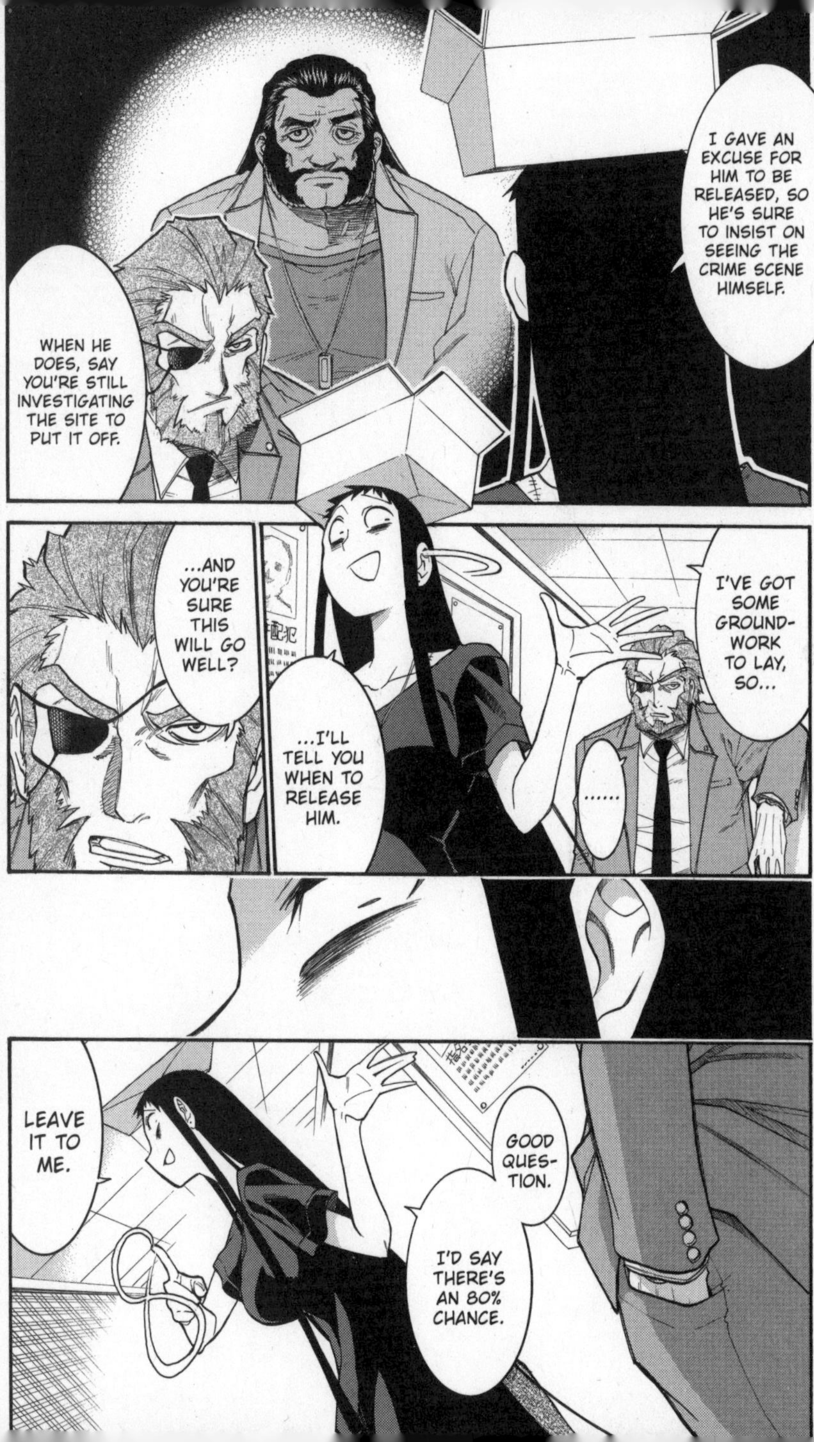
I GAVE AN EXCUSE FOR HIM TO BE RELEASED, SO HE'S SURE TO INSIST ON SEEING THE CRIME SCENE HIMSELF.
WHEN HE DOES, SAY YOU'RE STILL INVESTIGATING THE SITE TO PUT IT OFF.
I'VE GOT SOME GROUND-WORK TO LAY, SO...
......
...I'LL TELL YOU WHEN TO RELEASE HIM.
...AND YOU'RE SURE THIS WILL GO WELL?
GOOD QUES-TION.
I'D SAY THERE'S AN 80% CHANCE.
LEAVE IT TO ME.

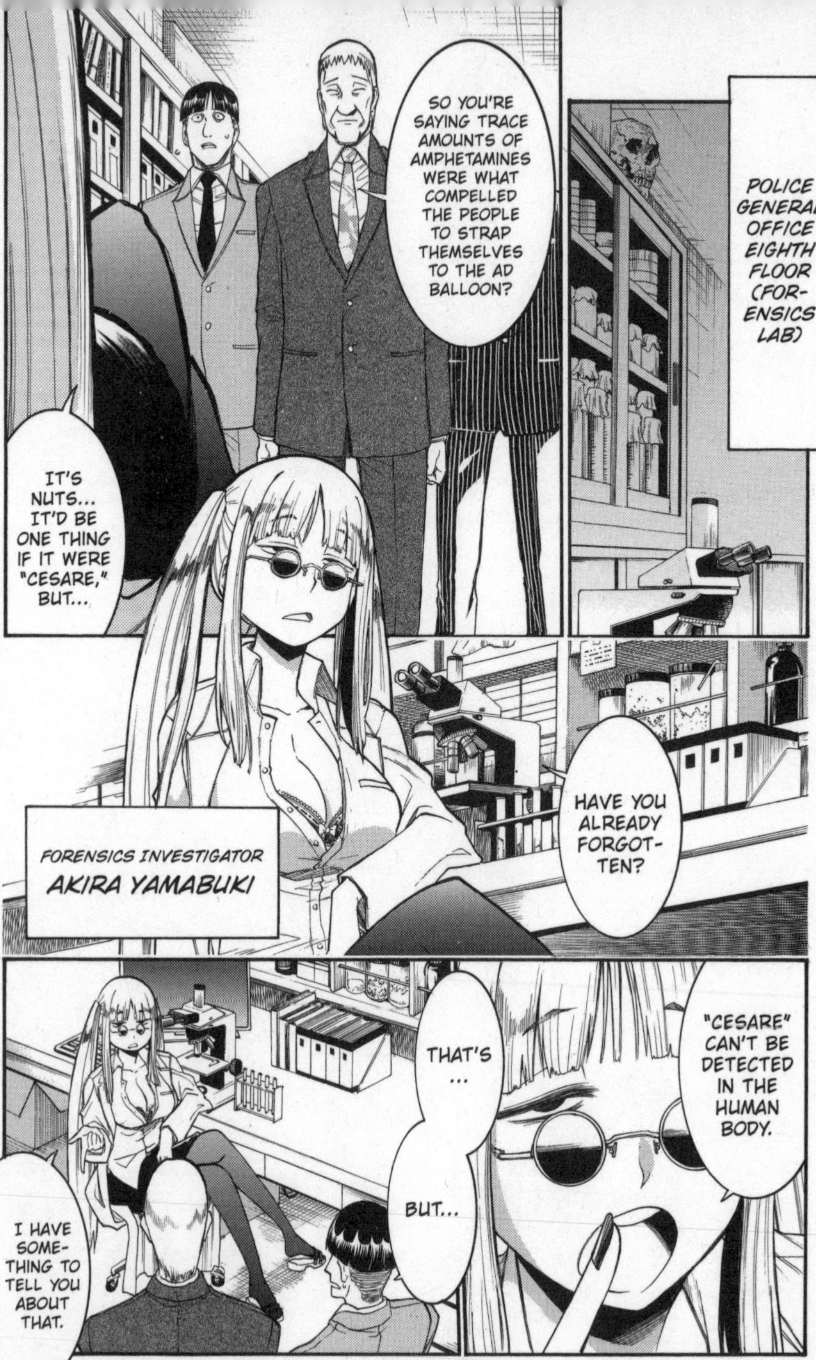
POLICE GENERAL OFFICE EIGHTH FLOOR (FOR-ENSICS LAB)
SO YOU'RE SAYING TRACE AMOUNTS OF AMPHETAMINES WERE WHAT COMPELLED THE PEOPLE TO STRAP THEMSELVES TO THE AD BALLOON?
IT'S NUTS... IT'D BE ONE THING IF IT WERE "CESARE," BUT...
HAVE YOU ALREADY FORGOT-TEN?
FORENSICS INVESTIGATOR
AKIRA YAMABUKI
"CESARE" CAN'T BE DETECTED IN THE HUMAN BODY.
THAT'S ...
BUT...
I HAVE SOME-THING TO TELL YOU ABOUT THAT.

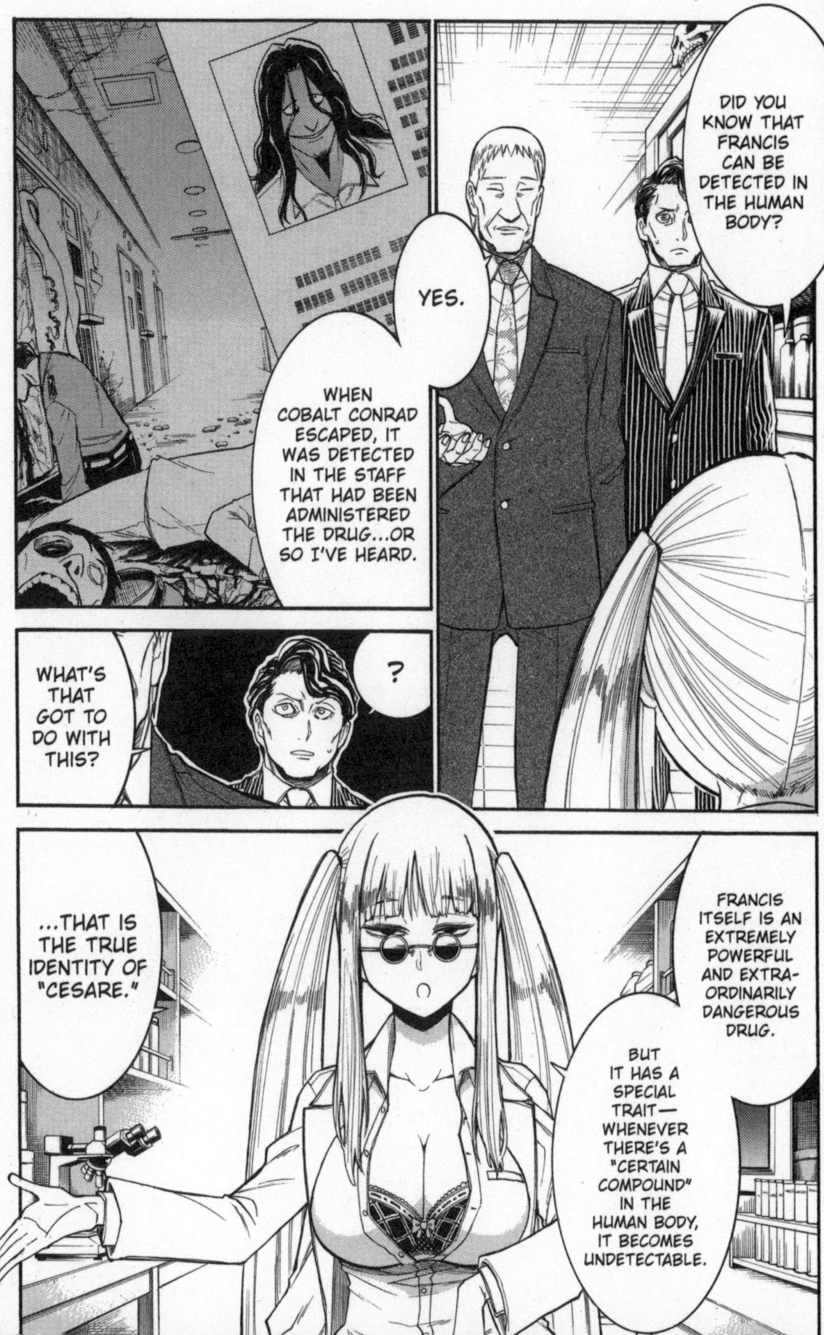
DID YOU KNOW THAT FRANCIS CAN BE DETECTED IN THE HUMAN BODY?
YES.
WHEN COBALT CONRAD ESCAPED, IT WAS DETECTED IN THE STAFF THAT HAD BEEN ADMINISTERED THE DRUG...OR SO I'VE HEARD.
?
WHAT'S THAT GOT TO DO WITH THIS?
FRANCIS ITSELF IS AN EXTREMELY POWERFUL AND EXTRA-ORDINARILY DANGEROUS DRUG.
BUT IT HAS A SPECIAL TRAIT—WHENEVER THERE'S A "CERTAIN COMPOUND" IN THE HUMAN BODY, IT BECOMES UNDETECTABLE.
...THAT IS THE TRUE IDENTITY OF "CESARE."

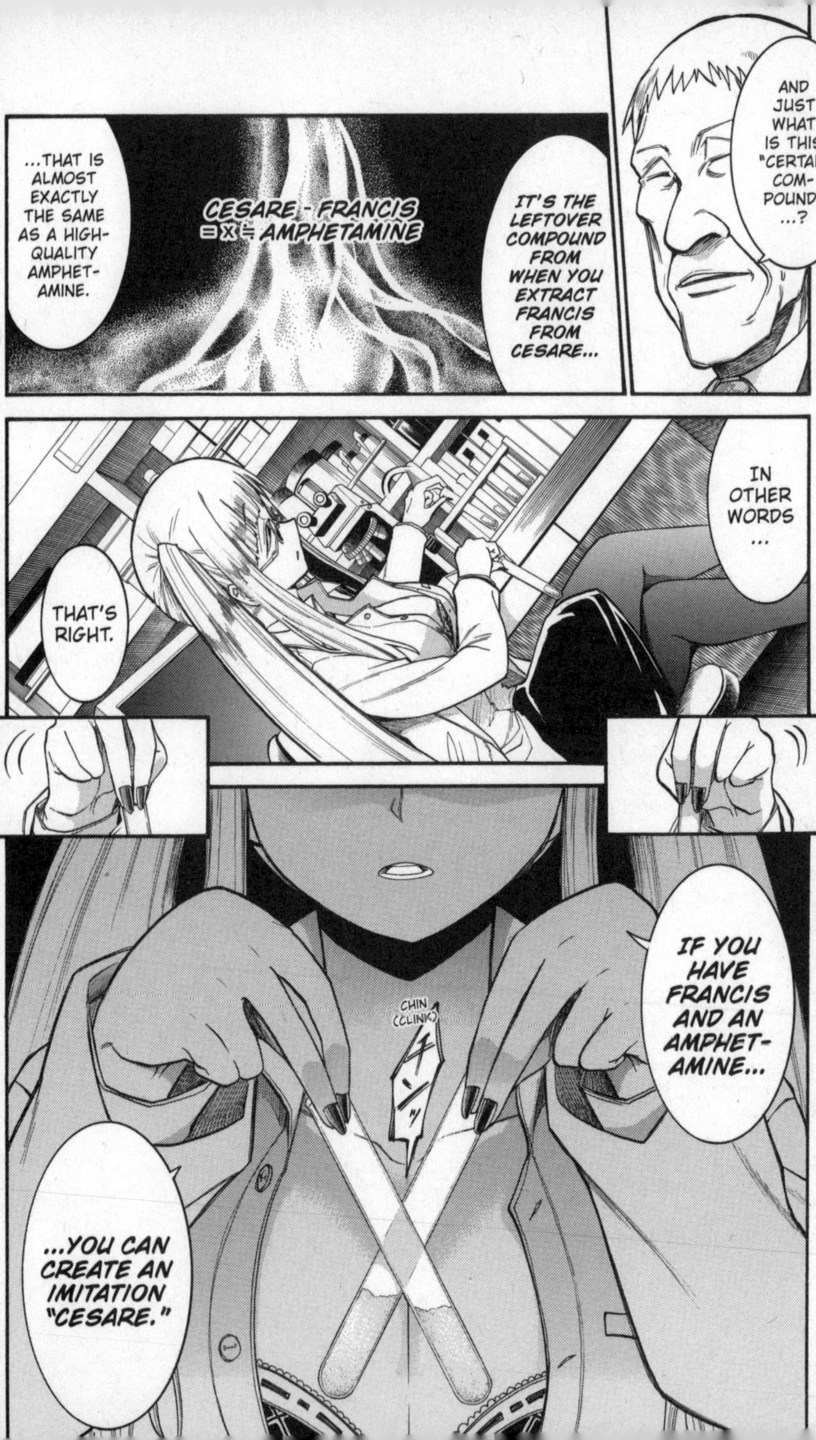
AND JUST WHAT IS THIS "CERTAIN COMPOUND" ...?
IT'S THE LEFTOVER COMPOUND FROM WHEN YOU EXTRACT FRANCIS FROM CESARE...
CESARE - FRANCIS = X ≒ AMPHETAMINE
...THAT IS ALMOST EXACTLY THE SAME AS A HIGH-QUALITY AMPHETAMINE.
IN OTHER WORDS...
THAT'S RIGHT.
IF YOU HAVE FRANCIS AND AN AMPHETAMINE...
CHIN (CLINK)
...YOU CAN CREATE AN IMITATION "CESARE."

MURCIÉLAGO

MURCIÉLAGO

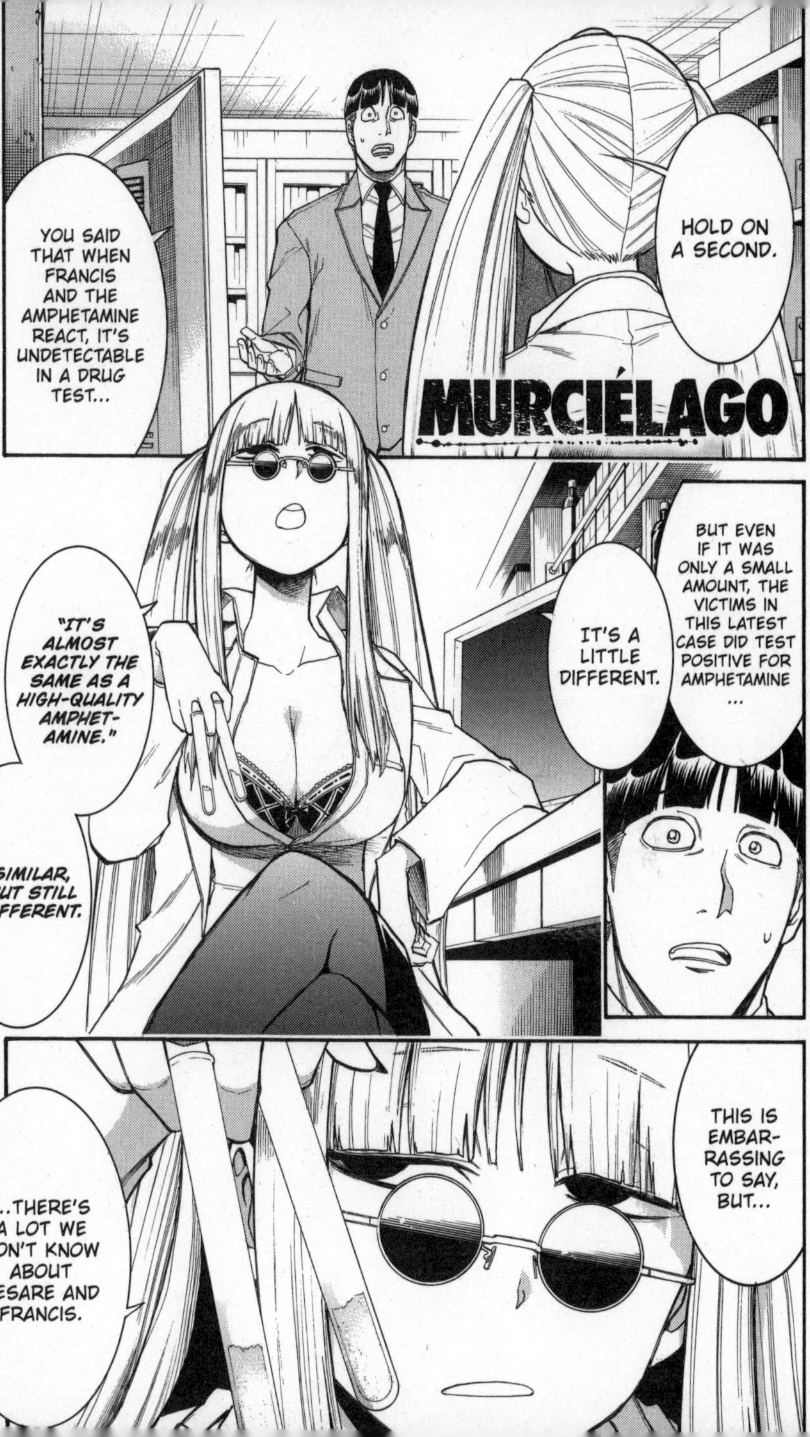
MURCIÉLAGO
HOLD ON A SECOND.
YOU SAID THAT WHEN FRANCIS AND THE AMPHETAMINE REACT, IT'S UNDETECTABLE IN A DRUG TEST...
BUT EVEN IF IT WAS ONLY A SMALL AMOUNT, THE VICTIMS IN THIS LATEST CASE DID TEST POSITIVE FOR AMPHETAMINE...
IT'S A LITTLE DIFFERENT.
"IT'S ALMOST EXACTLY THE SAME AS A HIGH-QUALITY AMPHET-AMINE."
SIMILAR, BUT STILL DIFFERENT.
THIS IS EMBAR-RASSING TO SAY, BUT...
...THERE'S A LOT WE DON'T KNOW ABOUT CESARE AND FRANCIS.

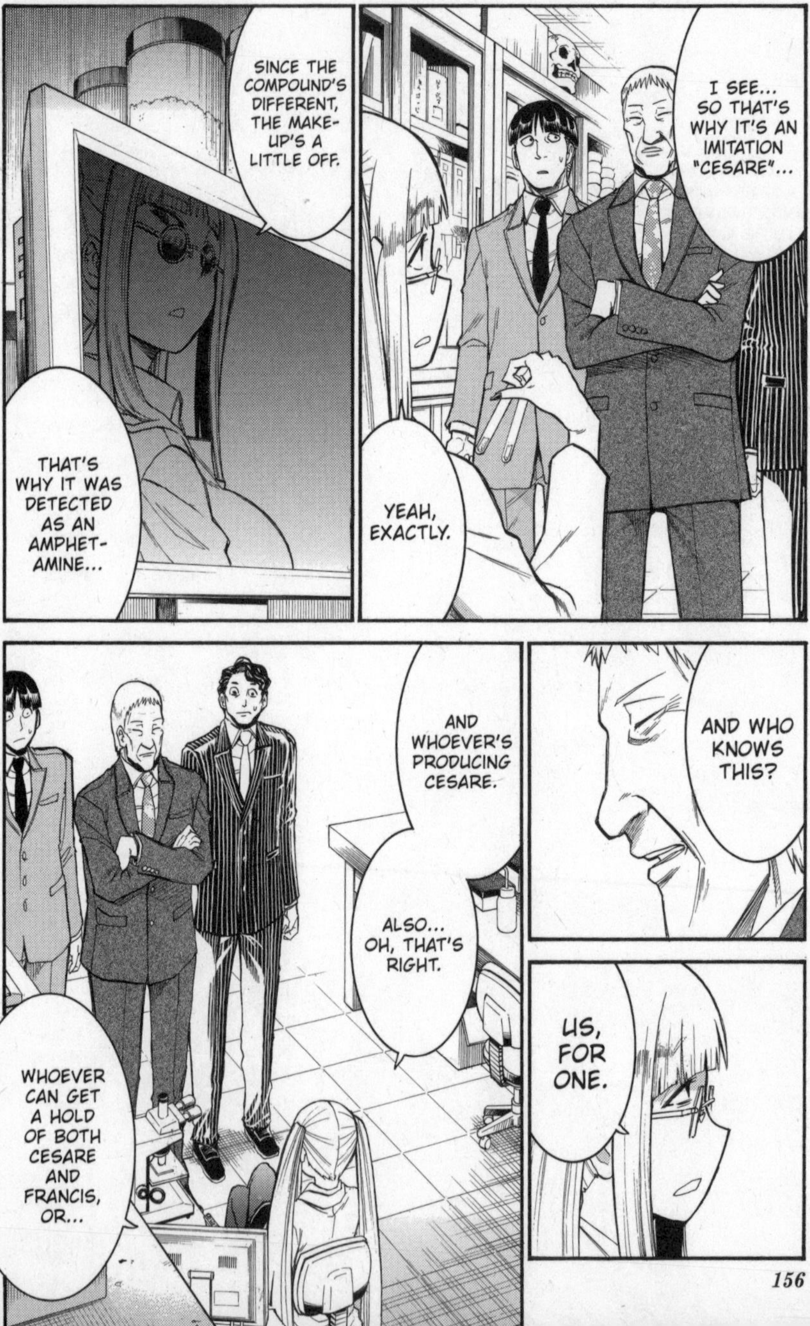
I SEE... SO THAT'S WHY IT'S AN IMITATION "CESARE"...
YEAH, EXACTLY.
SINCE THE COMPOUND'S DIFFERENT, THE MAKE-UP'S A LITTLE OFF.
THAT'S WHY IT WAS DETECTED AS AN AMPHET-AMINE...
AND WHO KNOWS THIS?
US, FOR ONE.
AND WHOEVER'S PRODUCING CESARE.
ALSO... OH, THAT'S RIGHT.
WHOEVER CAN GET A HOLD OF BOTH CESARE AND FRANCIS, OR...

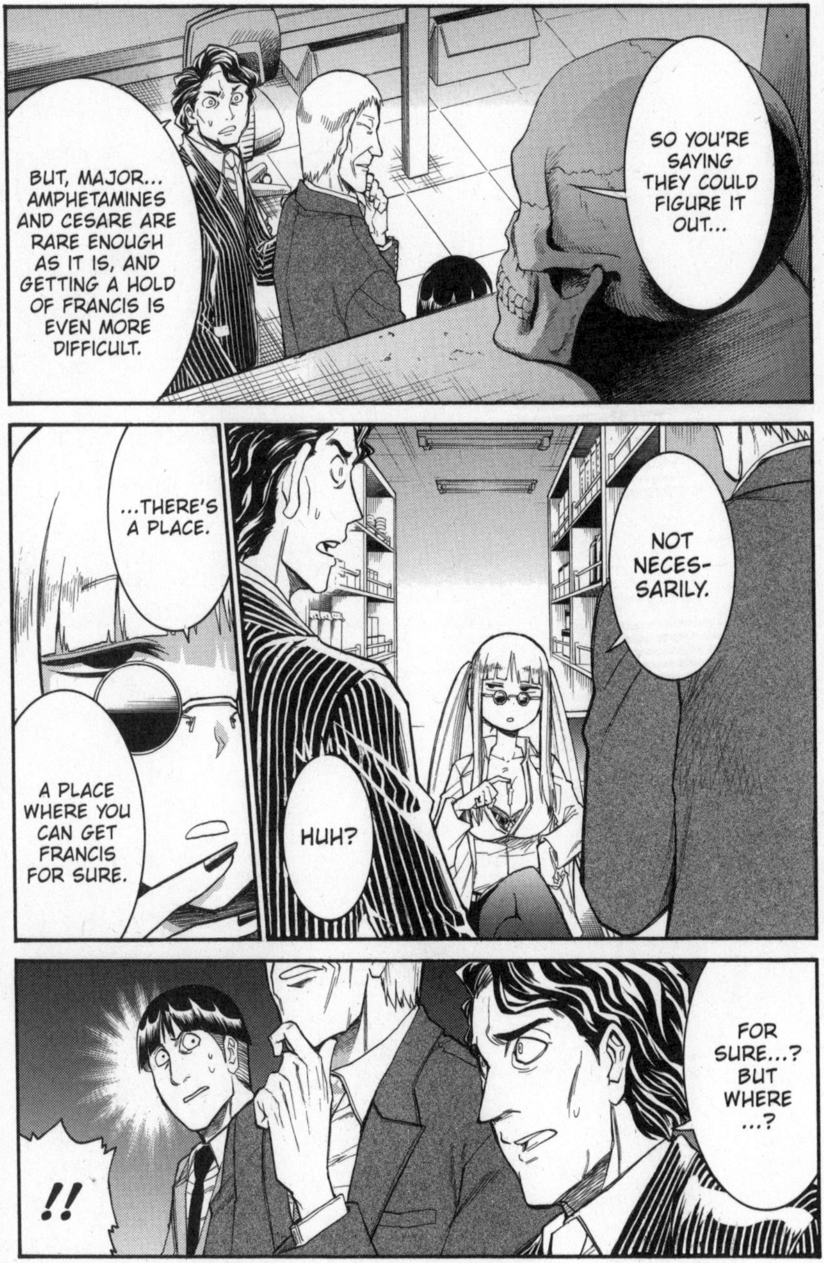
SO YOU'RE SAYING THEY COULD FIGURE IT OUT...
BUT, MAJOR... AMPHETAMINES AND CESARE ARE RARE ENOUGH AS IT IS, AND GETTING A HOLD OF FRANCIS IS EVEN MORE DIFFICULT.
NOT NECES-SARILY.
HUH?
...THERE'S A PLACE.
A PLACE WHERE YOU CAN GET FRANCIS FOR SURE.
FOR SURE...? BUT WHERE ...?
!!

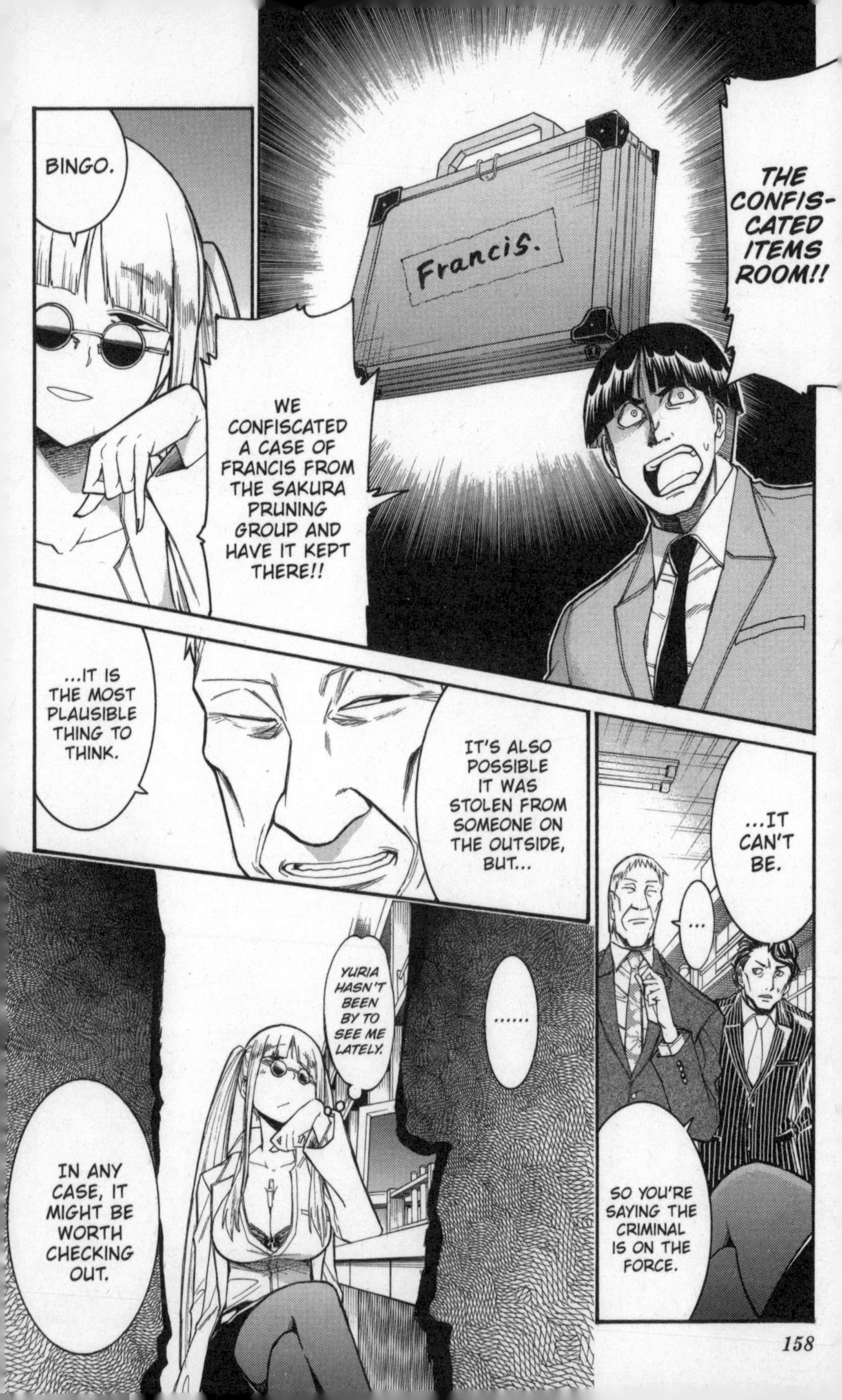
THE CONFISCATED ITEMS ROOM!!
Francis.
BINGO.
WE CONFISCATED A CASE OF FRANCIS FROM THE SAKURA PRUNING GROUP AND HAVE IT KEPT THERE!!
...IT CAN'T BE.
...
SO YOU'RE SAYING THE CRIMINAL IS ON THE FORCE.
IT'S ALSO POSSIBLE IT WAS STOLEN FROM SOMEONE ON THE OUTSIDE, BUT...
...IT IS THE MOST PLAUSIBLE THING TO THINK.
......
YURIA HASN'T BEEN BY TO SEE ME LATELY.
IN ANY CASE, IT MIGHT BE WORTH CHECKING OUT.

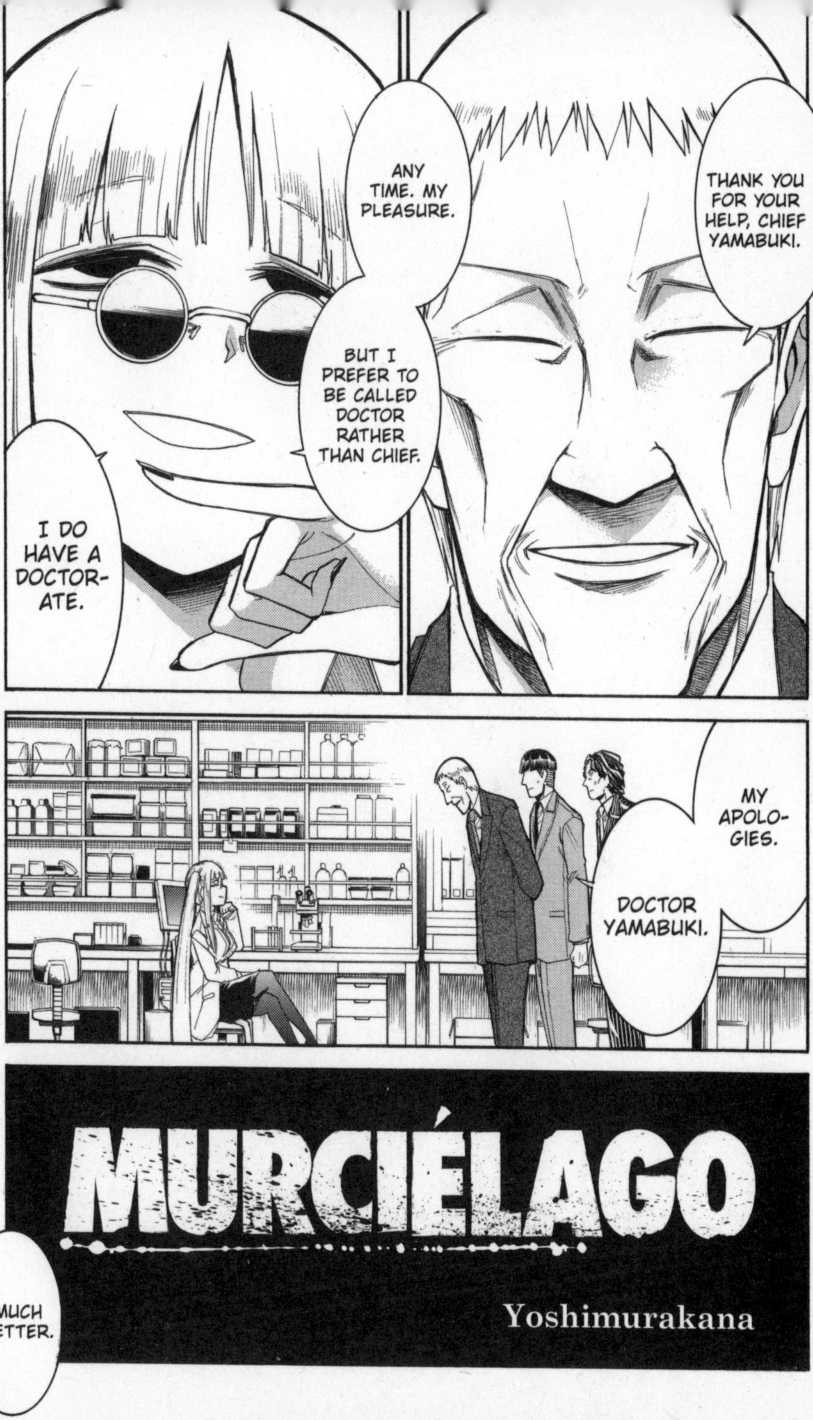
THANK YOU FOR YOUR HELP, CHIEF YAMABUKI.
ANY TIME. MY PLEASURE.
BUT I PREFER TO BE CALLED DOCTOR RATHER THAN CHIEF.
I DO HAVE A DOCTOR-ATE.
MY APOLO-GIES.
DOCTOR YAMABUKI.
MUCH BETTER.
MURCIÉLAGO
Yoshimurakana

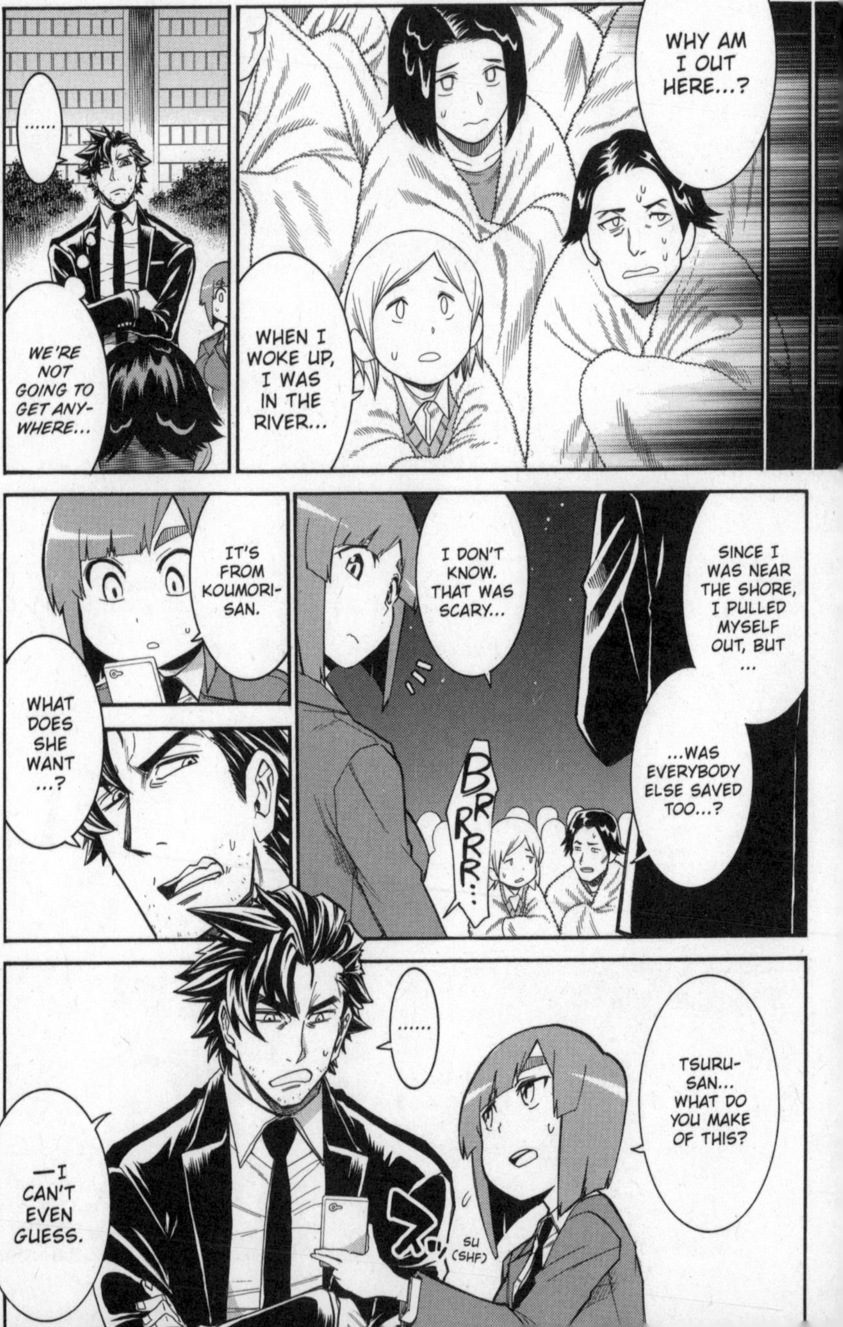
WHY AM I OUT HERE...?
WHEN I WOKE UP, I WAS IN THE RIVER...
......
WE'RE NOT GOING TO GET ANY-WHERE...
SINCE I WAS NEAR THE SHORE, I PULLED MYSELF OUT, BUT ...
...WAS EVERYBODY ELSE SAVED TOO...?
I DON'T KNOW. THAT WAS SCARY...
BRRRR...
IT'S FROM KOUMORI-SAN.
WHAT DOES SHE WANT ...?
TSURU-SAN... WHAT DO YOU MAKE OF THIS?
......
SU (SHF)
—I CAN'T EVEN GUESS.

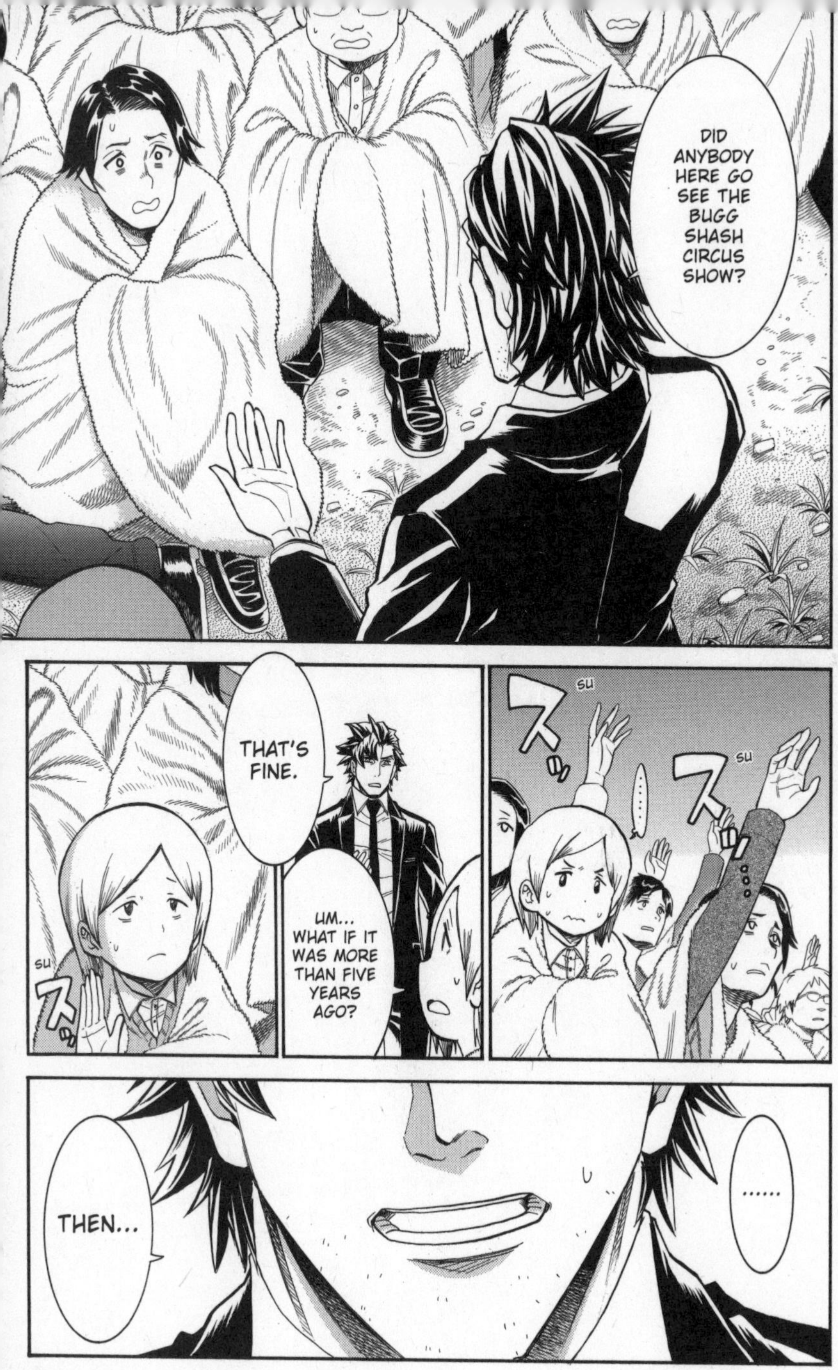
DID ANYBODY HERE GO SEE THE BUGG SHASH CIRCUS SHOW?
SU
ス
SU
ス
...
UM... WHAT IF IT WAS MORE THAN FIVE YEARS AGO?
THAT'S FINE.
SU
ス
......
THEN...

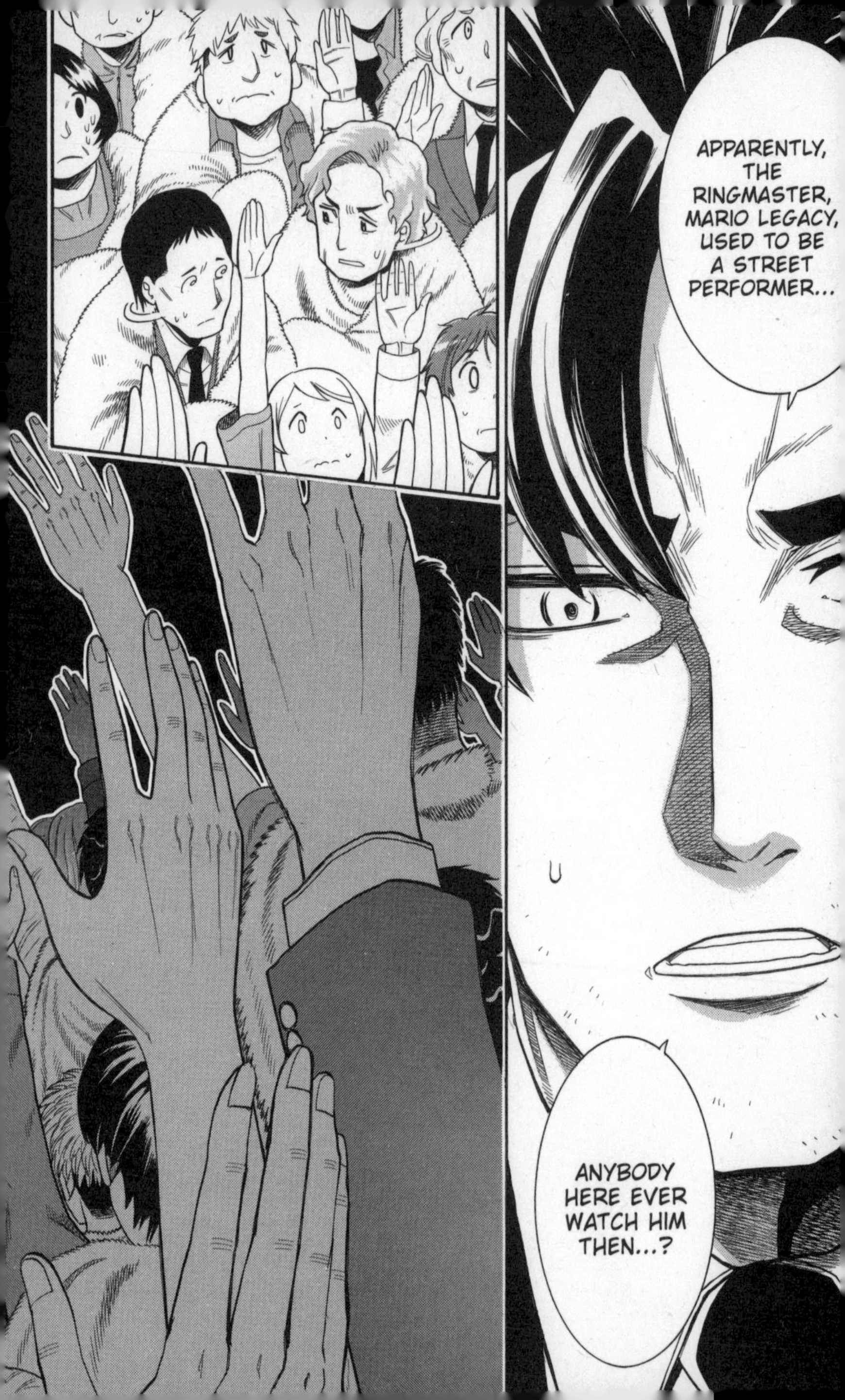
APPARENTLY, THE RINGMASTER, MARIO LEGACY, USED TO BE A STREET PERFORMER...
ANYBODY HERE EVER WATCH HIM THEN...?

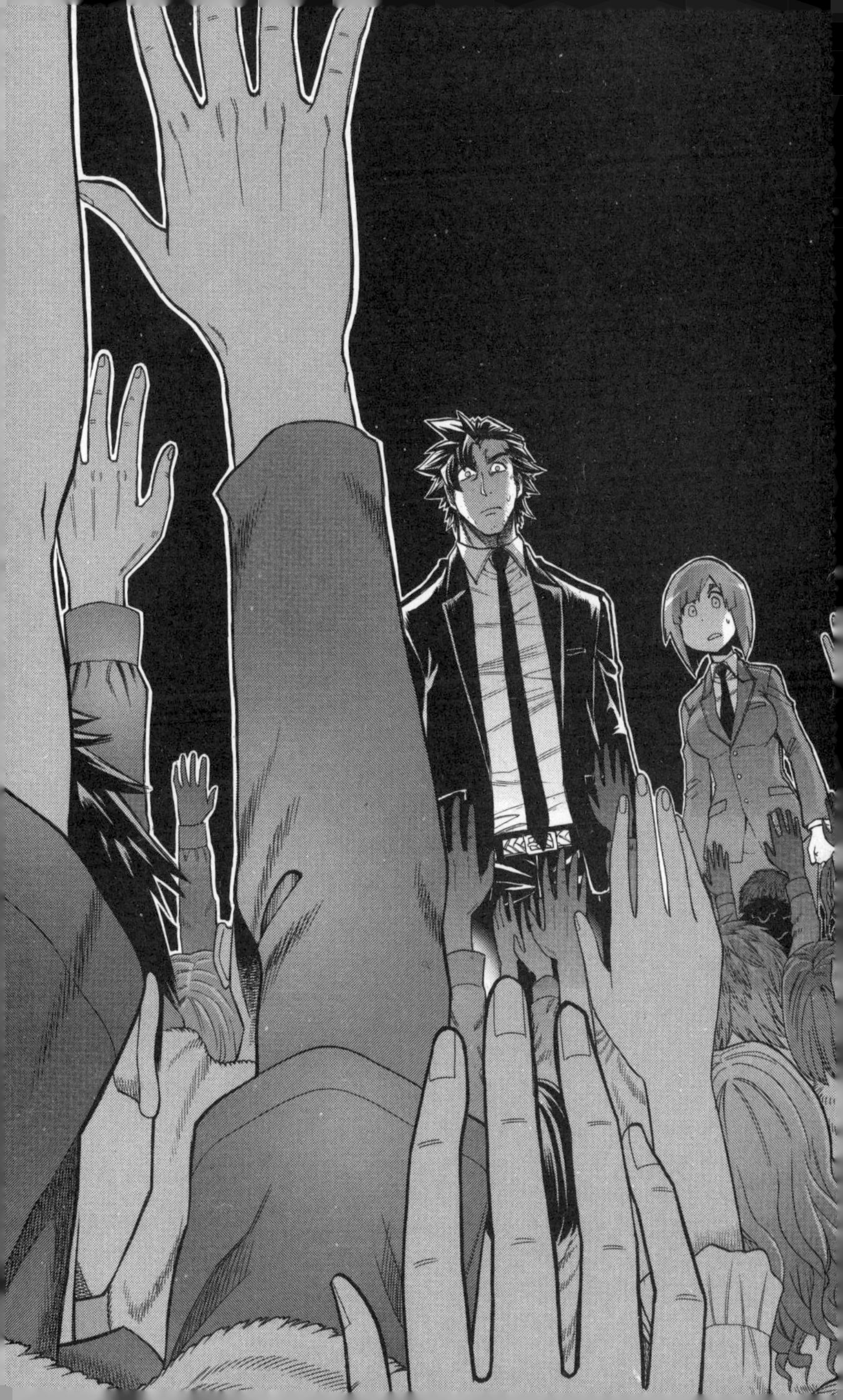

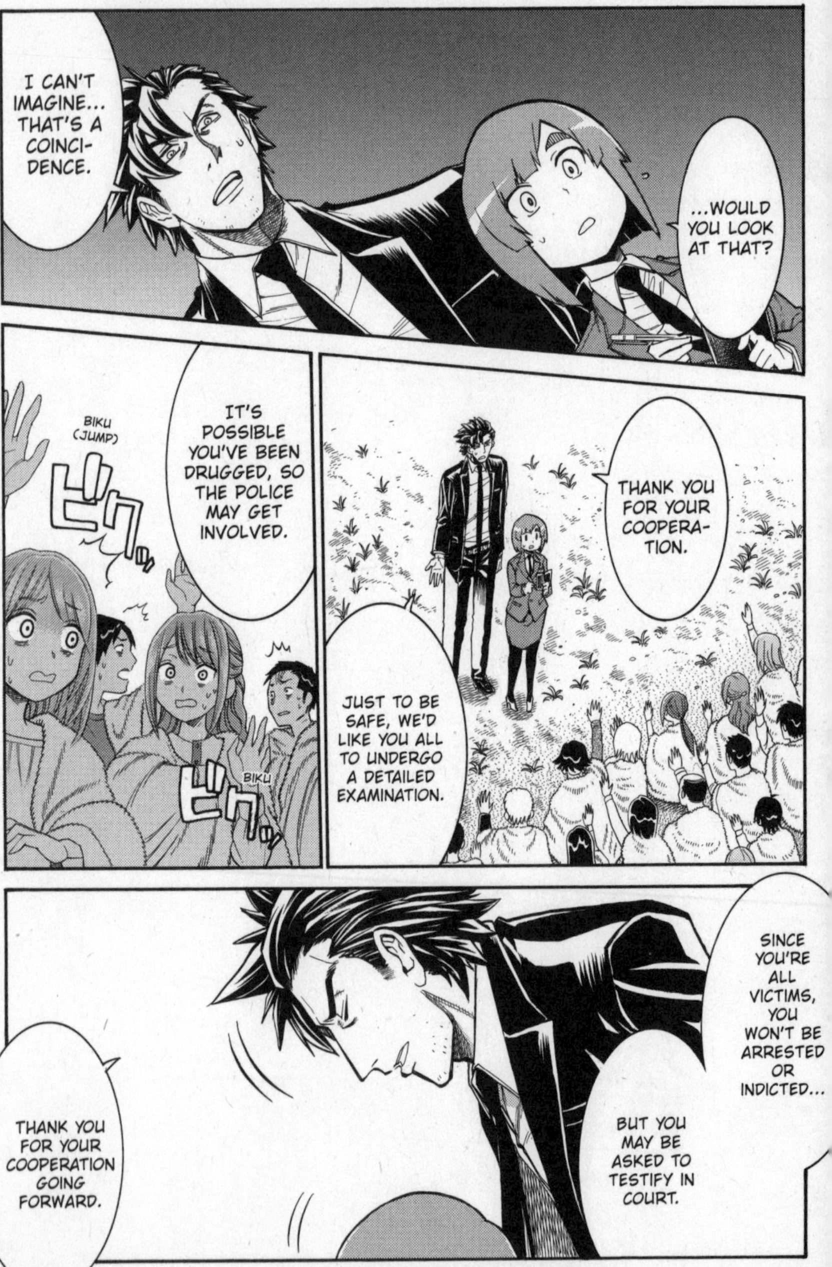
...WOULD YOU LOOK AT THAT?
I CAN'T IMAGINE... THAT'S A COINCI- DENCE.
THANK YOU FOR YOUR COOPERA- TION.
JUST TO BE SAFE, WE'D LIKE YOU ALL TO UNDERGO A DETAILED EXAMINATION.
IT'S POSSIBLE YOU'VE BEEN DRUGGED, SO THE POLICE MAY GET INVOLVED.
BIKU (JUMP)
BIKU
SINCE YOU'RE ALL VICTIMS, YOU WON'T BE ARRESTED OR INDICTED...
BUT YOU MAY BE ASKED TO TESTIFY IN COURT.
THANK YOU FOR YOUR COOPERATION GOING FORWARD.

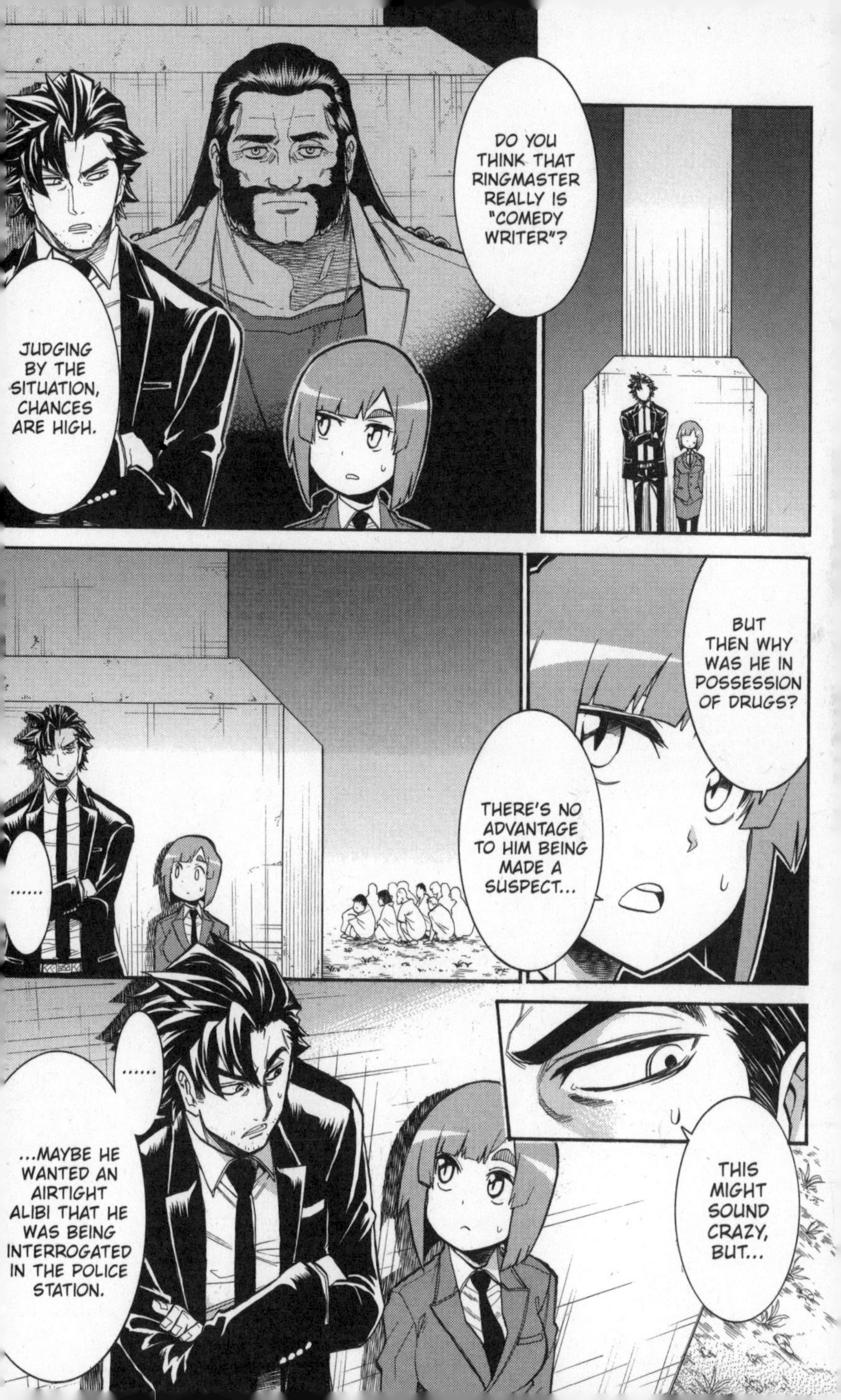
DO YOU THINK THAT RINGMASTER REALLY IS "COMEDY WRITER"?
JUDGING BY THE SITUATION, CHANCES ARE HIGH.
BUT THEN WHY WAS HE IN POSSESSION OF DRUGS?
THERE'S NO ADVANTAGE TO HIM BEING MADE A SUSPECT...
......
THIS MIGHT SOUND CRAZY, BUT...
......
...MAYBE HE WANTED AN AIRTIGHT ALIBI THAT HE WAS BEING INTERROGATED IN THE POLICE STATION.

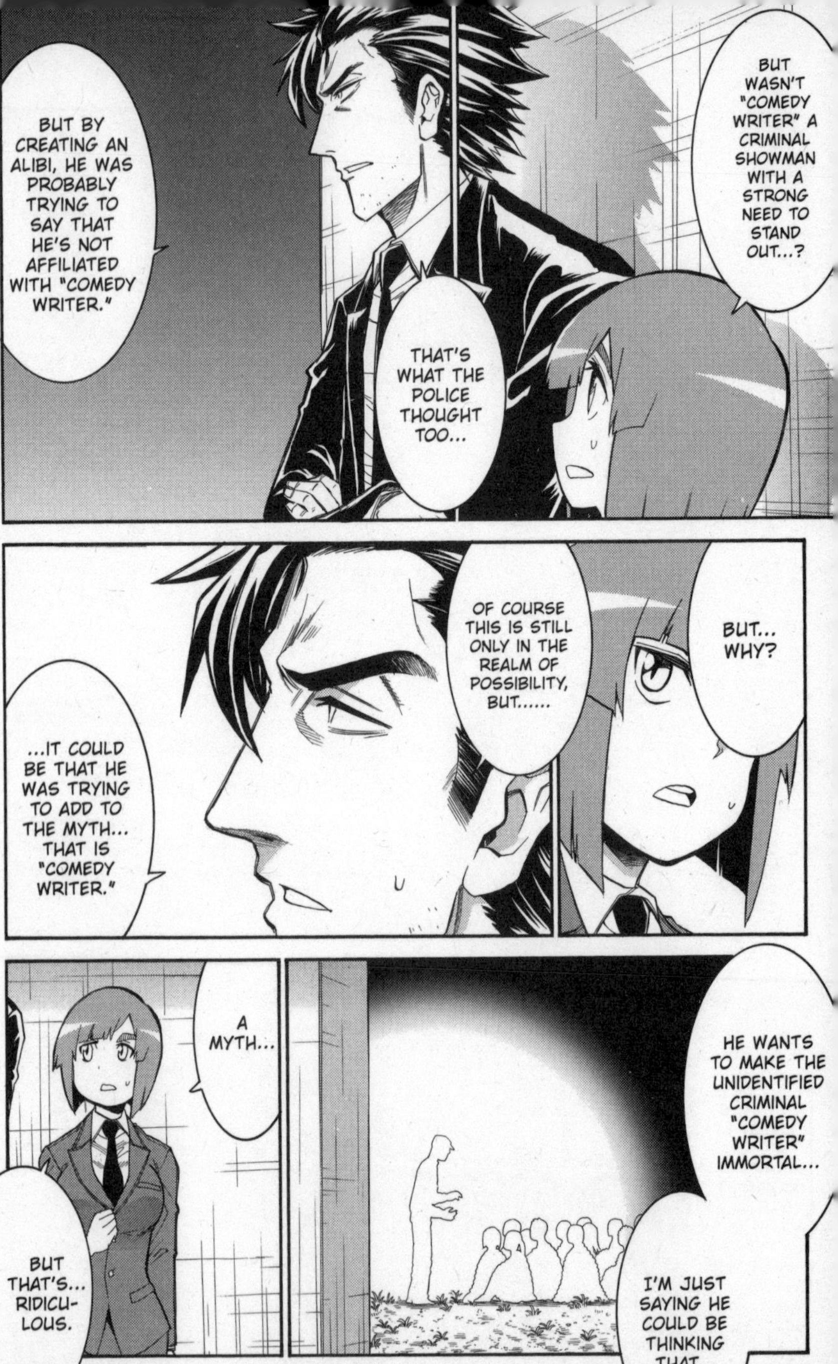
BUT WASN'T "COMEDY WRITER" A CRIMINAL SHOWMAN WITH A STRONG NEED TO STAND OUT...?
THAT'S WHAT THE POLICE THOUGHT TOO...
BUT BY CREATING AN ALIBI, HE WAS PROBABLY TRYING TO SAY THAT HE'S NOT AFFILIATED WITH "COMEDY WRITER."
BUT... WHY?
OF COURSE THIS IS STILL ONLY IN THE REALM OF POSSIBILITY, BUT......
...IT COULD BE THAT HE WAS TRYING TO ADD TO THE MYTH... THAT IS "COMEDY WRITER."
HE WANTS TO MAKE THE UNIDENTIFIED CRIMINAL "COMEDY WRITER" IMMORTAL...
I'M JUST SAYING HE COULD BE THINKING THAT...
A MYTH...
BUT THAT'S... RIDICULOUS.

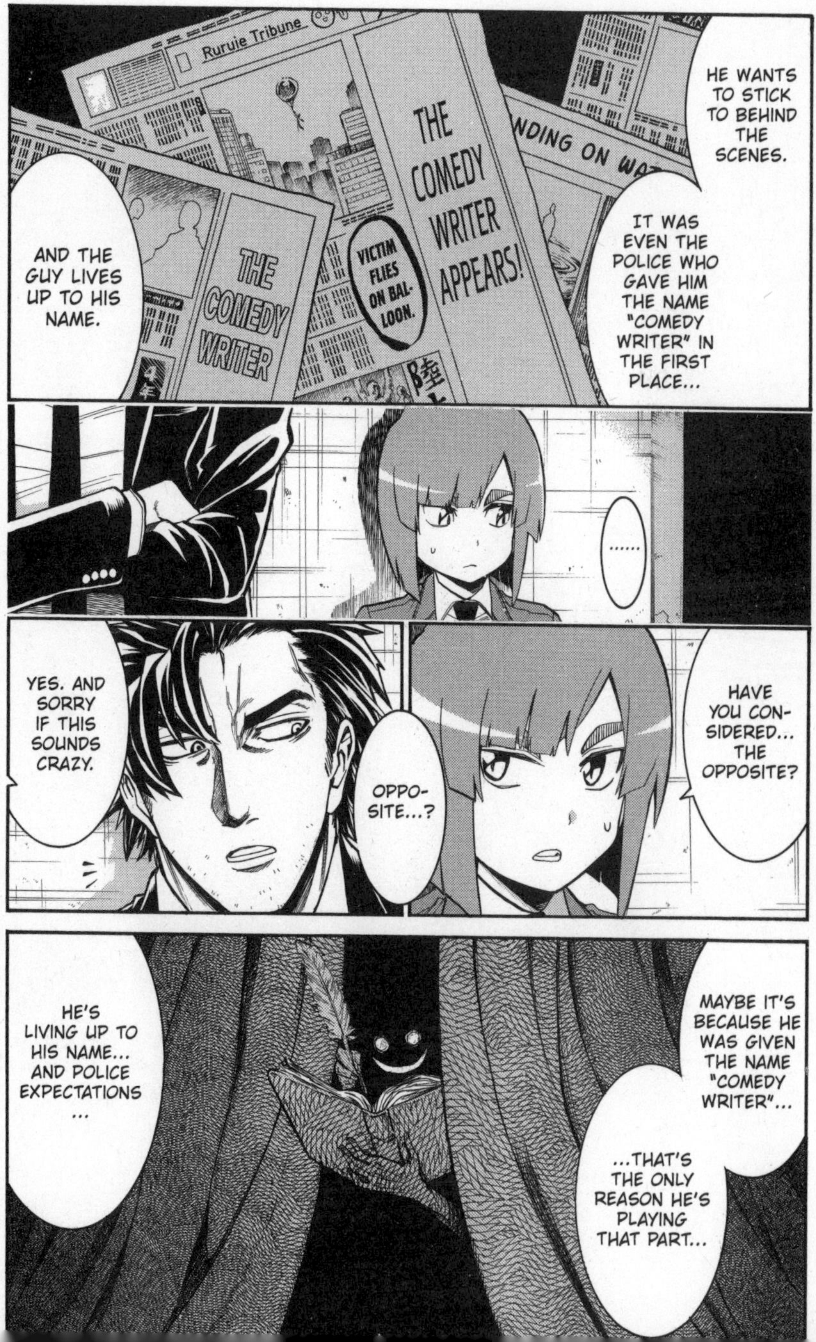
HE WANTS TO STICK TO BEHIND THE SCENES.
Ruruie Tribune
THE COMEDY WRITER APPEARS!
IT WAS EVEN THE POLICE WHO GAVE HIM THE NAME "COMEDY WRITER" IN THE FIRST PLACE...
VICTIM FLIES ON BALLOON.
THE COMEDY WRITER
AND THE GUY LIVES UP TO HIS NAME.
......
HAVE YOU CONSIDERED... THE OPPOSITE?
OPPO-SITE...?
YES. AND SORRY IF THIS SOUNDS CRAZY.
MAYBE IT'S BECAUSE HE WAS GIVEN THE NAME "COMEDY WRITER"...
...THAT'S THE ONLY REASON HE'S PLAYING THAT PART...
HE'S LIVING UP TO HIS NAME... AND POLICE EXPECTATIONS ...

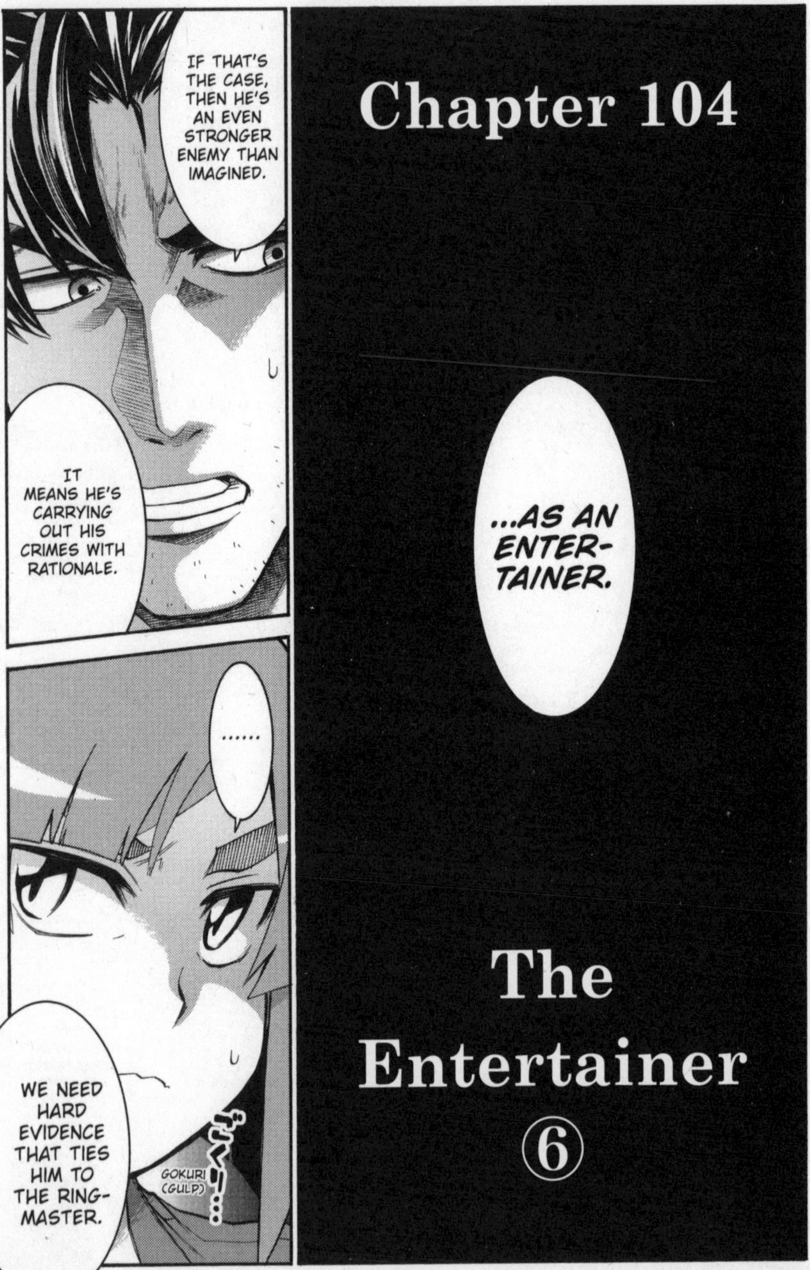
Chapter 104
...AS AN ENTERTAINER.
The Entertainer ⑥
IF THAT'S THE CASE, THEN HE'S AN EVEN STRONGER ENEMY THAN IMAGINED.
IT MEANS HE'S CARRYING OUT HIS CRIMES WITH RATIONALE.
......
WE NEED HARD EVIDENCE THAT TIES HIM TO THE RING-MASTER.
GOKURI (GULP)

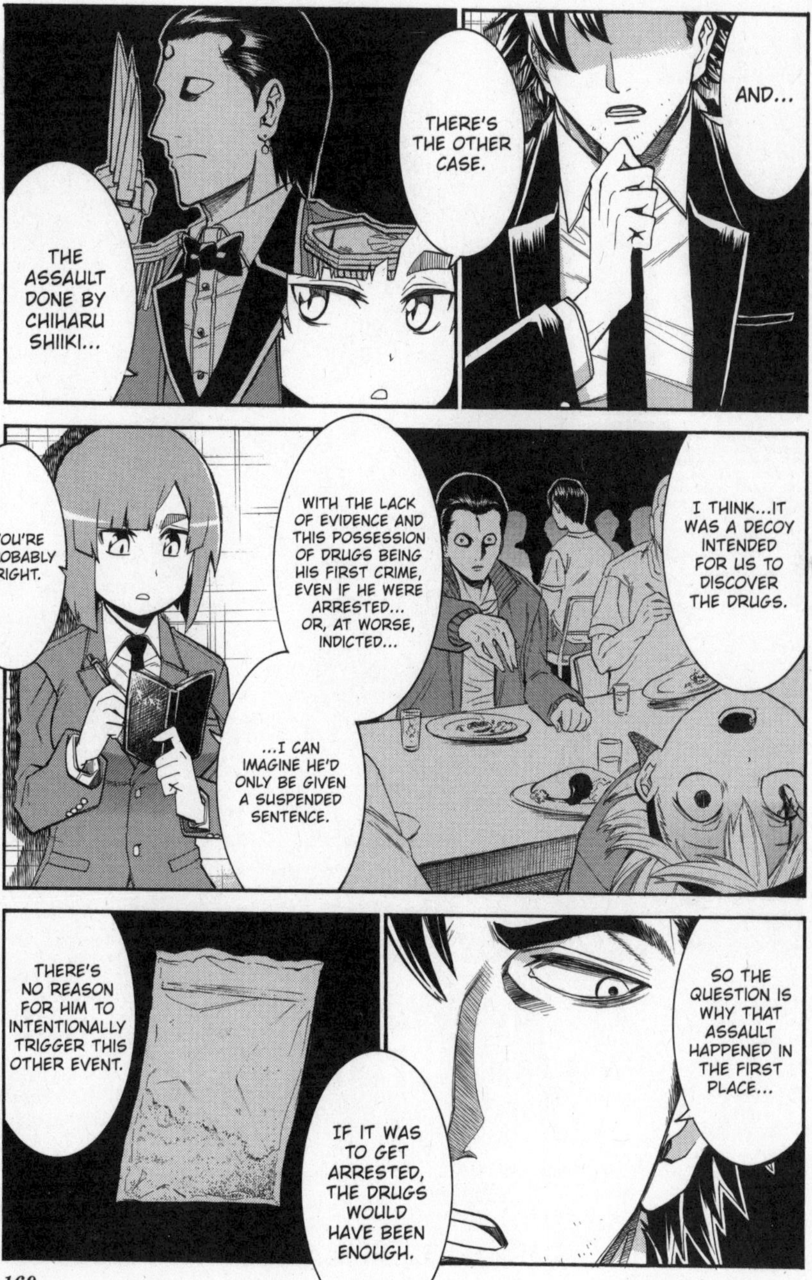
AND...
THERE'S THE OTHER CASE.
THE ASSAULT DONE BY CHIHARU SHIIKI...
I THINK...IT WAS A DECOY INTENDED FOR US TO DISCOVER THE DRUGS.
WITH THE LACK OF EVIDENCE AND THIS POSSESSION OF DRUGS BEING HIS FIRST CRIME, EVEN IF HE WERE ARRESTED... OR, AT WORSE, INDICTED...
...I CAN IMAGINE HE'D ONLY BE GIVEN A SUSPENDED SENTENCE.
YOU'RE PROBABLY RIGHT.
SO THE QUESTION IS WHY THAT ASSAULT HAPPENED IN THE FIRST PLACE...
IF IT WAS TO GET ARRESTED, THE DRUGS WOULD HAVE BEEN ENOUGH.
THERE'S NO REASON FOR HIM TO INTENTIONALLY TRIGGER THIS OTHER EVENT.

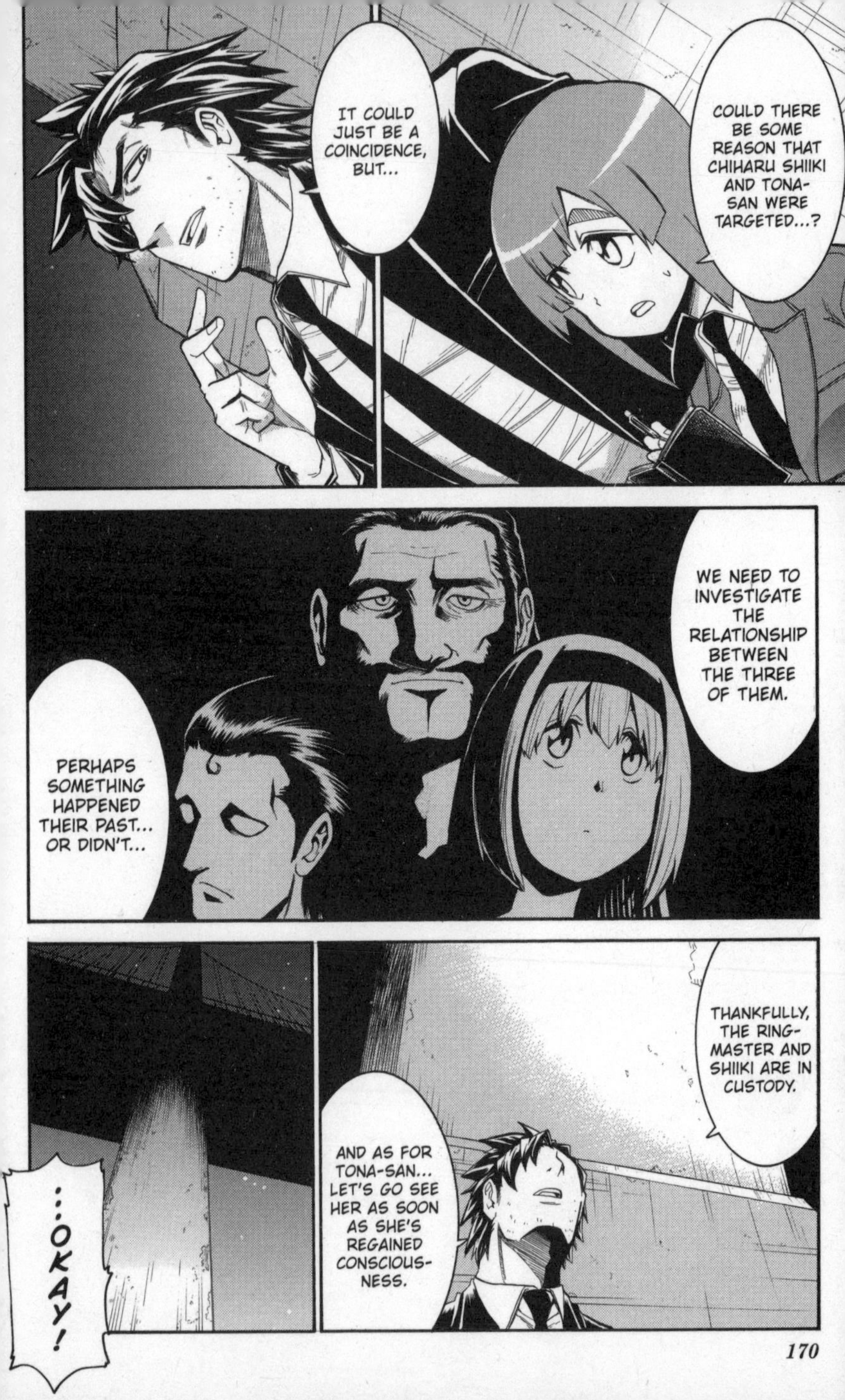
COULD THERE BE SOME REASON THAT CHIHARU SHIIKI AND TONA-SAN WERE TARGETED...?
IT COULD JUST BE A COINCIDENCE, BUT...
WE NEED TO INVESTIGATE THE RELATIONSHIP BETWEEN THE THREE OF THEM.
PERHAPS SOMETHING HAPPENED THEIR PAST... OR DIDN'T...
THANKFULLY, THE RING-MASTER AND SHIIKI ARE IN CUSTODY.
AND AS FOR TONA-SAN... LET'S GO SEE HER AS SOON AS SHE'S REGAINED CONSCIOUS-NESS.
...OKAY!

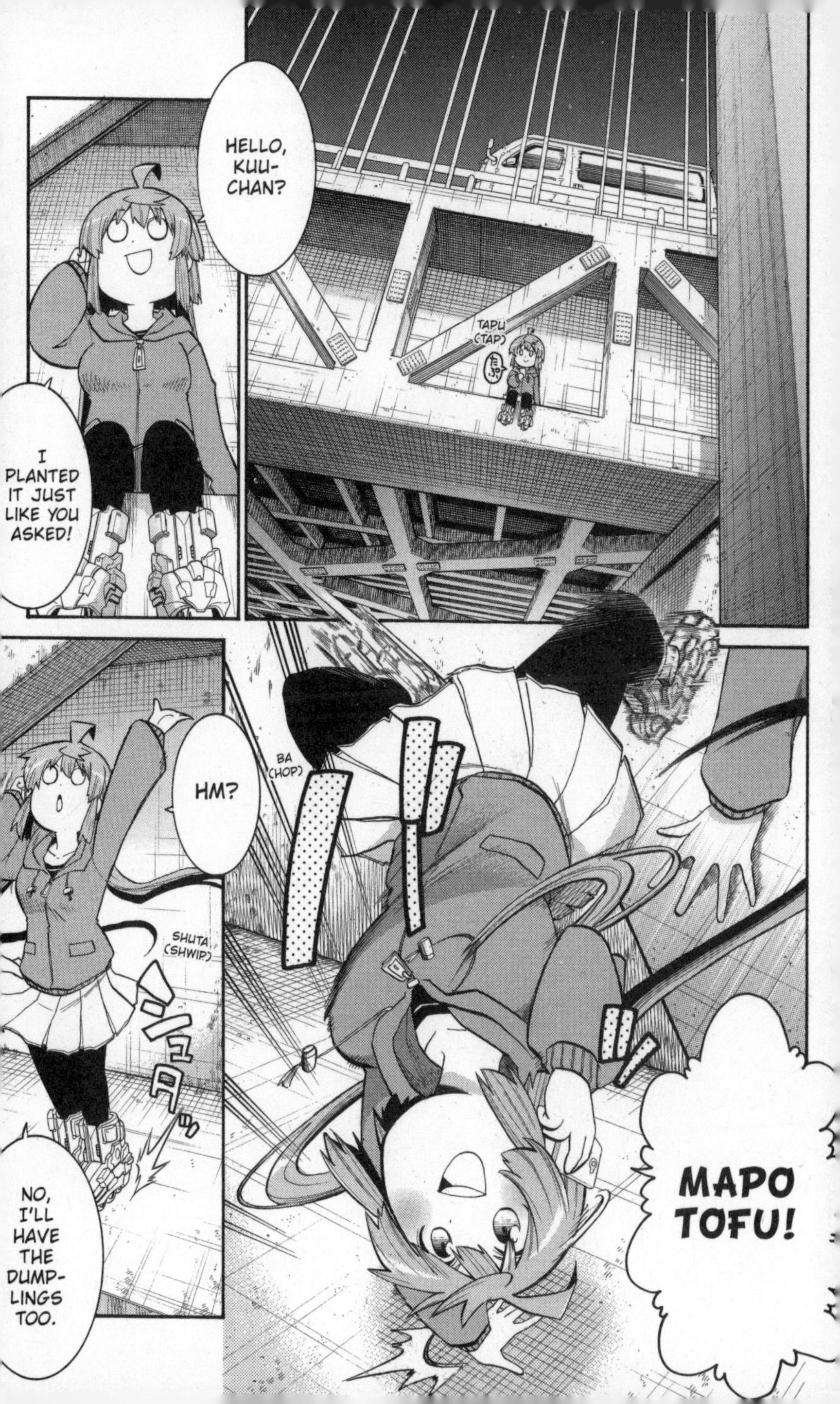
TAPU (TAP)
HELLO, KUU-CHAN?
I PLANTED IT JUST LIKE YOU ASKED!
BA (HOP)
MAPO TOFU!
HM?
SHUTA (SHWIP)
NO, I'LL HAVE THE DUMPLINGS TOO.

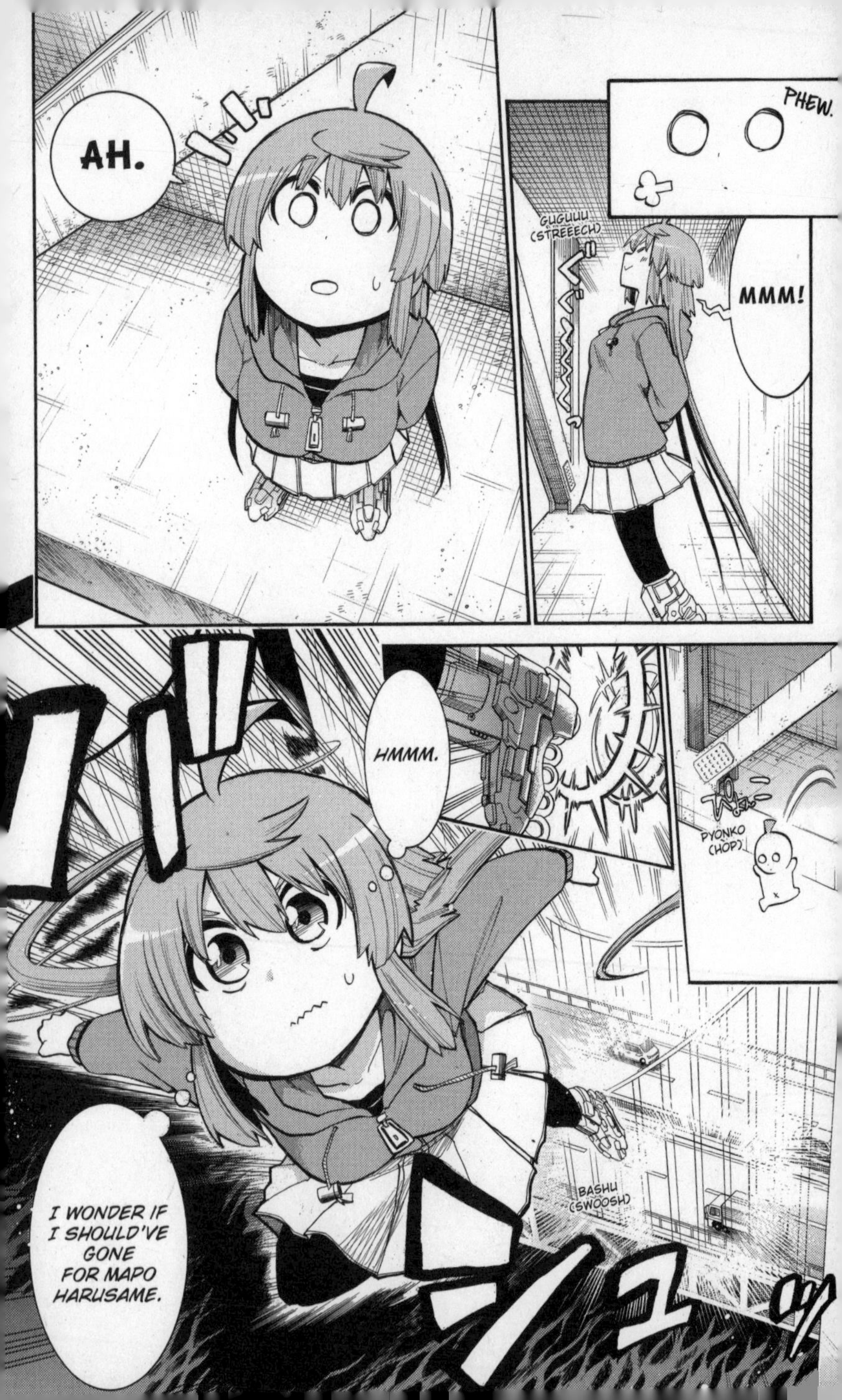
PHEW.
MMM!
GUGUUU (STREEECH)
AH.
PYONKO (HOP)
HMMM.
BASHU (SWOOSH)
I WONDER IF I SHOULD'VE GONE FOR MAPO HARUSAME.

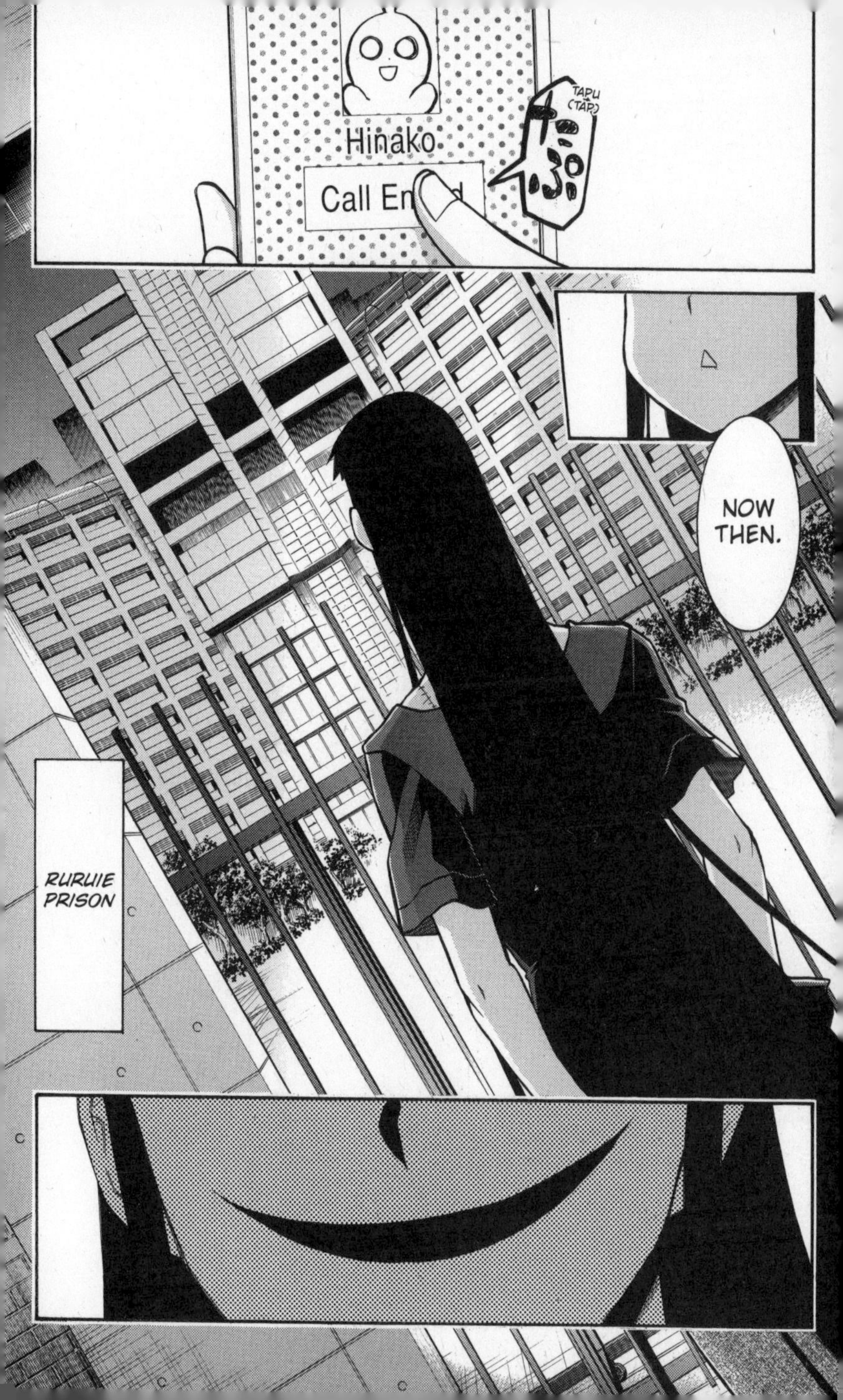
TAPU (TAP)
Hinako
Call En
NOW THEN.
RURUIE PRISON

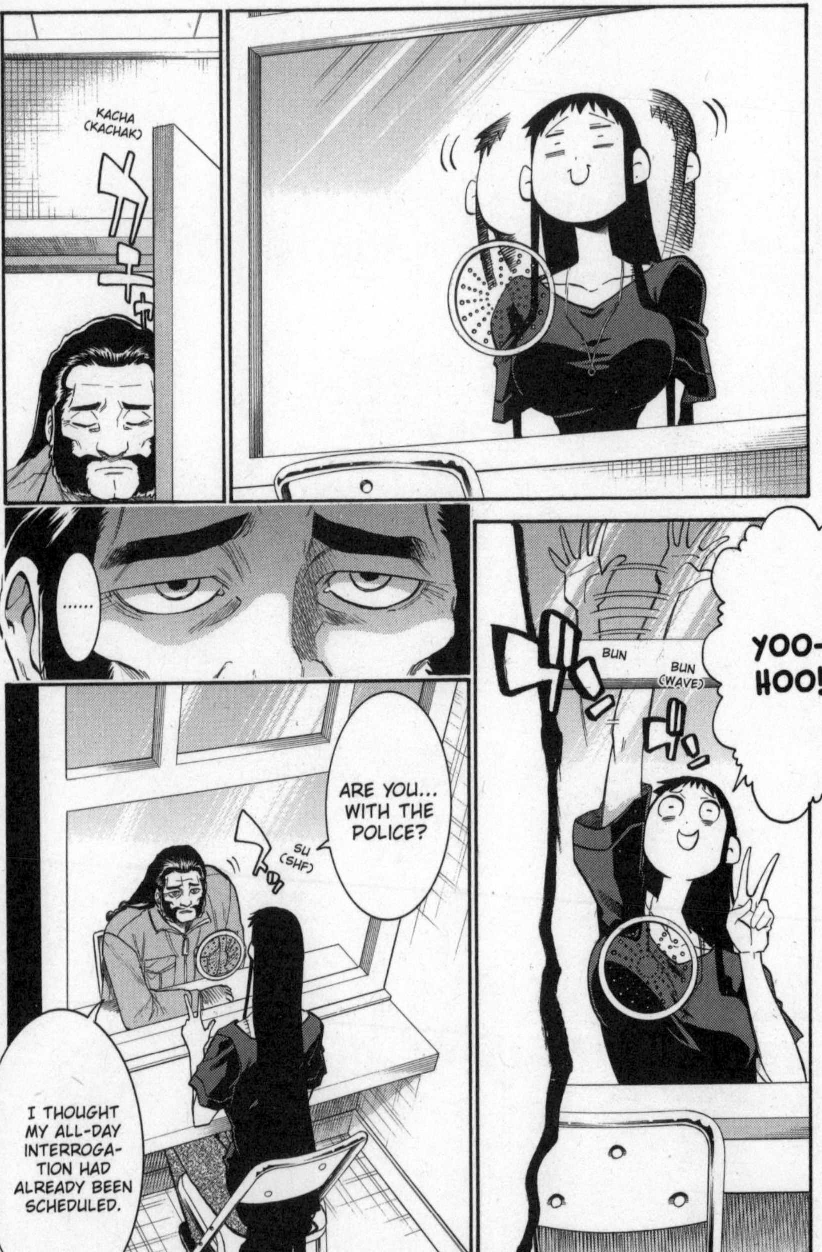
KACHA (KACHAK)
YOO-HOO!
BUN
BUN (WAVE)
......
ARE YOU... WITH THE POLICE?
SU (SHF)
I THOUGHT MY ALL-DAY INTERROGATION HAD ALREADY BEEN SCHEDULED.

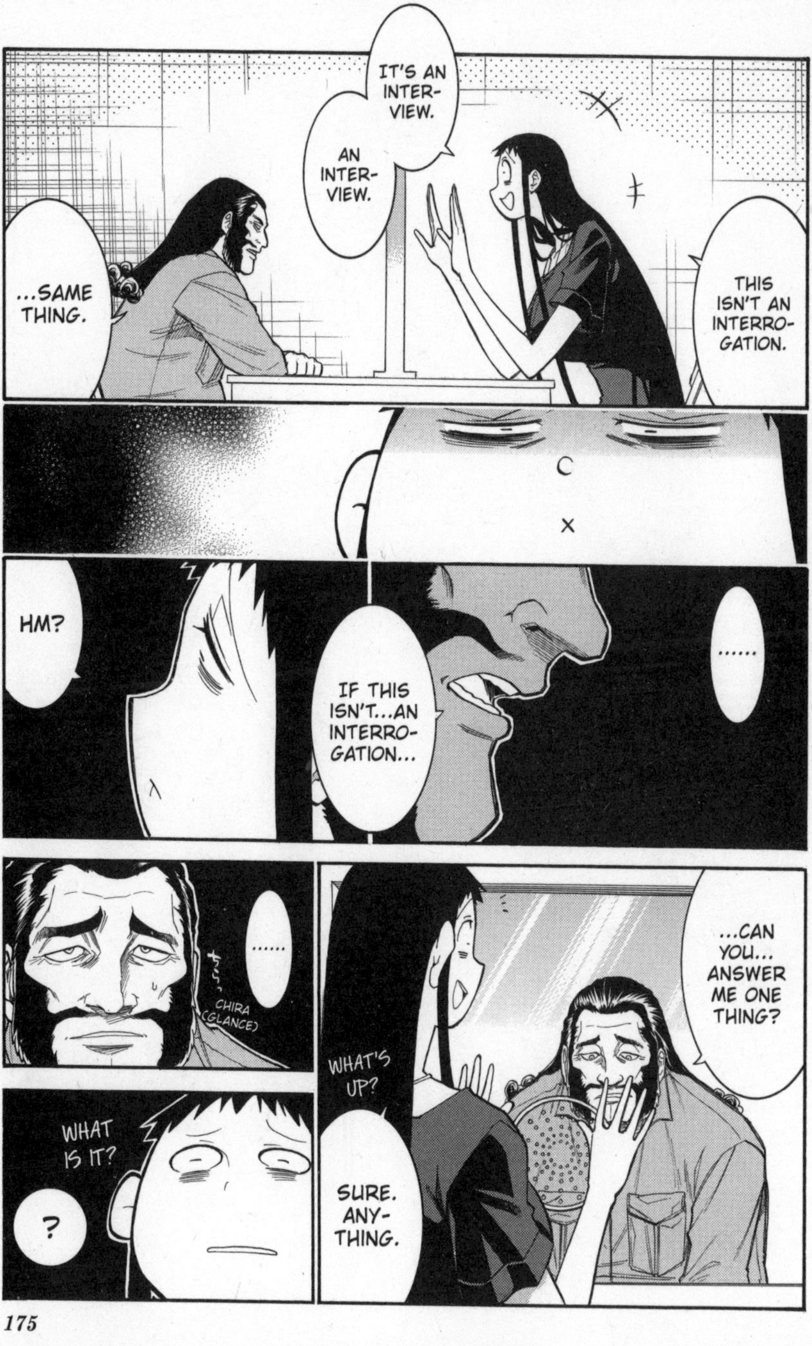
THIS ISN'T AN INTERROGATION.
IT'S AN INTERVIEW.
AN INTERVIEW.
...SAME THING.
......
IF THIS ISN'T...AN INTERROGATION...
HM?
...CAN YOU... ANSWER ME ONE THING?
WHAT'S UP?
SURE. ANYTHING.
......
CHIRA (GLANCE)
WHAT IS IT?
?

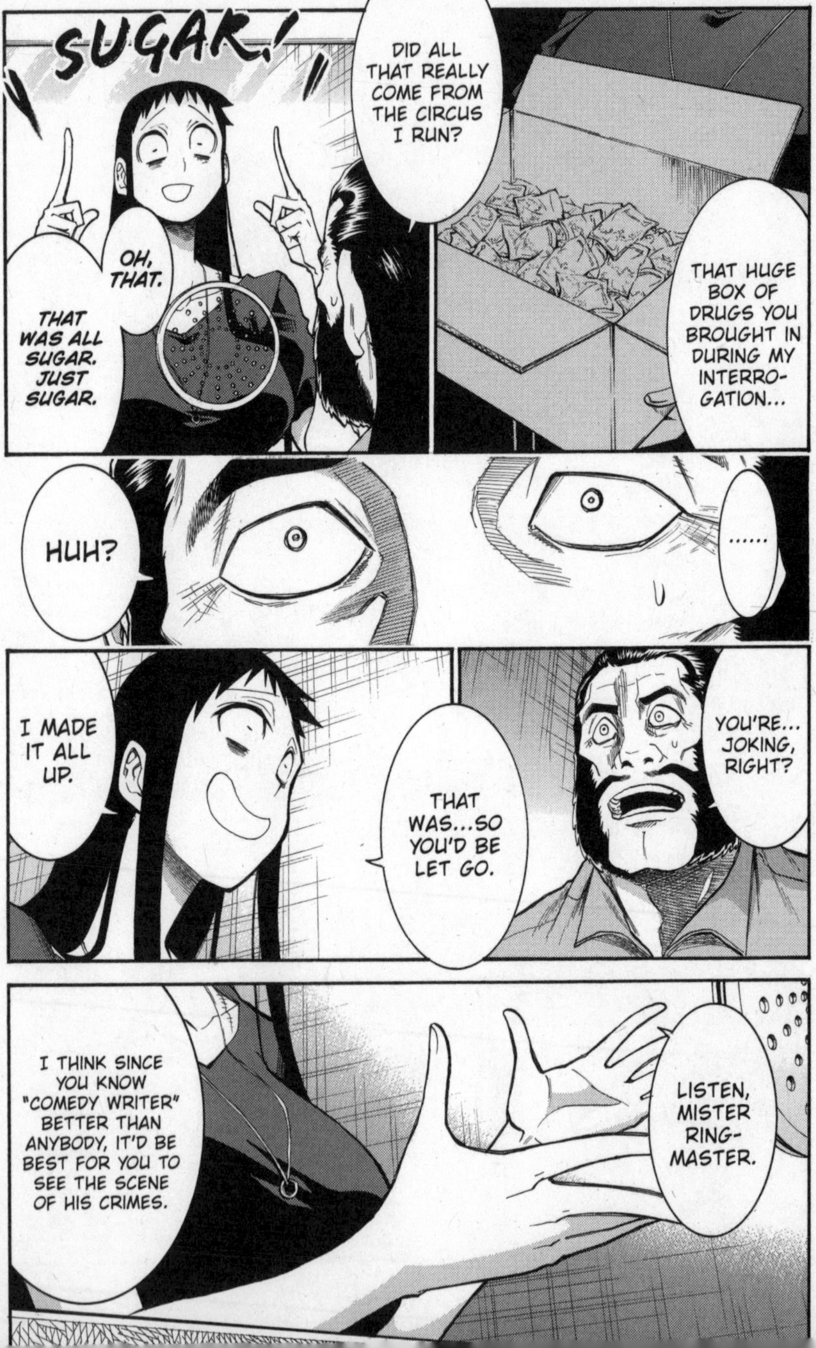
THAT HUGE BOX OF DRUGS YOU BROUGHT IN DURING MY INTERRO-GATION...
DID ALL THAT REALLY COME FROM THE CIRCUS I RUN?
SUGAR!
OH, THAT.
THAT WAS ALL SUGAR. JUST SUGAR.
......
HUH?
YOU'RE... JOKING, RIGHT?
I MADE IT ALL UP.
THAT WAS...SO YOU'D BE LET GO.
LISTEN, MISTER RING-MASTER.
I THINK SINCE YOU KNOW "COMEDY WRITER" BETTER THAN ANYBODY, IT'D BE BEST FOR YOU TO SEE THE SCENE OF HIS CRIMES.

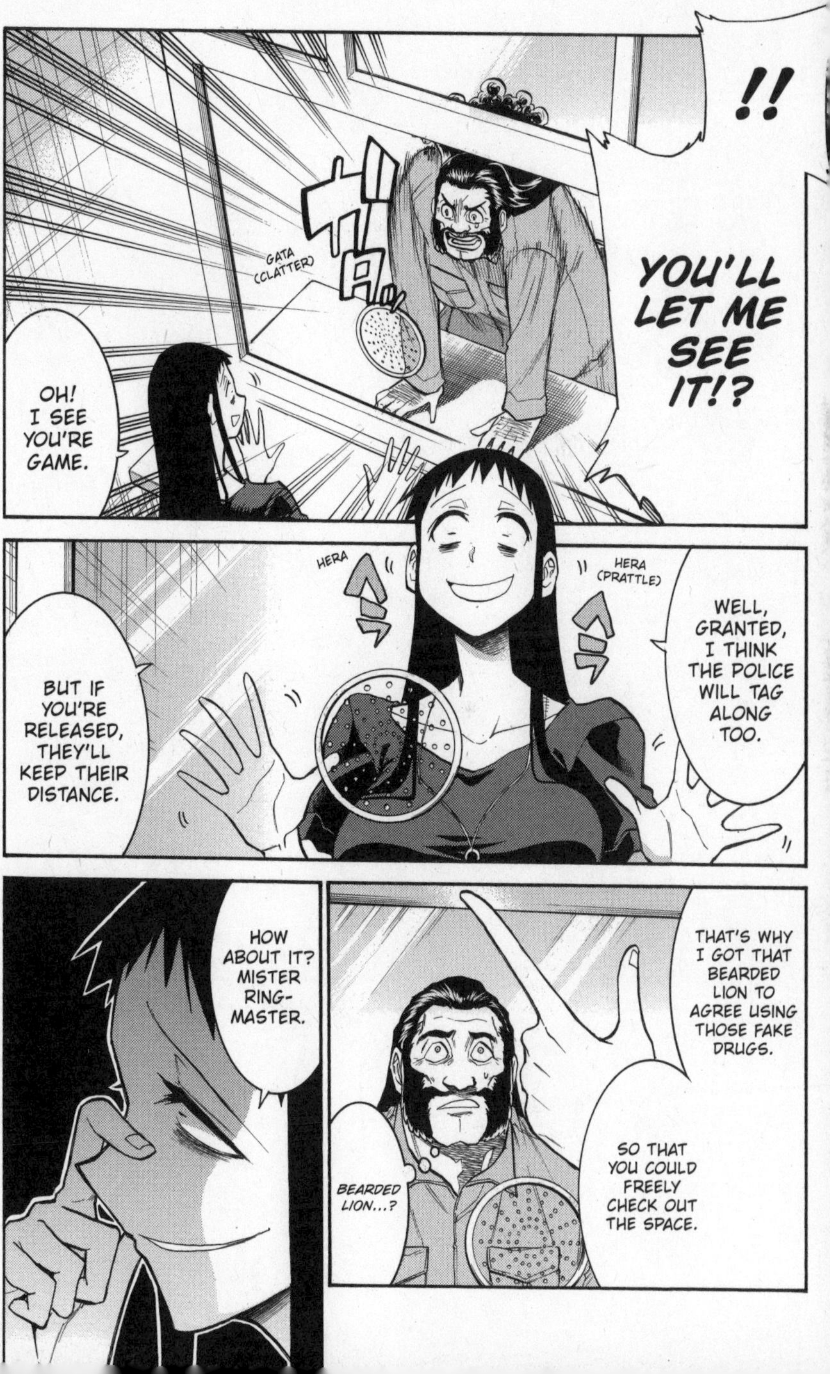
!!
YOU'LL LET ME SEE IT!?
GATA (CLATTER)
OH! I SEE YOU'RE GAME.
HERA (PRATTLE)
WELL, GRANTED, I THINK THE POLICE WILL TAG ALONG TOO.
HERA
BUT IF YOU'RE RELEASED, THEY'LL KEEP THEIR DISTANCE.
THAT'S WHY I GOT THAT BEARDED LION TO AGREE USING THOSE FAKE DRUGS.
SO THAT YOU COULD FREELY CHECK OUT THE SPACE.
BEARDED LION...?
HOW ABOUT IT? MISTER RING-MASTER.

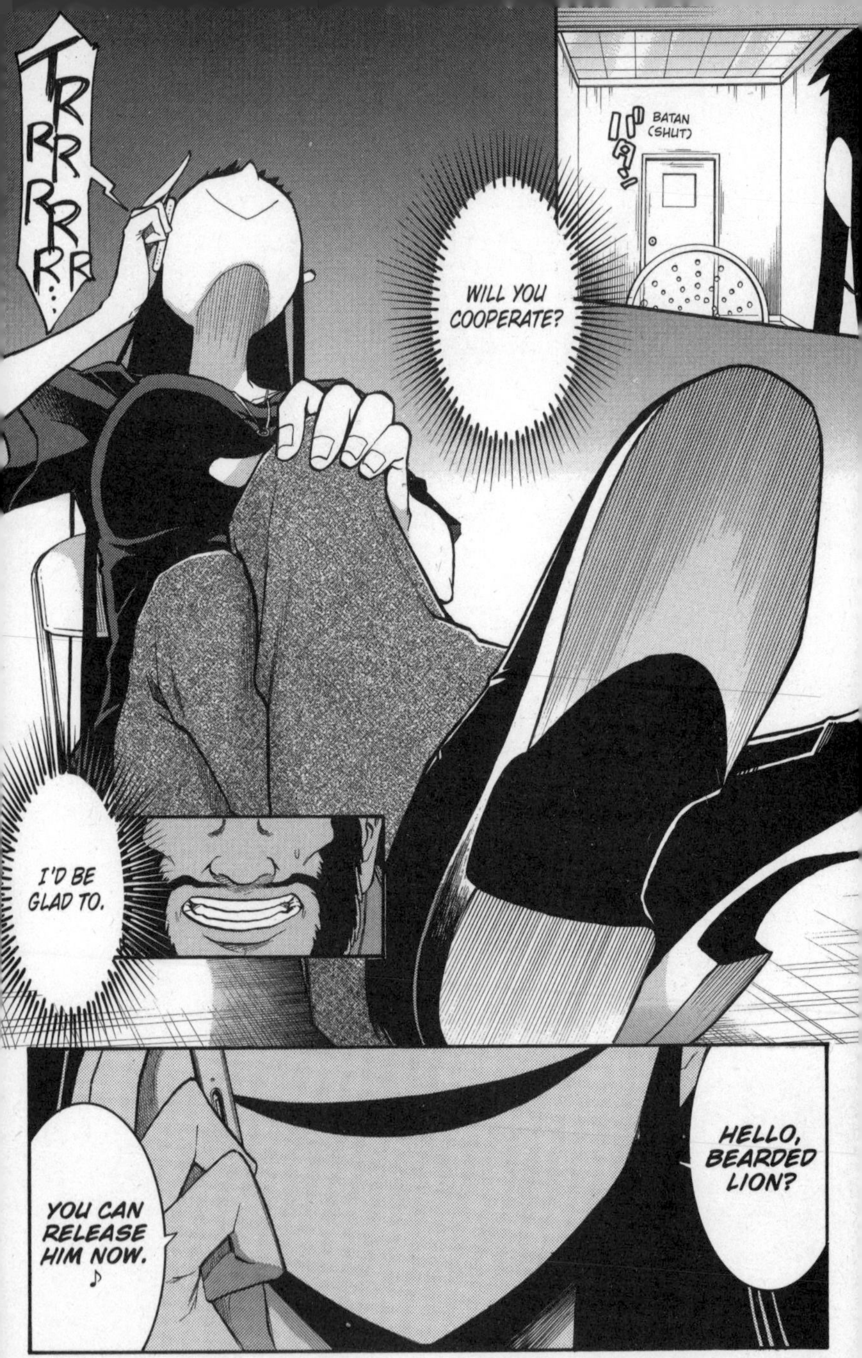
バタン
BATAN (SHUT)
WILL YOU COOPERATE?
TRRRRRRRR...
I'D BE GLAD TO.
HELLO, BEARDED LION?
YOU CAN RELEASE HIM NOW. ♪

MURCIÉLAGO

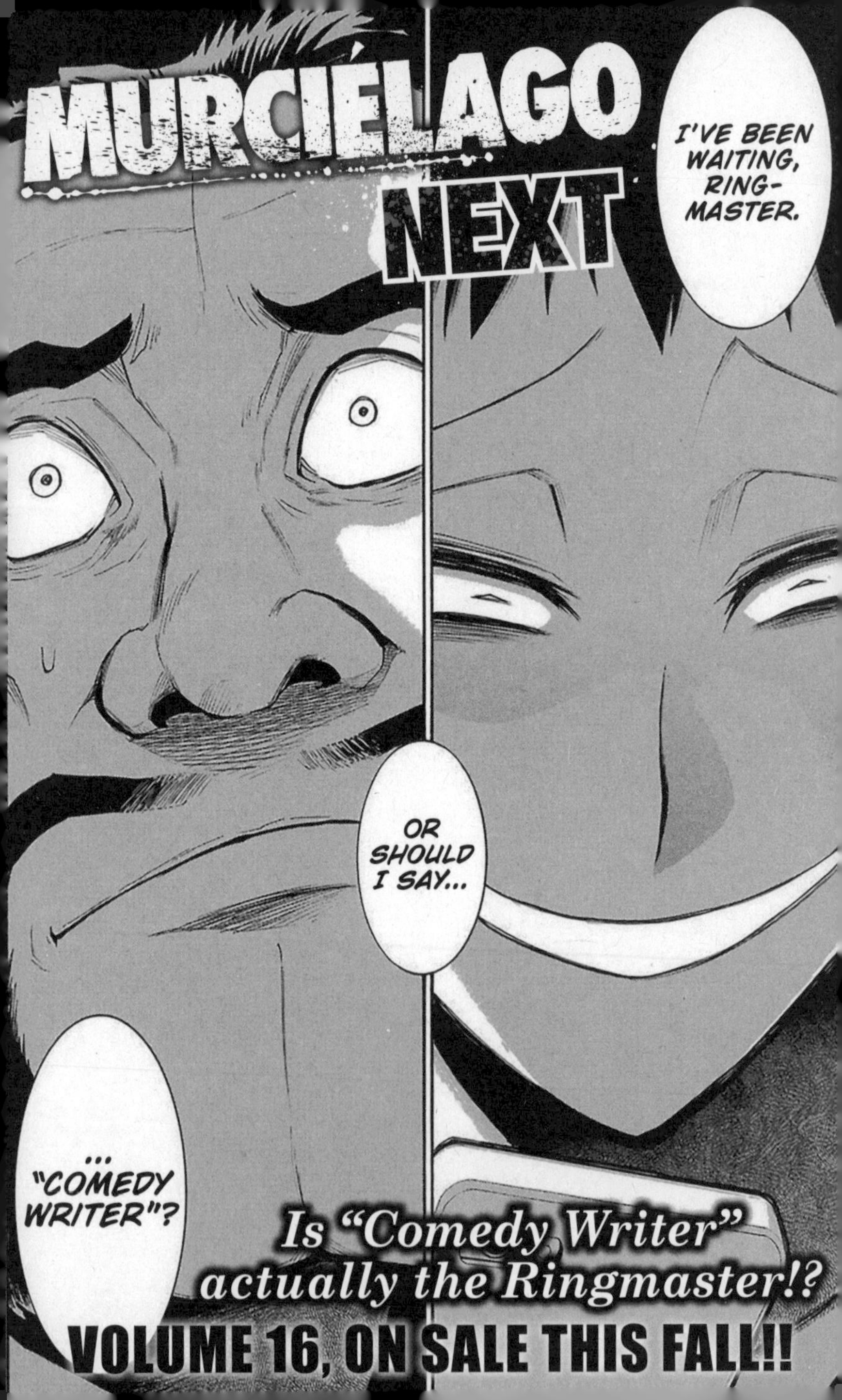
MURCIÉLAGO
NEXT
I'VE BEEN WAITING, RING-MASTER.
OR SHOULD I SAY...
..."COMEDY WRITER"?
Is "Comedy Writer" actually the Ringmaster!?
VOLUME 16, ON SALE THIS FALL!!

MURCIÉLAGO

MURCIÉLAGO

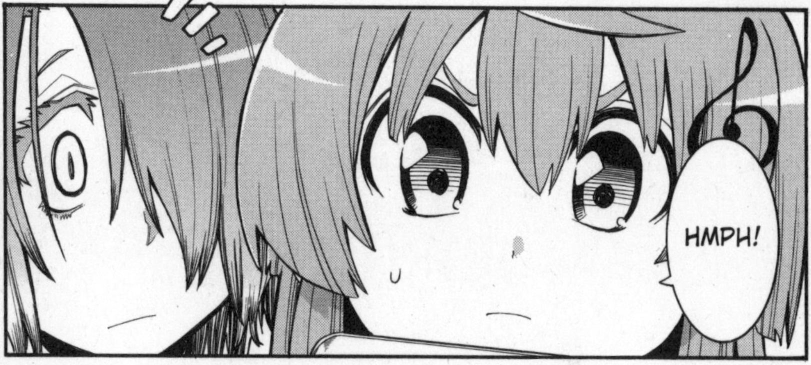
HMPH!

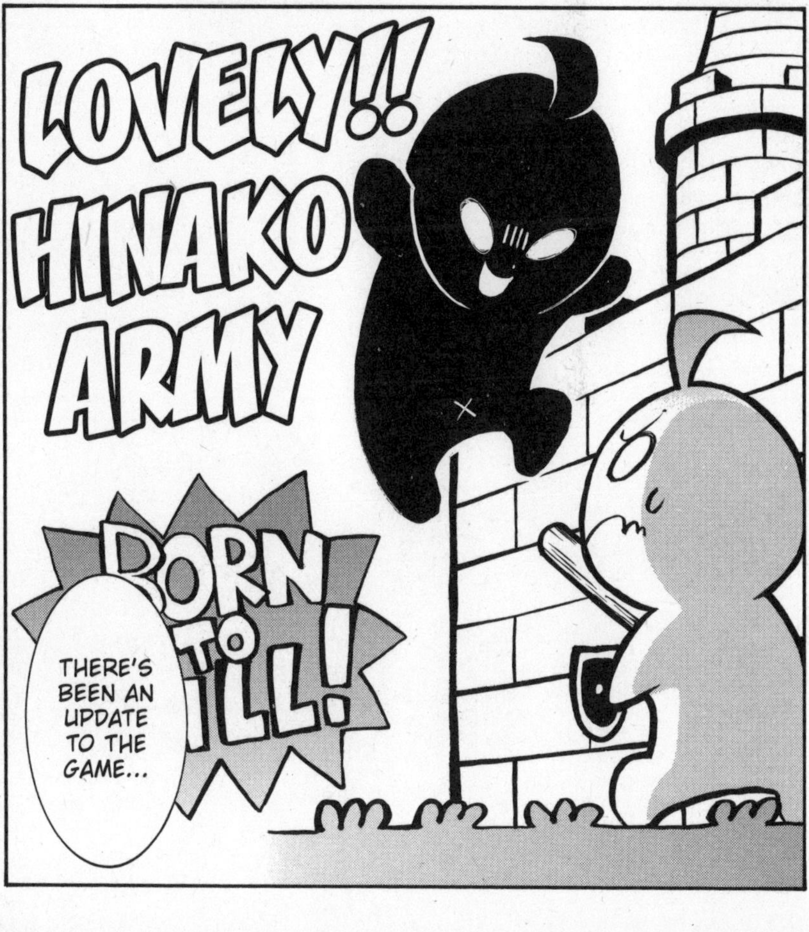
LOVELY!! HINAKO ARMY
BORN TO ILL!
THERE'S BEEN AN UPDATE TO THE GAME...

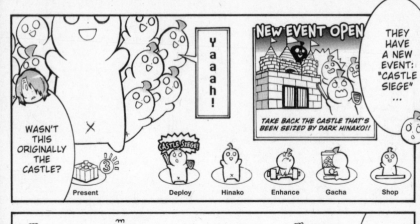

THEY HAVE A NEW EVENT: "CASTLE SIEGE"...

**NEW EVENT OPEN!**

TAKE BACK THE CASTLE THAT'S BEEN SEIZED BY DARK HINAKO!!

Yaaah!

WASN'T THIS ORIGINALLY THE CASTLE?

CASTLE SIEGE!

Present    Deploy    Hinako    Enhance    Gacha    Shop

THERE'S A CASTLE ON THE MAP!

LOOKS MORE LIKE A FORTRESS TO ME.

YAAAH!

LET'S HIT THE DOOR TO KNOCK IT DOWN.

OH NO! IT'S NOT WORKING!!

CASTLE

I MEAN, IT IS, BUT JUST BARE-LY!!

POKO

POKO (BONK)

POKO

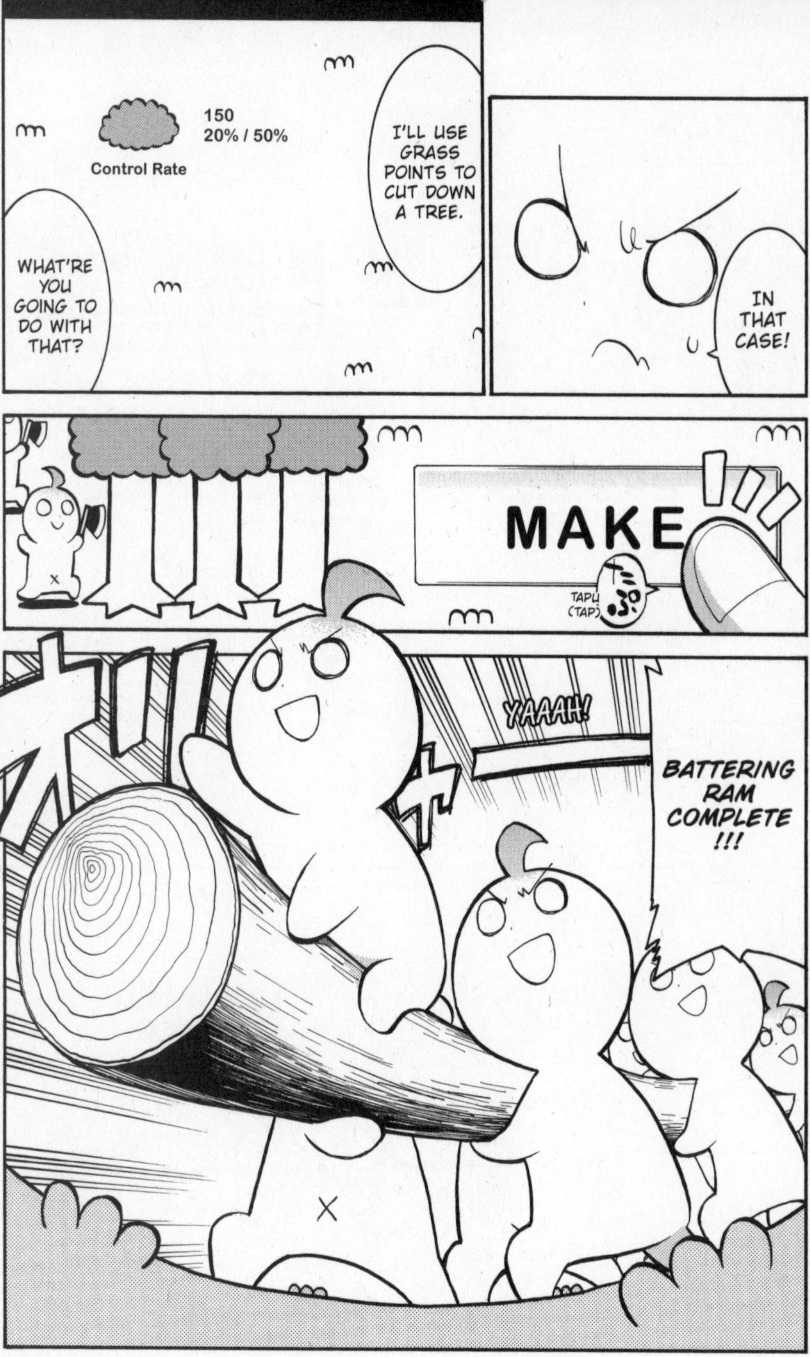
IN THAT CASE!
I'LL USE GRASS POINTS TO CUT DOWN A TREE.
150
20% / 50%
Control Rate
WHAT'RE YOU GOING TO DO WITH THAT?
MAKE
TAPU (TAP)
BATTERING RAM COMPLETE !!!
YAAAH!

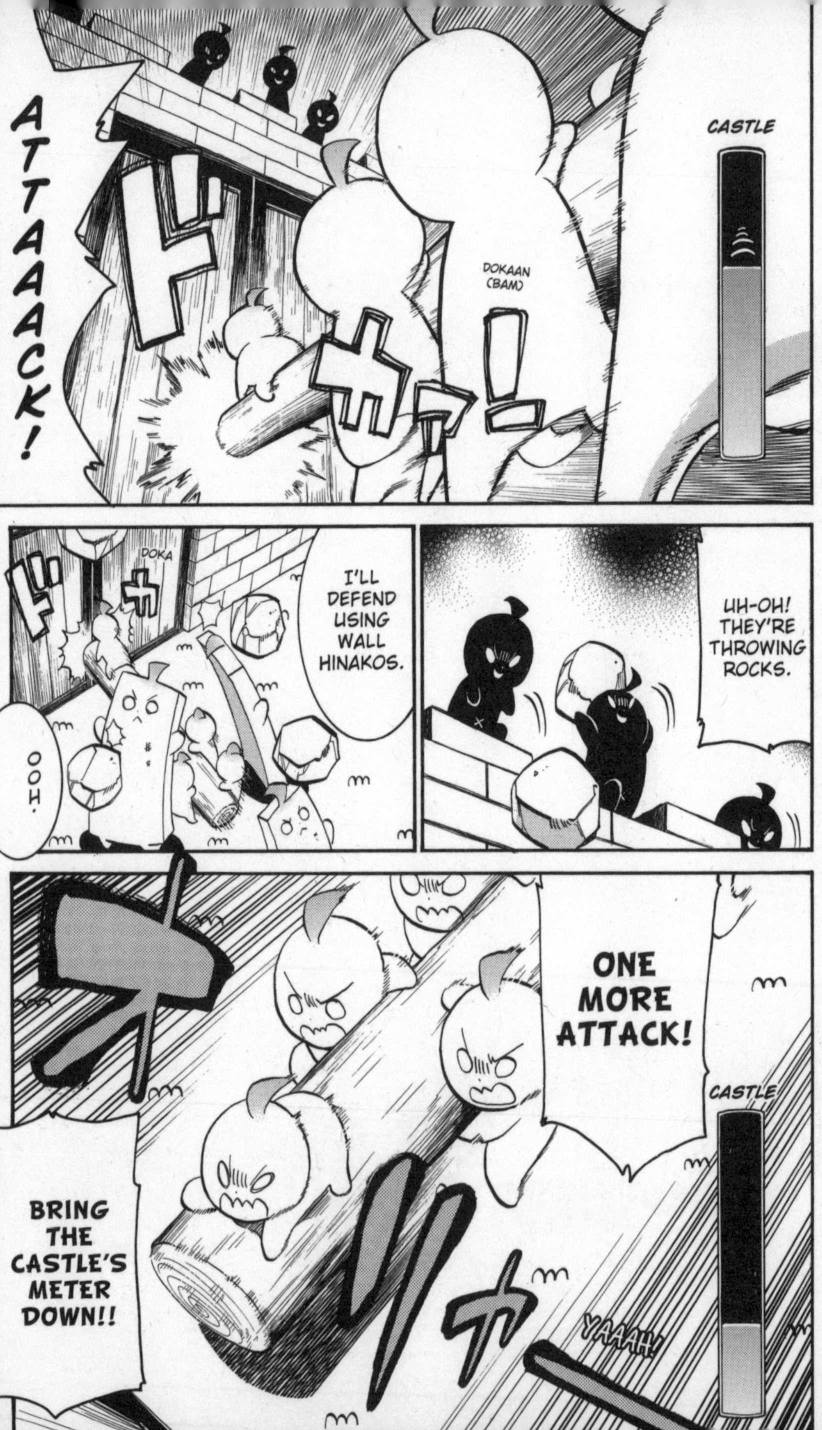
CASTLE
DOKAAN (BAM)
ATTAAACK!
UH-OH! THEY'RE THROWING ROCKS.
I'LL DEFEND USING WALL HINAKOS.
DOKA
OOH.
ONE MORE ATTACK!
CASTLE
YAAAH!
BRING THE CASTLE'S METER DOWN!!

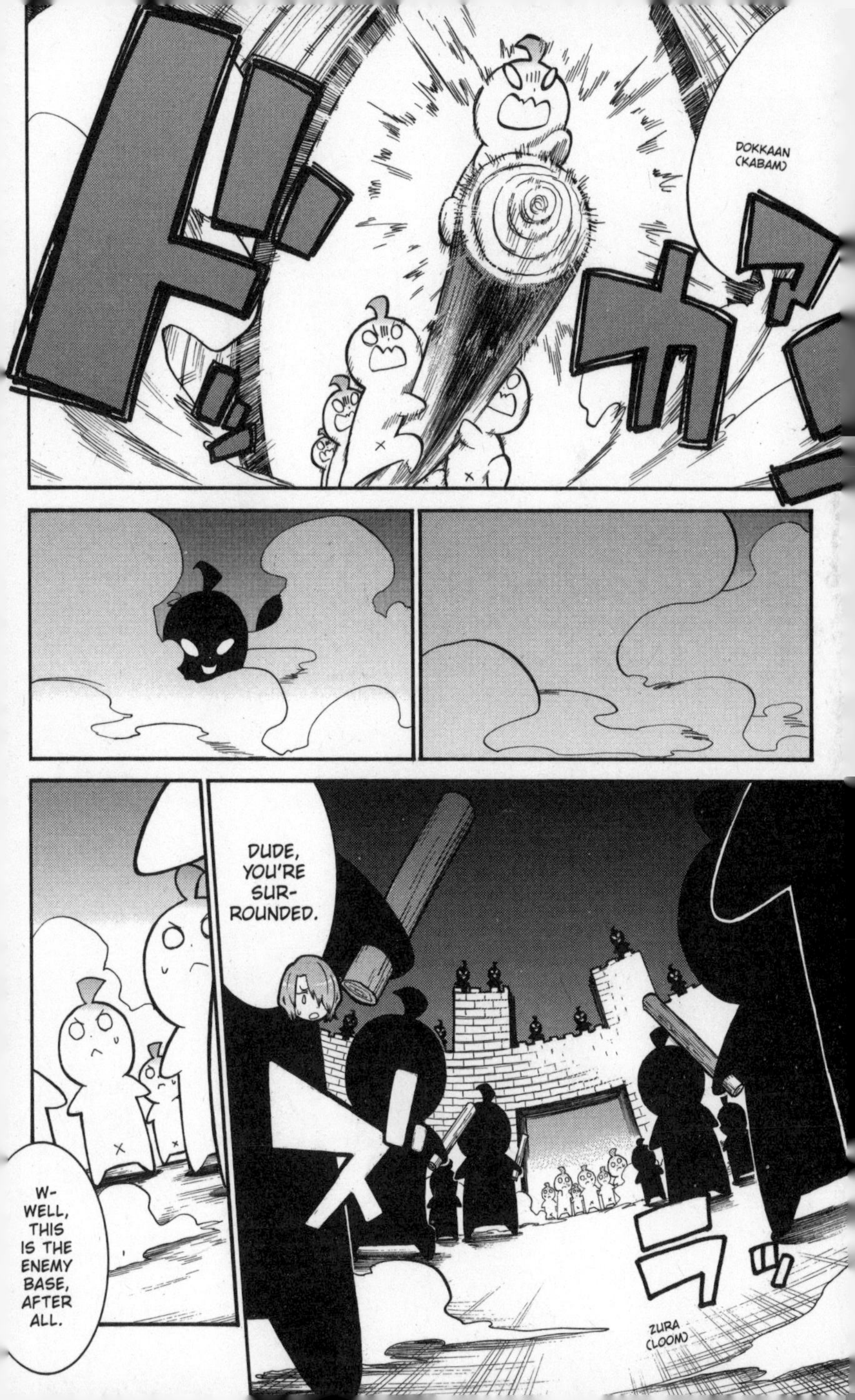
DOKKAAN (KABAM)
DUDE, YOU'RE SURROUNDED.
W-WELL, THIS IS THE ENEMY BASE, AFTER ALL.
ZURA (LOOM)

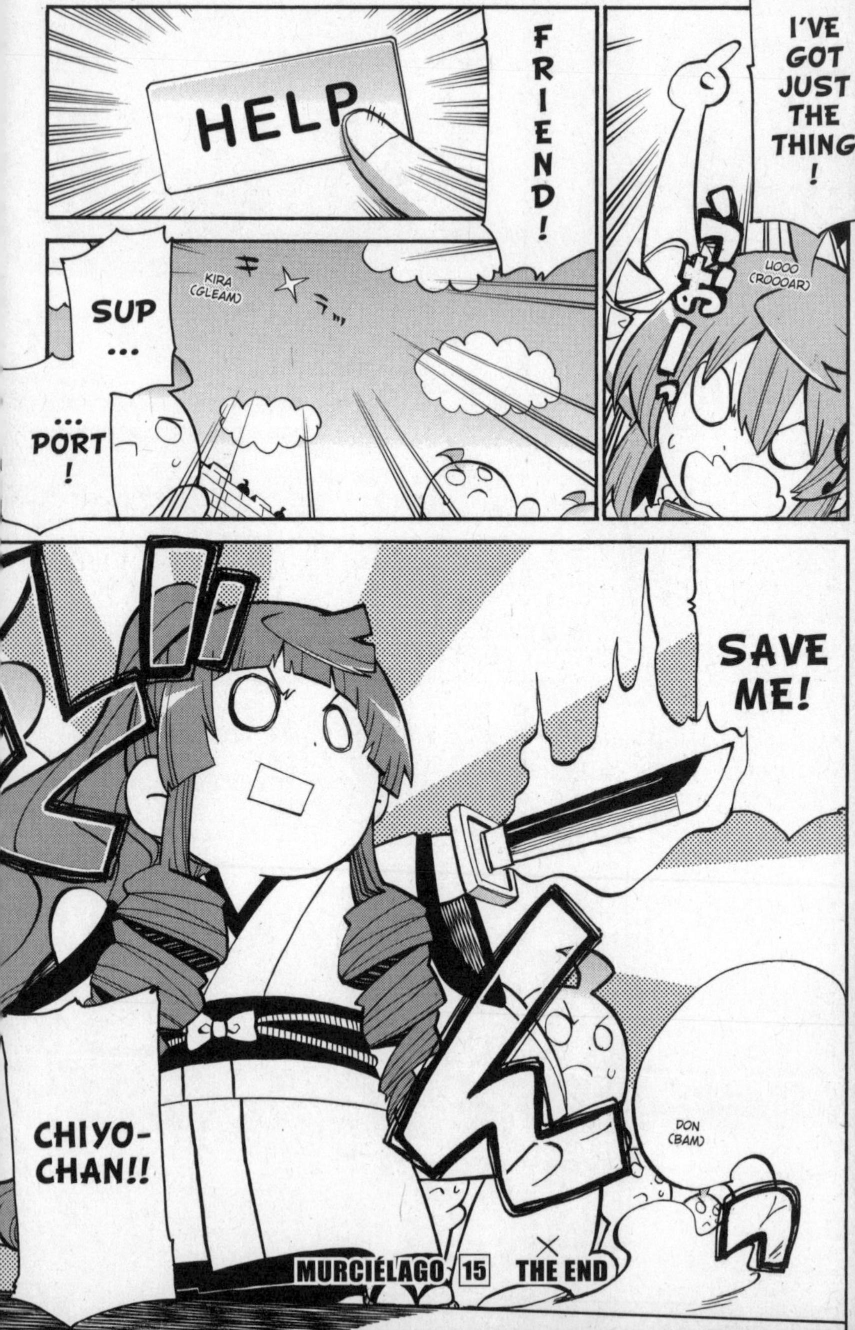
I'VE GOT JUST THE THING!
UOOO (ROOOAR)
HELP
FRIEND!
SUP...
...PORT!
KIRA (GLEAM)
SAVE ME!
DON (BAM)
CHIYO-CHAN!!
MURCIÉLAGO 15 THE END

**MURCIÉLAGO**

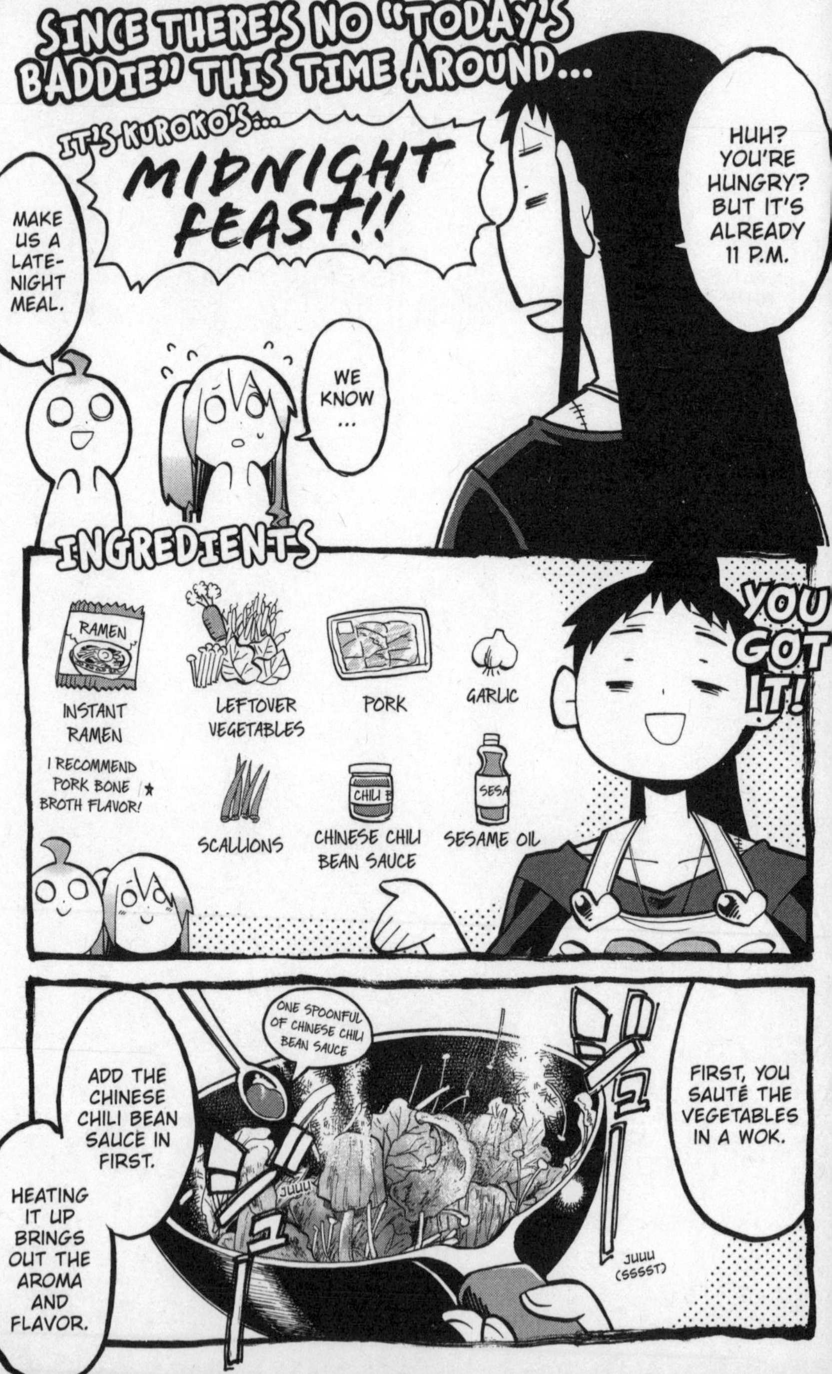
SINCE THERE'S NO "TODAY'S BADDIE" THIS TIME AROUND...
HUH? YOU'RE HUNGRY? BUT IT'S ALREADY 11 P.M.
IT'S KUROKO'S... MIDNIGHT FEAST!!
MAKE US A LATE-NIGHT MEAL.
WE KNOW ...
YOU GOT IT!
INGREDIENTS
RAMEN
INSTANT RAMEN
I RECOMMEND PORK BONE BROTH FLAVOR! ★
LEFTOVER VEGETABLES
PORK
GARLIC
SCALLIONS
CHILI
CHINESE CHILI BEAN SAUCE
SESA
SESAME OIL
FIRST, YOU SAUTÉ THE VEGETABLES IN A WOK.
JUUU (SSSST)
ADD THE CHINESE CHILI BEAN SAUCE IN FIRST.
ONE SPOONFUL OF CHINESE CHILI BEAN SAUCE
JUUU
HEATING IT UP BRINGS OUT THE AROMA AND FLAVOR.

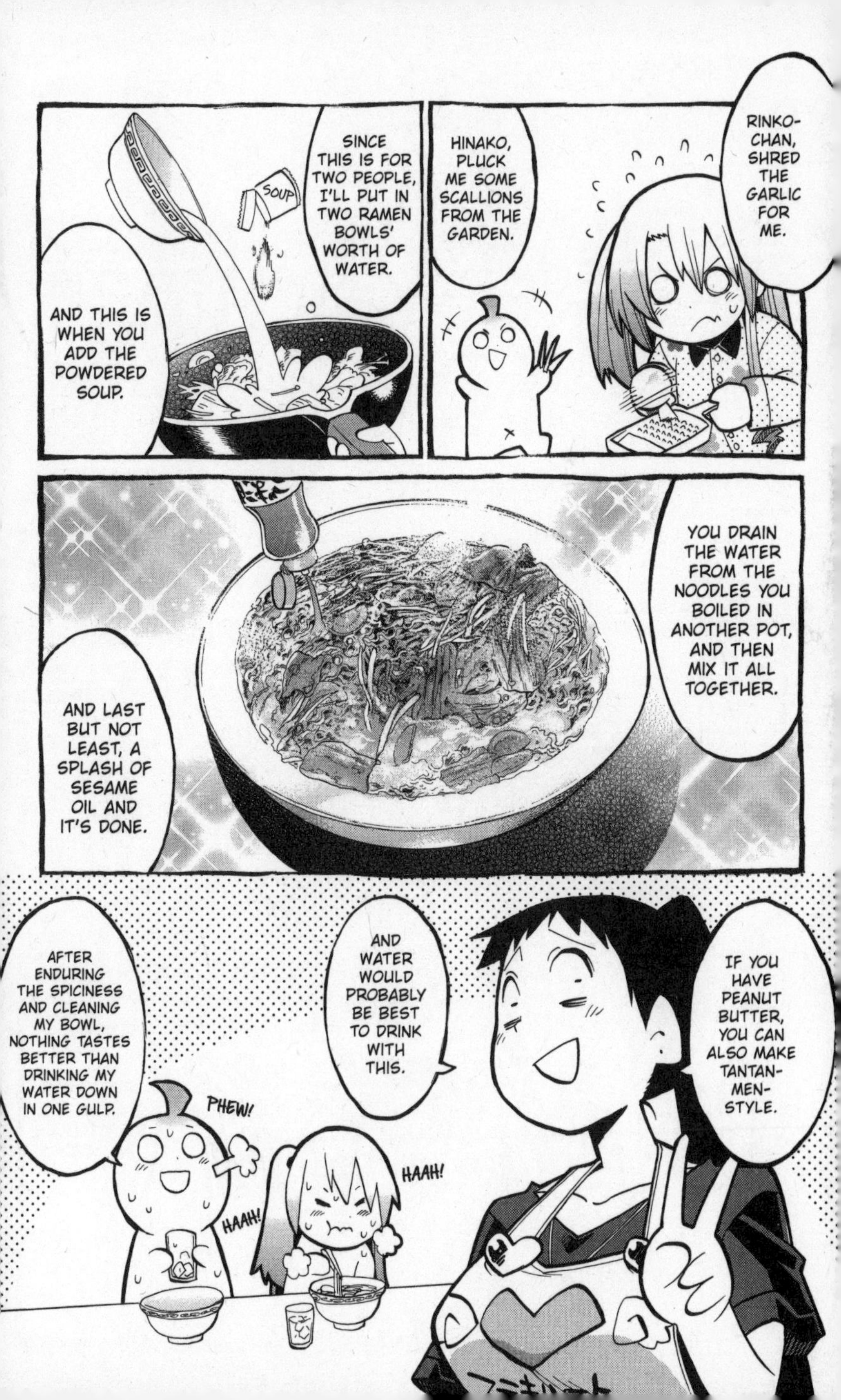
RINKO-CHAN, SHRED THE GARLIC FOR ME.
HINAKO, PLUCK ME SOME SCALLIONS FROM THE GARDEN.
SINCE THIS IS FOR TWO PEOPLE, I'LL PUT IN TWO RAMEN BOWLS' WORTH OF WATER.
SOUP
AND THIS IS WHEN YOU ADD THE POWDERED SOUP.
YOU DRAIN THE WATER FROM THE NOODLES YOU BOILED IN ANOTHER POT, AND THEN MIX IT ALL TOGETHER.
AND LAST BUT NOT LEAST, A SPLASH OF SESAME OIL AND IT'S DONE.
IF YOU HAVE PEANUT BUTTER, YOU CAN ALSO MAKE TANTAN-MEN-STYLE.
AND WATER WOULD PROBABLY BE BEST TO DRINK WITH THIS.
HAAH!
HAAH!
AFTER ENDURING THE SPICINESS AND CLEANING MY BOWL, NOTHING TASTES BETTER THAN DRINKING MY WATER DOWN IN ONE GULP.
PHEW!

General
**Murciélago** is Spanish for "bat."

**Suteki** is Japanese for "lovely."

**Kuroko** means "black lake" in Japanese, and is a Cthulhu Mythos reference to the Lake of Hali, where the dark god Hastur dwells.

The city of **Ruruie** is a reference to R'lyeh, a fictional lost city in H. P. Lovecraft's "The Call of Cthulhu."

### Page 12
**Yuri Indulgence** is a pun of the famous sushi restaurant chain "Sushizanmai" and her pose is very similar to the one of the owner on most of its signs. *Zanmai* translates to "indulgence."

### Page 27
The **Bugg Shash Circus** is named after Bugg-Shash, a creature from the Cthulhu Mythos. A gelatinous entity with innumerable eyes and mouths, it can turn humans into mindless puppets.

### Page 40
This "**frozen performance**" is in reference to the mascot of the Japanese Chunichi baseball team, Doala, who is infamous for freezing and holding a pose rather than joining in choreographed dances at publicity events.

### Page 69
The drug **Cesare** is a reference to a character in the 1920s German silent horror film *The Cabinet of Dr. Caligari*. Cesare is hypnotized by Dr. Caligari into a dream-like state, during which he murders people. **Francis** is one of the main characters in the film as well.

### Page 71
**Pikyuririiin** is the sound of the "Newtype reaction flash" from the Gundam franchise, where people with psychic abilities have heightened senses.

### Page 71-72
In Japanese, Hinako's misinterpretations are both rice-based puns (*Okome* Rider, or "Rice Rider," and *yukari gohan*, or rice sprinkled with red perilla, is a mishearing of *yukaihan*, or a criminal who does things to get a reaction). This English translation aims to keep the joke within the realm of grains.

### Page 95
**Oda Nobunaga** was a Japanese warrior and government official from history who ended a long period of feudal wars by unifying half the provinces of Japan under his rule. **Cesare Borgia** was similar in that he was a very ambitious politician and military leader.

### Page 120
**Nakoto Bridge** is a reference to the Pnakotic manuscripts, a fictional arcane text from the Cthulhu Mythos.

### Page 171
**Mapo tofu** is a spicy Sichuan dish made of tofu.

### Page 172
**Mapo harusame** substitutes noodles in place of the tofu in mapo tofu.

### Page 191
**Tantanmen** is a Japanese take on *dandanmian*, a Sichuan spicy noodle dish that sometimes incorporates a peanut butter sauce.

MURCIÉLAGO

# MURCIÉLAGO

## Yoshimurakana

Translation: Christine Dashiell ✦ Lettering: Alexis Eckerman

This book is a work of fiction. Names, characters, places, and
incidents are the product of the author's imagination or are used fictitiously.
Any resemblance to actual events, locales, or persons, living or dead, is coincidental.

MURCIÉLAGO vol. 15
© 2019 Yoshimurakana / SQUARE ENIX CO., LTD.
First published in Japan in 2019 by SQUARE ENIX CO., LTD.
English translation rights arranged with SQUARE ENIX CO., LTD. and Yen Press, LLC
through Tuttle-Mori Agency, Inc.

English translation © 2020 by SQUARE ENIX CO., LTD.

Yen Press
150 West 30th Street, 19th Floor
New York, NY 10001

Visit us at yenpress.com
facebook.com/yenpress
twitter.com/yenpress
yenpress.tumblr.com
instagram.com/yenpress

Yen Press is an imprint of Yen Press, LLC.
The Yen Press name and logo are trademarks of Yen Press, LLC.

The publisher is not responsible for websites (or their content) that are
not owned by the publisher.

First Yen Press Edition: August 2020
Library of Congress Control Number: 2016958266

ISBNs: 978-1-9753-0897-1 (paperback)
978-1-9753-0898-8 (ebook)

10 9 8 7 6 5 4 3 2 1

WOR

Printed in the United States of America